SILK ROADS

When they could not think what else to do they moved another thousand miles, set out another garden: beans and squash and sweet peas carried from the last place. The past could be jettisoned, children buried and parents left behind, but seeds got carried.

Joan Didion, *Where I Was From*

DK
[RED]

SILK
ROADS

A Flavour Odyssey
with Recipes from
Baku to Beijing

ANNA ANSARI

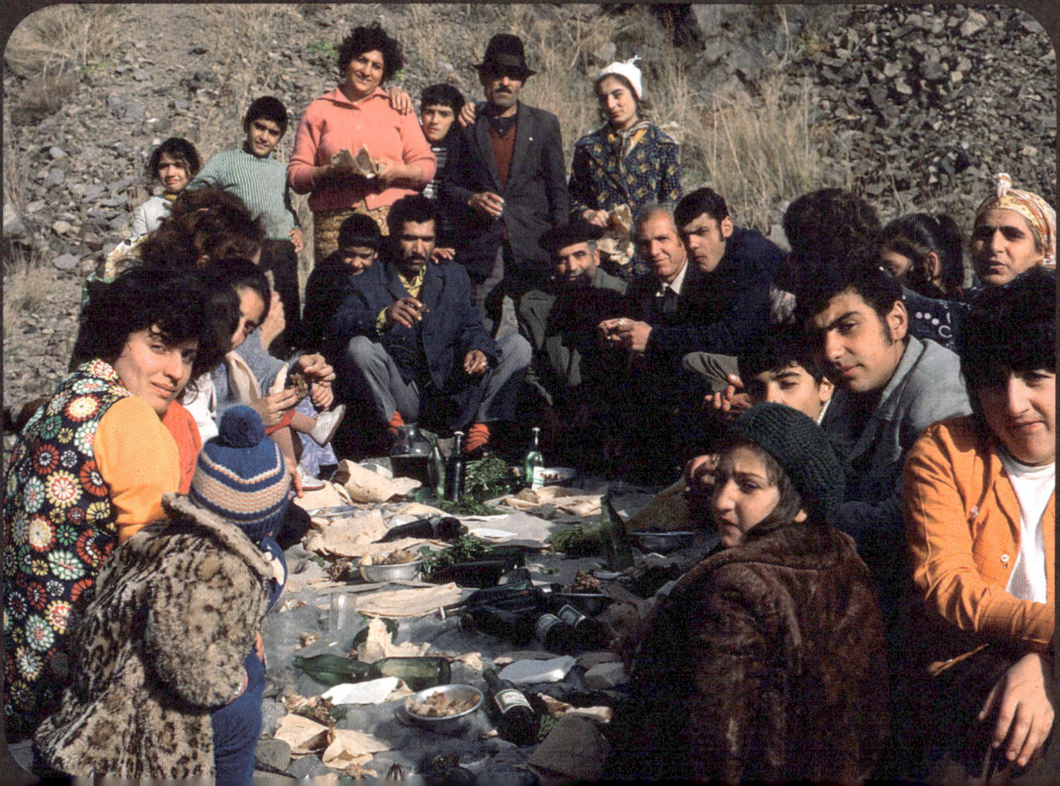

CONTENTS

INTRODUCTION
The Golden Peaches
Melons of Samarkand
6

Cook's Notes
16

COLD SALADS
18

SOUPS & STEWS
42

FERMENTS & PICKLES
70

EGGS, VEGETABLES & TOFU
88

QUADRUPEDS, FISH & FOWL
110

RICE
136

NOODLES
160

DUMPLINGS & BREAD
182

SWEET TREATS
214

Acknowledgments
250

Index
252

THE GOLDEN ~~PEACHES~~ MELONS OF SAMARKAND

It all started with a melon.

The melon in question was an Uzbek one intended as a souvenir from a three-week trip to the USSR my father and a group of American doctors took in late 1978. Travelling across the Soviet Union, the physicians had been invited ostensibly to bear witness to and learn from the "great advances" being made in Soviet medicine.

Instead, my father's takeaway on the Soviet system was that it was doomed to fail. A newspaper kiosk across from his hotel in Tashkent kept its bright lights on 24 hours a day; when my father asked why, the kiosk custodians casually stated that they didn't need to turn off the lights because *they* weren't the ones paying for the electricity – the state was. In Moscow, a restaurant bathroom tap was left on, water running continually, no one caring about the waste or cost – other than my dad, whose post-handwashing attempt to shut off the tap failed. Those were the Brezhnev days, an era of political and economic stagnation that eventually lead to Gorbachev, perestroika, and the ultimate dissolution of the USSR. My dad is no political fortune-teller, but he can spot a crisis when he sees one. He is also excellent at spotting good melons.

He doesn't know when or how he learned, but my father has been an expert melon-selector since he was a child. The house he grew up in in northwestern Iran was on a large lot replete with a cornucopia of fruit trees – plum, pomegranate, apricot, sour cherry, apple, and probably others long forgotten. My grandfather taught my dad how to choose and pick the ripest apricots and plums from their trees, so perhaps the knowledge of how to select melons also came from him.

My father's favourite childhood summer game was to compete with his siblings and neighbours to find the ripest melon in the nearby fields. If a watermelon was at its ripest, it would be heavy, thick, and tense with liquid – so much so that a knife dropped on it from above would cause the melon to crack and explode, sending shattered shards of rind flying everywhere. Whoever chose the ripest melon – and whosever melon shards flew the furthest – won. My father always won.

Other melons didn't react the same way to knives from above as watermelons did, my dad says, but he could still tell by their connection to the vine whether they were ripe and ready to eat. That knowledge grew as he did and, by the time he arrived in Uzbekistan in 1978, a middle-aged American citizen who had been living in Michigan for nearly 15 years, my father recognized at a Tashkent market a melon similar to one he used to eat in Iran – specifically a variety from the eastern part of his native country, near the Turkmenistan border. The hotel in Tashkent had served melon to the group of Americans, but it had been disappointingly bland and mealy – "not quality" melon, my dad tells me. The market melons, on the other hand, were superlative.

My father brought a melon back and started carving it up in the hotel dining room. There is a smile in his voice as he recounts how "it was like a riot": him, holding court at a drably covered table, cutting pieces of melon with surgical precision, doling out samples to his fellow physicians. "This is like heaven," said one doctor, while another cried, "So sweet! So juicy! Why haven't we had anything like this here?"

Complaints were lodged with the tour leader and the hotel. Mealy melon no more! The Americans demanded quality fruit! And so they were promised it ... and so the Soviet hotel managers failed to follow through on their promises. Customer service, my father noted – like medicine,

The golden (and green-and-white speckled) melons of Tashkent, Uzbekistan. October 1978.

electricity, and water conservation – was yet another thing at which the USSR wasn't great. Determined to satisfy their melon cravings, the following day, my father's travelling companions urged him to take them to the market and help them select quality melons. Melon needs thus satisfied – at least, for the majority of the group. Not for my father. Not ever.

On his final day in Tashkent, my father spotted "a real winner" of a melon. It was so beautiful and perfect he decided it must accompany him back to the United States. His children, my older brother and sister, needed to taste this melon; it would be the ultimate souvenir. No such melon existed in the US. Nothing in Iran was comparable either. This melon *must* come to America. It became a talking point among the doctors – "Ansari's melon" – as it accompanied the group from hotel to bus to hotel to airport to bus to hotel and, eventually, to a final airport, where it waited patiently in the lounge with its travel sponsor, ready for a journey to the other side of the world. Back then, the overhead bins on aeroplanes weren't closed. They had no doors, only a horizontal bungee-cord system to stop things from falling out. My dad's melon flew to America in one of those wide-open overhead bins, rolling back and forth, making noise, eliciting cries of, "Hey, do you hear it? It's Ansari's melon again! It's on the move!"

Unlike my father, who would continue his journey on to Michigan, family, and home, the Uzbek melon's first and final stop in the United States of America was Washington DC's Dulles Airport. Upon arrival, US customs agents were, unsurprisingly, full of questions for a group returning from the USSR during the still-raging Cold War.

"Did you bring anything from the Soviet Union?" an agent asked.

"No. Nothing." My father thought he had it made. The agent didn't even notice the melon … until my father volunteered, "Well, I just have this one melon."

"Melon?! Let me see. No. No. You cannot bring this in."

INTRODUCTION

My dad begged. "Please. I have carried this all the way from Uzbekistan. I have brought it so far. It is for my children. Please."

"No way. Absolutely not. You cannot bring that into the country."

And so, the agent took the melon, deposited it into a bin and sent my father on his way, souvenirless, melon-free, back to Detroit, back to his family and home, carrying with him only the memory of the most delectable fruit he had ever tasted.

For years, I have loved and been fascinated by *The Golden Peaches of Samarkand*, a 1963 treatise on the trade of material objects between Tang Dynasty China (618–907 CE) and Central Asian kingdoms written by the late American historian Edward H. Schafer. The book is divided into 18 categories, ranging from men to plants to textiles to pigments, jewels, books, and, of course, foods. Supposedly, yellow peaches "as large as goose eggs" made their way from the kingdom of Samarkand to the dynastic capital of Chang'an (modern-day Xian) on a diplomatic caravan, across treacherous deserts and mountain passes. Though Schafer, in his introduction, notes that the titular "golden peaches" might not have been peaches at all, for him, as for the people of the Tang court, this fruit, whatever it may have been, represented something so prized and beloved by the Samarkandians that it merited being carefully packed and guarded, and shipped overland nearly 3,000 miles to the Tang capital as tribute.

This always reminded me of my father and his attempted import of the Uzbek melon — a fruit so singular that all he wanted was to bring it to his children. So that they could taste this golden melon of Samarkand, if you will, he hand-transported it across the world, a treasure, a tribute to my siblings.

There is actually a very easy way of taking Uzbek melons home, one that goes back centuries. One of the earliest written mentions of Uzbek melons comes from the 10th-century Arab traveller, writer, and geographer Muhammad Abu al-Qasim

The Ark of Bukhara, a fortress dating to the 5th century CE, looms over (sadly melon-less) fruit stands. Bukhara, Uzbekistan. March 2024.

THE GOLDEN ~~PEACHES~~ MELONS OF SAMARKAND

ibn Hawqal, who describes Khorezm melons as "ugly" but of the "highest sweetness". He tells us the melons are cut up, dried, and "sent for export to numerous places of the world". In the 13th century, Marco Polo writes about them as well, noting that "they are preserved as follows: a melon is sliced … then these slices are rolled and dried in the sun, and finally they are sent for sale to other countries, where they are in great demand for they are as sweet as honey".

Like ships stocked with citrus to ward off scurvy, camel caravans travelled across Central Asia laden with strips of dried melon, pregnant with sweetness, vitamins and the taste of home, comforting and nourishing their human members on their long journeys. (You can, by the way, still find dried melon strips throughout Uzbekistan today, often studded with nuts and/or raisins, exploding with sweetness in the mouth of a modern traveller just as they have in the mouths of those travelling Central Asia for centuries.) Eventually, they also carried fresh fruit; by the mid-to-late 1800s, massive caravans of 1,000–2,000 camels transported ripe and ripening melons across Central and East Asia.

Melons have not only been exported from Uzbekistan as trade commodities and prized tributes to rulers in India, China, and Russia, but also as flavour-memories yearned for by immigrants and exiles. In his memoir, *The Baburnama*, Prince Babur, great-great-great-grandson of Tamerlane, the famous Turkic-Mongol ruler and founder of the Timurid Dynasty, complains about the dearth of good produce in the region of India he has conquered, despairing that there are "[n]o grapes or muskmelons, no good fruits … no good bread or food". Territorial advancement and empire-building be damned – Babur missed his melons, the melons of Uzbekistan! Like so many immigrants, Babur carried with him only the memory of the fruit of his homeland, even as he built a new one thousands of miles away.

Today, many Uzbek melons are harvested in autumn, left to ripen in sheds called *qovunxona*, and then sold in the winter for nearly 10 times what they command at the start of the season. (I paid 45 USD for an elusive winter melon in early April, the most money I have ever spent on a fruit.) Not only do these slow-ripened melons provide a much-needed supply of nutrients in the depths of winter, but the ripening process also amplifies their sweetness, as the melon starches slowly convert to sucrose over time, turning undoubtedly already incredible melons into unforgettable ones.

I can't tell you how long Uzbek melon-growers have been ripening and storing their melons in *qovunxona*, but I can tell you that the British balloonist, swashbuckler, and intelligence officer Frederick Burnaby detailed this traditional storage practice in his 1876 book *A Ride to Khiva*. Even then he called it an "old method", so one can only conclude that *qovunxona* have been used for ages.

Captain Burnaby, the lucky bastard, tasted one of these slow-ripened melons on his travels in Central Asia, enjoying it in the middle of a harsh Uzbek winter, proclaiming that "anyone accustomed to this fruit in Europe would scarcely recognize its relationship with the delicate and highly perfumed melons of Khiva". Truly, these are melons worth longing for. They are melons so prized as to be sent to neighbouring kingdoms as political gifts, melons worth their hefty and inflated winter prices, melons given to adventurers returning from outer space (I kid you not: Soviet cosmonauts, upon returning to Earth, were presented with Uzbek melons). In short, they are melons worth writing about.

"The melons of this countryside are abundant and very good, and at the season of Christmas there are so many melons … it is a wonder how many are sold and eaten in the market," proclaimed Ruy Gonzalez de Clavijo, the 15th-century ambassador sent by Henry III of Castille to Tamerlane's court in Samarkand. A century earlier, Ibn Battuta, the traveller and writer from Morocco, also praised Uzbek melons: "There are no melons like Khorezmian melons," he wrote, "maybe with the exception of Bukharian ones, and the third best are Isfahan melon." Isfahan – that's Iran. Bukhara – that's Uzbekistan. And Khorezm – well, that's an ancient name used to describe both the Uzbek city of Khiva, as well as an area that once covered most of present-day Uzbekistan, Turkmenistan, Tajikistan, Afghanistan, and Iran. We are in melon-land now, ladies and gentlemen, deep in the heart of it, deep in the heart of the Silk Roads. And it's been melon-land forever, apparently. Long-for-it, write-home-about-it, try-to-(AHEM, DADDY)-illegally-bring-it-home, melon-land.

These days we talk a lot about where our food comes from. Let's find out the carbon footprint of our bread. Let's make sure we know how our chickens were reared. I do it too. And I fully support and applaud the mainstreamification of seasonality and localism. But in these discussions of where our food comes from, of how many miles away from us our strawberries, leeks, and lettuces are grown, we aren't really asking where our food is really *from*, where its origins are, where the roots first took hold of the earth, in the earth. But I can tell you right here and now – that melon you're eating, that cantaloupe, that honeydew, that Galia – all of those sweet, fleshy orbs, they all come from Uzbekistan, from Central Asia, from the heart of the Silk Roads. In fact, archaeobotanists and geneticists posit that melons have been cultivated in this region for millennia. In 2015, during an excavation in an Uzbek village, a historian discovered carbonized melon seeds dating to between 800 and 1100 CE. Melon-land, indeed.

These melons were transported across deserts, carried as seeds in pockets, carried as sweets in dried strips, carried to us, today, here and now, by generations before us. My father may have failed to bring an Uzbek melon to my brother and sister (an aside from him: "I bet that customs agent took it and ate it himself, that son-of-a-bitch"), but he still succeeded in giving the dream of that melon to his children, including the ones yet to come (me! I'm talking about me!). He made it bigger than life. He made the melon the most magical, flavourful, beautiful fruit. He imbued it with a sense of wonder, longing, and joy – pure joy for what the land can give us, for what storytelling can give us, for what our heritage, memory, and history can give us. He gave that to me, and I give it to you now, here: my imagined golden melon of Samarkand, an emblem of everything the Silk Roads have given – and continue to give – to us all.

Though it lives in my imagination, my father's melon was real. The supremacy of Uzbek melons is real. The Silk Roads were not. Not exactly. Let me explain.

What we talk about when we talk about the "Silk Road" is a vast, informal overland trading network that connected (if not still connects) East Asia with Western Europe. I support the recent trend to pluralize the so-called road in question, a linguistic move that underscores the multi-directional, -faceted, -dimensional, and -geographical nature of these fabled routes. The Silk Roads. Plural. But even that's not an accurate moniker. The routes in question were rarely ever actual roads. Paths, maybe. If you were lucky. Tracks in the dirt, in the sand? Sure. But roads? Nope. And as for silk? Well, it certainly was traded between Asia and Europe, as far back in history as ancient Rome. But the diaphanous luxury was one of myriad goods that traversed the deserts, plains, and mountains between China and Italy. No, the Silk Road, the Silk Roads – this was a name invented by a 19th-century German geographer, Baron Ferdinand von Richthofen. "*Die Seidenstraße:*": a European moniker for a decidedly Asian trade and travel network. Go figure.

Despite its limitations, the term has been embraced by Europeans and Asians alike, and has also come to embody cultural, geographical, and political linkages, as well as historical achievements – both real and imagined. For many, to say in 2025 that one's family, city, country, and/or culture was part of the "Silk Roads" is to proudly situate oneself on an imprecise yet historically, economically, and culturally significant plane. Even if sometimes untrue or imagined. As my dearly departed Great-Aunt Myrna used to say: "No one is around to correct me, so I guess I can say whatever I want!"

I recently saw a theatrical performance called *Legend of the Camel Bell* in Xian. The description of the show in the *China Daily* is what initially intrigued me: "From the Tang capital … to ancient Rome, it tells the story of a group of young men heading toward unknown adventure and great fortune along the Silk Road … *Legend of the Camel Bell* uses 20 camels and 30 wolves onstage to recreate the authentic environment of the desert and the bitter wilderness along this historical route." Camels! Wolves! The Silk Road! Sold! In the end, the live animals weren't what stuck with me. Rather, it's the volcanos I can't stop thinking about. And the Chinese acrobats performing alongside whirling dervishes and gladiators at the Coliseum. It's the fact that I was the only non-Chinese audience member, and probably one of the only ones not to return home secure in the knowledge that the dangers of the Silk Roads included not only snowstorms and wolves, but also volcanic lava explosions. In the Himalayas …

But the reality doesn't matter, does it? The story the show tells is one of perseverance, hardship, and strength, and of economic, cultural, and political engagement. It makes sure its audience knows not only of China's participation in the global economy and world, but also of the longevity and supremacy of this role. It is a didactic show most definitely geared to a native Chinese audience. And, in the end, there really are only two actors of note – China and Europe. Everything else is just, as we would say in America, "flyover country".

A nomadic camel caravan in northern Iran. Sometime in the early to mid-1970s.

Fast-forward 30 minutes, and I'd be eating a meal that would change my life. Beijing, August 1998.

It bothers me. It frustrates me. The puzzled looks I get when I say my father is Azeri. The assumption that I'm going to Atlanta when I announce I'm travelling to Georgia. The incredulity that I would travel in Uzbekistan by myself. "Is it safe?" people ask. "Where is that? Why are you going there? Is that where Borat is from?"

The countries and cultures beyond the Bosphorus Straits remain, for the most part, unknown to the West. *Hic sunt dracones*: here be dragons. Not just dragons, though. Kingdoms once ruled by khans. Plagued by marauding bandits, frightening in their barbarism. Or else mythical, gilded, magical poetic lands, replete with shimmering turquoise minarets, stately pleasure domes, gold, jade, and ever-flowing opulence. I call fucking shenanigans. On all of it. There is so much more to the Silk Roads than that which people imagine, romanticize, Orientalize, or fear. And there is so much more to the transport network's impact on global foodstuffs than squabbles over whether Marco Polo brought noodles to Italy from China.

As a teenager, I lived with a Chinese family for nearly one year, a member of the first group of Western high-school students to spend an entire academic year in China. On one of our early days in Beijing, a classmate who had been to China before wanted to introduce us to a restaurant at which he had previously eaten. A group of us set out on our newly purchased bicycles. After a minor bike/car crash and a little bit of blood, we wound up down an alleyway in a small restaurant with signage in a script that looked vaguely familiar and not at all Chinese, and we gorged on noodles and lamb. This was my first taste of Uyghur food. Though I had only been in Beijing for a short time, from the first bite I knew this food was something different.

Our meals up until that point had typically consisted of wilted mystery greens with garlic, sautéed tomatoes and scrambled eggs, aubergine stewed so long it nearly liquified, fried tofu in a brown sauce, *gong bao* chicken, brothy soup, and bowls of steamed white rice. Don't get me wrong – it had all been delicious. I didn't know what I was

THE GOLDEN ~~PEACHES~~ MELONS OF SAMARKAND

eating most of the time, but I loved it. It tasted somewhat similar to the Chinese food from my favourite Michigan Chinese-American restaurants, but better, fuller, more exciting and flavourful.

The Uyghur food, on the other hand, was something else. No white rice appeared. No stewed aubergine and mystery greens. Instead, platters were piled high with skewers of lamb, glistening with fat, partially charred from the coals, speckled with cumin seeds and red chilli flakes, a freshly baked flatbread underneath to catch the dripping juices. Then, a large bowl of noodles appeared, coated in a faint tomato sauce, topped with chopped red and green peppers, sliced onions, and chunks of lamb.

This was not the Chinese food of suburban Michigan, and this was not the Chinese food of China. And yet there I was, eating this seemingly non-Chinese food in an alleyway in China's capital city, my teenage mind and world expanding with every bite. This was a whole new world of flavour – but flavours I knew and loved almost intuitively. This food was simultaneously new and exciting to a 17-year-old American, yet familiar and comforting to the palate of a first-generation Azeri-Iranian. Lamb with toothsome noodles was strange and different, while lamb with cumin tasted like something I had eaten all my life.

In Beijing, starting with that first bowl of Uyghur noodles, I discovered that I was connected to something much bigger than I had previously understood. Together, my father's food habits, his memories of food, and the flavours of Uyghur cuisine built a bridge for me to a rich and complex food culture – one that simultaneously existed in Iran, in China, and in immigrant communities across the globe. This was a food culture whose proliferation, transmission, and evolution could be traced back generations and centuries to intrepid travellers and traders who moved across the routes that would one day be dubbed the Silk Roads by a German nobleman. It was my father's food culture. It was my food culture. And it was the Uyghurs' food culture. All at the same time.

A few months after that first Uyghur meal, I took my visiting father to an upscale Uyghur restaurant. We dined and danced, and he chatted with the wait staff – in Turkish. Thousands of miles from the town in Iran where my father had grown up, across an ocean from our home in America, there we were – father and daughter, in 1998 Beijing – unexpectedly experiencing fruits of the Asian heartland's ancient trade routes together, routes that had spread language, religion, people, flavours, food, and culture for centuries.

My father has been always proud of his background and heritage – perhaps to a fault. For as long as I can remember, he has driven home the fact that he is – that we are – ethnically Turkish, and not Persian. We may eat *ghormeh sabzi* and refer to it as such, but it's "Iranian food" in our family, not "Persian food". The crispy layer of rice at the bottom of the pot in our house is called *gazmakh*; we do not refer to that deliciousness by the increasingly well-known word *tahdig*. *Gazmakh* is Turkish. *Tahdig* is Persian. We are Azeri. We are Turkish. And so are the Uyghurs.

A Turkish-speaking, Islamic people who primarily live in China's Xinjiang Province, today's Uyghurs are descended from the Songdians of old, a fierce and powerful Turkic-European people who once made their capital at Samarkand in modern-day Uzbekistan. Until, that is, Alexander the Great made his way westward, arrived at and conquered Samarkand in 329 BCE, and famously proclaimed: "Everything I heard about Samarkand is true, except for one thing: it turned out to be more beautiful than I could imagine." (Gotta say, I agree with the guy; it really is spectacular, even today.) Reeling from their defeat and the loss of their capital, the Songdians turned to trade, and, until the end of the Tang Dynasty, were the main Silk Roads traders, due to both their physical control of desert oases and trading posts, as well as the fact that Songdian was the lingua franca of Central Asian trade.

An earlier significant period of time, for our purposes at least, was China's Han Dynasty (206 BCE–220 CE), during which goods, including silk, made their way overland to ancient Rome. It was in the Han Dynasty that China first truly looked to and engaged with the lands to its west, gaining control over a swathe of the Tarim Basin as well as the Hexi Corridor in modern-day Gansu Province, a traversable strip of land linking China's central plains to Central Asia and a key Silk Roads passageway. This is when grapes came to China. Peas, cucumbers, and sesame too. But this was nothing compared to what the routes would carry a few centuries later, during the Tang Dynasty (618–907 CE), the second of the three golden ages (if I can call them that) of our titular trade networks.

The Tang Dynasty. The age of golden peaches. Of poetry. Of imported horses, asbestos, Bactrian camels, saffron, borax, kohlrabi, and spinach. A time during which Chang'an was the most populous city in the world, if not the most cosmopolitan and diverse, both ethnically and religiously. A time of expansions, both territorial and in popular mindset. However, after the An Lushan rebellion (see p54), China turned inward and remained as such, for the most part, and for a number of reasons, until the founding of the Mongol Yuan Dynasty (1271–1368) by Kublai Khan.

Under Mongol rule, the Silk Roads thrived as never before and never since. It was a third golden age of Central Asian trade, and the one about which we know the most, thanks to travellers, merchants, missionaries, and observers, including that oft-referenced Venetian, Marco Polo. The Pax Mongolica – the peace and stability the realm provided for trade and travel – cannot be underestimated.

Here's the thing. I'm not a historian. And I don't claim to be, so I'm not about to try to synthesize millennia of Central, East, and Middle East Asian history in a cookbook. But I do know and can tell you that, with the rise in sea trade after the fall of the Mongol Empire, the overland Asian trade networks dwindled in size and significance, eventually becoming little more than epic routes traversed by British and Russian envoys wanting to claim the regions for their home countries, pawns in a paternalistic so-called "Great Game". Today there's a new game being played, but not necessarily a great one, and you don't leave Georgia, Azerbaijan, Uzbekistan, or Kazakhstan without feeling Russian and Chinese influences, whether political, cultural, or culinary.

Influences, ingredients, flavours, and foods have criss-crossed the world since time immemorial. Tomatoes made their way from the New World to Italy. Chillies crossed oceans to arrive in India. Cinnamon. Corn. Potatoes. They have emigrated and integrated, become embedded in and integral to cultures and cuisines where they began as nothing more than foreign and unknown imports. Books on food and history, and even books on trade, focus generally on the sea routes, trading patterns, and economies of Western European empires and nations and, later, America. Little time and few words have been spent on the transmission of food, flavours, and ingredients over land and by non-Western players, at least in the English language.

Guide-posted by the fabled routes once traversed by merchants, travellers, adventurers, and pilgrims, this book traces flavours, ingredients, and dishes of the Silk Roads, from Baku to Beijing and beyond, across generations and continents. Together, we travel from the mountainous region in northwest Iran where my father was born and raised, across the Central Asian plains, mountains, and desert oases, and into the Uyghur neighbourhoods of China where I spent formative years of my youth and early adulthood.

Kargar Street in the Amir Abad district of Tehran, Iran. Sometime in the mid-1970s.

The food culture that I connected to in Beijing in 1998, with that first bowl of Uyghur noodles, is one that spans thousands of miles, from the shores of the Black Sea, over the Caucasus and Pamir Mountains, and across the Tamalakan and Gobi Deserts. It is a culture that encompasses ancient Mongol soldiers, Kazakh eagle-hunters, Persian merchants, Zorastrian prophets, Chinese imperial envoys, and all those who have travelled and lived along the so-called Silk Roads. These routes carried not only individuals and goods, but ideas, flavours, and memories – all informing and linking to each other across time and space, to this day. Indeed, the Silk Roads take us through the arteries of Asia in centuries past to my father, a 20th-century Iranian immigrant in Detroit, Michigan, and all the way to me, an Iranian-American putting dinner on the table for my family in east London.

This is a book about food and cooking, but it is also one about leaving home – and coming home. It's an immigrant story of what gets taken with us when we leave our homes, what we introduce to others as a way of introducing ourselves, and what remains when we are gone – what pieces and tastes of one culture are introduced and absorbed into new ones. It's a book about what we bring to the table, and about what we leave behind. It is a book to remind us that borders are geopolitical constructs, and that authenticity and ownership can oftentimes be shared, fluid, or imagined.

I hope you come away with a deeper understanding and enjoyment of not only the foods of the Silk Roads, but also of its people, history, and legacy. I hope you feel connected to places and dishes you may have only intangibly, fuzzily, dreamily pictured before, if at all. I want to take you on a journey across cultures, generations, and continents. And, of course, I want to feed you some incredible food in the meantime.

Zou ba!

COOK'S NOTES

Below you will find a few little tidbits that I hope will make your *Silk Roads* reading and cooking experiences fuller.

Determining how to best represent non-Roman scripts in an accessible, respectful, and useful way was legit challenging. Accordingly, in an attempt to be equitable I have opted to exclude the use of any and all non-Roman scripts. For Mandarin Chinese words and phrases, I have used the well-known and accepted *pinyin* system of transliteration and romanization, and have chosen to separate and space out words and phrases on a word basis rather than a character one. For other languages, things get a bit trickier. There is no *pinyin*-like system in place for Uzbek, Azeri, Farsi, and Arabic; that's why different spellings of Iranian dishes abound (e.g. *tachin, tacheen, tahchin, tahcheen*). In this book, I have used what makes most sense to me, and my family and food traditions. Such determinations involve not only word choices (e.g. *khoresh* versus *khoresht*), but also linguistic ones. The crispy bits at the bottom of the pot of Iranian rice? As I explained on page 13, in my world and family, that's *gazmakh*, a Turkic word, not *tahdig*, the Farsi one you see and hear bandied about more and more frequently. So it's *gazmakh* in this here book, for these here recipes. This is just to say: I have been eating the *gazmakh* in the bottom of the pot for 43 years and calling it by that name. Forgive me: it is still delicious and crispy and golden.

I have opted to italicize only foreign-origin words that were not included in the *Oxford English Dictionary* at the time of writing. I hemmed and hawed over how to handle this. Who determines when once-foreign language becomes so commonplace in English that it needs no visual emphasis to indicate its foreignness? Who gets to be the gatekeeper, and who appointed them? In this book, the answer is simple: I'm passing the buck to the *OED* because I don't want to be the one making the choices – because I don't think I *should* be the one making the choices.

OK, that was the complex stuff. The rest is easy.

- I've given **serving quantities** for all the dishes, but these are not set in stone. Most of the dishes are designed to be served family-style alongside many others; keep appetites and overall menu design in mind when it comes to serving quantities.

- "**Neutral oil**" means vegetable, rapeseed, avocado, or a similar super mild-flavoured oil. Furthermore, any time a recipe calls for **ghee**, I give you my leave to use olive oil instead.

- Unless otherwise specified, all **lemon/lime juice should be freshly squeezed**.

- Whenever a recipe calls for **MSG**, it is optional, but highly recommended.

- **To toast spices**, heat a heavy-bottomed pan over a medium heat. Add your spices to the pan. Give the pan a good shake. Keep shaking the pan on and off for 2–4 minutes, or until the spices start to smell (and, in some cases, pop). Empty your toasted spices into a bowl to stop them from toasting any further. Let them cool and then use as directed in the recipe.

- **To brew saffron**, add your saffron threads and the specified amount of sugar to a mortar and grind well with a pestle. Then, add the specified amount of hot water and/or other liquid. Let it steep for at least 2 minutes, and then use as directed in the recipe. As for saffron quantities, in my opinion, you can never have too much, but most of my recipes call for an easily eyeballed amount based on a portion of the typical weight of saffron as sold in British supermarkets. This weight varies, but is usually around 0.5g. My recipes typically call for 0.25g, 0.5g, or 1g.

- **To sterilize glass jars**, place both the jars and their lids in a deep saucepan. Fill the pan with water and bring it to the boil over a high heat. Once boiling, reduce the heat to medium and boil the jars for 10 minutes. Carefully remove the now-sterilized jars to a paper towel-lined baking tray to dry. Once dry and cool, your jars are ready to be filled. Apparently, you can also sterilize jars in the oven or dishwasher, but this is how I do it.

- **To brown butter**, melt small pieces of butter in a small saucepan over a medium heat. The melting butter will start to foam up and change colour. When it's foamy and yellow, make sure you're paying attention and stirring it near constantly. At this point, you should start to see little flecks in the foam – that's the milk solids separating out. Keep stirring, because you don't want them to burn. The French call brown butter *beurre noisette*, a phrase that translates to "hazelnut butter", and, once you get to this point, you'll understand why: the butter will turn a deep brown and emit an incredible nutty smell, and the milk solids will start to rapidly darken. Once that happens, immediately remove the pan from the heat, and pour the brown butter (milk solids included) into a heatproof bowl. This whole process should take minutes, so be quick on your feet.

My dad, on the side of a long and winding road to somewhere, in Azerbaijan, 1975.

INTRODUCTION

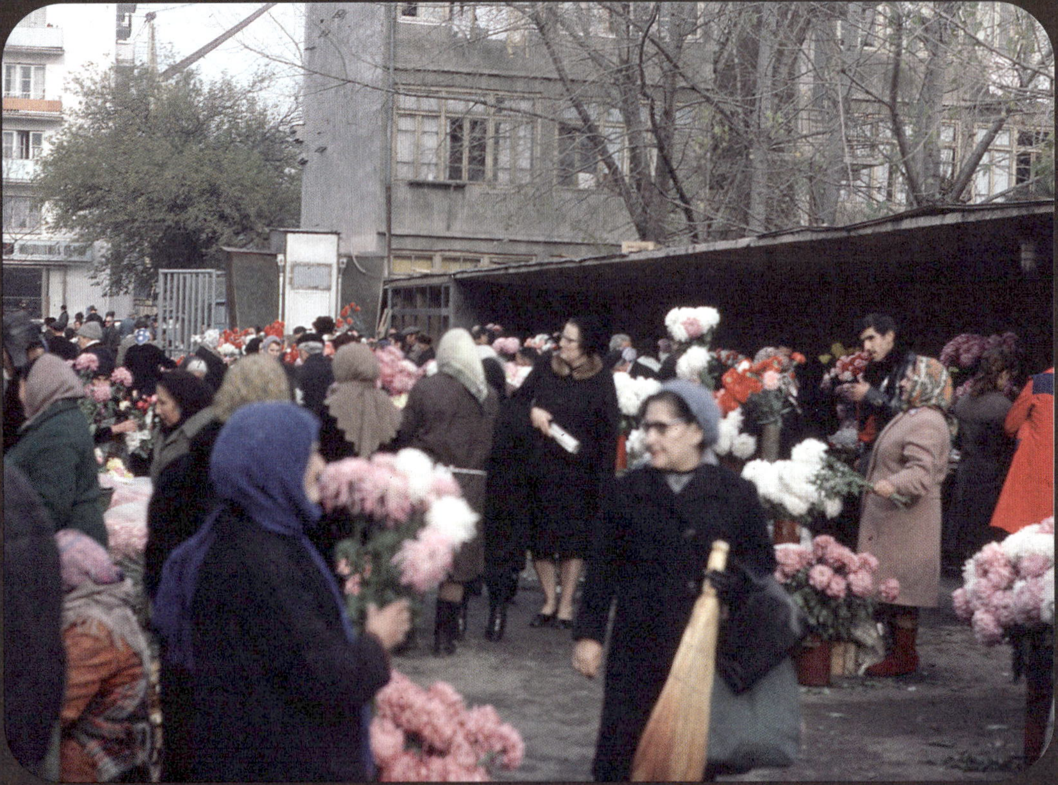

COLD SALADS

THE MARKET ECONOMY
20

ACHICHUK
Uzbek Tomato & Onion Salad
24

MORKOVCHA
Korean-Style Carrot Salad
27

SHALGAM
Kazakh Radish Salad
28

NOKOT
Uyghur Chickpea & Carrot Salad
28

QURUTOB
Tajik Bread Salad
31

AN AZERI TOMATO SALAD
32

A CENTRAL ASIAN SLAW
35

A GEORGIAN SUMMER SALAD
36

ROVOCH SALAT
Uzbek Rhubarb & Radish Salad
39

THE MARKET ECONOMY

I never enjoyed our trips to Detroit's Eastern Market. My father loved them, though, and so did his best friend, Dr Frugh, a fellow Azeri-Iranian and physician who lived just over the Michigan–Ohio border. Like my father, Dr Frugh had a Midwestern American wife and half-American children who spoke neither Farsi nor Turkish. Shireen was a year younger than my little sister, Sara, and like a sister to us both, while Dr Frugh's children from his first marriage were older and out of the house, just like my older siblings. Our families had great fun together for years – camping, boating, caravanning to Niagara Falls, trick-or-treating – all those wholesome, Midwestern, American things. Plus, Dr Frugh and my dad had their own kind of expatriate, exile, immigrant fun together – reciting poetry, drinking tea, talking politics and medicine, joyfully dancing through our house in their underwear upon learning that Ayatollah Khomeini had died, dragging their kids and wives to Eastern Market ...

Not only was Dr Frugh a talented neurologist, but he was also an exceptional Iranian cook – a grill-master extraordinaire whose interest in Eastern Market lay squarely with his ability to source there particular cuts of lamb that were impossible to find in Toledo. My father went for fresh fruit and vegetables; Dr Frugh for kebab and *khoresh* ingredients. I imagine they both went for comfort as well, if only subconsciously. For these two immigrants from northern Iran, Eastern Market, with its bounty of fruit and veg, meat, and "imported" grains, was undoubtedly a bit of home: an Americanized, Detroit-ified slice of culinary comfort. For me, a kid accustomed to organized aisles of dry goods at a suburban Kroger's grocery store, walking through Eastern Market's towering brick arches and into an open-air plaza full of foodstuffs and farmers was uncomfortable, foreign, and even a bit scary.

No – wait. That's not true. The market wasn't full. Not with farmers. And not with market-goers, either.

Like so much of Detroit in the 1980s, Eastern Market was depressed. However, unlike so much of Detroit in the 1980s, the market's decline had not been precipitated by either the fallout of the 1967 race riots or the automotive industry's slow-but-sure decampment from its birthplace. Eastern Market, which began in the mid-19th century as a spot to buy and sell wood and hay, and which eventually welcomed farmers selling food in 1891, was, in its heyday, so popular with Detroiters and so crowded that, in 1917, the city council required shoppers entering with baby carriages to have an actual baby in their carriage, because empty ones were being used as proto-shopping trolleys. After World War II, as American appetites and wallets turned to affordable and popular refrigerators and ready-made foodstuffs, and away from fresh fruit and vegetables, so too did Detroiters turn away from Eastern Market. Of course, the population and economic exodus certainly didn't help things, and by the time we were making our Saturday trips to Detroit, you could practically count on one hand the number

> **EASTERN MARKET, WITH ITS BOUNTY OF FRUIT AND VEG, MEAT, AND "IMPORTED" GRAINS, WAS UNDOUBTEDLY A BIT OF HOME: AN AMERICANIZED, DETROIT-IFIED SLICE OF CULINARY COMFORT.**

Top: Dried fruit and nuts galore. Teze Bazaar. Baku, Azerbaijan. January 2016.

Bottom: A vegetable seller and his wares. Siyob Bazaar. Samarkand, Uzbekistan. March 2024.

of fellow patrons and stall-holders present in the once-teeming market sheds. But still we went. My younger sister hilariously/devastatingly recalls our trips in a sepulchral manner, telling me: "It is always winter in the Eastern Market of our childhood. Cold and inhospitable. Occasional passers-by holding their bodies close and bracing themselves against either the bitter chill or a bitter pedestrian who may or may not have had a gun. I remember peanut shells on the ground."

I remember peanut shells, too – because our Eastern Market trips invariably ended at the Rocky Mountain Peanut Company, where we were allowed some penny candy and bags of shell-on nuts. Something to placate the kids, to pacify us, to bribe us into returning. Our Detroit day wasn't over yet, as we would drive across the dying city to Greektown to quickly ride the People Mover, browse the shops at Trapper's Alley, and, if we were lucky, eat saganaki and souvlaki at Hellas or Golden Fleece. *Opa!* Flaming cheese was always the highlight of those trips for me. The market itself was always the nadir.

At some point in my young adulthood, I learned to love markets. I recall wandering through Yunnan and Sichuan wet markets, snapping photos as I went. Fish heads in a pile, bowls of entrails, mountains of chicken feet, blocks of congealed blood. I was so taken with the living (or very recently living) wares that I frankly didn't even notice the fruit and vegetable offerings; even now, I can't summon them up in my mind's eye.

No, I was at the market for the live skinning of frogs, not for fruit, and I certainly didn't connect the Chinese markets I loved with the Detroit market I hated. Not until years later. Not until I went to Teze Bazaar in Baku, Azerbaijan, with my father.

Maybe it was because I had become so accustomed to markets in China. Maybe it was because I was in my pseudo-ancestral home. Maybe because the first vendor we encountered knew my father from television ("The doctor! From America! Hello! Welcome!") and quickly struck up a conversation (about the merits of Uzbek grapes, naturally). Maybe it's fucking Maybelline. I don't know, but I was immediately at ease in the market, grinning from ear to ear, smiling to the vendors, making kissing noises at the prowling cats. I was completely at home, and yet I was also astonished. Teze Bazaar was nothing like the Chinese markets I had been to in either scale or size. The place was massive. There was an area just for fruits and nuts. Another for meat and fish and caviar. A building for cheese and dairy products. And then there was the section for fresh fruit and vegetables, teeming with bags overflowing with onions, potatoes, aubergines, peppers. Tables covered in heaps of spinach, sorrel, green herbs, and tomatoes. Cucumbers stacked in pyramids. Jars of pickles and jams and preserves. I was in love. But, as I would learn a few years later, Baku's markets had nothing on Uzbekistan's.

> **I WAS AT THE MARKET FOR THE LIVE SKINNING OF FROGS, NOT FOR FRUIT, AND I CERTAINLY DIDN'T CONNECT THE CHINESE MARKETS I LOVED WITH THE DETROIT MARKET I HATED. NOT UNTIL YEARS LATER.**

Jet-lagged and bleary-eyed, my husband Ed and I made our way to Chorsu Bazaar a few hours after landing in Tashkent. The word *chorsu* itself means "four waters" in Persian, a fitting name for a market situated at the literal crossroads of ancient routes connecting the four great Uzbek cities of Tashkent, Bukhara, Samarkand, and (lesser-known-in-modern-times-but-massively-significant-in-antiquity) Shahrisabz. Where the relatively new turquoise-and-blue dome that acts as Chorsu's central hub sits (by the way, good on you, 1980s Soviets, for coupling concrete modernism with an aesthetic nod to Islam), a market has operated continuously since at least the 13th century, when Silk Roads travellers and merchants made their way to Tashkent from across Central Asia to a bazaar that became and remains one of the region's biggest.

Today, the dome houses concentric circles of foodstuffs: heaps of technicolour carrot salads, tubs of fragrant kimchi, horse sausages that would make Ron Jeremy blush, bins of fresh noodles and dumplings, pile after pile of spices — both familiar and not — wet and dry dairy products. And, upstairs, oh my god, dried fruits and nuts galore.

This 1930s description of Turpan's bazaar, written by British missionaries, intrepid travellers, and eloquent writers Mildred Cable and Francesca French, is near identical to what Ed and I saw at Chorsu in 2024, suggesting (to me, at least) a continuity of sales and wares that stretches far back in time, and underscores the timeless nature of these Silk Roads centres of commerce.

The dried-fruit market is one of the most varied and certainly the cheapest in the world. The vendor sits amid piles of sultanas of varying quality — the dark, the pale, the golden and the jade-green; these are kept carefully apart, and only the cheapest and commonest are ever mixed. On one side of him are mounds of minute currants, and on the other large, fleshy raisins, with dried black plums and apricots of different kinds ... There are also dried peaches, nectarines and mulberries, piles of shelled walnuts and dried jujube fruit.

Wow. What a market. And have you checked out the photo on page 21? That's some continuity, right there, if you ask me.

There's a greeting card I've seen a few times that says something like, "No great love story starts with a salad." And maybe no great love story has ever begun with a salad, but this book will. These are not just any salads — they are ones whose deliciousness, hidden by the simplicity of their ingredients, reveals itself at first forkful and astonishes. And this is not just any book — it may not be a love story, but it is an ode and homage to a region of the world whose claim on my heart is as deep, intense, and epic as any fabled romance.

Oh, and PS: I now love going to Eastern Market. And I'm not the only one. A confluence of Detroit's so-called rebirth and the embrace of seasonality and farm-to-table cooking and shopping has rejuvenated the market, which, on an average Saturday, now sees 50,000 visitors. My father isn't one of them, though. There's a closer farmers' market to him these days, and grocery stores carry the Middle Eastern foodstuffs once so difficult to source. Shopping habits have changed — in America, at least. The bazaars of Central Asia tell a different story; I hope you like it.

ACHICHUK

Uzbek Tomato & Onion Salad

Serves 2–4 as a side

The tomato, a South American fruit, entered Asia via China via the Philippines via the Spanish Empire seven hundred-some years ago. And the plant ended up in Uzbekistan, which is now a massive greenhouse tomato-growing nation, and made its way into this delightful salad.

Achichuk is sneaky. It doesn't sound like much – tomatoes, onions, and maybe some herbs – but it tastes like everything and everywhere. With dill on top, it reminds me of Iranian food. With coriander, it takes my taste buds to Mexico. And with some basil, it suggests the Mediterranean. And with no herbs, it still tastes amazing, refreshing, light, and bright. And in each of its iterations, *achichuk*, though transporting, tastes unmistakably Uzbek. Serve with An Uzbek Plov (see p149) or whenever you need a bright, refreshing salad.

---

1 tbsp bicarbonate of soda

1 onion, preferably white, thinly sliced into half-moons

3–4 tomatoes, cut into large chunks, juice reserved

fine sea salt

Optional toppings

fresh herbs

dried chilli flakes

thinly sliced fresh chilli

freshly ground black pepper

In a bowl, mix the bicarbonate of soda with 240ml (1 cup/8fl oz) cold water. Add the onion to the bowl and let it soak for 15 minutes. This takes the bite out of the raw onion.

After your onion has soaked, drain and rinse in cold water, then put it into a clean bowl. Add the tomatoes to the bowl, along with their juices. Gently mix the tomatoes and onion together. Season with salt to taste.

Add toppings, if you like, and enjoy.

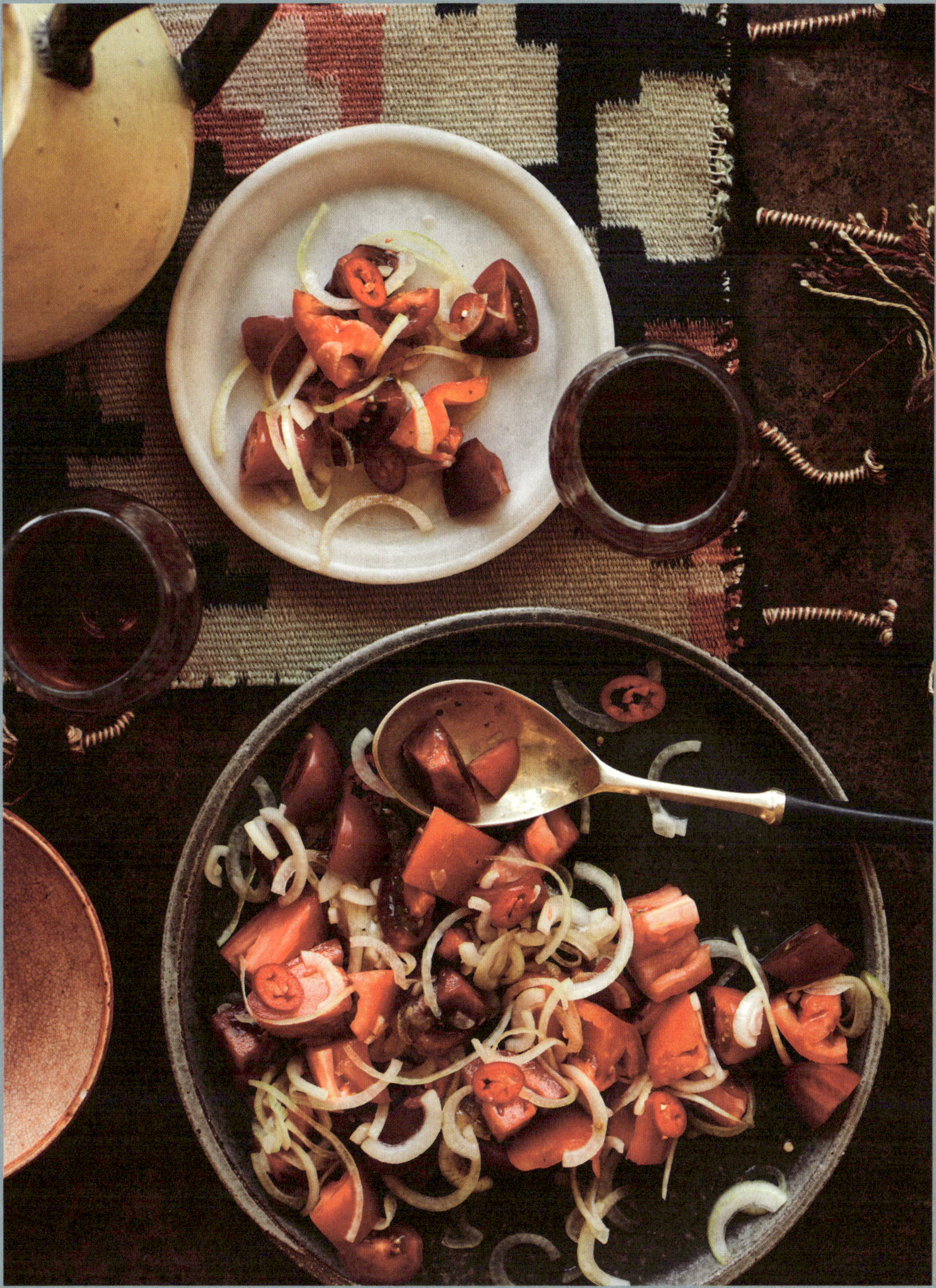

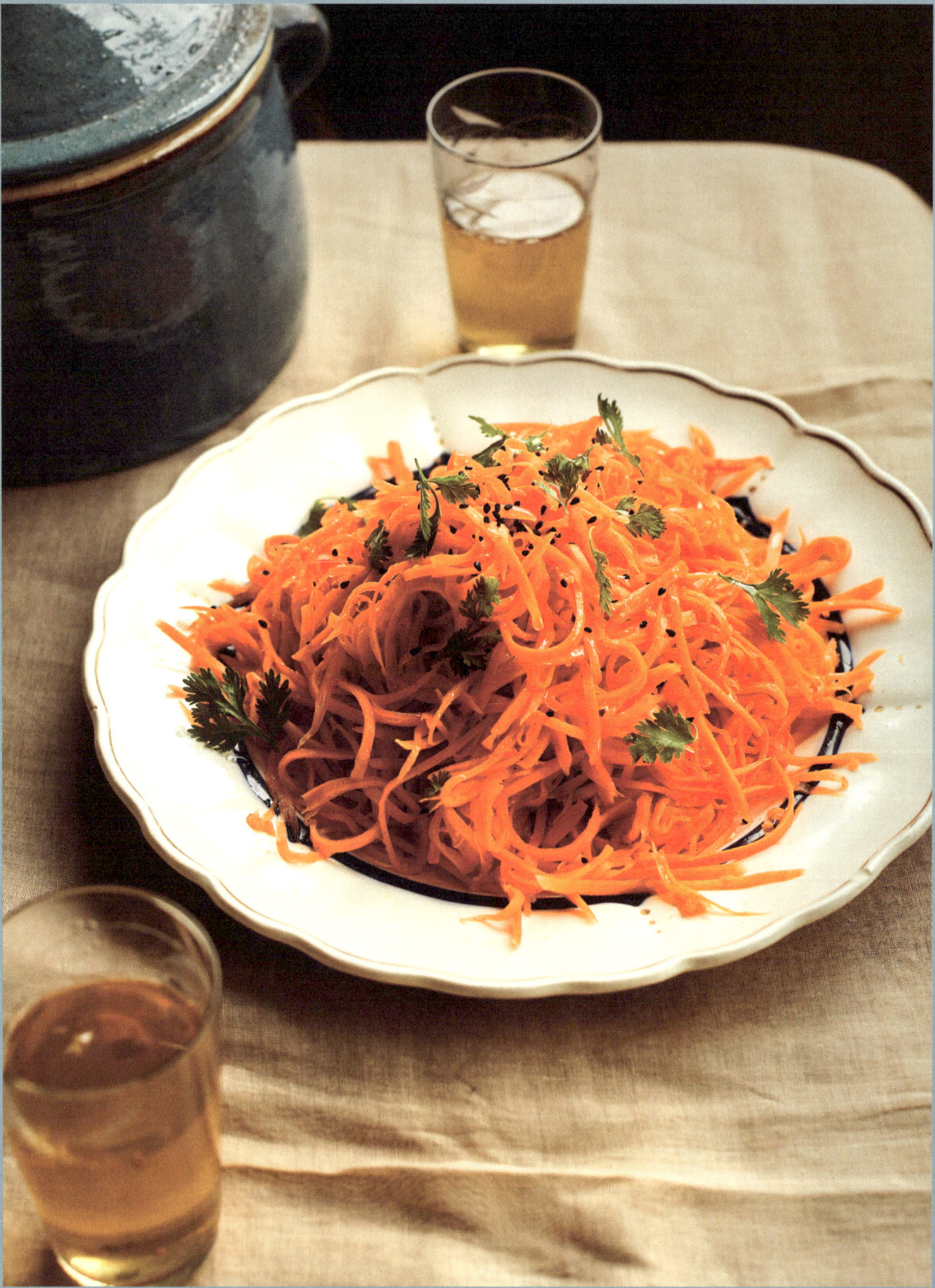

MORKOVCHA

Korean-Style Carrot Salad

Serves 3–4 as a side

When I brought this dish to the table to enjoy alongside Uyghur Roast Lamb (see p125), An Uzbek Plov (see p149), and some Uyghur *lamian* (see p171), I announced it as it had been announced to me: "This is a Central Asian carrot salad, but with a Korean spin. There are a number of ethnic Koreans throughout the region, so they have imported some of their flavours and cooking techniques, and—"

My friend Coley promptly interrupted me. "I know all about the Koreans! I think I had this in Kyrgyzstan when I was there! Hang on, I'll find my photos." He pulled out his phone and, lo and behold, he found a photo taken a decade prior of piles of carrots in a Kyrgyz market, and then one of a shredded carrot dish – a dish that looked strikingly like the one on my London dining table.

Coley took a bite. "Oh man, this is good! Yes – I remember this! It's amazing how you can taste something that just takes you back." I'd concur, but also point out that it's also amazing how you can taste something that takes you somewhere you've never been before. Try this and you'll see what I mean.

- 500g (1lb 2oz) carrots, peeled and julienned
- 1 tsp fine sea salt
- 120ml (½ cup/4fl oz) neutral oil
- 1 onion, thinly sliced into half-moons
- 4 garlic cloves, finely minced
- 1 tbsp rice wine vinegar
- ½ tsp white granulated sugar
- 1½ tsp ground coriander
- ½ tsp sweet paprika
- fresh coriander leaves and nigella seeds, to garnish (optional)

Place your carrots in a bowl with the salt and set aside for 20 minutes. The salt will enhance the sweetness of the carrots, while also drawing out their moisture, creating a pickled-like tartness when eventually combined with the rice wine vinegar – so don't skip this step.

Heat the oil in a sauté pan over a medium heat. Add the onion, watching out for any sputters. Keep a close eye on the pan: you want to imbue the oil with onion flavour, as it's the oil, not the onion, you will be using. But you want only the *faintest* hint of flavour, so the moment you see the onion start to turn brown, turn off the heat and, using a heatproof sieve, strain the oil into a heatproof mixing bowl. Discard the onion or find a use for it elsewhere. Set aside the bowl of oil.

Once your carrots have been salting for 20 minutes, grab a handful of them and squeeze. Hard. Get as much water out of them as you possibly can, then deposit the carrots into a second, medium-sized mixing bowl. Squeeze all the carrots this way and discard the salty carrot water. Add the minced garlic, vinegar, sugar, and spices to the bowl of carrots, and mix everything together.

Drizzle a tablespoon of the onion-flavoured oil into the carrots and stir with a fork. Taste, and decide what you want more of. Nothing? That's cool. Oil? Drizzle in another spoonful. Paprika? Add a pinch. Coriander? Go on, now. Taste. This is your adventure.

If you like, top with some coriander leaves and a sprinkling of nigella seeds to serve.

SHALGAM

Kazakh Radish Salad

Serves 4–6 as a side

Jane Grigson wrote: "It insults radishes, the most ancient of appetizers, to chop them and bury them in a salad." She clearly never tried *shalgam*. Typically a side, I also like to serve this as an *al fresco* lunch with avocado, walnuts, and bread. A little bit of Central Asia in East London. *Pictured right.*

- 1 daikon radish (about 300g/10oz), peeled and cut into 5cm (2in) matchsticks
- 1 carrot (about 300g/10oz), peeled and cut into 5cm (2in) matchsticks
- 2 red peppers, cut into 5cm (2in) matchsticks
- 2 garlic cloves, minced
- 2 tbsp white wine vinegar
- 6 tbsp olive oil
- ½ tsp fine sea salt
- freshly ground black pepper

To serve (optional)
- a few fresh dill fronds
- 2 red or purple radishes, thinly sliced

Combine your daikon radish, carrot, and peppers in a bowl.

Make a simple vinaigrette by whisking together the garlic, vinegar, olive oil, and salt in a small bowl until emulsified. You will end up with more vinaigrette than you need for this dish, and that is not a bad thing. Refrigerate the rest to use within the next 3–4 days.

Dress your salad with as much of the tangy dressing as you like, and crack some black pepper over the top. You can further spruce up this lovely salad with a few fronds of dill and a couple of thinly sliced red or purple radishes, if you are so inclined.

NOKOT

Uyghur Chickpea & Carrot Salad

Serves 2–4 as a side

This Uyghur-inspired chickpea salad will knock your socks off. Promise.

- 400g (14oz) can chickpeas, drained and rinsed
- 1 medium carrot, peeled and julienned
- 1 spring onion, chopped
- 1 garlic clove, minced
- 1 tsp white wine vinegar
- 1 tbsp olive oil
- 1 tsp honey
- 1 tsp fine sea salt
- handful of fresh coriander leaves
- ground cumin, for sprinkling

Combine the chickpeas, carrot, and spring onion in a medium bowl.

In a separate bowl, make a simple vinaigrette by whisking together the garlic, vinegar, olive oil, honey, and salt until emulsified.

Dress your salad with as much of the vinaigrette as you like. Top with coriander leaves and a sprinkling of ground cumin to serve.

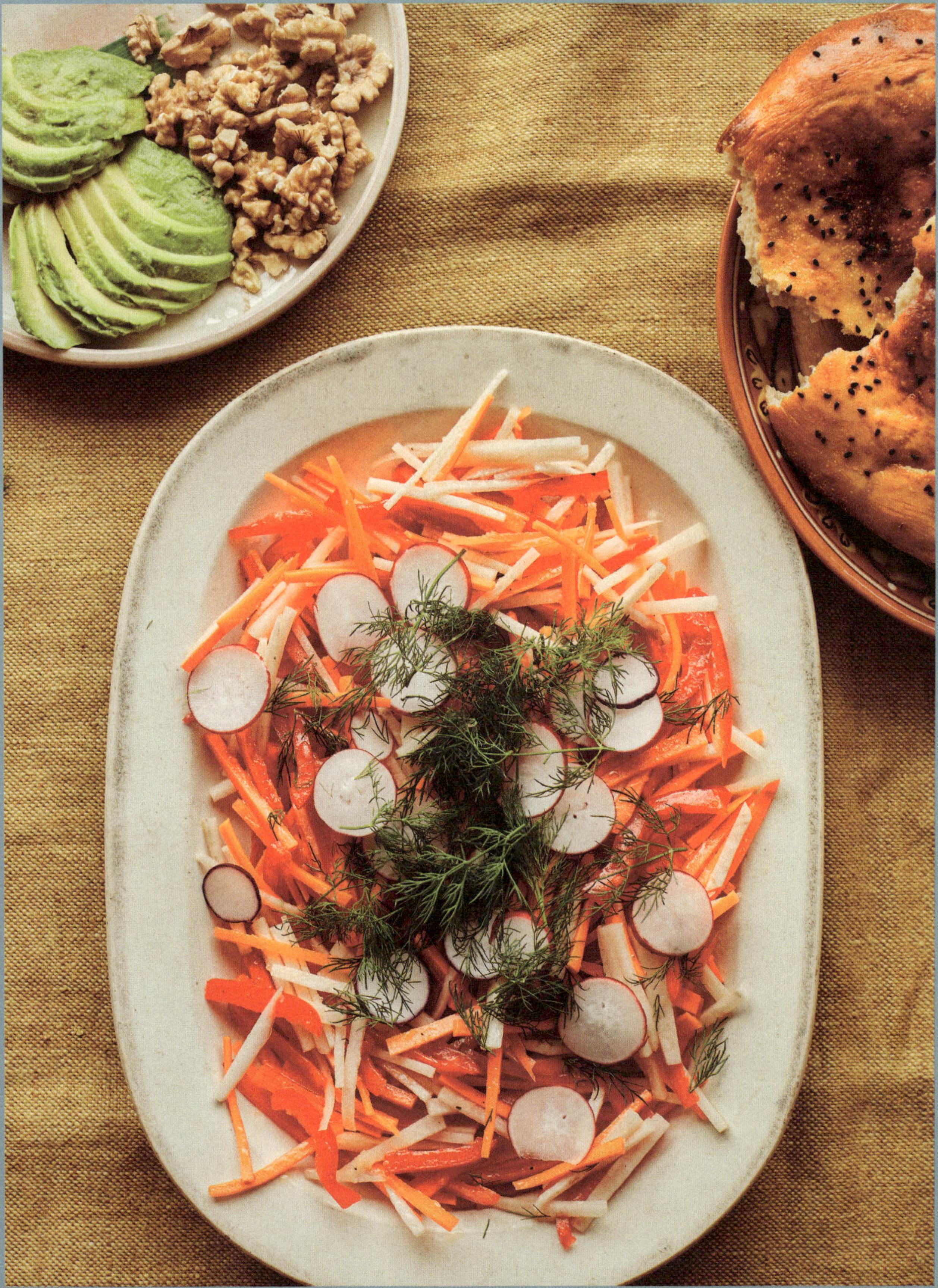

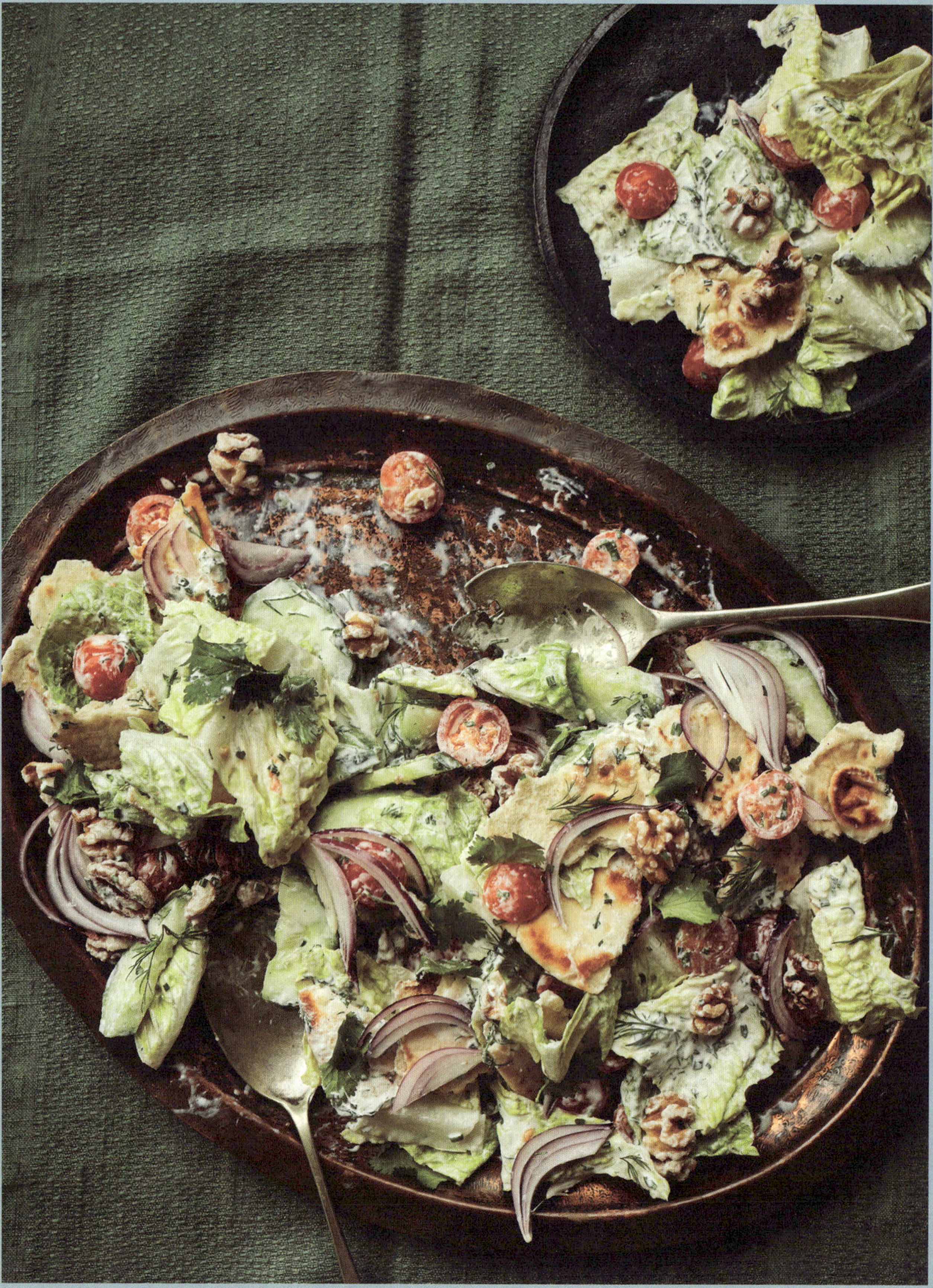

QURUTOB

Tajik Bread Salad

Serves 4–6 as a side

The *"qurut"* in *qurutob* is what Tajiks, Turkmen, and Uzbeks call the dehydrated dairy preparation known to Iranians as *kashk*, Armenians as *chortan*, and Turks as *kurut*. Ubiquitous and beloved across the Middle East, the Caucasus, and Central Asia, today's dried dairy balls are not so dissimilar from those with which, according to Marco Polo, Genghis Khan's soldiers once fortified themselves:

> *They ... have dried milk, which is solid like a paste. It is dried like this: they boil the milk and skim the cream off the top, putting it in another vessel to make butter ... Then the milk is put out in the sun to dry. And when they go to war, they each carry about ten pounds of this [dried] milk. In the mornings, they each take half a pound of the milk and mix it with water in a little leather flask shaped like a bottle, which they keep with them as they ride until the milk has been shaken up and has dissolved into a syrup. Then they drink it for breakfast.*

Lucky you – you don't need any *qurut* to make this salad (though, by all means, if you have some, go for it!). Instead, I've given you a recipe for a tangy yogurt dressing, redolent of the American ranch dressing of my youth, but healthier and much more delicious, with which to dress this Tajik bread salad. And, honestly, is there anything better than bread in a salad, soaking up a vinegary dressing while occasionally maintaining a crunch? No. The answer is no, there is not anything better, and there are not many salads better than this one either.

Note: These amounts will give you more dressing than you need for this salad, so you'll have some for next time. It will keep in the fridge for about 1 week.

---

2 Layered & Fried Flatbreads (see p211), 1 round of Central Asian Bread (see p205), or 3 toasted store-bought pita breads, roughly torn into pieces

1 head of romaine lettuce, roughly chopped

1 cucumber, sliced

50g (1¾oz) walnuts, shelled

250g (9oz) cherry tomatoes, halved

½ red onion, very thinly sliced

freshly chopped herbs (e.g. coriander, dill, or chives), to garnish

For the dressing (makes 320ml/ generous 1¼ cups/11fl oz)

250g (9oz) full-fat Greek yogurt

2 tsp garlic powder

¾ tsp onion powder

10g (¼oz) chives, chopped

5g (⅛oz) dill, chopped

5g (⅛oz) coriander, chopped

1 tsp fine sea salt

1 tbsp white wine vinegar

dash of Worcestershire sauce

freshly ground black pepper

In a medium bowl, combine all the dressing ingredients. Mix well, then add cold water, a tablespoon at a time, to thin out the dressing to your liking. Give it a taste. You may find you want more of a certain flavour; by all means, add it.

Combine the bread, lettuce, cucumber, walnuts, and tomatoes in a large bowl. Mix well, then toss with a generous (or stingy) few tablespoons of your personally seasoned salad dressing. Serve the *qurutob* either in that bowl or on a platter, topped with the red onion and some herbs.

AN AZERI TOMATO SALAD

Serves 4–6 as a side

The walnut. A portable, nutrient-dense, high-calorie nut beloved across the world, but most particularly in Iran and Central Asia, from whence it originated. Though generally believed to have first been cultivated in Iran, competing claims place the walnut's origin in modern-day Kyrgyzstan or northern China. Not up for debate, however, is the timeline: one of the oldest tree foods eaten by humans, we have been cultivating walnuts for at least 7,000 years.

The ancient Greeks loved the walnut and, later, so too did the Romans, who bestowed upon the nut its esteemed Latin name, *Juglans regia*, which translates directly to "royal acorn of Jupiter". Evidence of the ancient Roman walnut affinity can still be seen today in the form of unshelled walnuts, preserved forever in volcanic ash, at Pompeii's Temple of Isis.

As technology and science advance, so too does our understanding of the walnut's history. Recent research further supports Iran as the ancestral home of the walnut, and also suggests that traders and travellers planted walnut trees as they traversed the Silk Roads, giving themselves and their travel routes long-lasting food supplies.

Iranians love walnuts. Azeris love walnuts. And I love this salad – which has walnuts in it. The sweet juices of the tomatoes mix with pomegranate juice, walnuts, flat-leaf parsley, red onion – and nothing else. No oil. No vinegar. A salad of pure alchemy, pure harmony. A surprise. A revelation.

½ red onion, peeled

7g (¼oz) fresh flat-leaf parsley, plus extra to garnish

75ml (5 tbsp/2½fl oz) pomegranate juice

½ tbsp pomegranate molasses

500g (1lb 2oz) whole walnuts, plus extra to serve

750g (1lb 10oz) mixed ripe tomatoes (large ones cut into full circles or chunky wedges, smaller ones quartered or halved)

handful of pomegranate arils, to garnish

flaky sea salt

Combine the onion, parsley (stems included), pomegranate juice, and molasses in a food processor. Blend on a high speed until everything is well mixed, then add the walnuts. Pulse 6–10 times, or until the nuts have broken down into small gravel-sized pieces; you want them to have a bit of a bite, so try not to blend them into a paste.

Place your tomatoes in a large bowl and pour the blended walnut mixture over them. Mix well and, if you can, let the salad sit for an hour or two so that the tomatoes release more of their juices.

Toss the salad once more, before garnishing with additional parsley and walnuts, as well as the pomegranate arils and a sprinkling of flaky sea salt to taste.

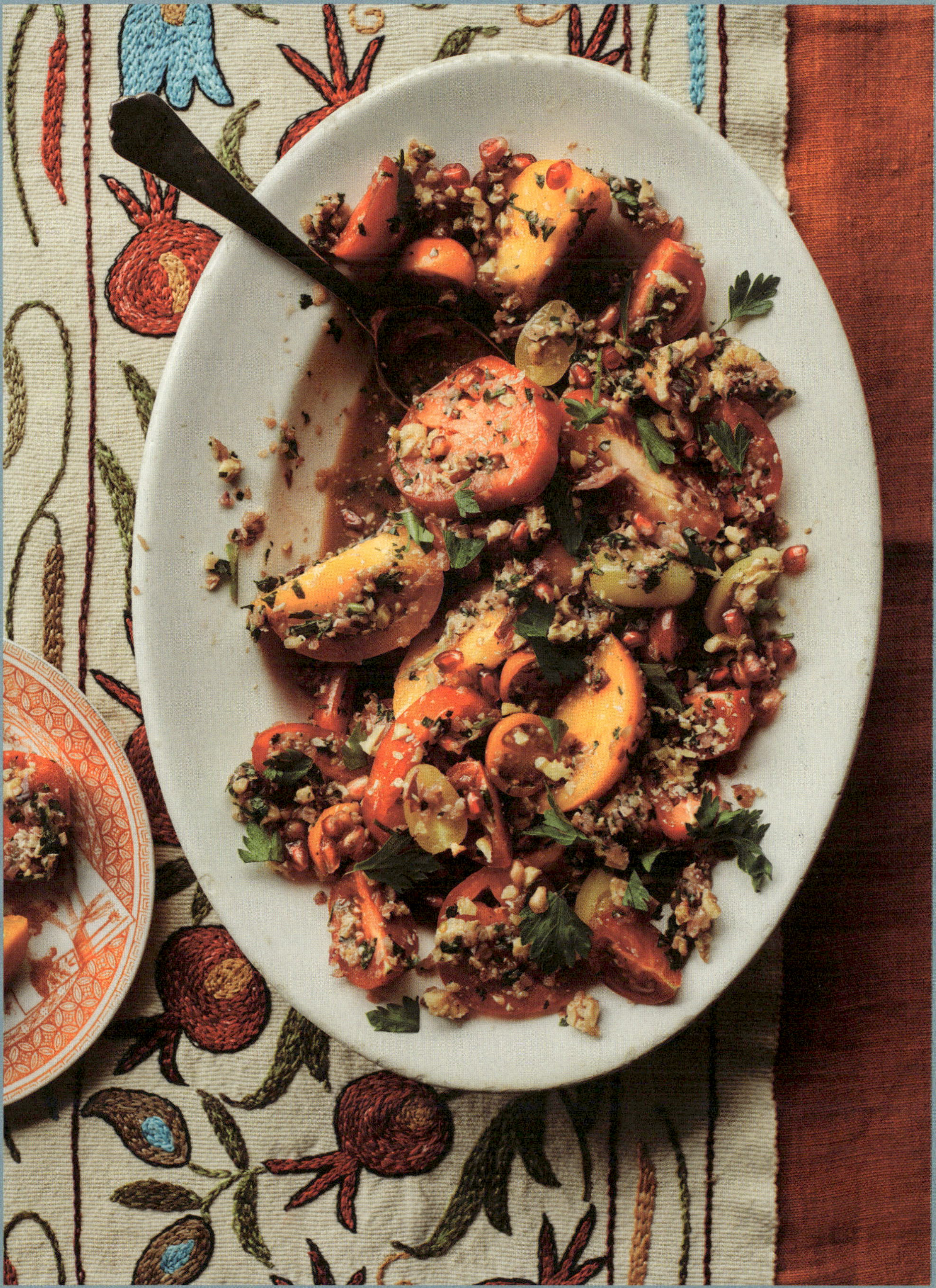

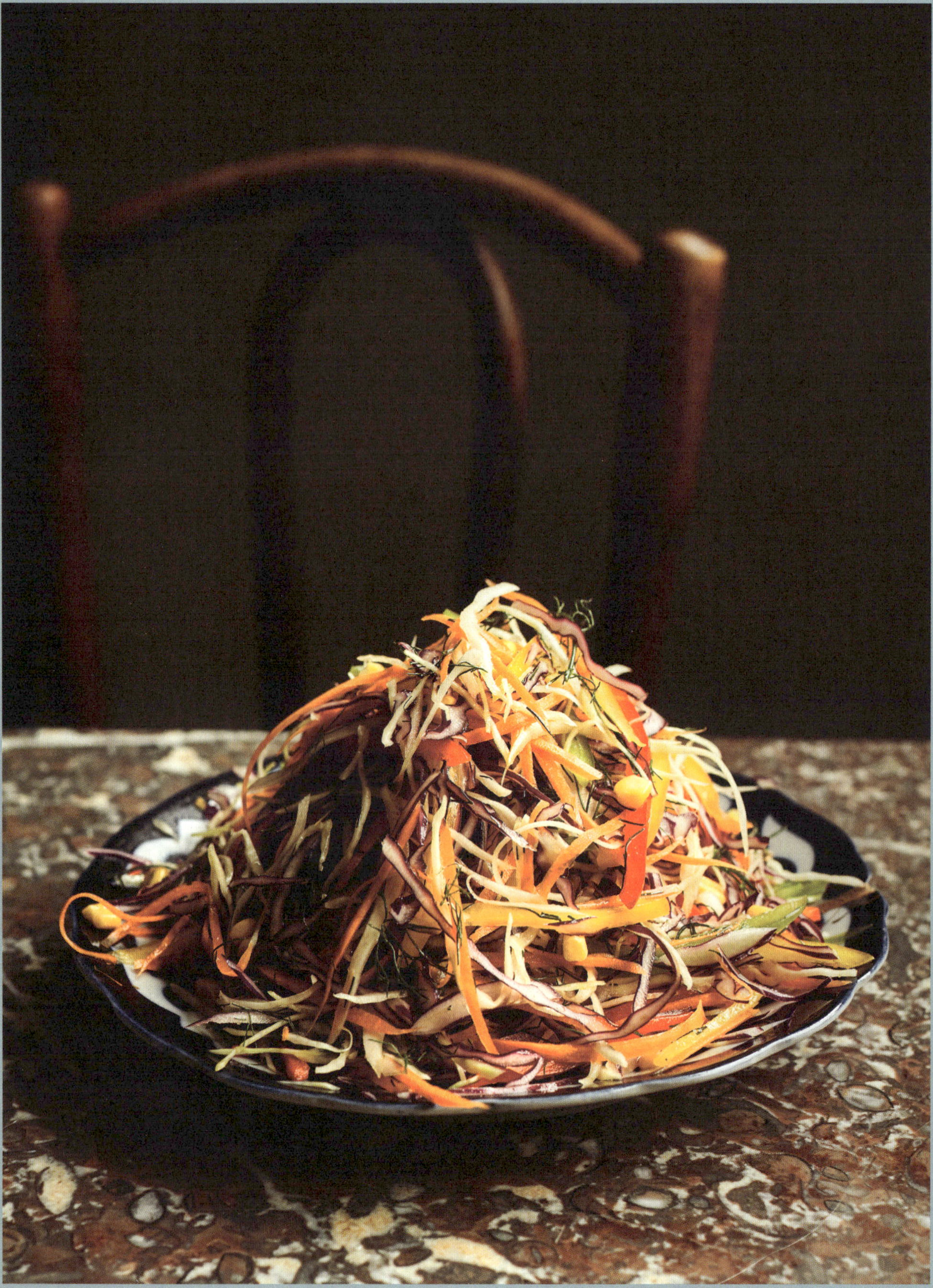

A CENTRAL ASIAN SLAW

Serves 4–6 as a side

Have you heard of "Asian slaw"? "Chinese chicken salad"? You might find one at a California Pizza Kitchen or a similar food joint in a shopping mall. Or even at a higher-end place: some say it was Wolfgang Puck who popularized the "dish". There are quotation marks there because the dish in question is nothing more than an imagined, exoticized, Orientalized flavour fantasy (often delicious, I must admit) that someone decided was "Asian" or "Chinese". I never gave the "dish" much thought until I had a thought-provoking conversation with my friend Jenny Lau, whose "Asian Slaw Alliance" sought to "reclaim and re-imagine the 'Asian' in 'Asian slaw'".

After chatting with Jenny, I saw the slaw everywhere. And it pissed me off, in the same way that calling something "Mediterranean" only because it is made with, say, capers, olive oil, and oregano annoys me. And then I got to Khiva, an Uzbek city whose name conjures up images of fierce, barbarous rulers doling out cruel punishments and growing rich off the back of the Central Asian slave trade and cotton industry, a city "preserved because forgotten", according to Jan Myrdal, the Swedish (and Maoist) writer – and a city in which my husband and I stumbled across this slaw. It blew my mind and blew open my notions of Asian food. A true (Central) Asian slaw, divorced of any Orientalist attempts at coupling cabbage with sesame oil and crispy wontons. And it was *everything*. A proclamation of the supremacy of salads.

Make it, and you'll see what I mean. Imagine you're on a rooftop in Khiva, overlooking the Itchan Kala, sun on your back, fresh, crisp flavours on your plate. And enjoy your Asian slaw, guilt- and racism-free.

For the slaw

300g (10oz) mixed red and white cabbage, thinly sliced

200g (7oz) carrots, peeled and julienned

1 red pepper, very thinly sliced

1 yellow pepper, very thinly sliced

½ green pepper, very thinly sliced

80g (3oz) frozen or fresh sweetcorn kernels (never canned – NEVER!)

10g (¼oz) fresh dill, finely chopped

For the vinaigrette

1 tbsp lemon juice

3 tbsp extra virgin olive oil

¼ tsp fine sea salt

½ tsp toasted coriander seeds

½ tsp honey (hot or not)

Combine all the slaw ingredients in a large mixing bowl. Toss well. (If you're using frozen sweetcorn, the kernels should defrost quickly enough that they're ready to eat by the time you are.)

Make your dressing by whisking together the vinaigrette ingredients in a bowl until emulsified.

Dress your salad with as much of the vinaigrette as you like.

A GEORGIAN SUMMER SALAD

Serves 4–6 as a side

There are few things I love as much as a good, ripe tomato or a perfectly sweet, juicy strawberry. And there are few salads I love as much as this one.

I visited Georgia for the first time in early June, when the country's tomatoes had just come into season. Strawberries had also just begun to make their appearance at Tbilisi's Dezerter's Bazaar and, undoubtedly, at similar markets around the country.

As I took in the sight of the mountains of berries and piles of tomatoes, my eyes widened and my mouth watered in anticipation of the meals and dishes that I imagined (not incorrectly) I would enjoy over the course of my stay in Sakartvelo – the native name for the country we know in English as Georgia.

Tarragon, I learned, is used with delightful abandon in Georgian cuisine; basil is omnipresent too. Nearly every meal I enjoyed that trip featured raw tomatoes, along with pickled *jonjoli*, a native edible green whose English name, "bladdernut", means less to me than its Georgian one does. We can't get *jonjoli* in the UK or US; the closest we can come is capers. And the closest we can come to a taste of Georgian summer in the UK or the US is this salad.

Serve with Suzma (see p77) and bread, or grate some halloumi cheese over the top.

400–500g (14oz–1lb 2oz) strawberries, thinly sliced lengthways

500g (1lb 2oz) mixed ripe tomatoes (large ones cut into full circles or chunky wedges, smaller ones quartered or halved)

10g (¼oz) fresh basil leaves, finely chopped

10g (¼oz) fresh tarragon leaves, finely chopped

2 tbsp capers

1 tbsp raw sunflower seeds

raw, unfiltered sunflower oil or high-quality olive oil, for drizzling

flaky sea salt and freshly ground black pepper

Combine the berries, tomatoes, herbs, and capers in a large bowl.

Just before serving, top your salad with the sunflower seeds and then give it a good drizzle of the oil, along with a generous pinch of sea salt and a few cracks of black pepper.

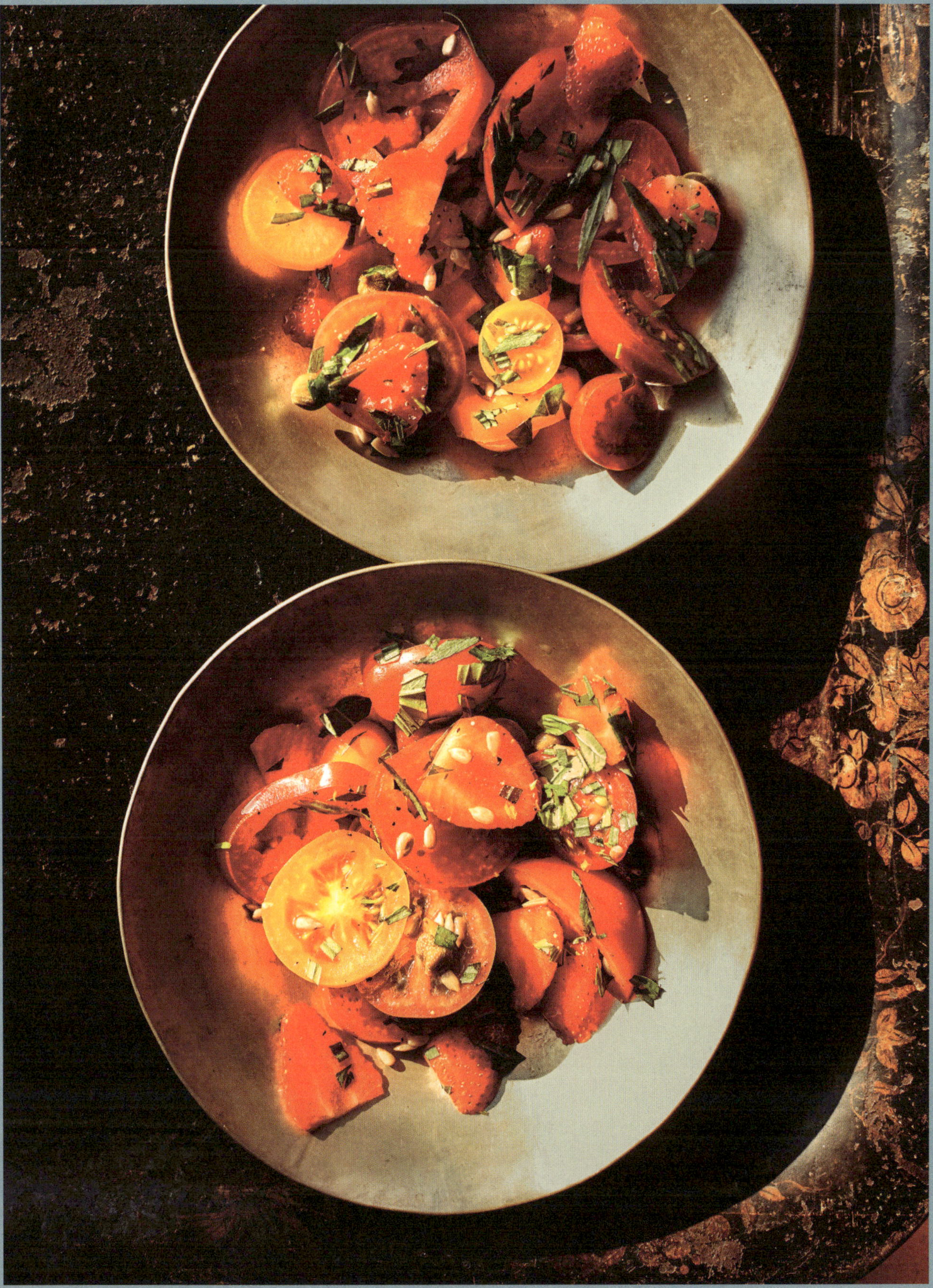

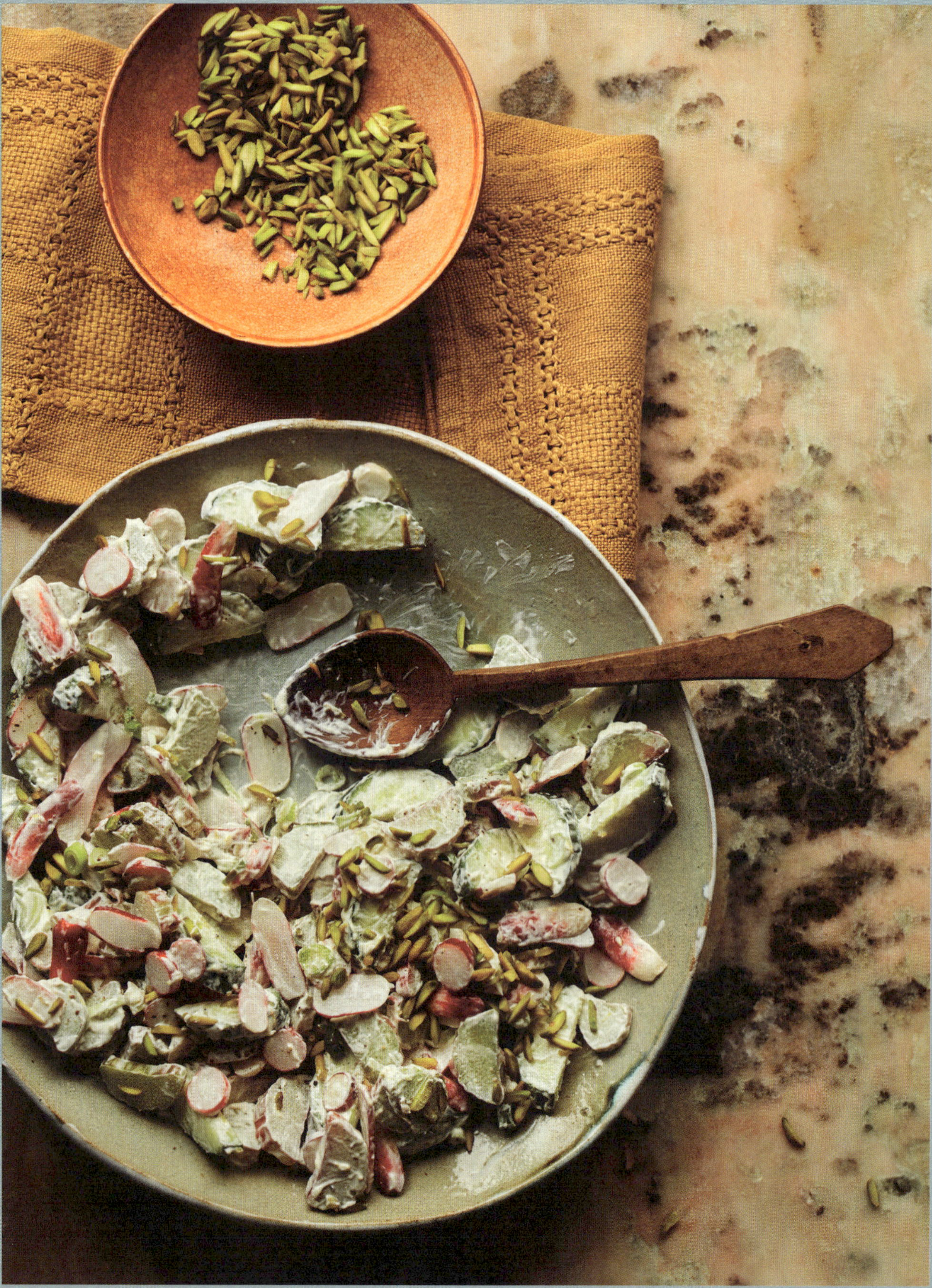

ROVOCH SALAT

Uzbek Rhubarb & Radish Salad

Serves 4–6 as a side

I associate rhubarb with my maternal grandfather, Grandpa Carl Carter, and his patch of rhubarb down by the creek in LaSalle, Michigan. A snippet of early childhood summertime and a slice of Americana pulled straight from the ground and eaten with a grimace and pride. Even as a little kid, I relished the puckering challenge of the bright pink, sweet-tart petiole.

I still love raw rhubarb. And I love the fact that rhubarb is an ancient Asian plant, the first written mention of which was by the 1st-century CE Greek pharmacologist Pedanius Dioscorides. The ancient Greeks called rhubarb *rha barbarum*, in recognition of the fact that the plant's origins lay far enough beyond the Bosphorus to belong to foreigners, to barbarians. They just didn't realize quite how far. By the 10th century, however, the trade of rhubarb from China to Western Asia (and the Mediterranean) was well established and the fruit well known. Marco Polo noted rhubarb's abundance in the mountains of China's Gansu Province, while de Clavijo included rhubarb in his list of the "best of all merchandise coming to Samarkand … from China".

This salad comes not from China, but from Uzbekistan, by way of my London kitchen and childhood love of raw rhubarb. You might be put off by the ingredients list, but I urge you to trust me on this one. If you do, you will be richly rewarded – and, if you're anything like my friend Greg, you'll find yourself licking your plate while repeatedly remarking on your incredulity that the combination of these ingredients comes together so magnificently.

300g (10oz) rhubarb, cut into 1cm (½in) pieces

200g (7oz) radishes, thinly sliced

300g (10oz) cucumber, either cut into 1cm (½in) slices or thinly sliced – or a combination of the two

1½ tsp fine sea salt

4 tbsp crème fraîche

zest of 2 lemons

8 spring onions, thinly sliced

2 tbsp pistachio nibs (or flaked almonds), to serve

freshly ground black pepper

Combine the rhubarb, radishes, and cucumber in a medium bowl. Sprinkle with the sea salt, then stir to mix and set aside for 10 minutes.

Now add the crème fraîche, lemon zest, and spring onions. Stir to mix well.

When you're ready to serve, top your salad with the pistachio nibs (or almonds) and a good grind of black pepper.

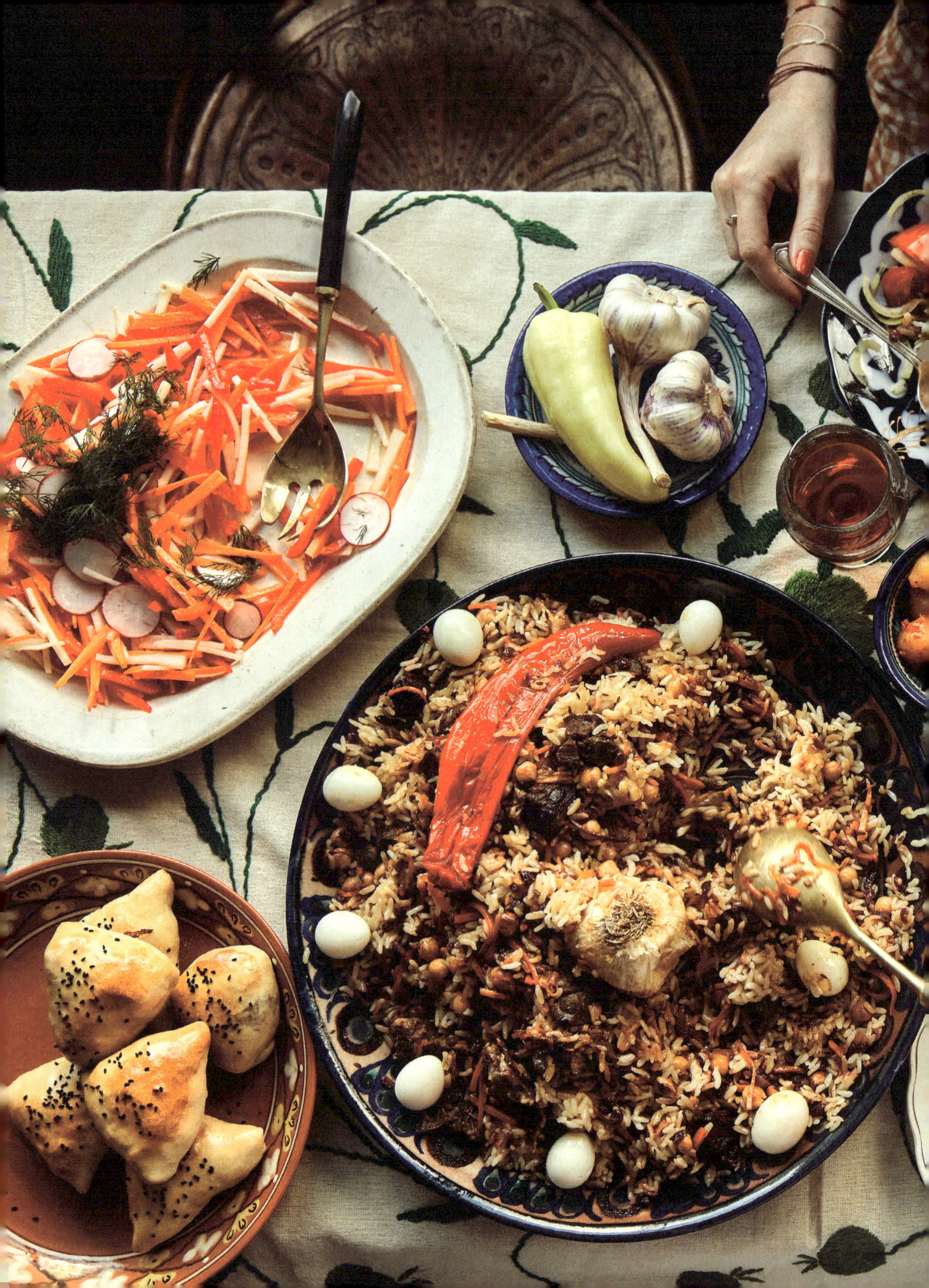

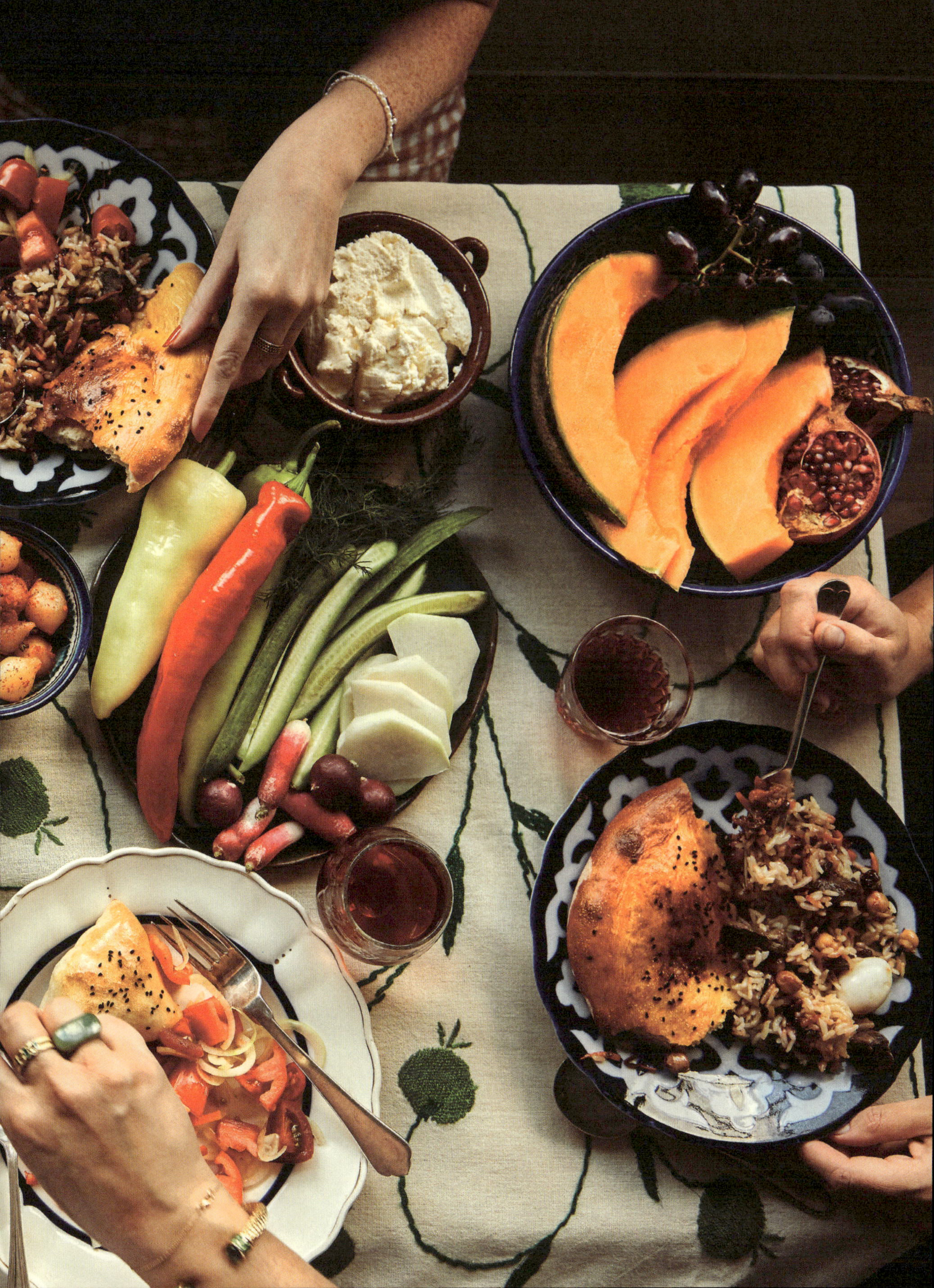

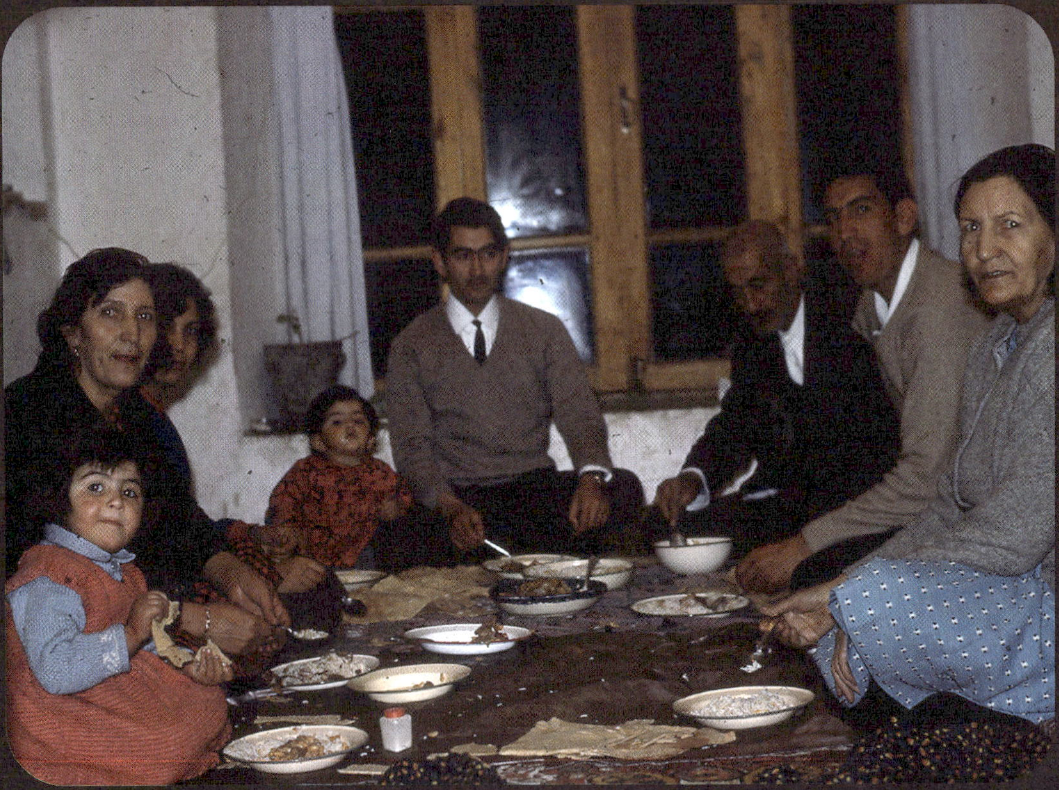

SOUPS & STEWS

**ROLOS, CHICKPEAS
& A WHOLE LOT OF STEW**
44

AB GOOSHT
Iranian Lamb & Chickpea Stew
49

DIMLAMA
Uzbek Harvest Stew
51

YANGROU PAOMO & DOGRAMA
Two Torn-Bread-and-Lamb Soups
54

(MUNG)BEAN & RICE SOUP
58

PITI
Azeri Lamb, Chickpea & Chestnut Stew
59

DOVGA
Azeri Warm Yogurt Soup
63

LOBIO
Georgian Bean Stew
65

ROLOS, CHICKPEAS & A WHOLE LOT OF STEW

Chickpeas (*Cicer arietinum*) are old. Really old. In fact, they are one of the oldest domesticated and cultivated crops, one of agriculture's so-called "founder crops". Full of protein, folate, fibre, zinc, and SO MUCH MORE, humans have been eating these little nutritional powerhouses since at least 9000–10,000 BCE. That makes chickpeas more than old: they're ancient. While *Cicer reticulatum* (the first cultivated chickpea and the ancestor of the legume we know and love today) is native to southeastern Turkey, a small debate remains as to whether their long-ago domestication occurred within the borders of modern-day Turkey or Syria. Either way, this nutrient-dense bean must have blown the minds of its early human Levantine cultivators with its versatility, stability, delectability, and transportability. From Turkey or Syria, the legume travelled east across trade routes, establishing itself as an indispensable part of cultures and cuisines from Iran to India, as well as westward, where it garnered fans in ancient Greece and Rome. Eventually, the chickpea went south, to Ethiopia, as well as further west to Spain, from whence its other well-known name, "garbanzo bean", originated.

Today, India is the world's biggest producer of chickpeas – but of the brown/black *desi* variety, not the creamy-coloured *kabuli* variety with which we in the UK and the US are most familiar. Smaller than *kabuli* ones, *desi* chickpeas tend to be hulled, split, and consumed as *chana dal*, or split yellow gram. While excellent in its own right, and closer in resemblance to its ancestral progenitor than the *kabuli* variety, the *desi* chickpea is not the one for us today – not the one for our *ab goosht*, for our *dovga*, for our *piti*. We are interested in the *kabuli* chickpea, my friends.

Kabuli. That looks and sounds a lot like Kabul, capital of modern-day Afghanistan and once an important stop on the southern-bound trading routes that connected Persia with India, doesn't it? Indeed, it was long believed that it was in Afghanistan where a *desi* chickpea was selectively cultivated into the *kabuli* variety we know and love. However, recent studies position Turkey as the ancestral home of both the *kabuli* and *desi* chickpea, suggesting that the two varieties each began their global travels from roughly the same place. And what roads these two travelled! What journeys they took! What a curiosity the chickpea must have appeared to a person in Sheki or Samarkand, produced, perhaps, from the pocket or saddle bag of a trader or traveller passing through. What a difference this legume would make in cuisine, culture, nutrition, agriculture, and economy, not just in Asia, but eventually across the globe: this delicious, geriatric, funny-looking little bean that could, did, and can do so much.

The role the chickpea plays in our stews, including *ab goosht* (see p49 for my recipe), is crucial. Not only does that little legume provide the dish with flavour, but it also acts as a textural base and binder, and bulks up the stew's volume

> **WHAT A CURIOSITY THE CHICKPEA MUST HAVE APPEARED TO A PERSON IN SHEKI OR SAMARKAND, PRODUCED, PERHAPS, FROM THE POCKET OR SADDLE BAG OF A TRADER OR TRAVELLER ...**

and nutritional force. The chickpea allows *ab goosht* to feed countless more mouths, to nourish countless more families, to strengthen countless more growing children than it would if it were yet another (chickpea-less) lamb stew.

My great-aunt Khalejan made *ab goosht* nearly every day when my father was growing up. Sick and weakened by malaria, he needed his aunt's cooking to help him regain his strength and health; he needed *ab goosht*. Decades later, she made *ab goosht* when my siblings visited Iran as kids, delighting them with her delicately but deeply flavoured stew, encouraging and teaching them how to whack the cooked lamb shank bone to dislodge the unctuous marrow within and enjoy it smeared on a piece of *sangkak* bread.

Khalejan's name was Fakhrintaj Chini, and she was born in 1915, in the same town in northwest Iran in which my father eventually entered the world. Maybe.

No one knows exactly when Khalejan was born. She's dead now, but even when she was alive, no one knew when her birthday was. She was born in the twilight of empire, in the final years of the Qajar Dynasty – a dynastic period in which once-mighty "Persia" was divided and conquered, both geographically and figuratively. With the signing of the Treaty of Turkmenchay in 1828, Northern Azerbaijan was ceded to the Russian Empire, and an artificial geopolitical division was created, one whose legacy outlived the empires that drew it. In 1907, the British and Russian empires carved up Iranian territory into "zones of influence". And then came World War I. And the Bolshevik revolution in Russia. And the Pahlavi ascension in Iran. The calendars were different back then, too, and shifted with the changing of dynastic rule. It was easy to forget a girl's birth date when far more than just calendars were in flux.

She was the youngest of three: all girls, all orphaned at a young age. City girls, daughters of a man who imported porcelain from China, a business with roots so long and deep that the family's name was inseparable from their trade. "Chini": a designation given generations and generations ago to Iranians who travelled overland to China and back.

An extraordinary cook whose talents touched the plates and palates of hundreds of people, and four generations of my family, Khalejan never married. My grandmother – her elder sister – and grandfather did not allow it. Instead, they insisted Khalejan live with them at their home. With no other assets to give, she made herself indispensable through her food. She was cook, housekeeper, and nanny, all wrapped up in one five-foot-eleven bow, until my grandmother passed away in 1979. Two years prior to her sister's death, Khalejan came to the United States for the first time to help my father care for my older siblings.

> **THE CALENDARS WERE DIFFERENT BACK THEN, TOO, AND SHIFTED WITH THE CHANGING OF DYNASTIC RULE. IT WAS EASY TO FORGET A GIRL'S BIRTH DATE WHEN FAR MORE THAN JUST CALENDARS WERE IN FLUX.**

Their mother had left. He needed support. He needed Khalejan. He needed her to do for him what she had done for his mother. And so she did.

Ironically, that first visit was in 1977 – the year Elvis Presley died. Khalejan loved Elvis, adored him, and was devastated by his death. She loved Elvis's pop-cultural contemporary Lucille Ball even more, and thought she was the funniest lady in the world. Khalejan named an impish cat after Ms Ball, and cackled with pure delight at the episodes of Lucille Ball's television show, *I Love Lucy*, that my mother

Top: "Prep station" at one of Xian's most beloved spots for *yangrou paomo*. Xian, China. April 2024.

Bottom: Khalejan at our home in Bloomfield Hills, Michigan. Spring 1997.

would record for her and send on VHS tapes to Iran whenever my father visited in the 1980s and 1990s. My cousin Shahpar tells me that she and Khalejan would sit next to each other on the sofa in Iran, watching those tapes over and over, tears in their eyes from laughter – and chocolate in their mouths.

My great-aunt loved chocolate – particularly Rolos, those oft-forgotten caramel-filled chocolate candies, along with Milky Ways. We sent bags of candy bars to Iran for her, along with those VHS tapes. And shoes; always shoes. Flats specifically, as she was a tall woman with very large feet. A towering, formidable woman, a beauty with olive skin, greenish eyes, and light-coloured hair that she dyed reddish with henna in her later years, she must have cut quite the figure to the would-be burglar she found in our home on a late 1980s visit to America, screaming at the top of her lungs in Turkish, one arm waving, the other brandishing a makeshift weapon – a frying pan – as she shooed the thief out the front door and down our street. Quite the figure indeed. She was a character. And a half.

For my great-aunt, food was more than sustenance. At least one of my family members confirms this, suggesting that cooking was survival for Khalejan. The same is true for a lot of women, particularly those with little to no agency, little to no property. Cooking as survival (lest we forget, her weapon of choice when confronting that would-be burglar was a frying pan). Cooking as labour. Cooking as an asset to be cherished and closely guarded, an asset of intangible wealth and value.

And, my goodness, what wealth and value she gave us all with her cooking! My older sister Maria tells me she can still see Khalejan when she eats *khoresh badmejan*, can still smell the rose petals on our aunt's hands. My mother waxes lyrical about Khalejan's *ash*, a rare vegetarian delight in an otherwise lamb-fuelled cooking repertoire.

Maybe my ancestors, Khalejan's ancestors, the "Chinis", carried chickpeas with them as they travelled across the Silk Roads. Who knows? We did send Khalejan Rolos, and got chickpeas in return. My dad used to carry them home to me, to his family in America, from his home and family in Iran. Dried chickpeas. Plain ones. Roasted ones. Salted ones. So, it's not inconceivable that someone whose blood runs through my veins today also carried the little legume with them on their long-ago arduous journeys across Asia. After all, for the chickpea to migrate as extensively as it did, someone had to do it. Many someones.

What a delicious little bean the chickpea is! And I can promise you, these recipes, with their deep historical roots, are also delicious. Let these soups and stews nourish, soothe, and care for you as my great-aunt cared for our family. Let them transport you across the Silk Roads to Iran, Azerbaijan, Uzbekistan, Turkmenistan, and China, as well as to any place where you feel warm, comforted, and alive.

> **MAYBE MY ANCESTORS, KHALEJAN'S ANCESTORS, THE "CHINIS", CARRIED CHICKPEAS WITH THEM AS THEY TRAVELLED ACROSS THE SILK ROADS. WHO KNOWS?**

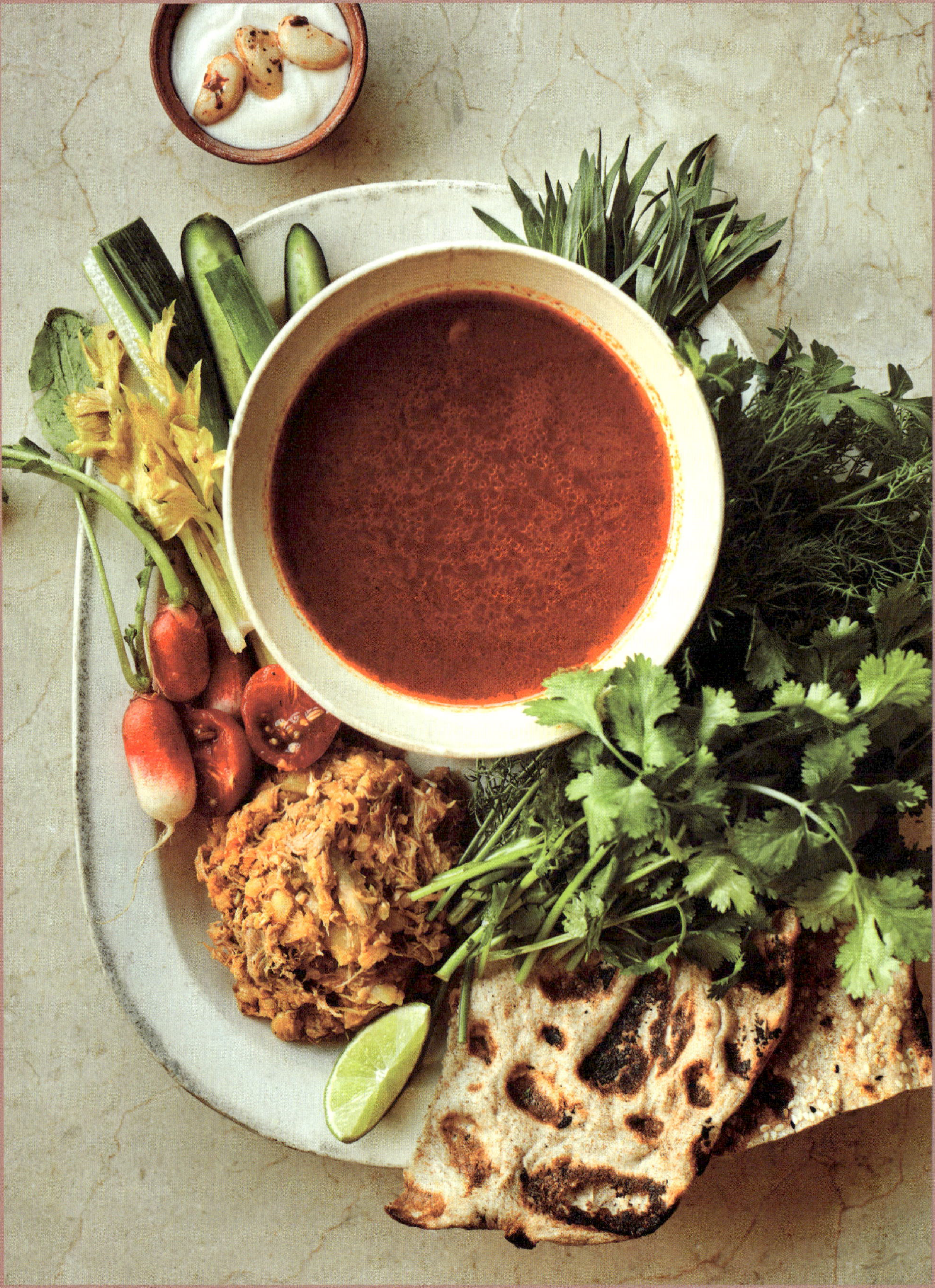

AB GOOSHT

Iranian Lamb & Chickpea Stew

Serves 6–8

A firm favourite with Iranians from all backgrounds, including those of us who have never even been to Iran, *ab goosht* requires very little effort in the way of cooking, ingredients, or money. It just requires time.

After the stew has cooked, the dish is most often served in two parts – the broth in a small bowl, and a scoop of the meat, beans, and potatoes, which have been removed from the broth and mashed together, on a plate. However, many enjoy *ab goosht* as a chunky stew, foregoing the mashing and separation part of the process. I prefer the former, but feel free to enjoy yours however you like. Either way, though, make sure to eat your *ab goosht* with some flatbread, herbs, and pickles.

- 800g–1kg (1¾lb–2¼lb) lamb shanks, on the bone
- 4¼ tsp fine sea salt, plus extra to taste
- 1½ tsp coarsely ground black pepper, plus extra to taste
- 3 tbsp ghee or olive oil
- 3 onions, quartered
- 4 tbsp tomato purée
- 2 tsp yeast extract (I use Marmite)
- 400g (14oz) can whole tomatoes in their juice, or 400g (14oz) large, very ripe fresh tomatoes
- 2 tsp Advieh (see overleaf)
- 1½ tsp ground turmeric
- 1 cinnamon stick
- 4 Iranian dried limes, each pierced with a knife
- 800g–1kg (1¾lb–2¼lb) starchy potatoes, well washed or peeled, cut into medium-sized chunks
- 400g (14oz) can chickpeas, drained and rinsed
- lime juice, to taste

To serve

- bread
- pickles
- fresh herbs (dill, coriander, and/or parsley)
- radishes

Season the lamb on all sides with 1½ teaspoons of the salt and 1 teaspoon of the black pepper.

Heat 1 tablespoon of the ghee or oil in a very large casserole pot over a medium–high heat. When it's hot and glistening, add the meat and brown it on all sides. Be patient. You can tell the meat has been properly browned and is ready to switch sides when it releases easily from the pan. For me, this process takes 2–4 minutes per side.

Remove the browned lamb from the pan, and set aside on a plate.

Add the rest of the ghee or oil to the pot and reduce the heat to medium. Add your onions, along with ½ teaspoon of the salt. Cook for 10 minutes, stirring often, or until the onions are golden and starting to brown.

Add the tomato purée and yeast extract. Stir and cook for 30 seconds, then add 150ml (²/₃ cup/5fl oz) water to the pot. Use a wooden spoon to scrape up any bits that may have stuck to the bottom of the pot – they are tasty flavour bombs and you want them!

Add your canned or fresh tomatoes, along with 1½ teaspoons of the salt and the *advieh*, turmeric, cinnamon stick, and dried limes. Stir.

Return the meat to the pan, along with any juices released, and stir again. Add 1.75 litres (generous 7 cups/3 pints) water, then cover the pot, increase the heat to high, and bring it to a boil. Once boiling, reduce the heat to low and let the stew simmer for 1½ hours, partially covered, stirring occasionally and skimming off any brown foam that rises to the top.

After 1½ hours, add a further 400ml (1¾ cups/ 14fl oz) water, along with the potatoes and chickpeas. Season with another ¾ teaspoon salt and ½ teaspoon black pepper. Stir everything together, then cover and leave to simmer for a further 1½ hours.

At this point, your house should be smelling like cinnamon and rose and lamb and soul – like comfort wafting from a pot. The lamb should be falling off the bone, and the potatoes should be cooked through.

For many, *ab goosht* is finished after this step – removal of bones and addition of salt, pepper, and lime juice notwithstanding – and is served as a chunky stew with some herbs, bread, and pickles on the side. But if you want to (and I encourage you to do so), keep going …

Using a big skimmer/spider, lift all the solid ingredients from the pot and transfer them to a large bowl. Make sure to find and discard the dried lime carcasses and cinnamon stick.

Remove any meat that is still attached to the bones – be careful, as they will be hot! Put the meat you pick off into the bowl with everything else you lifted out from the pot. If the bones have marrow in them, scoop it out, and add it to the meat-and-potato-filled bowl. Either discard the bones, save them to make stock, or give them to your dog.

Now mash all the solid ingredients in the bowl together into a rough, lumpy-textured paste. It's not beautiful, but it will be super delicious – make sure to add some salt, pepper, and lime juice to taste.

Taste and season the broth with additional salt, pepper, and a squeeze of lime juice.

To eat *ab goosht*, spread the mashed meat mixture on to a flatbread such as pita (or *sangkak* or *barbari*, if you can get some), then top with a few pickles and sprigs of herbs, and eat it as a sort of open-faced sandwich, with a bowl of the broth (also topped with some fresh herbs) on the side.

ADVIEH

Makes 4 tbsp

You can't make most Iranian dishes without *advieh*. I've tried; they just don't taste the same. At all. Not even worth it. So do yourself a favour – mix yourself up some *advieh* and make yourself some Iranian food.

1 tbsp dried rose petals, finely ground
1 tbsp ground cinnamon
1 tbsp ground cardamom
1 tbsp ground cumin

Mix together and store in an airtight container, where it will keep for a year (but I definitely go through my *advieh* stash a lot quicker than that).

DIMLAMA

Uzbek Harvest Stew

Serves 6–8

This stew is a gift to us from Uzbekistan, where it is a typical autumn dish, a celebration of the season, of the harvest, and of the earth. And it is exceptional, and extraordinary in its simplicity. It is a surprise and a chance to truly appreciate what the ground can give us.

Ingredients are layered in a pot, cooked slowly, and left undisturbed so that they release their moisture and create a broth in which their disparate flavours melt together and work in harmony to create something truly more than the sum of its parts.

Don't feel tied to my layering order (except for the cabbage – that should always be the final layer). Choose your own adventure. And, while I'm on that topic, don't feel tied to these ingredients or numbers, either.

Don't have five carrots? No problem. Use two. Or one. Or none. Do you have a turnip or three? Use those! You don't like tomatoes? No worries; leave 'em out! Ohh – what's that? A sweet potato hiding in the corner? Come on down – this stew's for you, little sweetie!

Dimlama is about seasonality and harvest and nourishment and simplicity, and making something wonderful out of what may seem commonplace. I want to eat this every autumn. I want to eat this every day. And I bet you will, too.

Note: I've used ox cheeks here, but you could just as easily use lamb or another cut of beef. You just want something that lends itself to slow-cooking.

---

3 tbsp fine sea salt

2 tbsp coarsely ground black pepper

2 tbsp cumin seeds

2 tbsp neutral oil

1kg (2¼lb) ox/beef cheek

4 onions, thinly sliced into half-moons

5 carrots, peeled and sliced into 2.5cm (1in) pieces

500g (1lb 2oz) tomatoes, quartered

1kg (2¼lb) starchy potatoes, peeled if you prefer, cut into medium-sized chunks

3 peppers (colour of your choosing), sliced lengthways

2 apples or quince, peeled, cored, and cut into medium-sized chunks

6 garlic cloves, minced

1 cabbage, separated into leaves

Put your salt, pepper, and cumin into their own separate small bowls. You will be using these seasonings over the course of your *dimlama* layering as you see fit, so I find it's best to have them all out and ready at the start.

Pat your meat dry with paper towels and season it on all sides with salt and pepper.

Heat 1 tablespoon of the oil in a heavy-based casserole pot over a medium heat. When the oil is hot and glistening, add the meat, making sure you don't overcrowd the pot, and brown it on all sides. Be patient. You can tell the meat has been properly browned and is ready to switch sides when it releases easily from the pan. For me, this process takes 2–4 minutes per side.

Remove your browned beef from the pan, place it on a plate and set it aside.

Add the remaining 1 tablespoon oil to the pot, along with half the sliced onions and a good pinch of salt. Cook, stirring occasionally, for about 10 minutes, or until they start to brown.

Spread the browning onions evenly over the bottom of the pot, then return the meat to the pot and reduce the heat to low. It's time to start layering your vegetables.

I like to add the ingredients in the following order, but as I said above, you do you – this is just what *I* do. On top of the meat, I layer the rest of the onions, adding some salt, pepper, and cumin. Then I add the carrots and tomatoes (and more salt and pepper and cumin). Next up: potatoes (and more salt and pepper and cumin). Now peppers are up to bat (and more salt and pepper and cumin), followed by apples or quince (and the final bits of salt and pepper and cumin). Then the garlic, sprinkled all over the top. Finally, lay cabbage leaves across the top of everything. The role of the cabbage is to keep the steam in, ensuring that everything cooks nicely and nothing dries out.

Once all your vegetables are layered, cover the pot with a lid and cook your *dimlama* over a low heat for 2 hours. At that point, take a little peek under the cabbage and see how things are going. Poke at a potato with a fork. You want your vegetables soft but not dissolving, and you want some broth. If you notice that your vegetables aren't releasing enough moisture to give you a broth, add 250ml (1 cup plus 1 tbsp/9fl oz) of water under the cabbage. Either way, let the *dimlama* cook for another hour (so it will have 3 hours in total).

Use a wooden spoon to push the cabbage leaves down into the stew, then stir everything together gently. The meat should be falling apart. The tomatoes should have disintegrated. The potatoes and carrots should be tender and yielding. The peppers should have collapsed. You should be excited. You're about to ladle earthly heaven into a bowl. Thank you, Earth. Thank you, Uzbekistan.

A bazaar in Bukhara, Uzbekistan. October 1978.

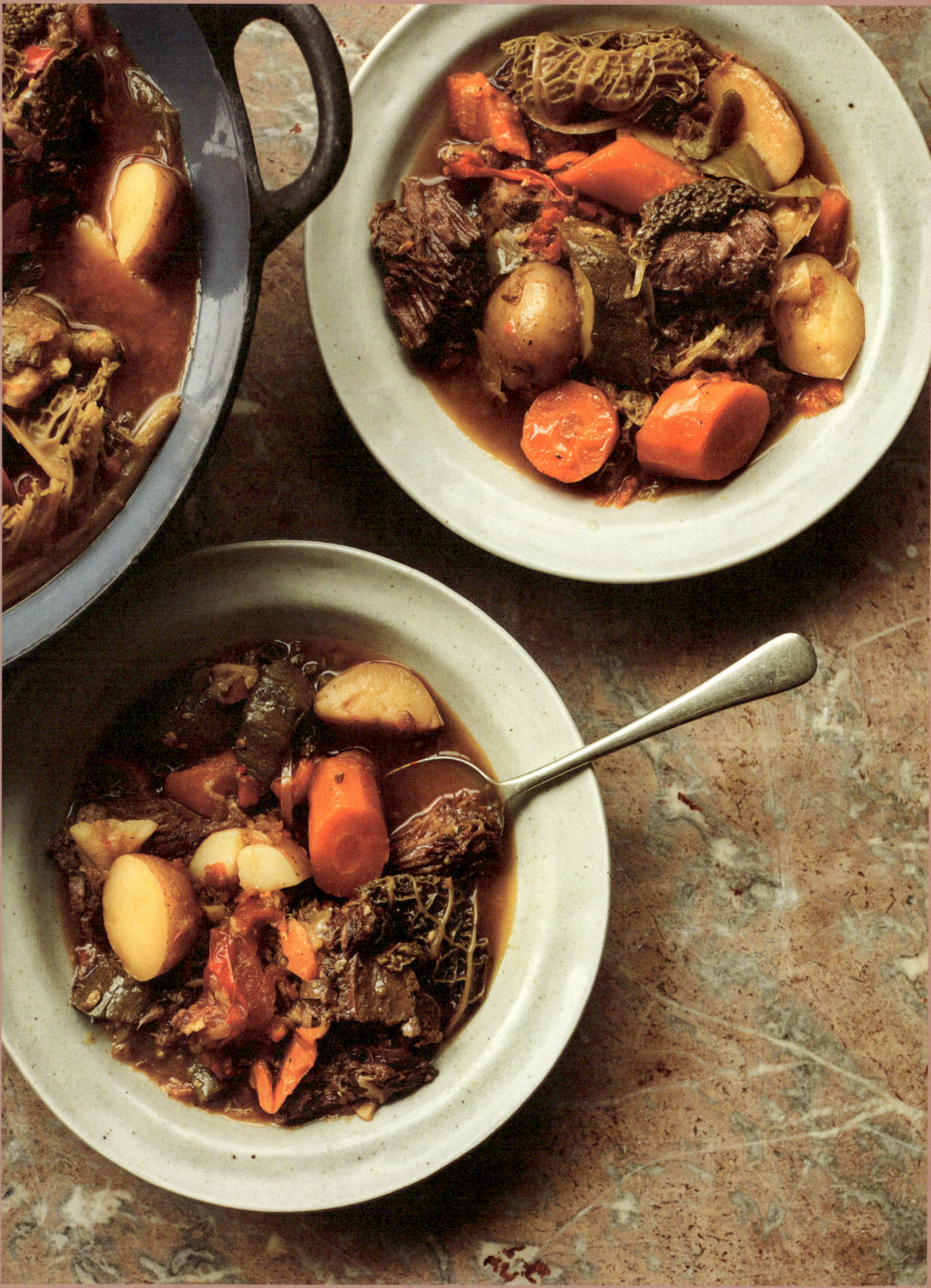

YANGROU PAOMO & DOGRAMA

Two Torn-Bread-and-Lamb Soups

Serves 4–6

Every student of Chinese history learns about the infamous eight-year-long Tang Dynasty-era An Lushan rebellion, which resulted in, amongst other things, the dynastic loss of control of Tarim Basin lands, and, despite its failure, precipitated the eventual decline of the Tang Dynasty itself. Like so many of Turkic and Songdian origin in 8th-century Chang'an, the titular rebel, An Lushan, started off as a merchant. Eventually, he garnered enough wealth, power, and influence to become both a general who commanded thousands of troops, and a court favourite – so much so that he was "adopted" by the Tang Emperor's consort, the (equally infamous) Yang Guifei.

An Lushan's non-Han ethnicity is believed to have played a role in the brutal massacres of foreigners by Tang forces during the rebellion, as well as the subsequent slow but sure dismantling of the multiethnic cosmopolis that was Tang Dynasty Chang'an. Distrust and suspicion of the "other" ran deep, especially when the "other" in question incited an uprising that saw 13–36 million people die.

Despite the resulting loss of territory and life, dynastic decline and inward orientation, some good – nay, great – did come of An Lushan's rebellion. I'm talking about Tang Dynasty poetry, of Li Bai, of Wang Wei. And of Du Fu, whose "*Chun Wang*", an aching, melancholic ode to a fallen capital, is considered by many as the apex of medieval Chinese verse.

> *The country shattered, mountains and rivers remain*
> *Spring in the city – grasses and trees are dense.*
> *Feeling the times, flowers draw forth tears.*
> *Hating to part, birds alarm the heart.*
> *Beacon fires for three months in a row;*
> *A letter from home worth ten thousand in gold.*
> *White hairs scratched grow even shorter—*
> *Soon too few to hold a hairpin on.*

Poetry wasn't the only great thing to come from the years of rebellion and blood loss. If the stories are to be believed, it was Turkic mercenary soldiers hired to defend Chang'an from An Lushan's forces that introduced *yangrou paomo* to China. They did not succeed in holding the line, those mercenaries, and An Lushan took the city – but, if we buy into the story that the locals enjoyed the mercenaries' lamb broth-soaked bread stew so much that they began incorporating it into their diet and adapting it to their culinary preferences, then, well, I think we can forgive their inability to hold down the proverbial fort. The Turks did a great thing for China: *yangrou paomo* is exceptional.

When I first encountered *dograma*, a light bulb went off in my brain. This stew, a celebratory meal typically prepared in an all-hands-on-deck fashion by the men in the family (or community, if making *dograma* for an ultra-grand occasion), immediately brought back decades-old memories of eating bowls of *yangrou paomo* in Xian's Muslim District. Chunks of bread. Lamb broth poured over top. Tender pieces of lamb. That's *dograma*, and that's *yangrou paomo*, and they are nearly the same, more or less.

Those three words – "more or less" – aye, there's the rub. That's where we run into questions of origin, ownership, and authenticity. Because *yangrou paomo* and *dograma* are not the same, however much they remind me of each other. Still, these dishes are so strikingly similar that I couldn't help but present them to you in this manner, side by side.

My friend Guncha, a Turkmen cook and musician, whose *dograma* was the first I ever ate, tells me that when Chinese students come to her cooking classes they exclaim upon seeing *dograma*, and tell her that their cuisine has a dish just like hers – *yangrou paomo*. And just as they are excited to share this commonality with Guncha, pleased to realize heretofore unbeknownst cultural closeness and culinary parallels, so too am I thrilled to share these recipes with you.

I once again invite you to choose your own adventure. Do you go east toward China and Xian and a bowl of *yangrou paomo*? Or do you head west, to Turkmenistan and *dograma*? That is the question that faces you in this recipe, or duo of recipes, as it were.

1kg (2¼lb) lamb shanks
1½ tsp fine sea salt
1½ tsp freshly ground black pepper
1 tbsp ghee or olive oil

To make *yangrou paomo* broth
1 tbsp fennel seeds
1 tbsp Sichuan peppercorns
2 bay leaves
1 tbsp fine sea salt
½ cinnamon stick
2–5 dried chillies (e.g. bird's-eye chillies)
2–5 spring onions
6cm (2½in) piece of fresh ginger
2 tsp dark soy sauce
2 tbsp Shaoxing wine

To make *dograma* broth
400g (14oz) can chopped tomatoes
1 onion, quartered
2 bay leaves
1 tbsp fine sea salt

To serve *yangrou paomo*
1 round of Central Asian Bread (see p205)
noodles of your choice – I like ramen or skinny rice noodles
fresh coriander
crispy chilli oil

To serve *dograma*
2 rounds of Central Asian Bread (see p205)
2 onions, finely diced
freshly ground black pepper

Season your lamb on all sides with the salt and pepper.

Heat the ghee or oil in a large casserole pot. When it's hot and glistening, add the meat and brown it on all sides. Be patient. You can tell it has been properly browned when it releases easily from the pan. For me, this takes 2–4 minutes per side. Once browned, remove your lamb and set it aside on a plate.

Discard any ghee or oil remaining in the pot before filling it with 3 litres (12²⁄₃ cups/5¼ pints) water.

Return the lamb to the pot, along with all the ingredients for your chosen broth. Bring to a boil. Once boiling, reduce the heat to low and simmer, uncovered, for 2–3 hours, or until the meat is fall-off-the-bone tender. Remove the shanks and set them aside on a plate. Keep the broth simmering on a low heat.

While your lamb is cooking, shred the bread into bite-sized pieces – remember, it's one round of bread for *yangrou paomo*, and two rounds for *dograma*.

• **For *yangrou paomo*,** set the bread aside until just before you plan on eating.

• **For *dograma*,** line a large mixing bowl with a clean tea towel. Fill the towel-lined bowl with the pieces of bread and the diced onion, and use your hands to mix them together. Pull the corners of the tea towel up and over to cover the mixture, then leave it until it's nearly time to eat.

Once cool enough to handle, pull the lamb off the bone and shred the meat into small bite-sized pieces.

• **For *yangrou paomo*,** set your meat aside and return your attention to the broth. Carefully remove the solids from the liquid with a fine mesh sieve; discard them and return the shredded meat to the broth. Taste the soup. Season to taste with additional salt if you like, then return the broth to a boil and add your noodles. Cook until they are ready; this will depend on what noodles you are using.

To serve *yangrou paomo*, place a handful of torn bread pieces in each bowl, then ladle some broth, lamb, and noodles over the top. Garnish with fresh coriander and maybe some crispy chilli oil. There you have it: *yangrou paomo*.

• **For *dograma*,** return the bones to the soup.

Open up your tea towel and add the meat to the onion/bread party, along with 120ml (½ cup/4fl oz) of the broth. Using your hands, mix everything together well. Squeeze the meat and its juices into the bread. Rub the bits of fat into the pieces of bread, dissolving it into nothingness.

Pull the corners of your tea towel up and over the mixture once again. Tie it up and let it rest for 30 minutes so that the flavours meld.

To serve *dograma*, add a scoop of the meat-bread-onion mixture to each bowl. Ladle the soup over the top along with plenty of ground black pepper.

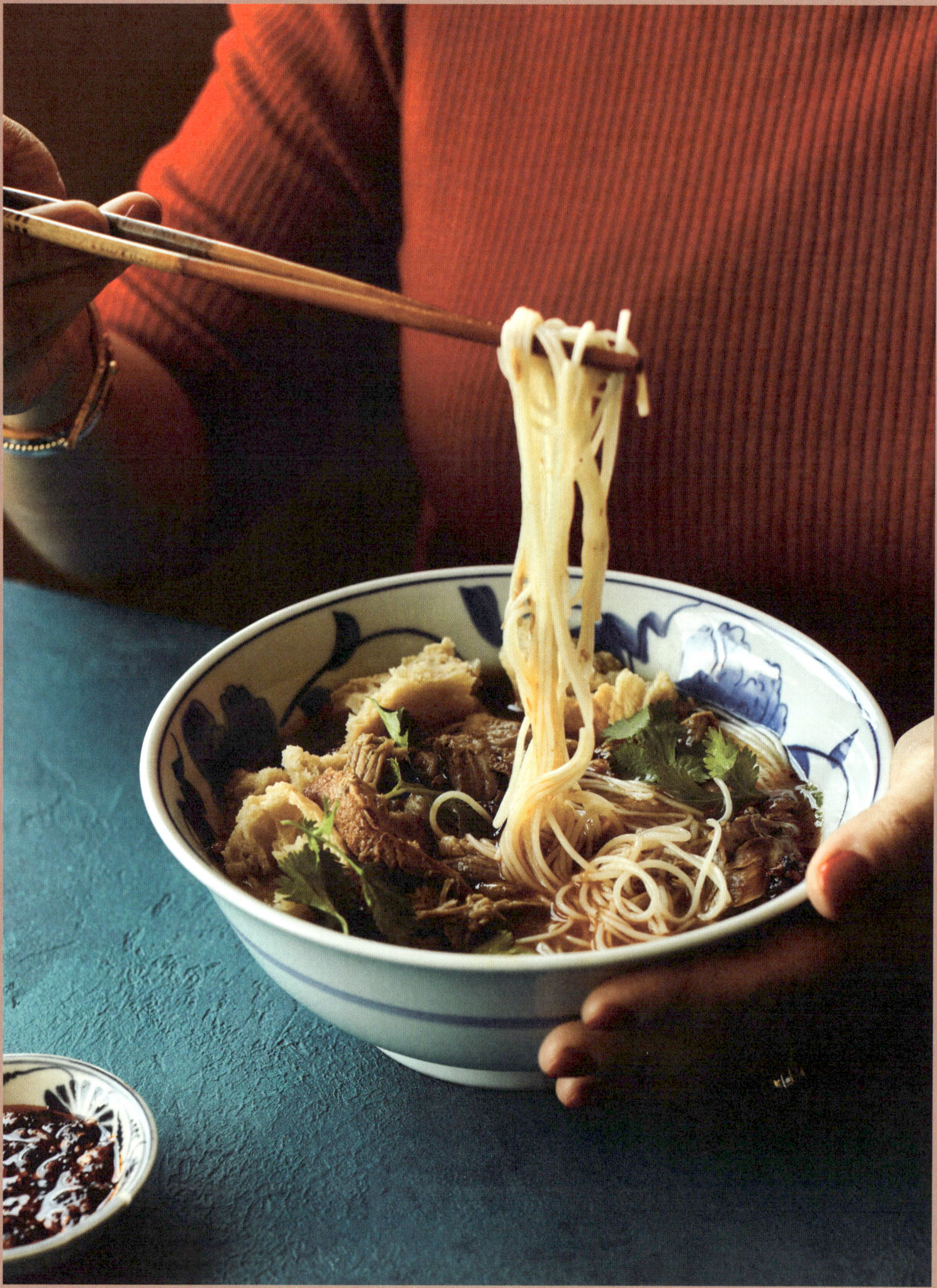

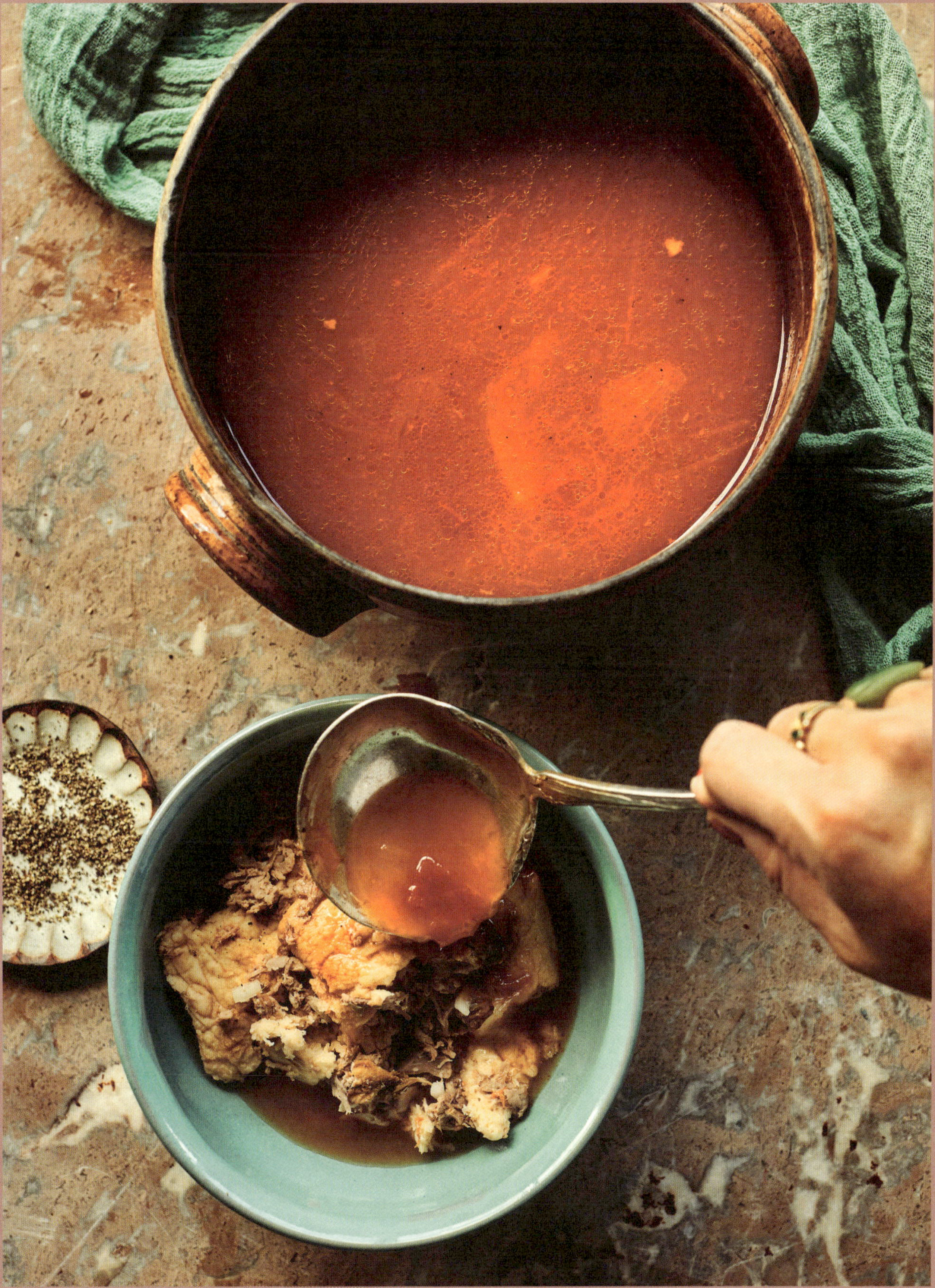

(MUNG) BEAN & RICE SOUP

Serves 4–6

A triumph of flavour, a harmonious union between legume and grain, and a testament to the majesty of simplicity, my take on a deceptively modest rice and bean soup, the likes of which can be found from Iran to Turkmenistan to Kazakhstan and back, begs to be enjoyed on a chilly day. Strike that: it should be enjoyed on any and every day. With some Central Asian Bread (see p205), of course. If you don't have mung beans, you can use whatever you enjoy or have on hand, other than black beans.

- 200g (7oz) dried mung or other beans (see above), soaked overnight, then drained and rinsed
- 100g (3½oz) risotto rice
- 1 bay leaf
- 2 litres (8½ cups/3½ pints) liquid (this can be a combination of stock and water; a well-seasoned homemade stock will make your soup shine, but I've made this before with three parts water and one part stock from a stock cube, and it was still exceptional)
- 3 tbsp ghee or olive oil
- 1 onion, finely diced
- 1 large carrot (140g/5oz), peeled and finely diced
- 1 large potato (250g/9oz), peeled and finely diced
- 1 tsp ground coriander
- 2 tsp ground cumin
- 2 tsp fine sea salt
- 2 tsp coarsely ground black pepper

To serve (optional)

- fresh coriander, chopped
- spring onions, chopped
- yogurt or Suzma (see p77)
- Central Asian Bread (see p205)

Bring a large pot of water to the boil over a high heat.

Add your drained and rinsed beans to the pot. Once the water returns to the boil, reduce the heat to low, then cover and cook for 1 hour.

Drain the cooked beans and discard the cooking water. Return the drained beans to your now-empty pot, along with the rice, the bay leaf, and your cooking liquid of choice. Bring to a simmer over a medium heat, then cover and leave to cook for 30 minutes.

Meanwhile, in a separate saucepan, heat the oil or ghee over a medium heat. Add the onion, then reduce the heat to low and cook, stirring occasionally, for 5 minutes, or until soft and translucent. Add the carrot and potato to the pan, along with all the ground coriander, and 1 teaspoon each of the ground cumin, salt, and pepper. Mix everything together and cook, stirring occasionally, for another 5–7 minutes.

Set this pan aside and wait for your 30-minute rice-and-beans timer to go off. Once it does, add the onion, carrot, and potato mixture to the soup pot. Stir to mix and cook, covered, over a low heat, for another 25–30 minutes.

Taste. Season your soup with the last of the salt, pepper, and cumin, adding more of each if you like.

Serve topped with some chopped fresh coriander and/or chopped spring onions, and perhaps a dollop of yogurt or *suzma*; and definitely eat it with a hunk of bread.

PITI

Azeri Lamb, Chickpea & Chestnut Stew

Serves 4–6

Like that initial meal of Uyghur food in 1998, my first bowl of *piti* shines brightly through the haze of food memories, and not only because it occurred relatively recently. A sunny afternoon. A rectangular wooden covered gazebo in the grassy courtyard of an 18th-century caravanserai. A live band playing in the corner. My family – my sisters and father and me – laughing, eating, talking.

Like so many before us, we came to the northern Azeri city of Sheki for three things: 1) the renowned local halva, a syrupy confection of rice flour, hazelnuts, cardamom, saffron, and coriander; 2) the Palace of Shaki Khans, a UNESCO World Heritage site and a magnificent building constructed in 1762, covered with ornate painted frescoes and fronted with stunning lattice-framed coloured glass and wood mosaics; and, 3) *piti*. Guess which one I was there for?

Founded in the 8th century BCE, the city of Sheki, with its location in the foothills of the Caucasus Mountains, a stone's throw from Azerbaijan's modern-day borders with Georgia and Russia, has, for centuries, attracted merchants, artists, travellers, and craftspeople. A Silk Roads stop on the cusp of Europe, by the middle of the 18th century, Sheki had become a powerhouse silkworm-breeding and silk-production centre, and remained one through the Soviet era. A powerhouse industry is nothing without its workers, though, and Sheki's silk workers needed something to eat. Enter: *piti*.

Traditionally made in individual pottery pots called *dopu* (another Sheki speciality, formed with dark red clay from the nearby mountains), *piti* typically consists of lamb or mutton, chickpeas, sour plums, chestnuts, saffron, and chunks of lamb fat. It is a hearty, filling, warming dish that is lovely as a chunky stew. Typically, though, like Ab Goosht (see p49), *piti* is a two-part meal, eaten as a bowl of strained broth and torn bread, and accompanied by a separate platter of the stew solids to be scooped up and enjoyed with more bread and some chunks of raw onion. I leave it to you to decide how you will eat it; just make sure to top either version with a shit ton of sumac.

I assume you, like me, have no *dopu* in your cupboard. I therefore give you leave to make your *piti* in a large casserole pot. If, unlike me, you have no access to quince as your substitute for sour plums, use pitted prunes instead; the flavour will be a bit different, but no less delicious. Then there's the matter of the fat, the chunks of lamb fat that course through and top every *dopu* of *piti*; I have no substitutions for you there. Let your heart thank me for that one; frankly, once you've made this, you probably will anyway.

Note: Any lamb stewing meat will do, if you can't get leg.

1kg (2¼lb) lamb leg, cut into 5cm (2in) chunks

2 tsp fine sea salt

½ tsp coarsely ground black pepper

200g (7oz) dried chickpeas, soaked overnight, then drained and rinsed

1 bay leaf

80g (3oz) unsalted butter

1 quince, well-washed and skin-on, cut into 2–3cm (¾–1¼in) chunks (if you cannot source quince, use 200–250g (7–9oz) pitted prunes)

180g (3oz) cooked chestnuts

1 onion, diced

0.25g saffron, ground with ⅛ tsp granulated sugar using a mortar and pestle, and then dissolved in 2 tbsp hot water

To serve

bread

raw onion, chopped into chunks

sumac

Preheat your oven to 180°C (160°C fan/350°F/Gas 4).

Season your lamb on all sides with 1 teaspoon of the salt and all the black pepper.

In a large ovenproof casserole pot or saucepan for which you have a lid, bring 1.9 litres (8 cups/ 3¼ pints) of water to a boil. Add the seasoned lamb and cook for 5 minutes, skimming off any brown foam that rises to the surface.

Turn off the heat, then use a slotted spoon to remove the lamb to a bowl and set aside. Don't drain away the liquid from the pot – you're going to use it as the base of your *piti* broth.

Add the drained and rinsed chickpeas to the pot of liquid, along with the bay leaf and the final teaspoon of salt. Cover the pot and place in your preheated oven. Cook for 1 hour.

Meanwhile, melt the butter in a sauté pan over a medium–high heat. Add the quince and cook for 5–7 minutes, or until it begins to brown at the edges, then set aside. (If using prunes, skip this step.)

After the chickpeas have cooked for 1 hour, pull your pot out of the oven, add the lamb, along with any juices released, then cover again. Return the pot to the oven and set a timer for another 30–35 minutes.

When your timer goes off, add the buttery quince (or prunes) to the pot, along with the chestnuts, onion, and saffron water. Return the pot to the oven to cook for a final 45 minutes.

Serve your *piti* as it is – a lovely, saffrony, chunky lamb stew – with some fresh bread on the side. Alternatively, strain the liquid broth from the solids and ladle it over torn bread in a soup bowl, serving the solids on the side, along with more bread and some chunks of raw onion – or just put it all together in a bowl, along with some bread, and dig in.

However you choose to enjoy your *piti*, make sure you top it with lots of sumac.

A conference of Hui Muslim men at the Great Mosque. Xian, China. July 2007.

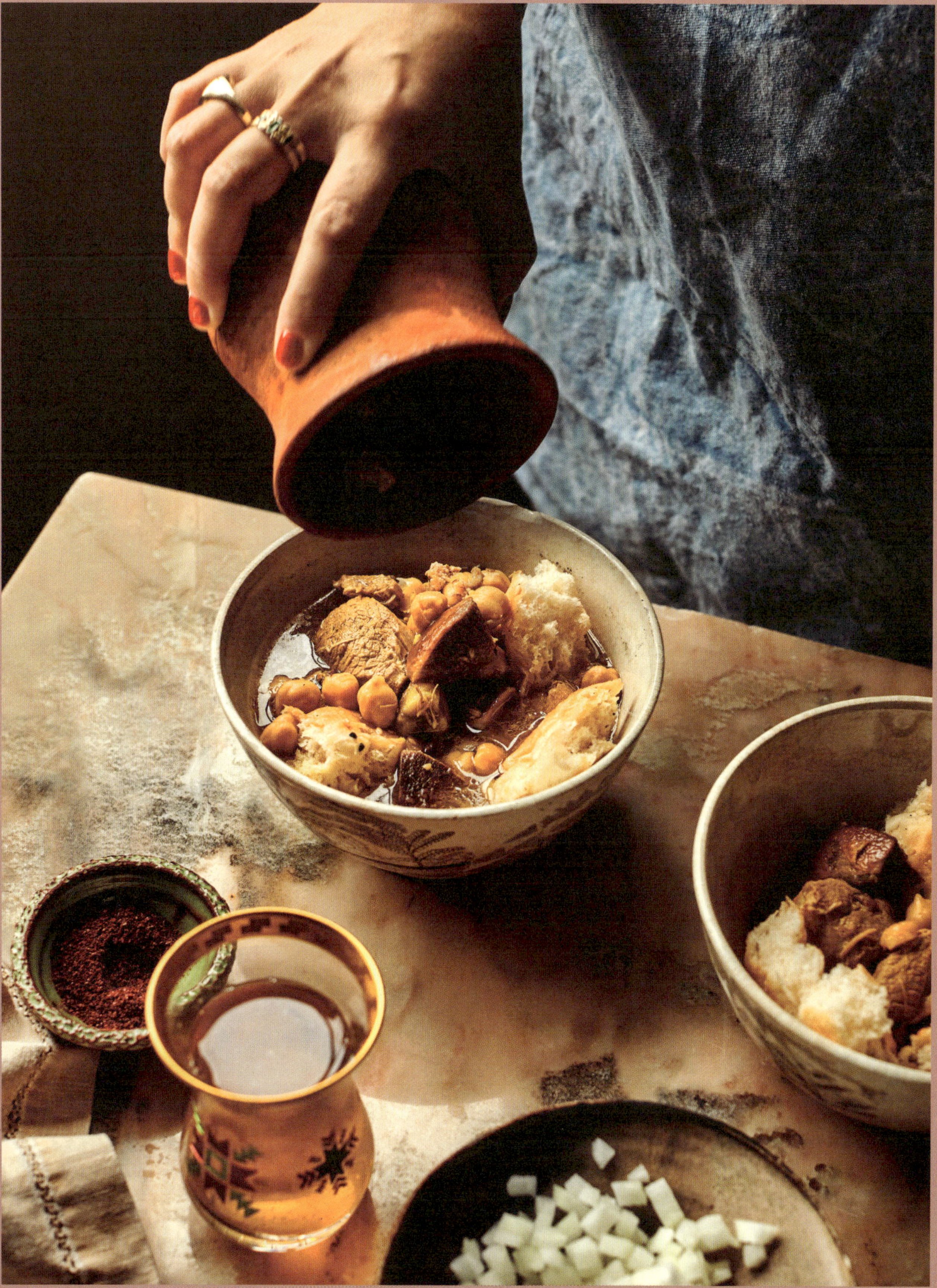

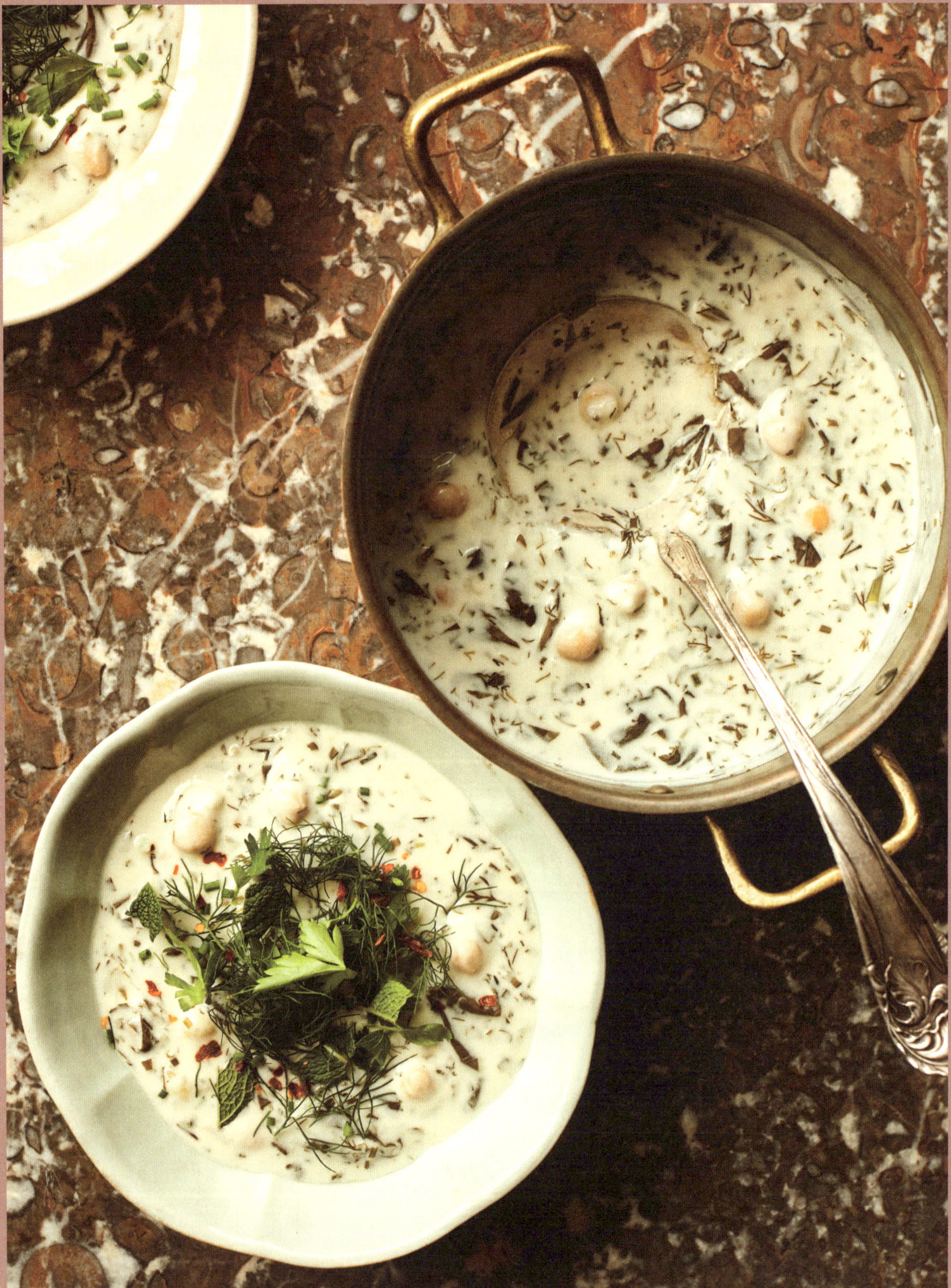

DOVGA

Azeri Warm Yogurt Soup

Serves 4–6

I was 19 years old when I had my first yogurt soup. It was refreshing and cold, and had cucumbers in it. I felt so grown up eating it; it was refined, cosmopolitan, a bit different, special – everything a 19-year-old in Manhattan thinks (or hopes) they are. I was probably wearing a suit (also my first) while I ate it, because I had that soup for lunch during my summer internship at the Azerbaijani Mission to the United Nations.

Like that dish enjoyed so long ago in Turtle Bay, Uzbekistan's *charlop* is a cold yogurt soup; it even has cucumbers. It is also delicious and cooling. This is not that soup. This is *dovga*, an Azeri yogurt soup that also happens to be a wedding soup. How's that for refined and special? And, while it can be and sometimes is eaten cold, *dovga*'s default temperature is warm. Yup. You read that correctly. This is a warm yogurt soup. And it's weird and wonderful, and kind of a game-changer.

- 750g (1lb 10oz) full-fat plain yogurt
- 1 egg, beaten
- 1 tbsp chickpea flour or plain flour (use chickpea flour to make this gluten-free)
- 70–100g (2¼–3½oz) risotto rice
- 80g (3oz) chopped spinach
- 75g (2½oz) fresh mixed herbs, chopped (e.g. dill, parsley, chives, coriander, tarragon, and mint; if using the final two, discard their stems), plus extra to serve
- 400g (14oz) can of chickpeas, drained and rinsed
- sea salt and freshly ground black pepper
- dried chilli flakes, to serve (optional)

In a medium heavy-based saucepan, whisk together the yogurt, egg, flour, and rice. Once everything is nicely combined, place your pan over a medium heat, and gradually add 950ml (4 cups/1½ pints) of water, stirring all the while.

Stir constantly until the mixture comes to a gentle boil. I'm serious here. Constant. Stirring. For a good 10–15 minutes. If you don't, this soup will fail – the yogurt will curdle and split, and you'll be deprived of something pretty incredible. And you don't want that.

Once the yogurt mixture is bubbling, reduce the heat to low and add the spinach, herbs, and chickpeas. Let the soup simmer for a further 15 minutes, or until the rice is cooked through. Constant stirring isn't required at this stage, but very frequent stirring is – and you know what? If you want to stand and constantly stir the pot, no one will stop you.

Another important caveat to this soup – don't add salt or pepper until you're about to eat it. Again, the salt could cause the yogurt to curdle and the soup to be ruined. And, don't forget: this is a wedding soup. You don't want to ruin a wedding soup, do you? No. I didn't think so. So, remember: constant stirring until it comes to a boil, and salt and pepper at the end.

Enjoy your *dovga* warm or cold, but either way, top it with salt and pepper to taste, some more fresh herbs, and maybe even some chilli flakes.

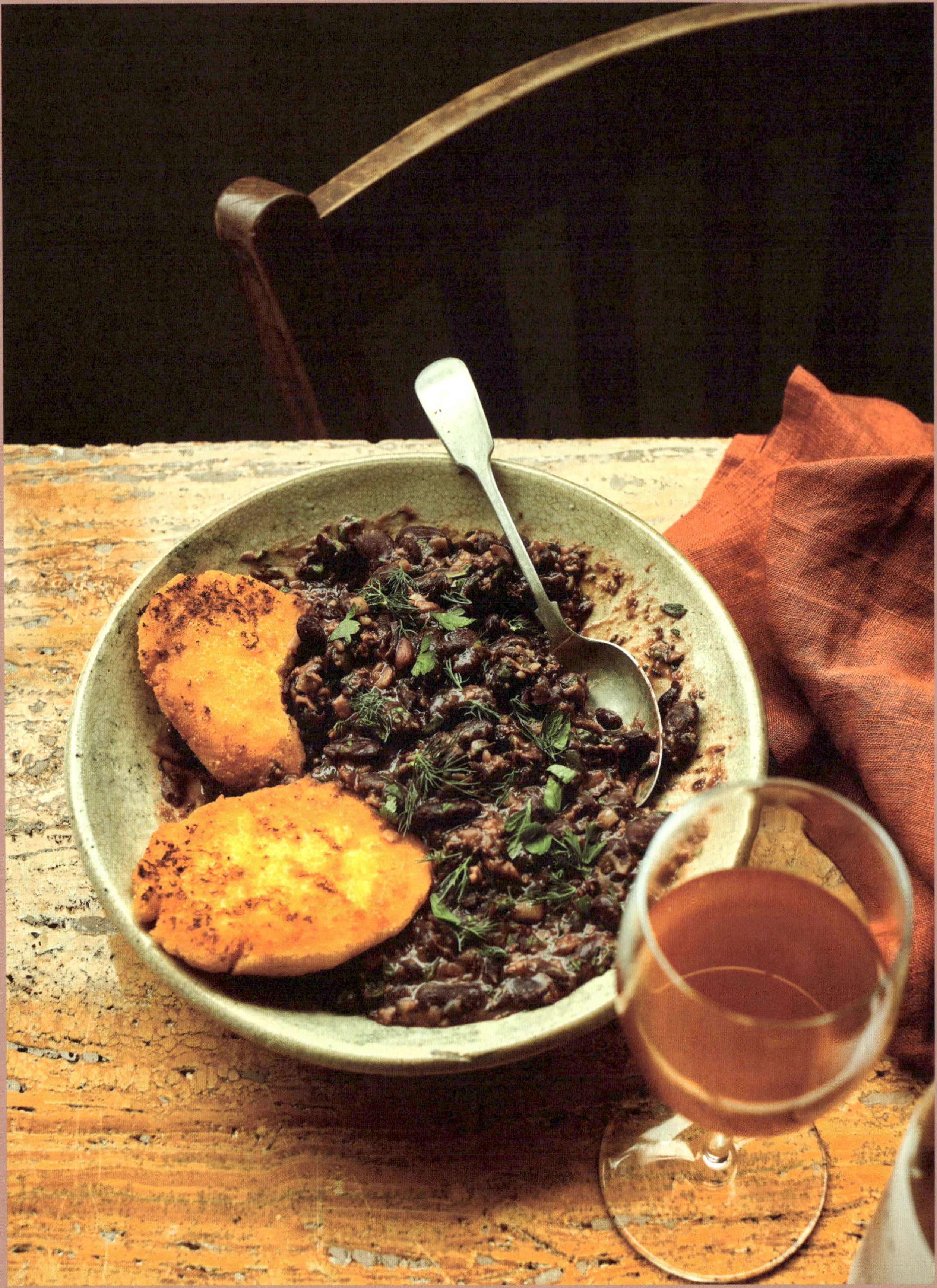

LOBIO

Georgian Bean Stew

Serves 4–6

As our hosts began to set the long table for our evening *supra* – the Georgian term for feast – the vista was otherworldly. Rolling green hills leading to snow-capped Caucasus mountains. A stone wall. A trio of young foxglove trees. Pink oleander bushes. A puppy underfoot. Cats lounging on the grass. A weathered wheelbarrow. An old red Lada parked under a walnut tree. And rows of grape vines. Kakheti, in northeastern Georgia, is the cradle of the country's wine culture, and is also where I had my first taste of *lobio*, a simple bean stew about which my two Georgian friends, Maka and Kristo, had much to say.

As I scooped spoonful after spoonful of *lobio* onto my plate, I asked the women how the dish was prepared. Their response was some sort of back-and-forth comedy routine.

"I first start by cooking my beans and browning my onions while the beans are softening," Kristo offered, just as Maka cut in:

"I don't brown my onions, Kristo. But I use tomato purée; you don't, do you?"

"No, no, no, Maka. You *must* brown your onions. And I don't like to use tomato purée. When my onions are browned, I add the herbs."

"*Lobio* really *should* have tomato purée, Kristo. But yes – any herbs!" Maka concurs. "Dried and fresh."

"No. I only use dried, Maka."

I was laughing at this point, thinking of duelling banjos and duelling bean recipes, of deep-seated opinions about what can and cannot, should and should not go into a dish, and of the casual, jocular nature of these two women and the warmth they brought to our table under the sun.

Kristo turned to me. "Anna. There are many variations. We all have our own way of making *lobio*. This is just how I make it."

Maka piped in. "Yes. You can make it however you like. But I like to have *lobio* with bread, not cornbread, because we didn't always have corn in Georgia."

"Oh, Maka," Kristo said, sighing. "You *must* have it with cornbread!"

You'll find a recipe for cornbread on page 209, but don't feel your *lobio* must be eaten with it. Bread will do just fine. In fact, anything will do – these beans are excellent when eaten the traditional way as a loose, soupy stew, but I also like them a bit stodgier, almost refried bean-like in texture, and eaten as a dip or slathered across a piece of toast, topped with a slice of tomato, flaky sea salt and some more fresh herbs. I do *lobio* my way, and if Maka and Kristo's back-and-forth is anything to go by, I think it's fair to say that when it comes to *lobio*, eat it however you enjoy it – and however you eat this version, I know you will enjoy it.

Note: If you don't have kidney beans, you can use whatever you enjoy or have on hand, other than black beans. I know the beans in the photo opposite might *look* like black beans, but I assure you they're just very well-cooked kidneys.

250g (9oz) dried kidney beans, soaked overnight, then drained and rinsed

1 onion, quartered

3 garlic cloves, 1 minced, 2 whole

1 bay leaf

1¾ tsp fine sea salt

2 tbsp olive oil

1 tsp ground coriander

1 tsp dried thyme

½ tsp dried chilli flakes

½ tsp coarsely ground black pepper

20g (¾oz) fresh parsley, dill, or coriander, or a combination of all three, chopped

Add your drained and rinsed beans to a large pot for which you have a lid. Pour in enough water to cover the beans by 5cm (2in), then place over a high heat and bring to the boil. Cook for 10 minutes at the boil before reducing the heat to low.

Add one onion quarter, two whole garlic cloves, and the bay leaf, then partially cover the pot with its lid and leave to cook for 1–3 hours, or until your beans are tender, checking on them occasionally and adding 1 teaspoon of the salt when they reach a just tender/al dente firmness. Note that the cooking time depends on the type and age of the beans.

While your beans are cooking, finely dice the remaining onion quarters. Heat the oil in a large sauté pan over a medium–high heat. Add the diced onion, along with ¼ teaspoon of the salt. Reduce the heat to medium and cook the onion, stirring occasionally, for 8–10 minutes, or until it is soft and golden.

Add the minced garlic, ground coriander, thyme, chilli flakes, and black pepper. Stir and cook for 60 seconds, or until fragrant. If necessary, take the pan off the heat and set aside while you wait for your beans to finish cooking.

Once your beans are ready, drain them from their pot, making sure to reserve the cooking water. Discard the garlic, onion, and bay leaf.

Add half the beans and 125ml (generous ½ cup/4fl oz) of the bean cooking water to the pan with the onions and spices. Use the back of a fork or a wooden spoon to mash the beans, water, and onions into a paste. Add the remaining ½ teaspoon salt to your bean paste, along with your chopped fresh herbs. Place over a medium heat and cook for 5–7 minutes so that everything warms up and the flavours meld. Mash any intact beans you encounter – or don't. It's up to you.

Return your whole, intact beans to their cooking pot, then add the maybe-mashed bean, onion, and herb mixture, and stir everything to mix. Place over a medium heat and begin adding the bean cooking water, 100ml (6½ tbsp/3½fl oz) at a time, until the contents of your pan reach your desired consistency. You can use water instead of the bean cooking water if you don't have enough of the latter, or if you accidentally tossed it, or if you (gasp!) used canned beans instead of dried ones. Cook for 5–7 minutes more, or until the *lobio* is nice and warm and begging to be eaten.

Opposite: Aperitivo hour chez Gio Togonidze at his home and vineyard in Georgia's Kakheti region. You can spy a glass of his wine on page 64. June 2024.

Left: The room in which I had some mind-blowing pork (see p132). Gio's house in Kakheti, Georgia. June 2024.

Bottom: A farewell ode before the heavens opened and forced us indoors. Ezo Restaurant. Tbilisi, Georgia. June 2024.

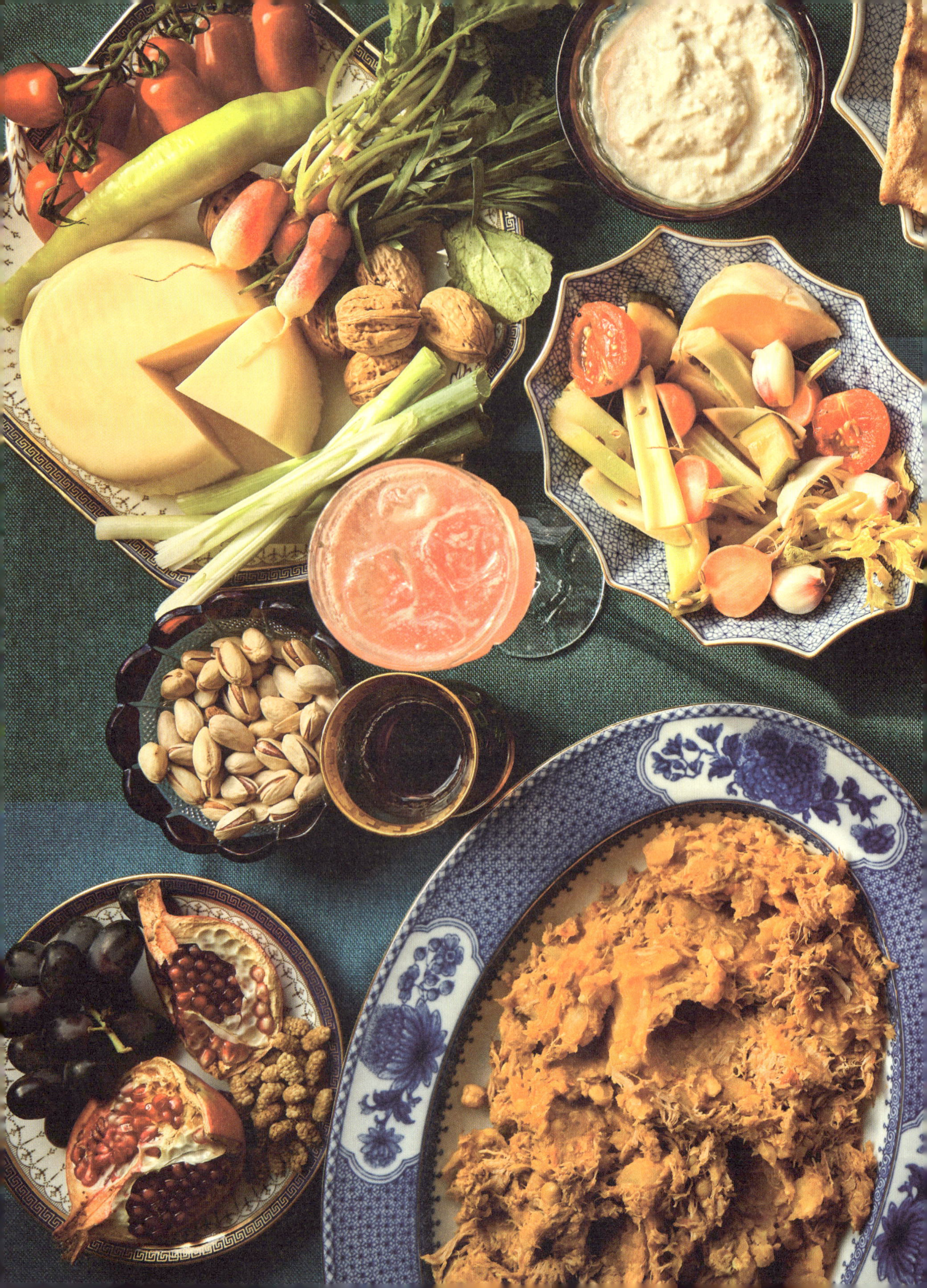

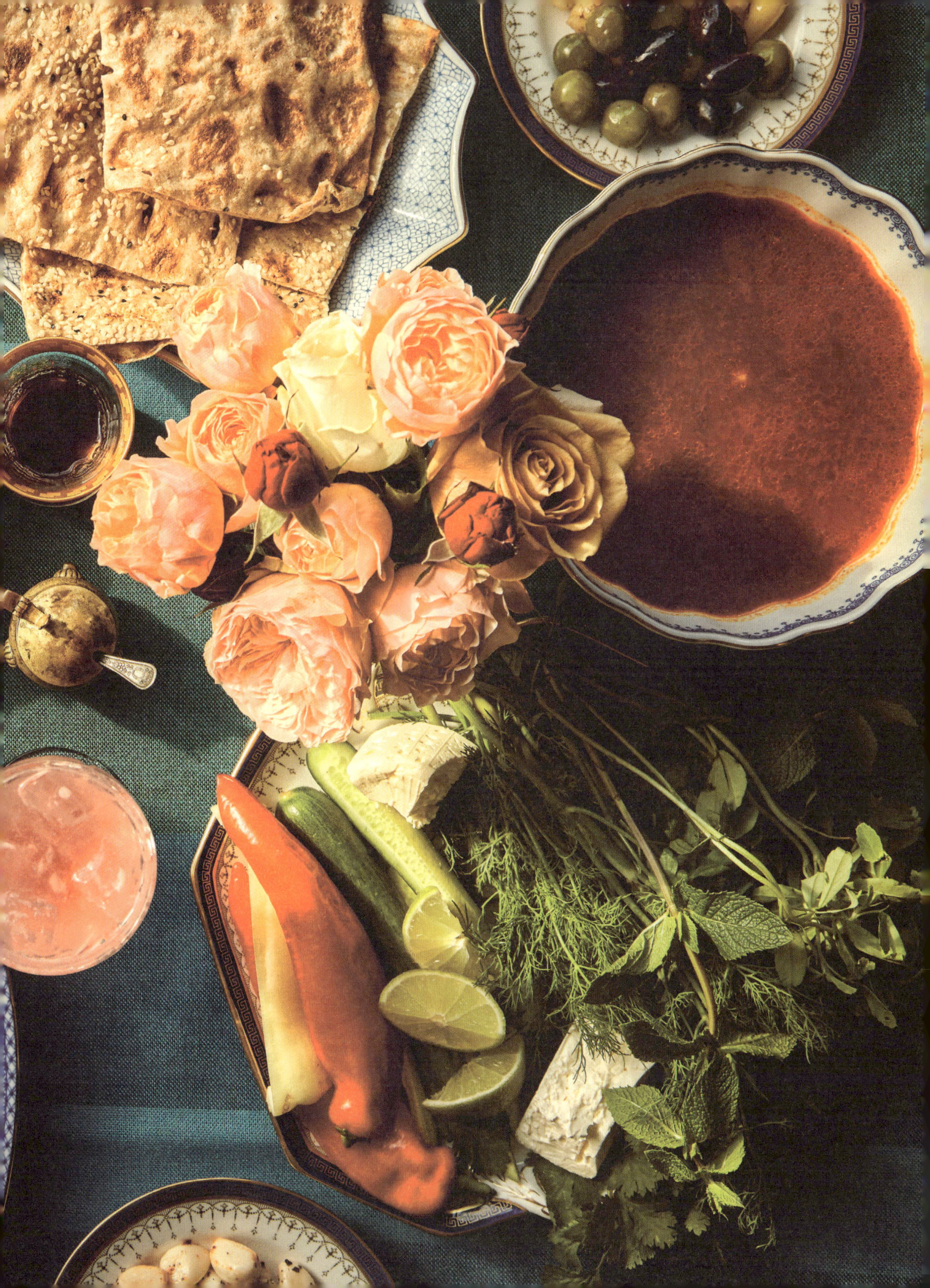

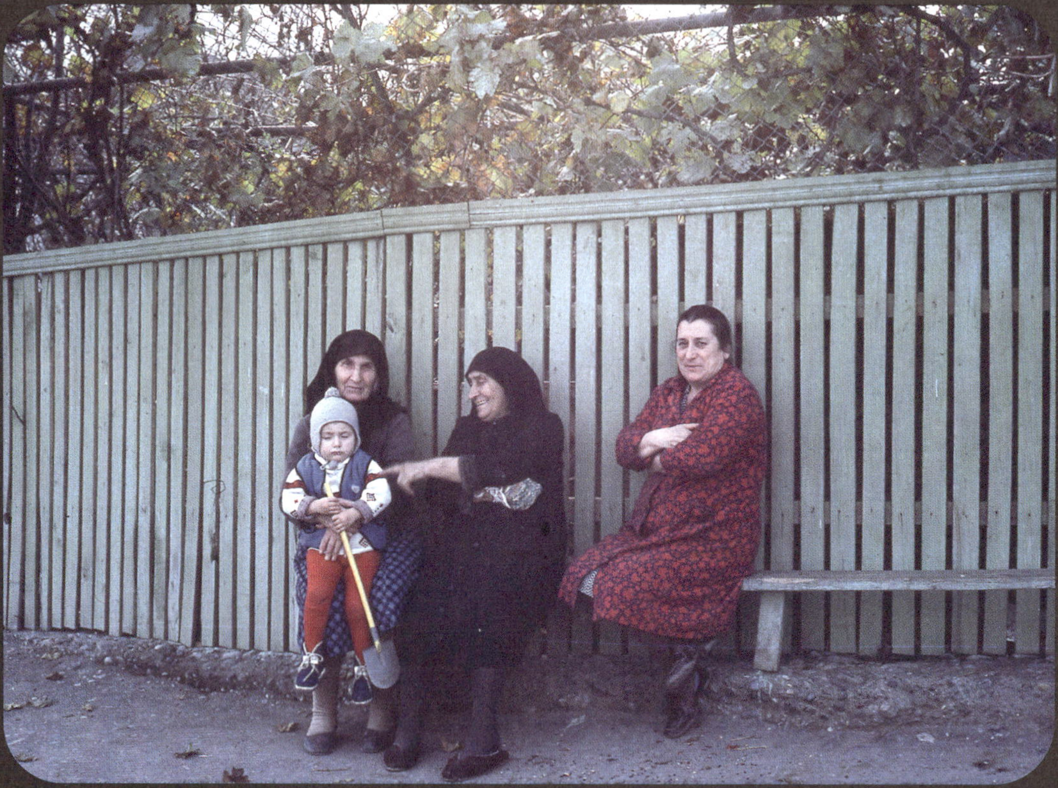

FERMENTS & PICKLES

PLEASE YOUR MOTHER.
EAT YOUR YOGURT. LIVE TO 100.
72

SUZMA
Uzbek Strained Yogurt
76

DOOGH
Iranian Yogurt Spritzer
78

GAYMAK
A Clotted Cream by Any Other Name
80

TORSHI
Iranian Pickled Vegetables
83

NO-WASTE BEETROOT BORANI
Iranian Yogurt Dip
84

PAOCAI
Chinese Fermented Pearl Onions
87

PLEASE YOUR MOTHER. EAT YOUR YOGURT. LIVE TO 100.

We eat a lot of yogurt in the US: by some accounts, around 120g (4¼oz) per person per week. Brits love yogurt even more than Americans, putting away nearly 200g (7oz) of it per person per week. In both countries, yogurt is a multi-billion dollar industry. But it wasn't that long ago that yogurt (in the US and UK, at least) was an unknown, foreign preparation made by and for pockets of immigrant populations.

Used to eating yogurt on a daily basis in Iran, my father, upon moving to Detroit in 1963, was keen to secure a means of continuing his fermented dairy habit. He asked his fellow medical residents where he could buy yogurt. He asked the nurses and the attending physicians. He asked grocers and neighbours. All to no avail. No one knew what yogurt was, let alone where to procure it. "Go to Greektown," someone finally suggested. "Maybe they will know what you're talking about."

Though Greektown today consists of a few Hellenic-themed restaurants, a hotel, and a casino, it began in the 1830s as a residential neighbourhood settled by Greek immigrants, and remained as such until right around the time my father went poking around looking for yogurt. In the early 1960s, the neighbourhood's character began to shift from residential to commercial – and thank goodness it did, because my father was eventually able to find himself some yogurt, and, decades later, I was able to enjoy some flaming cheese after a visit to Eastern Market.

Yogurt's popularity steadily increased over the last quarter of a century, and, these days, the thick, strained yogurt we call "Greek" is America's favourite type. However, it wasn't the Greeks who popularized yogurt in America, or even introduced it to the country on a commercial basis. No, that distinction lies with a couple of Armenian immigrants living on the East Coast.

In 1929, Rosa and Sarkis Colombosian started what would become America's first commercial yogurt company in their home in Andover, Massachusetts. With a wood-burning stove and an old family recipe, Rosa began making batches of *matsun*, an Armenian fermented dairy preparation, and sharing it with friends and neighbours. Before long, Rosa and Sarkis were distributing Rosa's homemade concoction to a wider market, selling it via horse-drawn carriage as well as at local stores catering to immigrant populations who were thrilled to enjoy a dairy product similar to ones from their homelands (or as close to them as they could get in 1930s Massachusetts).

To appeal to a varied immigrant population, Rosa and Sarkis started calling their product "yogurt", the Turkish term for fermented, curdled, and thickened milk familiar to many of Middle Eastern and Mediterranean descent. They also renamed their business "Colombo", truncating the Colombosian name and pseudo-Italianizing it, a move intended to situate the product in the realm of the largest immigrant population of the area – the Italians – as well as to make it less "foreign" and more marketable to non-immigrant Americans. Their gambles paid off. By 1940, the Colombosian's yogurt was all over New England. By the mid-1960s, when medical reports praising yogurt's health benefits started appearing, Colombo yogurts also started appearing at grocery stores across the country. By 1975, Colombo was the best-selling yogurt in America. And, in the 1980s, when Rosa and Sarkis's sons, Bob and John, started including fruit in their yogurt tubs, their sales exploded. The Colombo sons, however, were not the first to do this.

Top: Red and green *adjika*, freshly pressed sunflower oil, and bottles of pickled delights — including green plums with tarragon. Telavi, Georgia. June 2024.

Bottom: A cheese vendor at a market in Telavi, Georgia. June 2024.

In the 1950s, the company Danone, known in the US as Dannon and founded in Barcelona in 1929 by Isaac Carasso, a Sephardic Jewish Greek, pioneered the idea of including fruit compote at the bottom of yogurt tubs. While Rosa and Sarkis were busy selling their yogurt to New England immigrants, Carasso, who in 1942 had moved Danone to the Bronx, was trying his hand with the New York City market. Though Danone succeeded in selling plain, unflavoured, unsweetened yogurt to the city's immigrant population, non-immigrant Americans simply didn't like it. They associated dairy products with sweet treats like ice cream and frozen sherbet, and the slightly sour taste of yogurt did not fit with these preconceptions. Danone hoped to sweeten things up by adding some fruit to the mix and, in doing so, to boost its sales. Fruit on the bottom or not, yogurt's popularity and yogurt makers' profits continued to stagnate until the late 1970s and early 1980s, due, in no small part, to a group of centenarians from Soviet Georgia's Abkhazian region.

The ad opens on a moustachioed man hoeing the ground in a vineyard. The text on the video says, "Taruk Lasuria. Age 96," as a voiceover announces: "In Soviet Georgia, there are two curious things about the people. A large part of their diet is yogurt. And a large number of them live past 100." Temur Vanacha, aged 105, then appears, sporting a massively bushy moustache that I have seen described as "Hungarian" in style, but which reminds me of Sir Didymus from the movie *Labyrinth*. Temur is stripping leaves from a branch.

Then comes Kashteh Tanya, aged 101, resplendent in a red waistcoat and chopping wood with an axe. "Now, we are not saying that Dannon yogurt will help you live longer," the voiceover continues, "but [it] is rich in nutrition." After Shadat, aged 103, rides through the vineyards on a horse, a grinning man in an Astrakhan fur hat appears: 89-year-old Bagrat Tabaghua, eating a cup of yogurt. The voiceover finishes by telling us that Bagrat apparently liked his Dannon yogurt so much that he ate two cups, which "pleased his mother very much". The ad closes with an elderly woman leaning on a cane, playfully tugging at Bagrat's ear.

That's it. That's the claim, the not-so-subtle suggestion, the golden ticket that lifts yogurt's popularity and pads the yogurt makers' pocketbooks. Yogurt is good for you. Yogurt is healthy. Yogurt might even help you live longer. Oh. And yogurt has been eaten by people in Georgia for centuries.

Though the ad's goal was to sell yogurt and its health benefits to an American audience, it simultaneously and perhaps unintentionally firmly situated yogurt outside America's borders, outside Western Europe, and in the lands of the unknown, exotic other. Sure, a lot of what has been sold and marketed as yogurt over the years would undoubtedly have not pleased Bagrat Tabaghua's mother very much, but somewhere along the line (and perhaps starting with Dannon's 1977 ad) Americans (and Brits too) accepted the foreign nature of their (now) favourite dairy breakfast and snack food.

These days, no one bats an eye at the term "Greek yogurt". No one questions the thickness of Icelandic skyr. No one is shocked to find kefir in the dairy aisle. As our world has become more global, in many ways so too have our mindsets and palates. Yogurt, a food once so foreign the request for it resulted in blank-eyed, confused stares in a Detroit hospital and a scavenger hunt in an immigrant neighbourhood, is now so firmly entrenched in British and American food culture that not only do we not realize "yogurt" is a Turkish word, but also we don't care. And even though eating it might not really help you live to be 100, yogurt is indeed good for you. Just ask my dad. He is 89 years old, and a large part of his diet is yogurt. Plus, it is fucking delicious.

Left: All the *qurut* (see p31), all the time. Siyob Bazaar. Samarkand, Uzbekistan. March 2024.

Bottom: Fresh, homemade (dare-I-call-it-"small batch") yogurt at Yaşil Bazaar. Baku, Azerbaijan. January 2016.

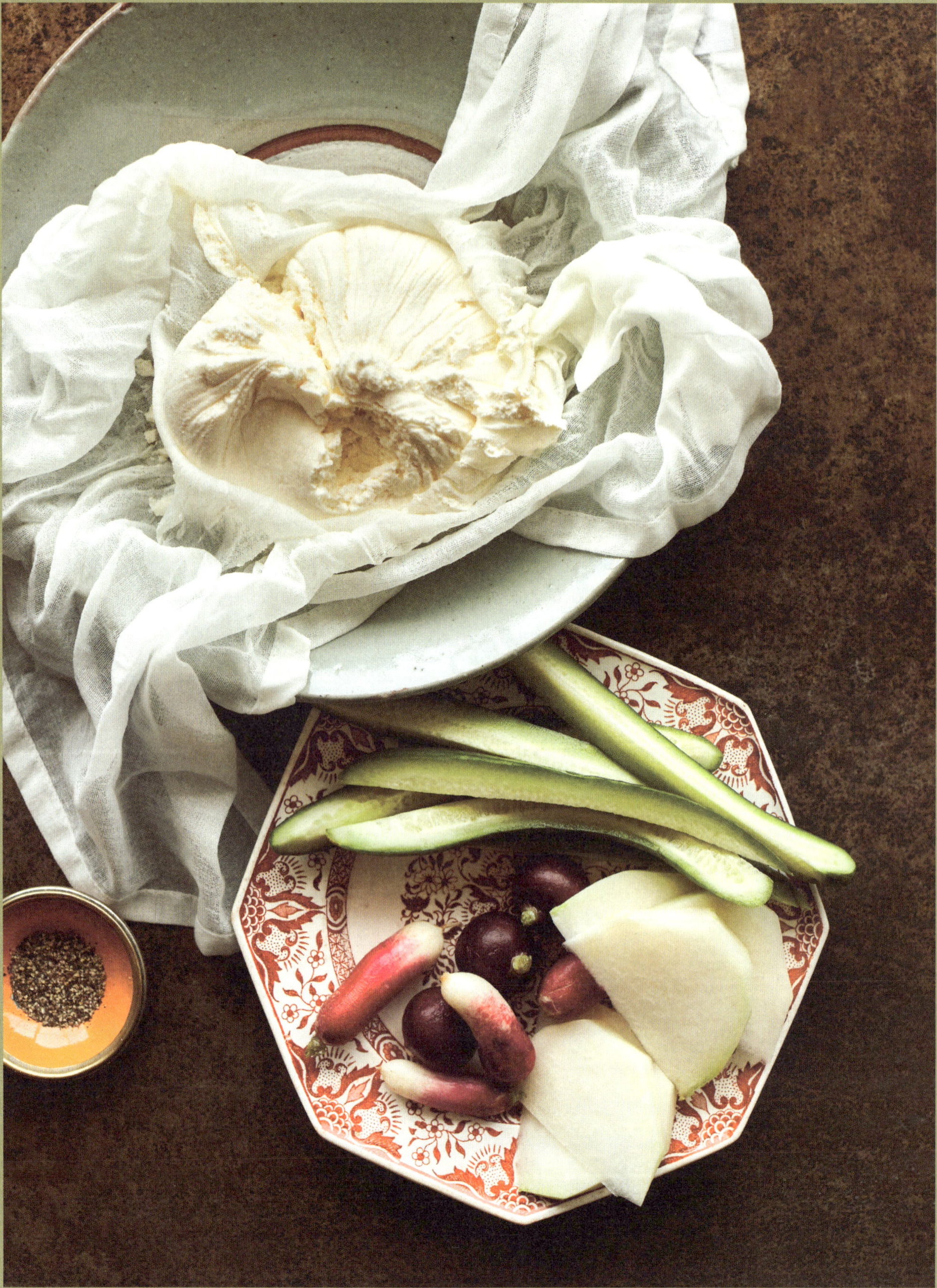

SUZMA

Uzbek Strained Yogurt

Makes 640g (1lb 6oz)

We were waiting for the goat when they brought out the yogurt. Little tubs filled with a white, dairy-looking substance, sprinkled with rock sugar. It was delicious – and not just because we were hungry. Cultivated and prepared by the same Tibetan villagers who would soon toss a caprine quadruped on the bonfire before us, it was cold and fresh and tasted of the farm, of the Gansu grasslands on which we stood.

But it wasn't goat yogurt. Nope: it was yak yogurt. Yes, you heard me right – yak yogurt. Yogurt from that hairy, horned ox associated mostly (for me, at least) with Himalayan sherpas and yak milk tea, a beverage so far removed from what I consider tea to be, and so far from what I consider delicious to be, that I cringe even thinking about it. I will be content if I never have a sip of yak milk tea again in my life, but disappointed if I never enjoy another spoonful of yak milk yogurt.

After the yogurt and some beers and a few dances around the bonfire, the goat materialized – and it dazzled us. We pulled the meat directly off the bone, eating it with our hands as the Milky Way spilled itself across the sky. I bet no one other than me remembers the yogurt – that night belonged to the goat and the dark, sparkling skies. But it was my first, unforgettable taste of non-commercially produced yogurt, and it was a revelation.

We don't and can't know exactly when or where the first yogurt was made. What we do know is that it happened a very long time ago, probably somewhere on the Central Asian steppe. The most plausible theory is that yogurt was an accident: milk was put into a saddle-esque bag made of animal skin (or stomach) for transport; bacteria from the "bag" seeped into the milk, which in turn was nestled up against the side of the animal (camel, horse, or what have you), whose body heat provided an ideal temperature for incubation, and whose jostling movement aided the curdling and mixing process.

Imagine the look on that well-travelled nomad's face when, arriving at his destination, he opens up his saddle bag for a much-needed libation and instead finds a sour, thickened milk. But he's thirsty, so he drinks it. And he doesn't die. In fact, he finds that he likes it. He tells all his friends, and they all ingest this new milk product they have accidentally created – and maybe they, like the Soviet Georgians, live to the ripe old age of 100. Or something like that.

Armenians call it *matsun*. Georgians call it *mastoni*. Azeris, Turkmen, Uzbekis, and Tajiks call it *qatiq/gatyk/katyk*. English-speakers call it yogurt. I call it delicious.

A double-strained Uzbek preparation, *suzma* is so thick it makes Greek yogurt look like milk, and is closer in consistency to cream cheese than to the spoonable breakfast dairy with which we are (now) familiar in the US and the UK. *Suzma* can and should be eaten à la cream cheese, too; it's delicious slathered on a bagel. And while I have given you a number of suggestions as to how to use it (see pp58, 97, and 192), my favourite way of eating *suzma* is the simplest, and the way I enjoyed it most in Uzbekistan: teetering on the edge of a crisp slice of daikon radish or kohlrabi, topped with a pinch of salt and a grind of black pepper.

1kg (2¼lb) full-fat Greek yogurt

1½ tsp fine sea salt

Mix the yogurt and salt in a medium mixing bowl.

Line a fine mesh sieve with a square of muslin or cheesecloth. Place the sieve over another larger, deepish bowl.

Pour the salty yogurt into the lined sieve. Gather up the edges of the muslin and tie them together with a rubber band. Transfer this set up – bowl, colander, tied baggie of dairy – to the refrigerator and leave it there to drain for 12–24 hours.

The liquid from the yogurt will drain away into the bowl below (discard, or use for another purpose), and you'll be left with a delicious thickened dairy product you can use like cottage or cream cheese. Store in an airtight container in the refrigerator for up to 2 weeks.

DOOGH

Iranian Yogurt Spritzer

Serves 2

The Oghuz Turks once ruled a swathe of Central Asia through a cobbled-together tribal federation, and provided modern-day Turkish, Azerbaijani, and Turkmen people with a supposed shared ancestor in the form of Oghuz Khan, as well as an epic collection of 8–10th-century tales of drama and morality in the form of *The Book of Dede Korkut*.

The first of the book's stories begins with an infertile royal couple begging God to bless them with a son. In preparation for a sacrificial ritual feast to accompany their prayers, the wife tells her husband:

> *Heat up meat in hillocks; let lakes of kumis be drawn.*
> *Make an enormous feast, then ask what you want and let them pay.*
> *So, with prayerful mouths singing your praises,*
> *God may grant us a fine hefty child.*

Kumis as a gift to God. *Kumis* for a fine hefty child. That's how important the fermented mare's milk beverage of the Central Asian steppe once was.

"I tasted it and [finding] it disagreeable passed it on to one of my companions." So writes Ibn Battuta, the 14th-century traveller from Morocco, of the *kumiz* given to him on his travels in Uzbeg Khan's Golden Horde. Still enjoyed today across Asia, *kumiz* (or *kumis* or *kumiss*) is an ancient beverage of great renown, and though Ibn Battuta didn't enjoy it, Marco Polo did, telling us that "[the Mongols] prepare [mare's milk] in such a way that it resembles white wine; it is a delicious drink".

This is not *kumis*. This is nowhere close to white wine. This is *doogh*, an Iranian carbonated yogurt drink, and it's awesome. (And no horses were milked in the making of it.) A probiotic, refreshing spritz, *doogh* will blow your notions of what and how yogurt can be consumed right out of the water. A little bit of salt, a little bit of tang, a little bit of mint, and a little bit of carbonation – a little bit of heaven on ice. I can't promise you a fine hefty child, but you will get a delicious drink that you won't want to pass to any of your companions.

250g (9oz) full-fat plain yogurt
½ tsp fine sea salt
1 tsp dried mint

250ml (1 cup plus 1 tbsp/9fl oz) soda water
ice

fresh mint leaves, cucumber, and dried rose petals, to garnish (optional)

In a large jug, mix the yogurt, salt, and dried mint together. Add the soda water and mix once more. Pour into ice-filled glasses and garnish with optional fresh mint, dried rose petals, and even a spear of cucumber. Bottoms up!

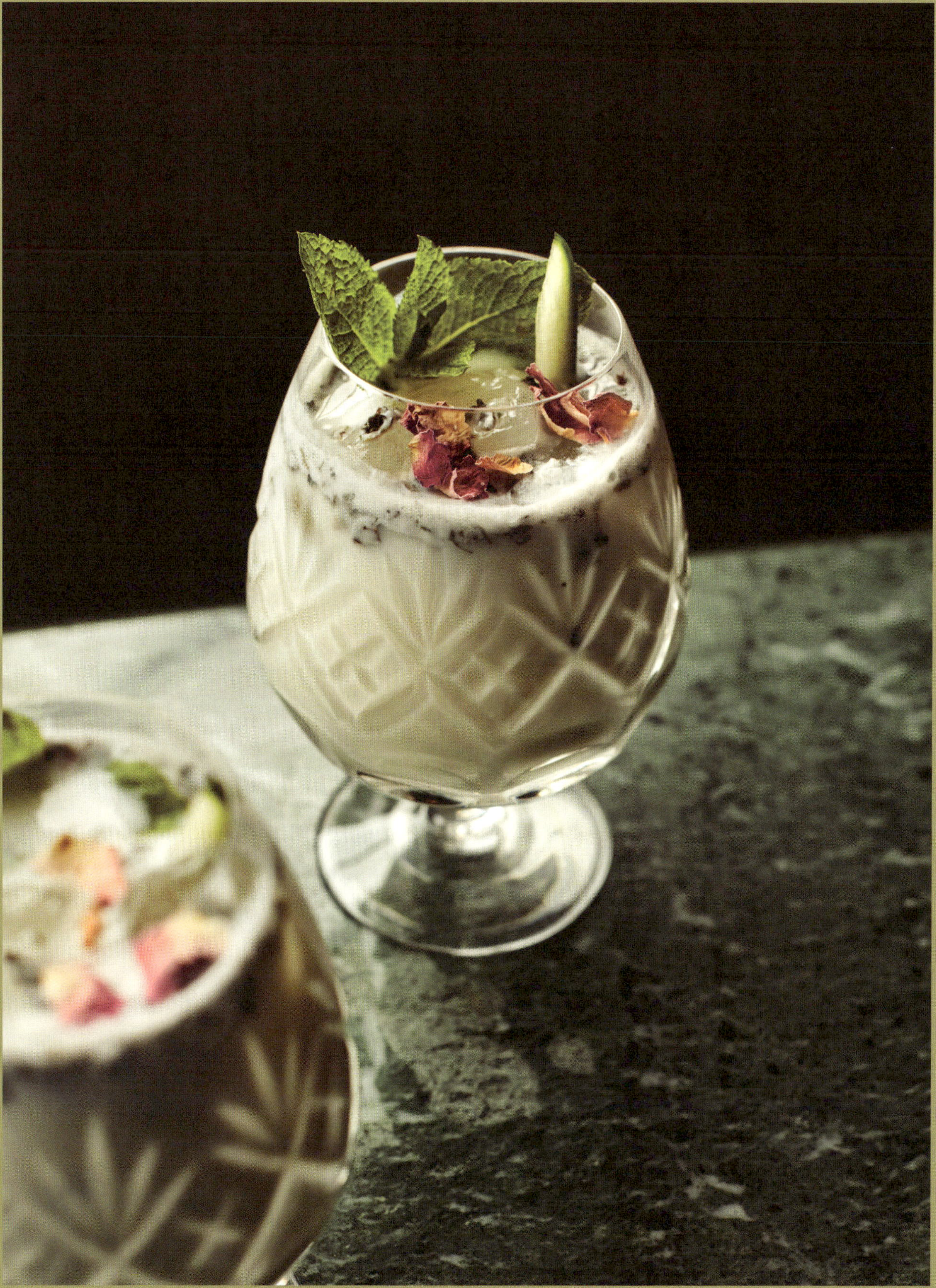

GAYMAK

A Clotted Cream by Any Other Name

Makes 200–300g (7–10oz)

Basically a Turkic clotted cream, *gaymak* (or *kaymak*, depending on who you're talking to) may be my father's favourite food. And it might be yours, too, after you try it.

Best (in my opinion) slathered on a fresh-from-the-*tendir* bread, with honey drizzled on top and accompanied by a strong cup of tea, enjoy *gaymak* as you would any clotted cream.

Or try using it to make ice cream – I'm told that what makes the ice cream from Andijan in Uzbekistan's Ferghana Valley so great is its *kaymak* base. You could (and should) also serve this dolloped on top of my Quince Bakewell Pudding (see p246).

4.5 litres (19 cups/scant 8 pints) whole milk (preferably raw)

1.2 litres (5 cups/2 pints) double cream

fine sea salt (optional)

Combine the milk and cream in the widest-based saucepan you have. I use a 30cm (12in) non-stick high-sided sauté pan, but a slightly smaller one would work as well.

Put your massive pan of milk and cream over the smallest, weakest burner you have. Turn the heat to medium and bring the mixture to a simmer. Let it simmer for 20 minutes, being careful to watch and ensure that it neither comes to a boil nor, (gasp!) even worse, boils over.

After 20 minutes, decrease the heat to its very lowest setting. Keep it on that low heat for another 1½–2 hours. You don't need to watch the mixture like a hawk, but don't stray too far from it either. It will bubble, but don't stir it, even if it threatens to erupt. Blow on it a bit if you need to, but generally avoid disturbing the mixture as best you can.

Eventually, it'll start to turn yellow at the edges – this is good; this is what you want. Once this happens, remove the pan from the stove and leave it to cool for 5–7 hours. During that time, a yellowish crust will develop – when you see it, you'll know that you're on your way to greatness. Once cool, carefully move the pan into your refrigerator, cover it with a lid, and keep it there to further chill overnight.

In the morning, remove your pan from the refrigerator, being very careful not to disturb the yellow top. With a slotted spoon, scoop up that golden layer and deposit it into a medium bowl. Get all of it, every last little bit of the buttery-looking crust, and if you get a bit of the liquid too, that's a-ok. (The leftover liquid milk can be discarded or used for yogurt-making, if you're into that kind of thing.)

Once you've got it all, mash it up a bit in the bowl and, if you like, add a pinch of salt.

You did it. You made *gaymak*. Congratulations. Your waistline and arteries may never forgive you, but your tastebuds will be forever grateful.

Store the *gaymak* in an airtight container in the refrigerator for 1–2 days.

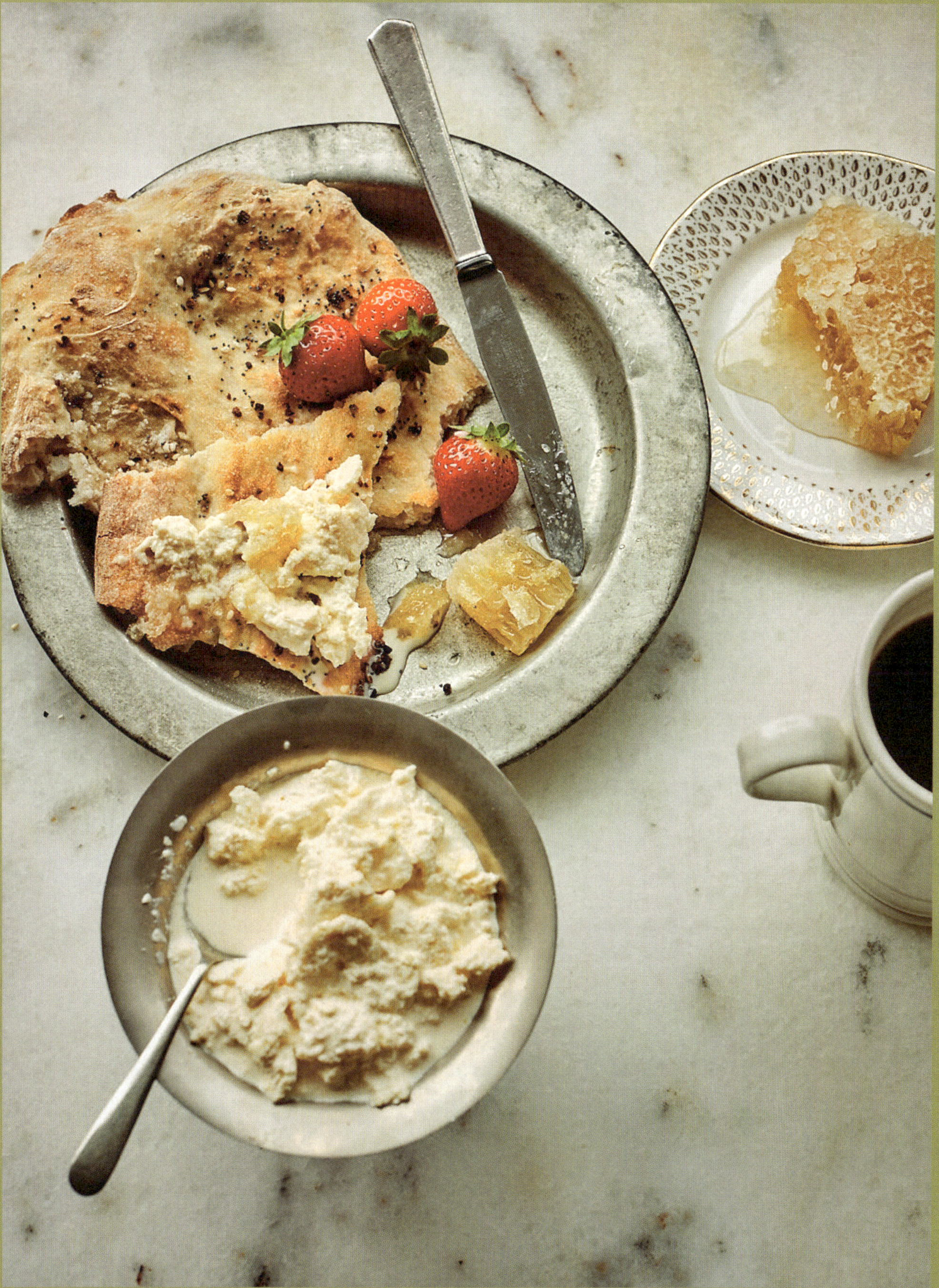

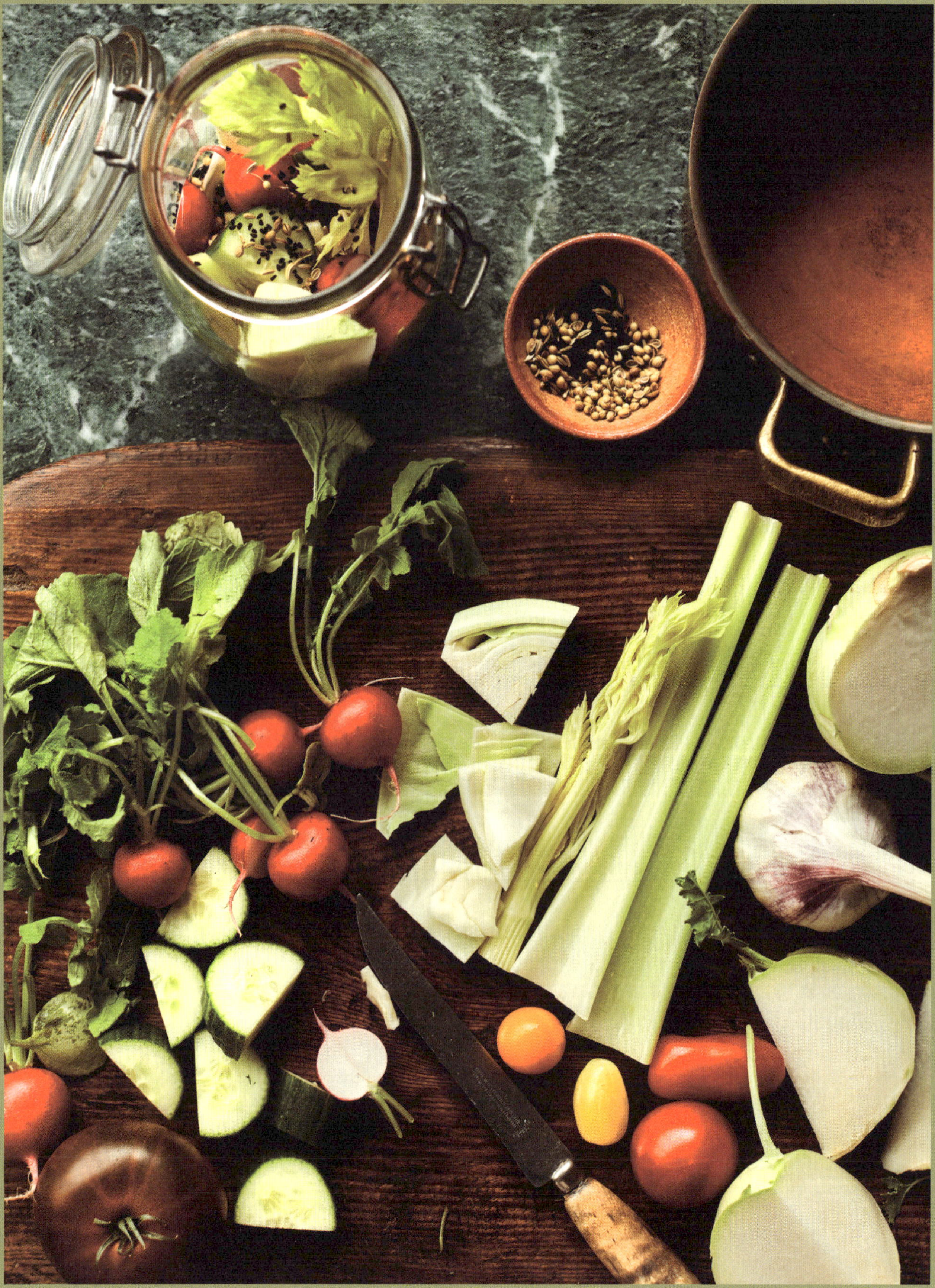

TORSHI

Iranian Pickled Vegetables

Makes a 1-litre (1-quart) jar

Depending on the time of year, the first thing you smell when you open the door to my father's house is vinegar. You take off your shoes, walk into the larder room, and open the refrigerator. Staring back at you will inevitably be jar upon jar upon jar of *torshi* – Iranian pickles. Cucumbers. Peppers. Tomatoes. Onions. Garlic. And not small jars, either; I'm talking 5-litre (5-quart) monstrosities, filled to the brim with summer and Iranian flavour. It can literally take your breath away ... and then later, at dinner, you eat one, with your rice and your lamb, and you think to yourself: *Ahhh, OK – a couple of days in a vinegar-scented home is totally worth it if this crunchy bite of joy is what I get.*

The recipe below is for a mixed-vegetable pickle in a vinegar brine. You could just as easily choose one single vegetable. Experiment and enjoy, and remember that the vinegar smell will fade, but the pickles will last for ages, just as they have in homes across the Middle East and Central Asia for centuries.

350ml (1½ cups/12fl oz) apple cider vinegar

1 tbsp fine sea salt

75g (2½oz) granulated sugar

3 tsp mixed whole spices (optional; I enjoy a mixture of coriander seeds, peppercorns, fennel seeds, and nigella seeds)

900g (2lb) vegetables, washed and chopped if necessary (cabbage, celery, cauliflower, beetroots, radishes, turnips, green beans, cucumbers, kohlrabi, peppers, garlic, tomatoes ... you get the picture, anything goes)

In a medium saucepan, combine the vinegar with 200ml (scant 1 cup/7fl oz) water. Add the salt and sugar, and bring to the boil over a high heat. Once boiling, reduce the heat to low and simmer for 10 minutes, making sure that the sugar and salt both dissolve. Turn off the heat, add your spices, if using, and allow the brine to cool.

Pack your vegetables into a sterilized 1-litre (1-quart) glass jar (see p17), cutting them down to size if necessary to fit.

Once your brine is cool, carefully pour it into the jar of vegetables, making sure to leave a 2.5cm (1in) gap at the top of the jar and ensuring that all your vegetables are fully submerged in the brine. Seal immediately. Place in refrigerator. Wait a day. Eat.

These will keep for up to a year – but they'll definitely be gone before then!

NO-WASTE BEETROOT BORANI

Iranian Yogurt Dip

Serves 4–8 as a dip

Borani laboo and *borani esfanj* are two of the most beloved Iranian yogurt preparations, the former made with beetroot and the latter with spinach. This is my ode to them, as well as to my commitment to kitchen-waste reduction, making excellent use of those gorgeous beetroot stalks and leaves you often find attached to the divisively delicious, incredibly nutritious earthy orbs and which, sadly, often find their way to the bin.

- 2 tbsp olive oil
- 1 onion, very thinly sliced into half-moons
- 200g (7oz) beetroot leaves and stalks, leaves roughly chopped, stalks finely chopped
- 1 garlic clove, minced
- 2 tsp dried mint
- 250g (9oz) cooked beetroot, coarsely grated
- 375g (13oz) Greek yogurt
- ½ tsp fine sea salt
- zest and juice of 1 lime

To serve (optional)

- pistachios
- flaky sea salt
- mint leaves

Heat the oil in a large saucepan over a medium heat. Once hot, reduce the heat to low, add the onion, and cook for 15 minutes, stirring occasionally, until golden brown. Add the beetroot stalks, garlic, and 1 teaspoon of the dried mint. Cook for a further 5 minutes, stirring frequently to prevent any burning. Add the beetroot leaves and cook for 3–5 minutes more, or until the leaves are soft and wilted. Set aside to cool.

In a medium bowl, combine the grated beetroot with the yogurt, salt, lime juice, and half the lime zest. Stir to mix well. When the onion and beetroot leaf/stalk mixture is cool, add this to the bowl and stir to mix everything together, before moving the bowl to the refrigerator. Chill for at least 1 hour so the flavours can come together.

Just before serving, sprinkle the *borani* with the last of the dried mint and lime zest. If you like, top it off with some pistachios and flaky sea salt, and garnish with some fresh mint leaves.

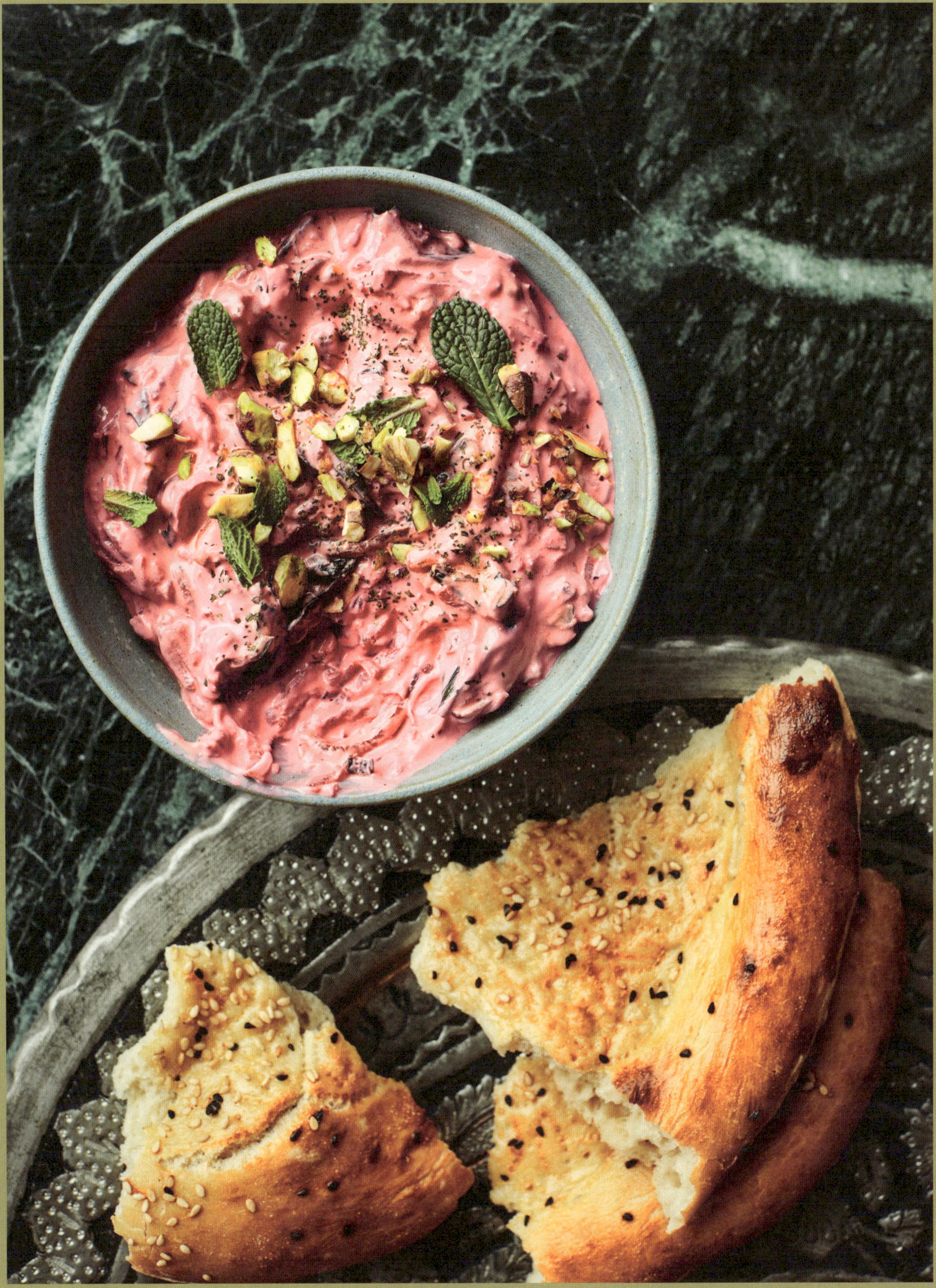

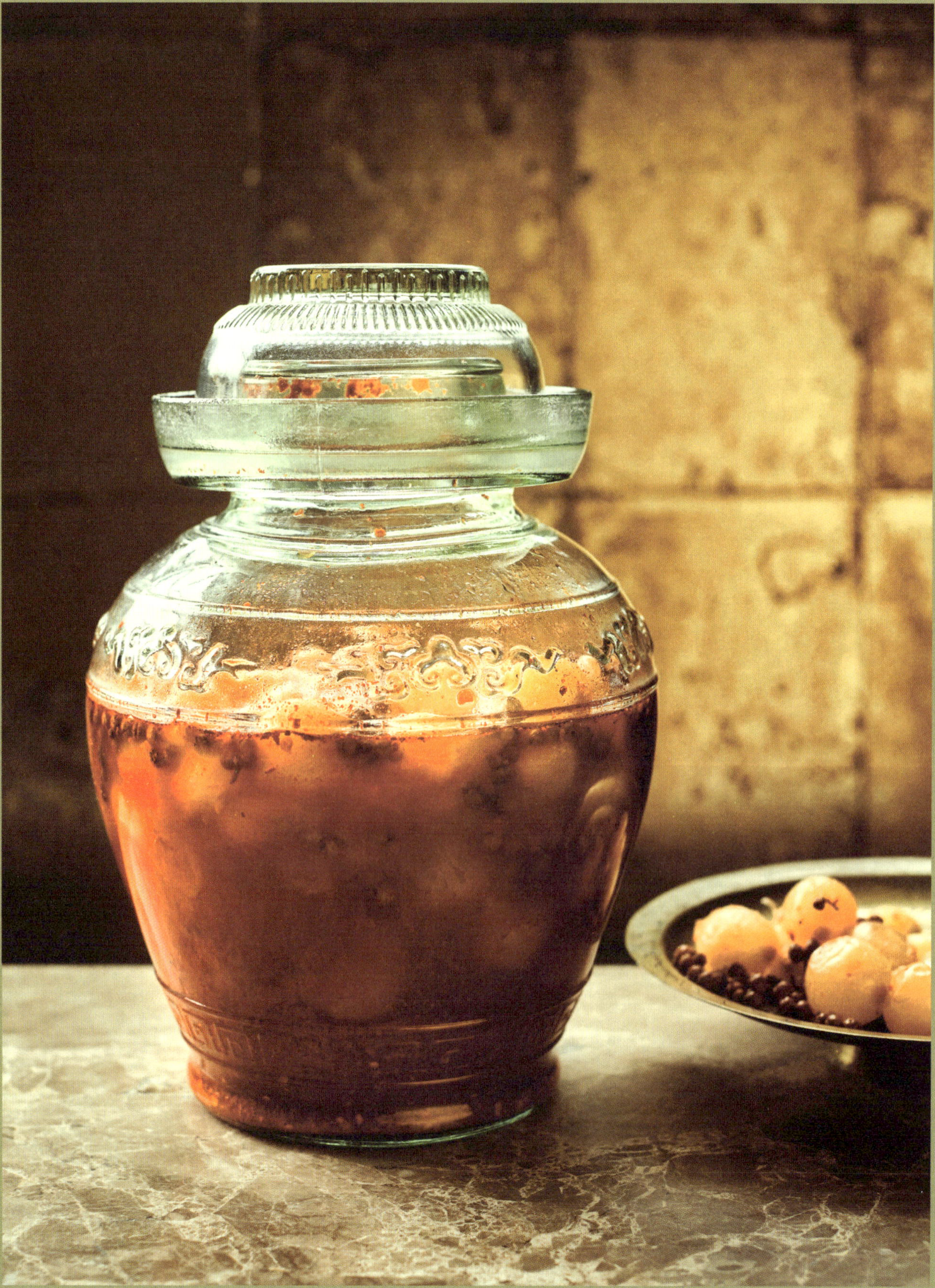

PAOCAI

Chinese Fermented Pearl Onions

Makes 1kg (2¼lb)

I easily ate spicy Yunnan pickled pearl onions every day for a month in 2003. The first time a few of them arrived on a tiny saucer, cosied up next to the simple fried rice I ate for lunch, I was perplexed. Why were they there? What did Homer, the English name the cook in Kunming had given himself, want me to do with them? I didn't get it. I wasn't used to pickles, other than Iranian ones, or the ones I would get as an accompaniment to a Reuben sandwich at Zingerman's Deli; and those were dill ones, cucumbers, either bright green if "new" or sage green if "old". Not bright red. Not onions. And not with fried rice. But, what the heck, I thought, and I tried one – right after a bite of rice. It was mouth-puckering and juicy and spicy and incredible, and it changed the way I viewed pickles – which, in this case, is to say lacto-ferments – and fried rice forever.

Make these and eat them with fried rice. Make these and eat them with An Uzbek Plov (see p149). Make these and use them in a martini, as my friend Tyler does. Make these and never look back.

This recipe calls for an optional addition of *baijiu*, the fiery clear Chinese liquor painfully familiar to anyone who has spent any time in China. You can find *baijiu* at most East Asian grocery stores, or you can head to a liquor store to score a bottle of Ming River, an upscale *baijiu* from my Qinghua and Columbia classmate and buddy, Bill, that will knock your socks off in the best way.

56g (2oz) fine sea salt
28g (1oz) white sugar

1kg (2¼lb) pearl onions
6 tbsp dried chilli flakes

2–3 tbsp Sichuan peppercorns
2 tbsp *baijiu* (optional)

Bring 900ml (4 cups/1½ pints) water to the boil in a large saucepan over a high heat. Once boiling, turn the heat off, and add the salt and sugar to the pan. Stir to dissolve. Set aside and let it cool to room temperature.

Meanwhile, add your pearl onions, chilli flakes, and Sichuan peppercorns to a large bowl and mix well. Tip your spicy onions into the base of a sterilized pickling jar (see p17). I encourage you to make these using a *paocai* jar, which you should be able to find online or at a Chinese grocer's.

Once your brine has cooled, add the *baijiu*, if using, then carefully pour your boozy brine into your pickling jar and over the onions. If you are using a Chinese pickle jar, pour a little bit of water into the jar's lip and cover with the lid. Otherwise, if using a regular jar, just put the lid on.

Set your pickles aside and watch the magic happen. Note that if you are using a regular jar with a lid, you will need to "burp" it every day once you see bubbles start to form. If you are using a Chinese pickling jar, make sure the water in the moat doesn't evaporate.

Taste your onions after 3–4 days. I like mine after about a week of fermentation, but to each their own.

I also like to remove my pickled onions, keep the brine in the jar, add some more salt and chilli flakes and more onions (or whatever vegetable I have in the house – currently green beans and radishes are swimming in my brine), and keep the fermentation party going.

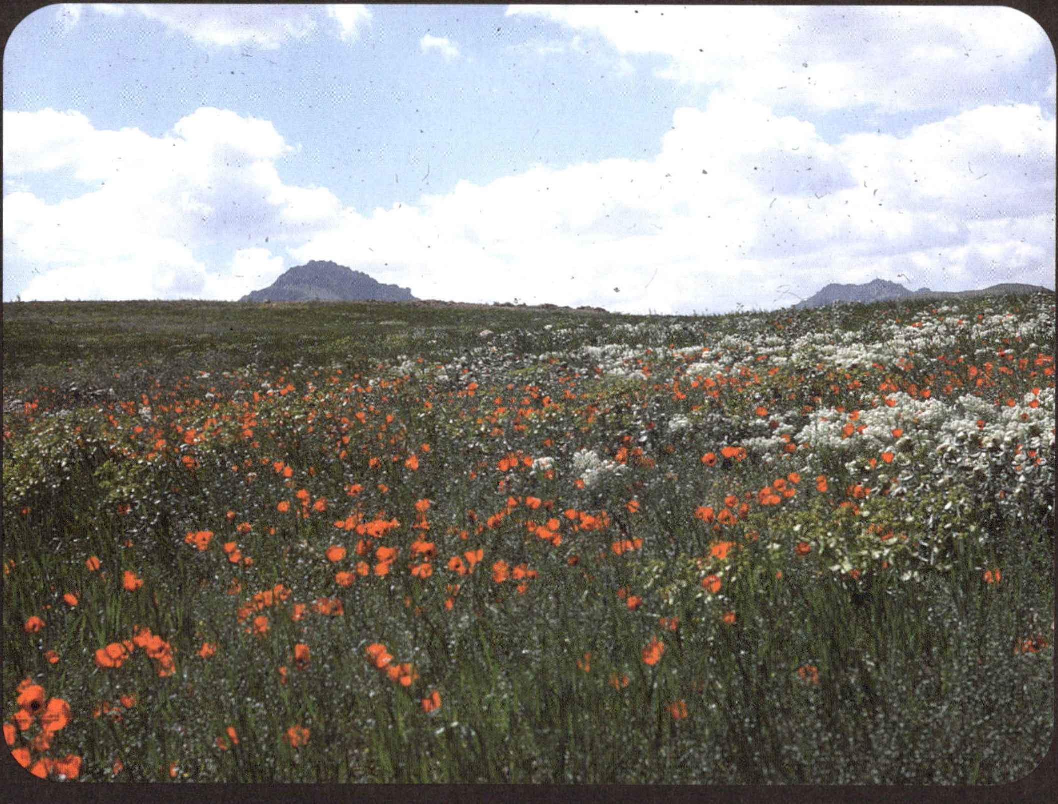

EGGS, VEGETABLES & TOFU

**EATING TOFU
IN DUNHUANG**
90

SPINACH CHIGIRTMA
Azeri Spinach & Eggs
94

CRUCIFEROUS KUKU
Iranian Broccoli Frittata
96

POMIDOR YUMURTA
Azeri Eggs & Tomatoes
97

CHICKEN CHIGIRTMA
Azeri Saffron Chicken & Eggs
98

**SPINACH, CARROT
& EGG BRAISE**
101

DI SI XIAN
Four Earthly Treasures
103

AUBERGINE FRITES
107

ZIRAN DOUFU
Uyghur Cumin Tofu
109

EATING TOFU IN DUNHUANG

The first tofu I liked – nay, loved – was a Japanese one. Deep-fried little cubes of melt-in-your-mouth silken tofu, sitting atop a smidge of dashi broth and underneath a dollop of grated radish. Spring 2000. A narrow yakitori joint on St Mark's Place in NYC's East Village. *Agedashi* tofu, ordered – alongside a plate of chicken meatball skewers and a shimmering bonito-topped *okonomiyaki* – by the Japanese classmate whom I would see in Tokyo a few months later on my way to Chinese summer school at Beijing's Qinghua University.

That was a golden summer. Of bike rides. Sweltering heat. Yanjing beers. Hours of Mandarin instruction. Sweat. Uyghur noodles. *Chaobing*. More beers. Extreme humidity. Sanlitun. *Mianbao che* rides. *Jianbing*s. Even more beers. I was 19, and full to the brim with the joy, confidence, and enthusiasm specific to that age, that in-between time when you're still a kid but think you're an adult and nothing can stop you. That summer, "The Real Slim Shady" was definitely the most frequently played track at every Qinghua East Gate bar. And *riben doufu* – "Japanese tofu" – was the most frequently ordered dish at our meals.

Riben doufu is not a Japanese dish; it's firmly Chinese. Perhaps it got its name from its resemblance to *agedashi* tofu, as they both consist of fried silken tofu, but that is where the similarity between the dishes ends. Unlike the pale delicacy of *agedashi* tofu, *riben doufu* uses a silken tofu made with eggs, whose yolks give it a characteristic yellow colour. The tofu is then typically squeezed out of a tube into round, coin-sized discs which are coated and fried before ending up on a platter with stir-fried greens, shiitake mushrooms, and a starch-thickened sauce. I loved it. We all loved it.

Funny thing is, we were in China. Eating "Japanese tofu" on a near-daily basis. Out of the myriad native tofu preparations to fall in love with, I had to fall for the one that was an approximation of another culture's cuisine. Go figure. Mock *agedashi* tofu. Chinese cooks, however, have been skilled at using tofu to approximate other things for centuries.

Tofu originated in China near the start of the Common Era and, by 965 CE, when the soy bean preparation makes its first written appearance, the consumption of tofu appears to have become sufficiently commonplace. However, its established presence and importance in Song Dynasty (960–1279) Chinese cuisine is undoubtedly due to the import and explosion in popularity of Buddhism, a religion that, like so much else, snaked its way through Asia via the trade routes of antiquity.

Siddhartha Gautama – the man who became known as Buddha – was born in either Nepal or India, in the 5th or 6th century BCE. Or not. Things are fuzzy. Records are old and conflicting – some folks think he was born in the 6th century BCE while others claim he died in the 8th, so, you know, take these dates with a big, flaky grain of sea salt. In any case, by the 3rd century BCE, the teachings of Buddha had been fully embraced by the Mauryan Emperor Ashoka.

Ashoka's support for Buddhism resulted in the religion's flourishing, not only within the confines of the Indian subcontinent, but also outside it; in 250 BCE, the Ashoka-sponsored third Buddhist Council decided that Buddhist missionaries and pilgrims should set off from India to proselytize. They made their way south

> OUT OF THE MYRIAD NATIVE TOFU PREPARATIONS TO FALL IN LOVE WITH, I HAD TO FALL FOR THE ONE THAT WAS AN APPROXIMATION OF ANOTHER CULTURE'S.

Top: The "Parents Bestowing Kindness on Their Children" section of the 12th-century Buddhist rock carvings at Dazu, Baodingshan, outside Chongqing, China. February 1999.

Bottom: A man inspects tomatoes. Siyob Bazaar. Samarkand, Uzbekistan. March 2024.

and southeast – and north, to Central Asia, where they were welcomed by the rulers and citizens of the Kushan Empire.

Kushan, which stretched across northwest India, Pakistan, Afghanistan, and up to Iran, the oases of the Oxus River valley, and the western Tarim Basin, not only proved to be fertile ground on which to spread the teachings of the Buddha, but also acted as an ideal geographical launchpad from which Buddhist missionaries and pilgrims could make their way east to China. Travelling already established commercial paths across deserts, mountains, and oases – across those Silk Roads into China – they came to the Middle Kingdom.

In 68 CE, the first Buddhist temple in China was established in Luoyang, the (relatively) newly declared capital of the Eastern Han Dynasty (25–220 CE), which, during the latter part of the Han Dynasty, served as the terminus (or starting point, depending on your perspective) of the era's Silk Roads. In its heyday, Luoyang was the most important centre of Buddhist learning and art in all of Asia. During the Tang Dynasty, however, Dunhuang, a strategic oasis nestled between the eastern end of the Taklamakan Desert and the western fringes of the Gobi Desert, supplanted Luoyang in both artistic and religious supremacy. A perfect stopping point for the early pilgrims and missionaries coming from India via the Kushan Empire, it was from Dunhuang that Buddhism travelled down the Hexi corridor – the only means of entering ancient China from Central Asia, and at the mouth of which Dunhuang strategically sat. The religion made its way down the corridor and into central China, where it caught the eye and devotion of the Tang Empress Wu, whose support for her new religion in part resulted in Buddhism's flourishing, as well as in tofu's increased usage.

Buddhism changed the way its followers structured and viewed their lives. It changed the way they saw humans and the beauty of the (fleeting) world. And it changed the way they ate.

Abstention from killing is one of the five main precepts of Buddhism and, while the religion does not strictly prohibit its followers from consuming meat, many Buddhists find meat-eating problematic if not immoral and sacrilegious. Accordingly, Tang Dynasty Buddhist monks and monasteries began experimenting with vegetarianism … and started turning tofu into mock meats, fish, and fowl.

It's worth pointing out that the Tang Dynasty saw not only the flourishing of Buddhism, but other religions, too. Tang era Chang'an was a multicultural, religiously diverse cosmopolis. However, Christianity, Judaism, Manichaeism, and Zoroastrianism's relation to tofu is non-existent, so they don't quite merit our current attention (and I'm on a strict word count limit). Plus: Dunhuang was all about the Buddhism, baby.

Far more than an oasis of commerce and religion, Dunhuang of the 7th century CE was a city of art, of hundreds of caves filled with colourful frescoes depicting Buddha's life, the mortal world, paradise, animals, scenes of commerce, portraits of patrons. They stand, in my mind at least, as a wonder of the world on par with, if not exceeding in grandeur, ancient sites far more famous. However, once the Tang Dynasty turned inward, once the Mongols and then Islam came, Dunhuang and its caves, its magnificence, were forgotten, hidden away, on the edges of two remote deserts – and we are so very lucky they were. No one destroyed them. No one plundered them. No one noticed them; until someone did.

It is Sir Marc Aurel Stein, Hungarian-born Brit, Knight Commander of the Indian Empire (WHAT a title, eh!?), Silk Roads scholar and adventurer, to whom we in the West owe the rediscovery of the Dunhuang art. Stein spent ages in Asia before ever setting foot in Dunhuang, gallivanting across lands from the Tarim Basin to the Pamir Mountains, crating treasure after treasure back to Britain, filling in holes on the murky British maps of an area the Empire wanted but didn't quite know how to take.

I have complicated feelings about these state-sponsored archaeologists, dragging their finds back to London, New Haven, Stockholm. I have complicated feelings about Stein. But I have always loved the fact that he kept naming his dogs the same thing, over and over: Dash. Dash II. Dash III. Seven of them in total. He replaced one after another, each accompanying him on his expeditions in Central Asia. Indeed, one of Stein's Dashes (VII, I believe) was with him on the fateful day in 1907 when he managed to gain access to a cave in Dunhuang which would have enormous historical importance.

> *The secret chamber was literally heaped from floor to ceiling with a great stack of neatly rolled documents and relics, which made a solid mass of material rising to a height of nearly ten feet. There was only just enough room for two men to stand in the space left by this amazing pile of documents which, it was later calculated, occupied five hundred cubic feet. Indeed there was so much weight of material that Stein was genuinely worried in case Wang Tao-shih, as he scrambled about tugging out samples, should topple the structure and be buried beneath the collapse of the pile of documents.*
>
> – Timothy Severin, *The Oriental Adventure: Explorers of the East*

Happily, the result of this encounter did not end with Wang Tao-shih, the Daoist priest who had taken it upon himself to guard and protect the caves (and sell off some of their contents to the highest bidders, naturally), being buried under the documents, but rather with Stein's returning to Britain with his Dunhuang haul ("24 cases of manuscripts and another five cases of embroideries, paintings, and art relics"), and a renewed attention to the once-famous-and-then-forgotten Silk Roads town. Chinese and Europeans alike descended on the region, vying for artifacts, vying for glory. Eventually, historic, artistic, and cultural preservation came to Dunhuang, the effects of which today enable intrepid travellers to visit a select number of caves. Like Aurel Stein, I too went to Dunhuang, but I didn't find a treasure trove. All I discovered was that I had the nerves to go paragliding over the desert. Oh yeah – and I got sexually harassed there too. It was *quite* the memorable trip.

NO ONE DESTROYED THEM. NO ONE PLUNDERED THEM. NO ONE NOTICED THEM; UNTIL SOMEONE DID.

You can have a better time in Dunhuang than I did. You can walk into the caves and be amazed by the immeasurable talent, devotion, time, love, and skill that went into the paintings and carvings before, beside, and above you. And then you can go back to your hotel, get ready for dinner, and maybe have some tofu, *riben* or not, and be amazed that the people who were responsible for painting the scenes forever etched in your memory and mind's eye were also the ones responsible for popularizing the curdled soy bean product on your plate.

And if you can't – if you don't make it to Gansu – that's OK. You can still eat some tofu – I have a few recipes for you here – and contemplate its origin as you avoid oil splatters from your wok. You could also contemplate, as I am as I write this, that in Chinese slang, "to eat tofu" means to take advantage of someone sexually, and that's kind of the same thing as sexual harassment, so it's all come full circle.

SPINACH CHIGIRTMA

Azeri Spinach & Eggs

Serves 2–4

My mind has been blown a few times while researching this book. Realizing that the Chinese word for spinach – *bocai* – which I have known for decades, means "Persian vegetable" is one of them. The "*bo*" in *bocai* refers to Bolinguo, an archaic designation for ancient Persia, from whence spinach originated. Oh – and the Western European words for spinach (e.g., *epinard*, *espinaca*, *spinaci*) are all derived from *esfanaj*, the Persian word for spinach. That's some iron-heavy etymology right there.

While scholarship has stumbled over the precise date and means of spinach's transmission from west to east, it is generally accepted that the so-called "chieftain of leafy greens" (as spinach was dubbed by the 12th-century Arab Andalusian agriculturalist Ibn al-'awwām) arrived in China, in seed form, from Iran via Nepal in the middle of the 7th century CE. Special and rare enough to be sent as tribute from the Nepalese king to the Tang Court in Chang'an, spinach is now a mainstay on tables across the world. Including mine. This is but one of a few spinach recipes in this book, a testament to both the versatility of the leafy green and its ubiquity in the culinary traditions of the regions we are exploring.

Serve with bread and cheese, or enjoy as part of a brunch spread (see p97).

---

4 eggs
1 tsp fine sea salt
¾ tsp freshly ground black pepper
300g (10oz) frozen chopped spinach

4 tbsp ghee, or 60g (2oz) unsalted butter
1 onion, finely diced
flaky sea salt
Aleppo chilli flakes or dried chilli flakes

Crack your eggs into a small bowl. Add ½ teaspoon each of salt and pepper, and use a fork to lightly whisk the eggs. Set aside.

Fill a medium saucepan with water and bring it to the boil over a high heat. Add the spinach and cook for 3 minutes, then drain in a fine mesh sieve.

With the back of a wooden spoon, press down on the drained spinach (still in the sieve) to get as much moisture out as possible. Set aside.

Melt the ghee or butter in a medium non-stick sauté pan (or a well-seasoned cast-iron pan) for which you have a lid over a medium heat. Add the onion, along with ¼ teaspoon each of the salt and black pepper. Cook, stirring occasionally, for 5–7 minutes, or just long enough for the onion to turn golden brown.

Meanwhile, see if you can press down some further on the spinach to get some more liquid out; if it's cool enough, you can try and squeeze with your (clean) hands. If you can't get any more liquid out, that's OK too.

Reduce the heat to low, and add the spinach to the browning onions, along with the final ¼ teaspoon of salt. Mix the spinach and onions together well, and cook them for a further 2 minutes, stirring frequently, before flattening out the mixture across the centre of the pan.

Add the eggs to the pan, spreading them out evenly across and through the spinach in the centre. Cover the pan and cook until the eggs are set, 6–7 minutes. Transfer to a serving plate and top with flaky sea salt and chilli flakes to taste.

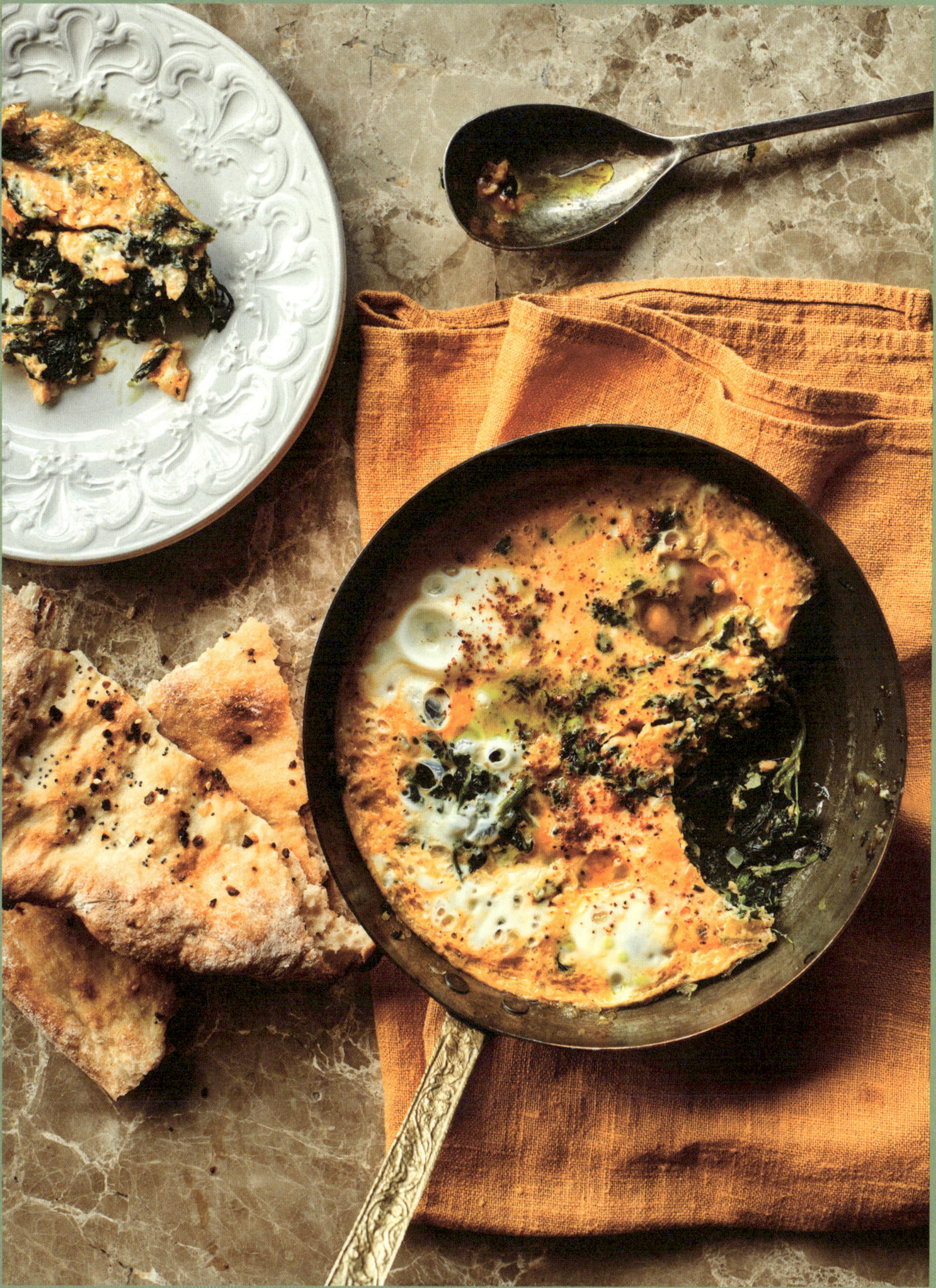

CRUCIFEROUS KUKU

Iranian Broccoli Frittata

Serves 4–8

I always hated *kuku*. It was too green for me, too herby, too beloved by my vegetarian sister, and I was a contrarian as a child, if nothing else. In recent years, however, I've grown to not just like, but to love *kuku*, and part of that was discovering that there is not just one type. The recipe below is for a broccoli *kuku*, simply because I had a head of broccoli in my refrigerator when I was writing it. Try it with other vegetables – I adore cauliflower *kuku*. You can make *kuku* from nearly anything; that's one of its most magical characteristics. It's a choose-your-own-adventure, Friday-refrigerator-clean-out dish that is (relatively) healthy, economical, easy, and delicious. The spices I've listed below are just suggestions and tastes that I enjoy. You can play around with what you like – there's no wrong answer. Just keep in mind that the eggs are only here to bind everything together; they're not the stars of this show.

Also, while *kuku* is fantastic served warm, it is also exceptional when cool or cold.

- 7 tbsp olive oil
- 1 onion, thinly sliced into half-moons
- 1 tsp fine sea salt
- 1 tsp ground turmeric
- 3 garlic cloves, minced
- 1 head of broccoli (about 600g/1lb 5oz), florets coarsely chopped
- 6 eggs
- 1 tbsp plain yogurt
- ½ tsp baking powder
- 1 tbsp plain flour
- juice of 1 lime
- ¼ tsp cayenne pepper
- ½ tsp ground cumin
- ¼ tsp freshly ground black pepper

In a medium sauté pan for which you have a lid, heat 4 tablespoons of the oil over a high heat. Once the oil is hot and glistening, reduce the heat to medium and add the onion. Cook, stirring occasionally, for 3–5 minutes, until soft, translucent, and just starting to brown at the edges.

Stir in ½ teaspoon of the salt, along with the turmeric, garlic and broccoli. Add 4 tablespoons water, then cover the pan and cook for 4–6 minutes, or until everything is soft. Transfer the contents of the pan to a bowl and set aside to cool. This is your *kuku* filling.

Meanwhile, in a large mixing bowl, combine the eggs, yogurt, baking powder, flour, lime juice, cayenne pepper, and cumin. Add the remaining salt and the black pepper, and whisk until well combined. Once the *kuku* filling has cooled down, fold it gently into the eggs.

Heat the remaining 3 tablespoons olive oil in a shallow ovenproof sauté pan. Once the oil is hot and glistening, reduce the heat to low and pour the *kuku* mixture into the pan. Use a spatula to push the vegetables down into the eggs and spread everything around evenly. Cook, uncovered, for 15 minutes, or until the eggs have set – you can check this by gently giving the pan a shake.

Once the eggs are set, turn off the heat and turn your oven's grill to high. Slide your *kuku* under the grill and brown the top for 1–2 minutes.

Enjoy *kuku* with bread, with a simple green salad, or on its own.

POMIDOR YUMURTA

Azeri Eggs & Tomatoes

Serves 2–4

OK. This might be my favourite egg dish, and it's a real reminder of how lucky we are. Take a look at the ingredients list. Eggs. Fat. Tomato. Salt. Pepper. It's practically nothing. But together, it's everything.

Cooking can be magic. This dish is magic. Enjoy this eggy Azeri delight with a hunk of bread, a chunk of cheese, and a strong cup of tea, or serve as part of a delectable brunch spread (see below).

---

4 eggs

½ tsp fine sea salt

½ tsp freshly ground black pepper, plus extra to taste

2 tbsp ghee, or 30g (1oz) unsalted butter

4–5 medium tomatoes (about 350–400g/ 12–14oz), diced

flaky sea salt

Crack your eggs into a small bowl. Add the fine sea salt and black pepper, and use a fork to lightly whisk the eggs. Set aside.

In a medium non-stick sauté pan (or a well-seasoned cast-iron pan), heat your ghee or butter over a medium heat until melted. Add the tomatoes and their juices. Reduce the heat to medium–low and cook the tomatoes for 8–10 minutes, or until they break down, prodding them a bit to help them along and stirring occasionally so that nothing burns. Don't rush your tomatoes. It's the slow release of their sweetness that makes this dish so special.

Reduce the heat to low and tip in your eggs. Gently mix the eggs into the tomatoes and add a couple more grinds of pepper, if you like. Cook the eggs, undisturbed, for another 5–7 minutes, until they are just set.

Transfer to a serving plate and top with flaky sea salt to taste.

Note: Enjoy this Azerbaijani egg and tomato preparation as part of brunch spread with freshly sliced cucumber, some Suzma (see p77), a salty cheese, warm bread (see Central Asian Bread, p205, or Layered & Fried Flatbreads, p211), and Spinach Chigirtma (see p94).

CHICKEN CHIGIRTMA

Azeri Saffron Chicken & Eggs

Serves 4–6

Though it includes chicken, I have chosen to place this Azeri dish in this chapter, nestled next to its fellow egg preparations, as it is the eggs that impart its essential character. That's right, this former customs and trade lawyer is applying the General Rules of Interpretation to her recipes: GRI 3(b), specifically, a rule that more or less says if you have mixtures of more than one thing (and other customs classification rules don't apply), then you classify those mixtures according to "the material or component which gives them their essential character". What constitutes a good's (or a recipe's) essential character is up for debate, argument, and sometimes lawsuits; but there's no one here to debate, argue with, or sue me (other than my editors, and they're awesome), so my classification choice wins every time.

I've applied this principle to a few recipes. To Dovga (essential character: soup, see p63). To Dushbara & Chochure (essential character: dumplings, see p197). It's a choice. It's an interpretation. And, when it comes down to it, it doesn't matter where in this tome you find these recipes; it just matters that you find them.

Enjoy this dish with rice, with bread – with rice *and* bread, if you like! – and a zesty cold salad.

- 1kg (2¼lb) skin-on, bone-in chicken thighs and/or drumsticks
- 3 tbsp ghee or olive oil
- 300g (10oz) onions, thinly sliced into half-moons
- 150g (5½oz) green peppers, thinly sliced
- 2 garlic cloves, minced
- 2 tbsp tomato purée
- ¼ tsp ground cinnamon
- 4 tbsp lemon juice
- 1g saffron, finely ground using a mortar and pestle
- 6 eggs
- sea salt and freshly ground black pepper

To serve (optional)
- freshly chopped tomatoes
- fresh coriander leaves

Season your chicken on both sides with salt and pepper. Heat the ghee or oil in a wide shallow casserole pot over a medium–high heat. When it's hot and glistening, add the chicken and brown it on both sides. Be patient. You can tell the meat has been properly browned and is ready to switch sides when it releases easily from the pan. For me, this process takes about 2 minutes per side. Once browned, remove your chicken and set it aside on a plate

Reduce the heat to medium–low and add the onions to the now-empty pan. Cook gently for 10–15 minutes until they are soft and golden. Add the green pepper and garlic, along with a generous pinch of salt and a few grinds of black pepper to taste.

Add the tomato purée to the pan and stir to combine. Add the cinnamon, stir to combine again, and then return the chicken to the pan, along with any juices released. Pour the lemon juice evenly over the chicken and then (also evenly) scatter over the ground saffron. Add 240ml (1 cup/8fl oz) water to the pan and stir, then increase the heat to high and bring the mixture to a boil. Next, reduce the heat to low, cover your pan, and leave to cook for 20 minutes.

In a bowl, whisk the eggs together with a big pinch of salt. Leave them to rest while the chicken cooks.

Once 20 minutes have passed, uncover your pan and pour the whisked eggs over and around the chicken, tilting the pan if necessary to distribute them evenly throughout. Cover once more and cook over a low heat for a further 5–7 minutes, until the eggs are just set.

Serve the chicken *chigirtma* in the pan, topped with chopped tomatoes and coriander leaves if you have them. If you don't, don't stress – just crack some more freshly ground pepper over the top, along with some flaky sea salt.

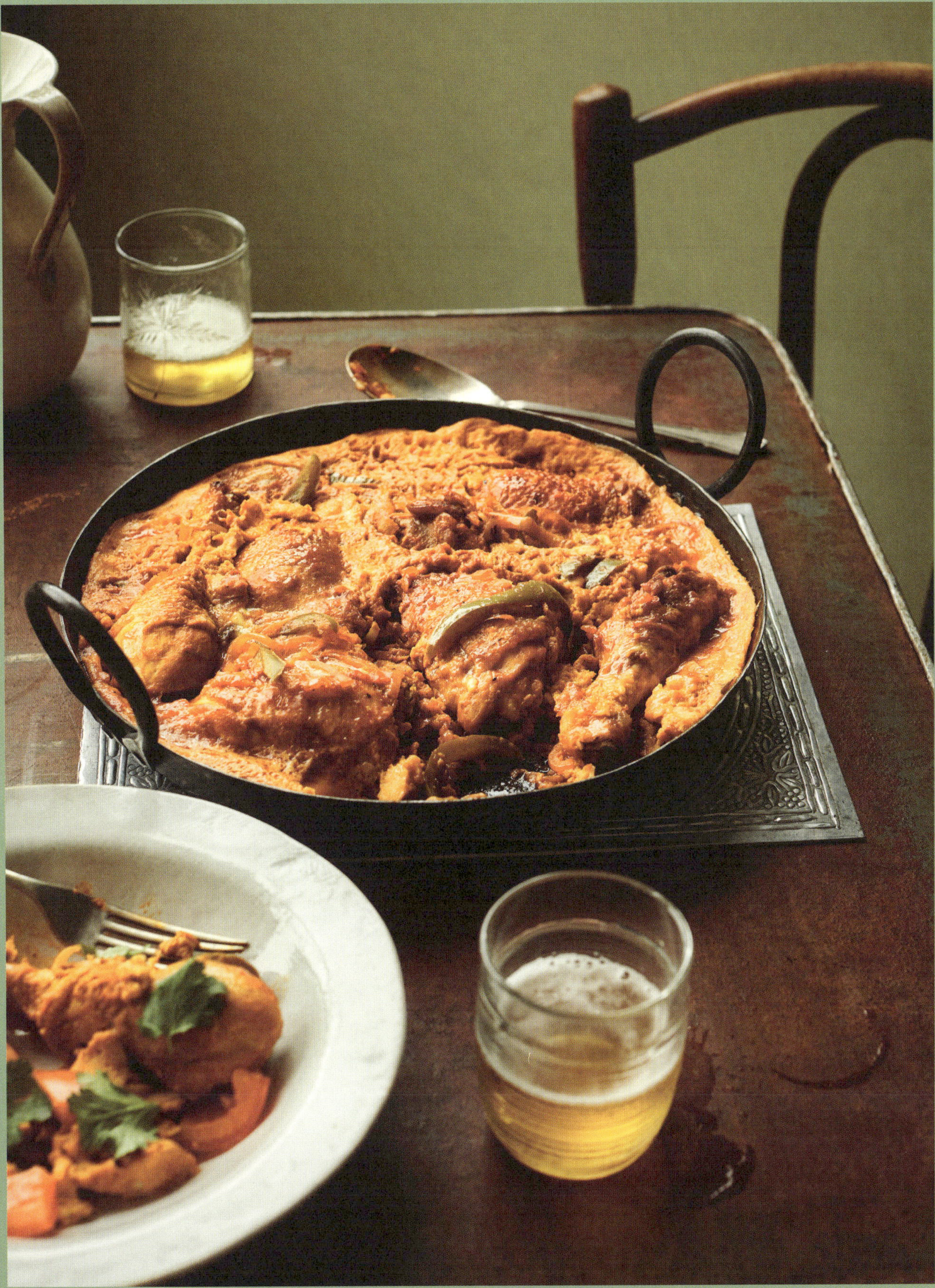

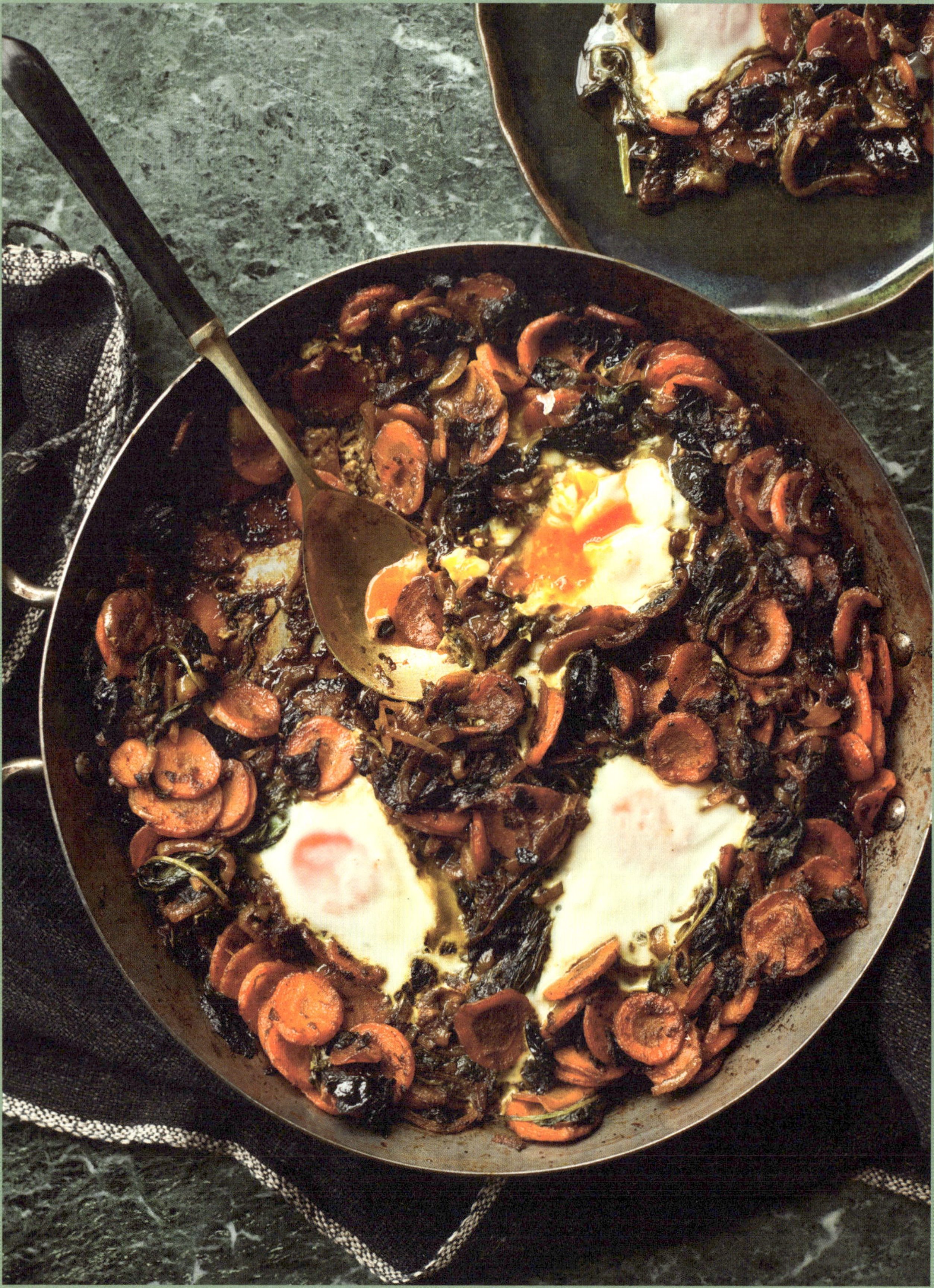

SPINACH, CARROT & EGG BRAISE

Serves 4–6

As promised, another spinach dish. This is a sweet-and-sour ode to *nargessi*, an Iranian spinach and egg dish, as well as to *khoresh havij*, an Iranian carrot and lamb braise.

I made this for the first time on a cold autumn night in the Cotswolds, not long after a 22-year-old Iranian woman, Mahsa Amini, died, likely from injuries sustained when she was arrested for allegedly not wearing her hijab "properly". As I cooked in our charming rental cottage, I thought about how fortunate and privileged I was. I thought about my son sleeping upstairs and my friends in the room next door, some of whom were gay. I was free to wear what I wanted, to paint my nails, to wear lipstick and a miniskirt if I so desired. My friends were free to love whomever they wanted. My son is free to grow up to be who he wants to be, to worship whom and if he pleases. No one is going to force him to wear a beard or shave it off, in the name of religion or the state, thank goodness.

Religious extremism can destroy more than lives. It can erase history. It can hobble and/or distort culture. It can bomb 6th-century CE Buddhist statues to bits, as the Taliban did in Bamiyan in 2001, disappearing in a few moments irreplaceable icons which had peacefully gazed down upon Silk Roads travellers, merchants, and pilgrims for centuries. What a waste. What a loss. What a tragedy for a girl to die because a few strands of hair peeked out from under a scarf.

If only the Afghan Buddhas had been forgotten, hidden away like the caves of Dunhuang, unmolested by exploitation, untouched by fanaticism …

Let us not take our rights, privileges, and freedoms for granted; we must make sure we protect, respect and champion them. Not everyone is as fortunate as we are. Access to healthy food, to fresh fruit and vegetables, to spinach and carrots, to hormone-free eggs: that is a privilege as well, and one so many of us (myself included) also often take for granted. Let's try to do better.

- 4 tbsp extra virgin olive oil
- 2 large onions, thinly sliced into half-moons
- 2 garlic cloves, minced
- 2 tsp fine sea salt
- ¼ tsp coarsely ground black pepper
- ½ tsp ground turmeric
- 1 tsp ground cinnamon
- 1 tsp ground cardamom
- zest of 1 orange
- zest of 1 lime and juice of 2 (about 5 tbsp), plus extra zest to taste
- 500–600g (1lb 2oz–1lb 5oz) carrots, peeled and thinly sliced into 5mm (¼in) coins
- 0.25g saffron, ground with ⅛ tsp granulated sugar using a mortar and pestle, and then dissolved in 2 tbsp hot water
- 3 tablespoons white wine vinegar
- 2 tablespoons soft light brown sugar
- 200g (7oz) pitted prunes, chopped
- 120g (4¼oz) fresh spinach
- 4 eggs
- flaky sea salt

Heat 2 tablespoons of the olive oil in a shallow ovenproof casserole pot over a medium–high heat. Once the oil shimmers, reduce the heat to medium, add the onions, and cook, stirring occasionally, for 10 minutes, or until they become soft and lovely and begin to brown.

Reduce the heat to low and add the garlic. Stir and cook for 30–60 seconds, or until fragrant.

Next, add the salt, pepper, turmeric, cinnamon, cardamom, and citrus zest. Stir everything together well before adding 250ml (1 cup plus 1 tbsp/9fl oz) water. Cover with a lid and turn your attention to the carrots.

Heat the remaining 2 tablespoons olive oil in a large non-stick sauté pan over a medium–high heat. Once the oil shimmers, reduce the heat to medium, add your carrots, and cook, stirring occasionally, for 7–8 minutes, or until the carrots are softened, but not soft, and browned, but not burnt.

When the carrots are ready, remove them from the pan using a slotted spoon/spider, leaving behind any excess oil, and transfer them to the casserole pot with the onions. Stir to combine, then add the lime juice, brewed saffron, vinegar, and brown sugar. Stir everything together, then add the prunes. Stir again to mix well. Keep the heat on low and let everything cook, covered, for 45 minutes.

After 45 minutes, taste your *khoresh*. It should be sweet, sour, and saucy. Adjust to taste with more salt, lime zest or juice, vinegar, or sugar, as you see fit. If it's overly watery, increase the heat a little and cook with the lid off for a few minutes to allow some liquid to evaporate. You don't want to lose it all, though, so be vigilant! Alternatively, if your *khoresh* looks to be drying out like the Aral Sea under Soviet planning, add a splash more water.

Add your spinach to the pan, one handful at a time. Push the raw leaves amongst and below the cooked mixture, letting each handful wilt before adding the next. Depending on the amount of carrots you used and/or your palate for spinach, you may or may not fit in all 120g (4¼oz). I always do, though – spinach really does cook down to nothingness rather quickly.

Once all your spinach is in and wilted, you could stop there, let your pan cool down and refrigerate it overnight. The flavours will continue to develop (and frankly often taste richer and more delicious) if left for even a few hours. What I like to do, though, is get to this point, leave the *khoresh*, covered, on the actual back burner, heat off, and cook the rest of my meal – usually rice, maybe a green leafy salad. I reheat the *khoresh* in an oven preheated to 200°C (180°C fan/400°F/Gas 6) until warmed through, and then proceed with the egg grilling.

Preheat your oven's grill to high. Using a large spoon or ladle, make four wells in the top of your *khoresh* and crack an egg into each. Sprinkle a bit of flaky sea salt on to each egg, and maybe even grate some fresh lime zest over top. Carefully put your pan under the grill.

Watch your eggs. You want the whites to be fully cooked and the yolks to be just a wee bit runny. You definitely don't want anything to burn, and my experience with grills suggests constant vigilance is necessary to avoid unwanted and charred outcomes. When your eggs are set, remove the *khoresh* from the oven, take it over to your table, and enjoy!

DI SI XIAN

Four Earthly Treasures

Serves 2-4

Di san xian: three treasures from the earth. Aubergine. Pepper. Potato. A warming delight on a cold winter's night, and a mainstay on Chinese menus and tables across the world, this hearty, comforting, typical northern Chinese dish made its way to my dinner table when I was a teen in Beijing more times than I can count. Here, I have added tofu to round out the dish, making it a one-wok dinner ready in under 30 minutes.

This dish also underscores the fluency with which once-foreign foodstuffs can be incorporated into and reinterpreted by a new cultural/culinary lexicon. Whereas aubergine has been present in Chinese cuisine since the start of the Common Era, peppers and potatoes are relatively new imports, products of the Columbian Exchange – the global spread of (among other things) plants, seeds, and crops from the Americas to the rest of the world that began in the late 15th century following Christopher Columbus' infamous 1492 voyage.

Its roots may be in the Americas, global trade, and colonialism, but this is a Chinese dish, through and through, while simultaneously an example of the interconnectedness of foods and flavours across geography and time.

Plus now with tofu, a fourth earthly treasure – as I'm sure the Buddhists of yore would agree. My six-year-old certainly does (and I hope you do too).

Note: This recipe calls for a delicious fermented chilli bean paste – *doubanjiang* – which you should be able to source at major grocery stores these days. Though it packs a heat, *doubanjiang*'s spice does not overwhelm, and here it lends the dish a beautiful tinge of spicy umami. If you shy away from spice, please just omit it.

- 1 aubergine, cut into 2.5cm (1in) chunks
- 3½ tsp fine sea salt
- 240ml (1 cup/8fl oz) plus 1 tbsp neutral oil
- 2 potatoes (about 270g/9½oz), well washed or peeled and roughly chopped into 2.5cm (1in) chunks
- 2 tbsp light soy sauce
- 1 tbsp dark soy sauce
- 1 tbsp Shaoxing wine
- 1 tbsp *doubanjiang* (optional, but highly recommended)
- ½ tsp ground white pepper
- 2 tsp caster or granulated sugar
- 4 tbsp cornflour
- 280g (9½oz) firm tofu, drained and cut into 2.5cm (1in) chunks
- 3 garlic cloves, minced
- 2 peppers (colour of your choosing), cut into 2.5cm (1in) chunks
- 3 spring onions, chopped

Tip the aubergine chunks into a bowl and cover with cold water. Add 2 teaspoons of the salt and leave to soak for 20 minutes. You may need to put a plate on top of the aubergine to keep everything submerged in the water.

Heat the 240ml (1 cup/8fl oz) of oil in a wok or large sauté pan over a medium heat, swirling the oil around to coat the base of the wok. Once hot, add the potatoes and fry for 8–10 minutes, turning occasionally, until golden brown on all sides.

While the aubergine soaks and your potatoes fry, make your sauce. In a small bowl, combine the two soy sauces, Shaoxing wine, *doubanjiang* (if using), white pepper, and sugar, along with ½ teaspoon of the salt and 1 tablespoon of the cornflour. Stir to dissolve the cornflour as best as you can.

Once your potatoes are ready and nicely browned, use a slotted spoon/spatula to remove them from the wok and set aside on a paper towel-lined plate. Turn off the heat but keep the oil in the wok, at the ready.

After their soaking time is up, drain the aubergine pieces and rinse them under cold water. Dry thoroughly with paper towels and then toss in a medium bowl with the remaining 3 tablespoons cornflour.

Return the wok to a medium–high heat, and add the aubergine pieces. Fry for 8–10 minutes, turning occasionally, until golden brown. Remove the aubergine from the pan with your slotted spoon/spatula, and set aside on the plate with the potatoes.

Discard the leftover oil, then add 1 tablespoon fresh oil to the wok. Once the oil is hot, add the tofu, garlic, and peppers. Cook, stirring frequently, for 3 minutes, or until the peppers begin to char at their edges. Return the potatoes and aubergine to the wok, and stir everything together to mix.

Grab your bowl of sauce. Stir it to make sure the cornflour is fully dissolved, then add the sauce to the wok, along with the spring onions and the final teaspoon of salt. Stir together and cook everything for 30 seconds, then serve.

Three treasures of the earth, plus tofu, on your dinner table.

An alleyway near the Great Mosque. Xian, China. July 2007.

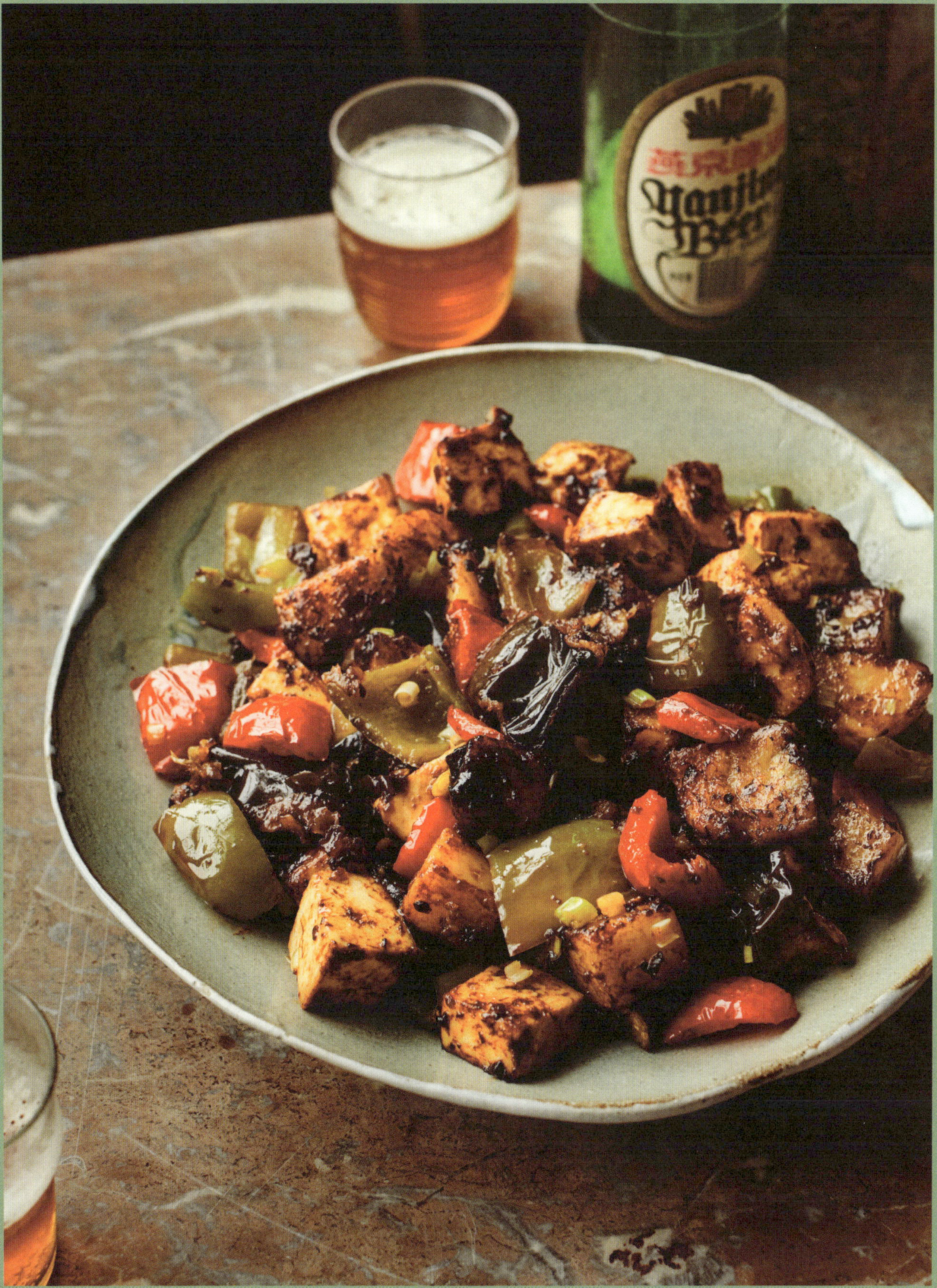

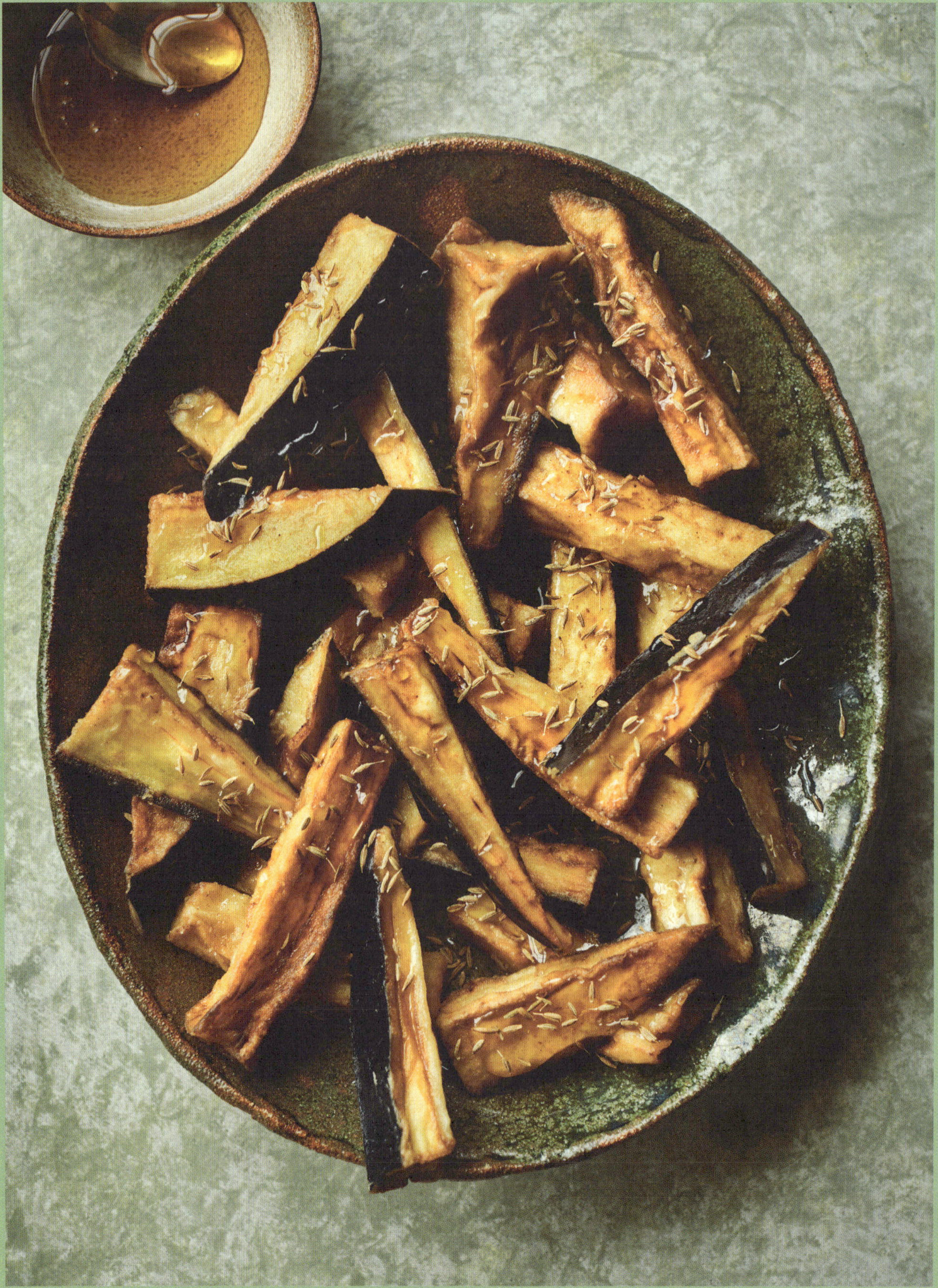

AUBERGINE FRITES

Serves 2–4 as a tapas

When I lived in Shanghai after university, my friends and I frequented a Uyghur restaurant on Yishan Lu, a stone's throw from one of our homes. We would feast on lamb and soups and noodles and *kao baozi* (see p200 for my recipe). And this dish – cuminy fried aubergine fritters – or something like it, at least.

I haven't seen this anywhere else. The most similar dish I can find is the Spanish *berenjenas fritas con miel*, one of my all-time favourite tapas. The Arabs brought the aubergine to Spain in the 8th century. They got it from Asia, where it has been cultivated and eaten since at least the start of the Common Era. And once the nightshade landed in Iberia, someone at some point started deep-frying it and drizzling it with syrupy sweetness.

A fellow American now living in Barca, Coley is my son's godfather, the first friend I made when I moved to Shanghai, and a man who loves to eat. Between Coley, myself, and his wife Zia, we cobbled together our collective food memories in an attempt to recreate the frites we ate together decades ago, and, in doing so, created something new – a dish tinged with memories not only of rowdy, lamby meals in Shanghai's Xujiahui District, but also with more recent ones – white tablecloths, dappled sunshine, the sparkling blue Mediterranean behind us, our children drawing pictures together on one side of the table as we finish another bottle of Albariño on the other. And fried aubergines, drizzled with honey.

The restaurant on Yishan Lu is still open, I hear. I hope they still have their aubergine frites on the menu. If they don't, that's OK – because I can always make these. And now you can, too.

---

1 aubergine (about 350g/12oz), cut into 2 × 2 × 8cm (¾ × ¾ × 3¼in) frites

750ml (3 cups/1¼ pints) milk, beer, or sparkling water, plus extra as needed

120g (4¼oz) plain flour

1 tbsp ground cumin

1 tbsp fine sea salt

vegetable oil or other neutral oil, for deep-frying

To serve

honey or date molasses

cumin seeds

Place the aubergine frites in a large bowl and pour your chosen liquid over the top, adding more as necessary to fully cover. Set aside and to soak for 30 minutes.

In another bowl, combine the flour and cumin.

Drain your soaked aubergine frites in a colander. Once they're looking decently dry, toss the frites (still in the colander) with the salt, and then dump them into the flour-and-cumin bowl. Turn to coat the aubergine pieces in the flour-and-cumin mixture, and get ready to deep-fry.

Pour oil into a large saucepan or sauté pan to a depth of 5cm (2in) and heat it over a medium–high heat until it's shimmering and nearly (but not!) smoking. Line a plate with paper towels and have it at the ready next to your stovetop.

Using chopsticks or tongs, carefully place some aubergine frites into the hot oil. Fill your oily pan with aubergine frites, but don't overcrowd it. It's better to work in batches here.

Fry the aubergine frites for 2–3 minutes on each side until golden brown, turning occasionally and paying close attention. Now, golden aubergine can devolve into burnt aubergine before you know it and, while there is a time and place for burnt aubergine, this is not it. Remove your golden frites from the pan and place on the paper towel-lined plate to drain.

Repeat until you have fried all your aubergine frites.

To serve, pile up your frites on a platter, drizzle with honey or date molasses, and sprinkle some cumin seeds on top for good measure.

ZIRAN DOUFU

Uyghur Cumin Tofu

Serves 2–4

Though widely used in cuisines across Asia, cumin is rarely found on the Western European or American table. And that is a true shame. I love cumin. A Central Asian spice so ancient it was once used as a mummification ingredient for Egyptian pharaohs and is mentioned in the Old Testament, cumin has an earthy pungency that is warm and deeply flavourful without being hot and spicy – and, as you may notice, it is the third most utilized seasoning in this book after salt and black pepper.

Known in both Farsi and Uzbek as *zira*, I also know cumin as *ziran*, the Mandarin Chinese phoneticization of the Uyghur word for cumin. *Ziran* is a word most closely connected to a dish found at every Uyghur restaurant within and outside China (and, for better and worse, increasingly at non-Uyghur Chinese restaurants as well): *ziran yangrou*, cumin lamb.

We are not working with lamb here. There is a LOT of lamb in this book. And I love *ziran yangrou*. I really do. But I love tofu, too, and I feel bad for vegetarians who keep missing out on tasting these flavours together. Luckily, they no longer need to.

Right now, I know what you're thinking: this looks like a LOT of cumin. Maybe even too much cumin. I hear you. But hear *me* out – the cumin is the whole point of this dish. It's the *name* of the dish. *Ziran*. It *should* look like a lot of cumin. It *is* a lot – but it's not too much. You may even find that you want more cumin than I've suggested the next time you cook this.

280g (9½oz) extra-firm tofu, cut into 4–5cm (1¾–2in) squares or rectangles, 2–3cm (¾–1¼in) thick

200ml (scant 1 cup/7fl oz) vegetable oil

½ onion, thinly sliced into half-moons

4 small dried red chillies (e.g. bird's-eye chillies)

3 tbsp cumin seeds, toasted

1 tsp ground cumin

1½ tsp ground Sichuan peppercorns

¼ tsp chilli powder

½ tsp caster sugar

¾ tsp fine sea salt

½ tsp MSG

handful of fresh coriander leaves

For the marinade

1 tsp potato flour or cornflour

1 tbsp ground cumin

1 tbsp neutral oil

1 tbsp dark soy sauce

1 tbsp Shaoxing wine

½ tsp ground white pepper

In a medium bowl, combine the marinade ingredients with 1 tablespoon water. Mix well, then add the tofu and turn to coat. Set aside and let the magic happen (or as much magic as can happen in 20 minutes).

When you're ready to cook, line a plate with paper towels and heat the oil in a wok or large sauté pan over a high heat for 1 minute – you want it hot, almost (but not!) smoking. Drain your tofu and add it to the pan. Fry for 2–3 minutes, or until golden on all sides. You will need to turn and flip your tofu to achieve an even cook, which means you need to be careful not to let the wok oil spurt out and burn you!

Remove your golden tofu to the paper towel-lined plate and set aside for now.

Carefully drain all but 3 tablespoons of the oil from your wok. Reduce the heat to medium and add the onion to the pan. Continue to be alert for oil splatters! Stir-fry the onion for 1 minute, then return the tofu to the wok, along with the dried chillies. Stir-fry for another 3 minutes, being careful not to let things burn. Once the tofu is nicely browned, reduce the heat to low. Add the cumin seeds, ground cumin, ground Sichuan peppercorns, chilli powder, sugar, salt, and MSG. Mix everything together and cook for a final minute.

Serve your tofu topped with fresh coriander. Take a bite. Pretend you're eating lamb – or be thankful you're not. To each their own.

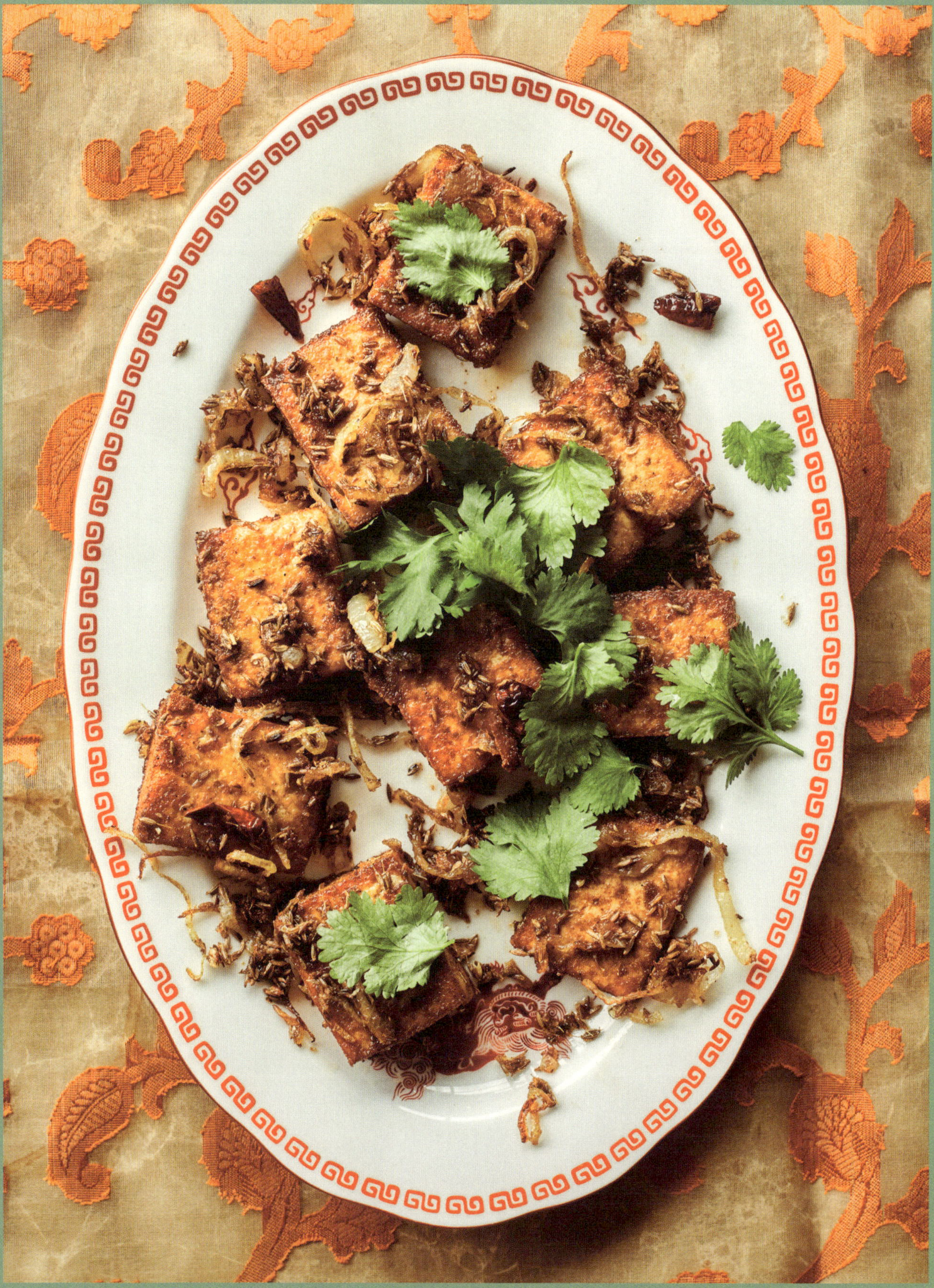

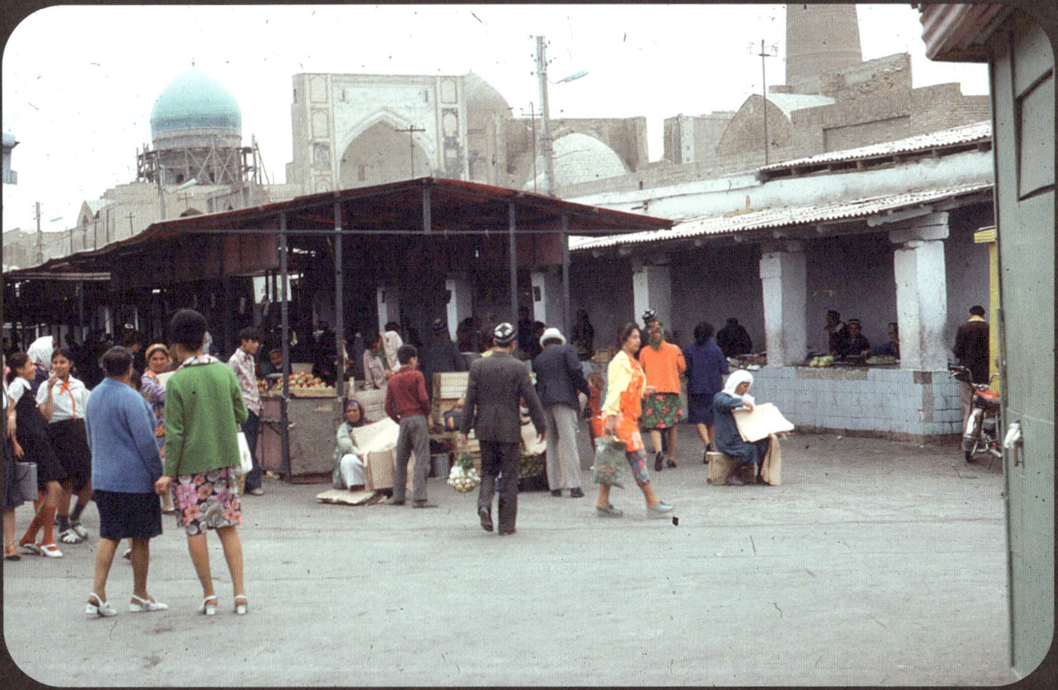

QUADRUPEDS, FISH & FOWL

CONSIDER THE FAT-TAILED SHEEP
112

DA PAN JI
Uyghur "Big Plate Chicken"
117

ROAST DUCK WITH CRANBERRY TKEMALI
118

JUJEH BRICK CHICKEN THIGHS
121

UYGHUR LAMB CHOPS
124

UYGHUR ROAST LAMB
125

QUINCE KHORESH
Iranian Quince & Chicken Braise
129

TUSHONKA
Soviet Stewed Beef Short Ribs
131

PORK MTSVADI
Georgian BBQ Pork
132

SILK ROADS STUFFED FISH
135

CONSIDER THE FAT-TAILED SHEEP

I spent countless hours of my childhood on a dairy farm, where my elementary school's after-school care programme was based. Each afternoon, we traipsed about, mostly unsupervised, checking in on the chickens, feeding the goats, chatting with the Clydesdales, spraying one another with fresh and direct-from-the-udder milk, laughing hysterically, stumbling across a lambing, becoming comfortable with animals: farm life in all its grassy, hay-and-manure-filled splendour. I saw kittens being born, trudged through actual pig shit, and saw a cow's placenta up close. And when I got home, I often walked into our living room to find my dad studying open-heart surgeries, watching and rewinding and then rewatching videos taken in the operating room – bloody, tissuey human gore filling our television screen. A ventricle here. An aorta there. A lung. A spurting, severed artery. I saw it all.

I learned early on in life to be comfortable with blood, guts, and bodily functions. Hell, for an eighth-grade project on sexually transmitted diseases, I dug out a medical textbook and had colour copies of gonorrhoea-addled genitals blown up to share with my class. With such a high tolerance for gore, it was a surprise that, in 1997, on my first trip to China, I was stopped dead in my tracks by a chicken.

It was in a cage in a Shanghai market, and I don't remember what it looked like, I just know it was alive. Until it wasn't. It all happened so quickly. A customer pointed, then the vendor took the chosen chicken, held it upside down, slit its throat, and ripped off all its feathers. Rapidly, expertly, aggressively, coldly. It took less than a minute. The chicken then went into some sort of cylindrical centrifugal force contraption in which it was speedily spun around before it was handed over in exchange for a banknote. This took less than a second minute. I was horrified. Shocked. Flabbergasted. I was 15 – and what the actual fuck had I just seen?

Eighteen months later, I walked through the back door of a restaurant in rural northern Yunnan Province in southwest China. A few men milled about, grinning with pride as they showed the gaggle of American teenagers a massive hog. And then they stunned it. A spike straight through the back of the pig's skull. I don't remember the actual killing, the inevitable knife to the throat; none of us do, so maybe they asked us to leave for that bit. But eventually the pig was strung up high by its hooves. Most of its hair was singed, then shaved off. They opened it up in front of us, removing organ after organ from the animal's cavity, carefully butchering, cleaning, and breaking down the carcass. I remember the blood. A friend recalls the smell of burned hair. And then we had lunch, mere feet from the slaughtering and butchering, mere yards from the yard where the pig was most likely born and raised. That's some real farm-to-table shit. And also the stuff of nightmares.

But why? Why was I so horrified and shocked by the death of a pig, of a chicken? Why was it that I, a young woman who didn't shy away from cow placentas, horse manure, and spurting arteries, was so taken aback by these experiences? I chalk it up to life and death. Literally. The blood and guts I was familiar with were those of birth, of life, of healing. The cow placenta didn't revolt me because the newborn calf enchanted me. Vivid images of aortas

> **THE VENDOR TOOK THE CHOSEN CHICKEN, HELD IT UPSIDE DOWN, SLIT ITS THROAT AND RIPPED OFF ALL ITS FEATHERS.**

Top: A beheaded porcine quadruped. Telavi, Georgia. June 2024.

Bottom: Ye olde bucket of Korean sharpbelly fish. Lankaran, Azerbaijan. April 2024.

and ventricles didn't traumatize me because my dad used them to grow as a surgeon and save people's lives. I was OK with all of that, but I didn't want to see death, to know viscerally from whence my food came.

When he was a kid, my dad would walk the 15 minutes from his house to his neighbourhood butcher a few times a week. He would tell the butcher what Khalejan was going to make and, after deftly chipping it away from one of the whole strung-up sheep dangling from ceiling hooks, the butcher would pass the meat over to my dad and send him on his way. If they were planning to cook chicken, they would kill one of the birds in their yard. Either way, my father knew where the food on his table came from and how it got there.

He also knew what the sheep he was eating had itself eaten when it was alive, and where it had dined. Northern Iran, like much of Central Asia, has been home to tribes of nomads for centuries – transhumant pastoralists, to be specific – who moved with their flocks of livestock on a seasonal basis. They typically summered in mountainous highlands and spent their winters in the warmer (often desert) areas, a lifestyle practised today only by a small percentage of Iranians. Since the 19th century, government policies across Central Asia have encouraged the settlement of nomad populations, and have mostly succeeded. Where my father once saw the nomads on a biannual basis, the children growing up in his village today don't see them at all.

Iran's most famous nomadic tribe, the Qashqai (for whom the Japanese car manufacturer Nissan named an SUV, explaining their decision to do so in a romanticized, bordering-on-if-not-actually-culturally-appropriating way as, "Freedom, movement, grace, beauty. You get the idea. Qashqai embodies the spirit of the ancient nomad, embodied to allow the 21st-century you to explore new boundaries. Or something like that"), are a Turkic people whose own proud origin story places them as having arrived in present-day Iran either as part of Tamerlane's conquering forces in the 14th century or with Hulegu Khan's a century prior. Though the latter man's fame pales in comparison to that of his grandfather, Genghis Khan, and his brother, Kublai Khan, without Hulegu's campaigns in western Asia (including the devastating siege of Baghdad in 1268, which effectively ended the glory of the Abbasid Caliphate and the Golden Age of Islam), Mongol rule would not have stretched from the East China Sea to the Black Sea and beyond – rule which brought with it the (relatively) safe passage of goods, ideas, and people that ushered in a third golden age of trade across the Silk Roads.

> WHERE MY FATHER ONCE SAW THE NOMADS ON A BIANNUAL BASIS, THE CHILDREN GROWING UP IN HIS VILLAGE TODAY DON'T SEE THEM AT ALL.

One of the reasons for the Mongol Empire's success was its ability to synthesize native practices and adapt to local habits while maintaining and championing its own traditions and values, perhaps the most significant of which was pastoral nomadism. Genghis Khan's early adoption and application of Chinese-inspired bureaucratic and land-management practices to disparate nomadic tribes resulted in a powerful military capable of conquering and maintaining control of lands far beyond the tribes' native steppe, while a commitment to the nomadic way of life ensured the continuation of itinerant animal husbandry – something which has been preserved, even if in an extremely limited fashion, to this day.

The Iranian transhumant pastoralists, whose seasonal migrations my father witnessed and whose sheep he ate as a child, were, in the mid-20th century, still as tied to and dependent on their flocks for their livelihoods as their Central Asian ancestors had been, whether under the rule of Hulegu, Genghis, Tamerlane, or Tsar Alexander II. And the sheep in question are not – and were not – just any sheep. They are fat-tailed little ovines, renowned for their chubby, dangling tails, which are full of blubbery fat that is frankly delicious to cook with and eat.

You might not believe it, but on average, one of these tails weighs 5kg (11lb). I cackled with glee at my first sighting of a cart full of fat-tailed sheep on their way to market in Uzbekistan's Ferghana Valley, tails all a-wiggle. It made me think of Glenn Miller's "Must be Jelly ('Cause Jam Don't Shake Like That)". Remarkable and unmissable to the foreign eye, the sheep's plump behinds evolved to provide their steppe- and desert-dwelling selves with a food store to call upon in harsh times; originally, it was the animal itself who was nourished by its own fatty tail, and now it is us.

In addition to having "the largest guts of any sheep in the world" (as noted by writers Mildred Cable and Francesca French in their book *The Gobi Desert*), the Karakul sheep breed, one of the most famous varieties of fat-tailed sheep, provides flavourful meat, as well as the prized-and-often-fashionable-but-morally-questionable *astrakhan* fur and skin. By the turn of the 20th century, Bukhara, then an emirate and protectorate of Tsarist Russia, was economically dependent on the brisk Karakul trade it did with Russia and Europeans – Germans, particularly – who bought the sheep's skin, fur, and casings for import into their home countries, where they turned the fur and skin into hats and jackets for the well-heeled ... and the casings into sausages for everyone.

One of the results of economic dependence on sheep, of having an animal so intertwined with one's life, one's livelihood, one's every movement in many ways, is a respect for and admiration of the animal in question. I like to think that that is the reason for including odes to sheep in Kirghiz poetry, for singing songs about the love of mutton, as Frederick Burnaby, author of *A Ride to Khiva* tells us his 19th-century Central Asian guide did, and for saying to a woman with nothing other than pure sincerity and admiration in one's heart: "Thou are lovelier than a sheep with a fat tail ... thy face is the roundest in the flock, and ... thy breath is sweeter ... than many pieces of mutton roasted over bright embers." I like to think that if we know where our food comes from, if we know where the animals we eat once lived, supped, and roamed, and if we truly understand that once they were living, and that killing them, no matter how humanely or well-intentioned, always involves violence and blood, then maybe we won't flinch, as my teenage self certainly did on those memorable occasions in China, from the reality of what is on our plates when we are confronted with how it got there.

Fortunately, we live in an era of increased awareness of and respect for the animals who feed us. And I am particularly fortunate and privileged to be able to choose the meat I bring to my table, and to pay a premium for products that I know have been sustainably and ethically raised, with (hopefully) less of an environmental impact than a hamburger from a fast-food chain. When you cook the recipes in this chapter, I hope you will love them, but I also hope you will consider what you are cooking – the chicken, the duck, the fish, the cow, the sheep. Consider the meat. Where it came from and what it cost for it to arrive on your plate.

"Kebab. Kebab. Kebab. That's all they eat here," a British Petroleum executive in Baku once dismissively complained to my dad. Well, first of all: that's not true. And secondly, while there are kebab recipes in this chapter, there are also whole ducks and fish, slow-roasted beef and lamb, and stovetop chicken preparations. Flavours from Tbilisi to Kashgar, from Tabriz to Bukhara, from Detroit to London and New York – from me to you.

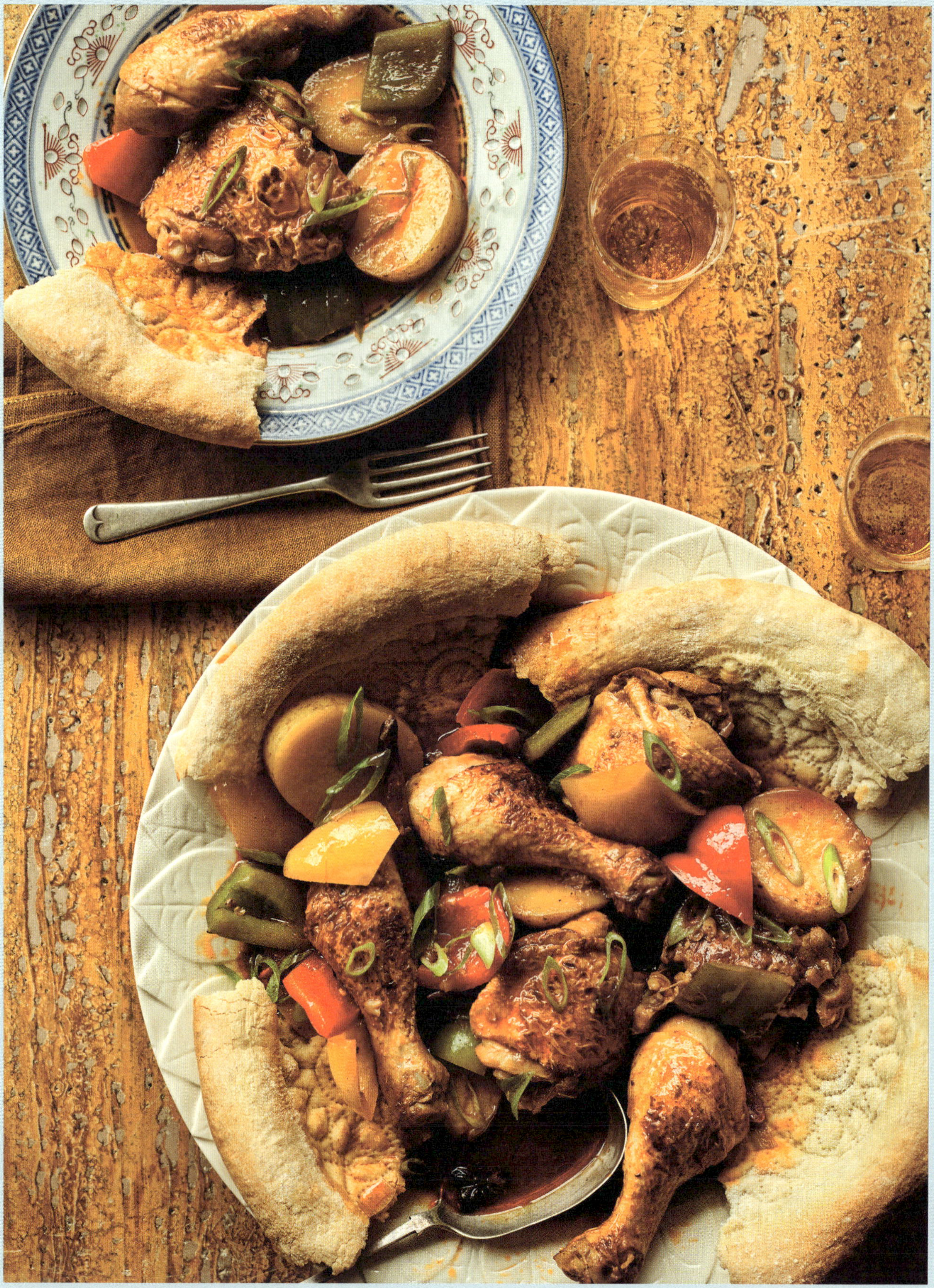

DA PAN JI

Uyghur "Big Plate Chicken"

Serves 6–8

Da pan ji – "big plate chicken" – is a relative newcomer to Uyghur cuisine, if not an import. Some say that a Sichuan transplant to Xinjiang, missing the punch and heat of his home province's spicy food, came up with the dish in the 1990s; others claim the dish has its roots in China's non-Turkic Hui Muslim community. Whatever and wherever its origins, *da pan ji* has become a staple in Uyghur restaurants both within and outside of China, served frequently on a bed of noodles or, as I prefer it and offer it to you here, noodle-free, but with a sauce that begs to be sopped up with some Central Asian Bread (see p205).

- 3 tbsp neutral oil
- 2 tbsp granulated sugar
- 1kg (2¼lb) chicken legs and/or thighs, preferably skin-on, bone-in
- ½ tsp sweet smoked paprika
- 2 star anise
- 10–15 dried chillies of your choosing (the amount you use will depend on their heat level and your heat tolerance)
- ¼ tsp ground white pepper
- ½ cinnamon stick
- 1 tbsp ground Sichuan peppercorns
- 2 bay leaves
- 2.5cm (1in) piece of fresh ginger, minced
- 3 fat garlic cloves, minced
- 1 mild red or green chilli, sliced into rings
- 2–4 spring onions, chopped, whites and greens separated
- 2 tbsp light soy sauce
- 2 tbsp tomato purée
- 2 tsp fine sea salt
- 3 peppers (colour of your choosing), cut into 3cm (1¼in) chunks
- 1kg (2¼lb) potatoes, (I suggest using all-rounders like Albert Bartlett Roosters or Yukon Gold), well washed or peeled and cut into 2cm (¾in) rounds

---

In a large pot for which you have a lid, heat the oil over a high heat. Add the sugar to the oil and whisk it until it dissolves. Add your chicken to the sugary oil, making sure you don't overcrowd the pan, and brown it on all sides. You can tell the meat has been properly browned and is ready to switch sides when it releases easily from the pan. For me, this process takes about 2 minutes per side. Once browned, remove your chicken and set it aside on a plate. You may need to do this in batches.

Reduce the heat to medium, then add the dried spices and bay leaves to the pan and fry for 1 minute, or until fragrant. Add the ginger, garlic, fresh chilli, and spring onion whites, along with your soy sauce, tomato purée, and salt. Stir well.

Return the chicken to the pan, along with any juices released. Stir to coat the chicken, then add 600ml (2½ cups/1 pint) water. Bring the mixture to the boil before covering the pot with its lid and reducing the heat to low.

Leave to simmer for 15 minutes before adding the peppers, potatoes, and an additional 150ml (⅓ cup/ 5fl oz) water. Stir to mix and then cook, covered, over a medium heat for another 20 minutes, or until the potatoes are fork tender.

Remove the pot from the heat, add the spring onion greens, stir through, and eat greedily.

ROAST DUCK WITH CRANBERRY TKEMALI

Serves 3–4

I ate a coot in a town on the Caspian Sea in southern Azerbaijan. You know the bird I'm talking about: a black waterfowl with a small patch of white on its forehead and beady little red eyes. I used to see them making their nests on the shores of Hyde Park's Serpentine Lake, but I never imagined I would eat one. Although it was smothered in a rich and beautiful sauce of pomegranate and walnuts, the coot was not to my liking. It was, dare I say it, pretty foul. Hehehe.

The Caspian Sea and its environs have a diversity of waterfowl and, unsurprisingly, a long tradition of eating those birds. Duck. Goose. Coot. What have you. More generally, Central Asia has historically teemed with game birds. Pheasant. Partridge. Grouse. Pigeon. With the exception of coot, I very much enjoy eating and cooking with all these birdies. Duck is my favourite, though. I love duck. We served duck at our wedding. We have duck on Valentine's Day. We lived off home-made duck confit during lockdown when it was difficult to source more in-demand animal proteins. And while I was nervous the first time I cooked a whole duck, I shouldn't have been; it's really not that hard at all, and the pay-off is incredible – especially when you end up with an elegantly spiced bird with crispy skin and a Georgian *tkemali*-inspired sauce. Serve this with simple roast potatoes.

---

1 whole duck (about 2kg/4½lb)

For the dry rub

1 tsp ground turmeric

2 tsp Advieh (see p50)

2 tsp freshly ground black pepper

2 tsp baking powder

2 tbsp fine sea salt

1 tbsp caster or granulated sugar

For the cranberry *tkemali*

200g (7oz) dried cranberries

¼ tsp coriander seeds, toasted and coarsely ground using a mortar and pestle

⅛ tsp fennel seeds, toasted and coarsely ground using a mortar and pestle

1 garlic clove, minced

10g (¼oz) fresh dill (stems included)

10g (¼oz) fresh coriander (stems included)

⅛ tsp dried chilli flakes

⅛ tsp dried mint

⅛ tsp fine sea salt

1 tsp pomegranate molasses

Combine all the dry rub ingredients in a small bowl. Set aside, and attend to your waterfowl.

Trim away any excess skin around the duck's neck and cavity openings. If your duck has come with a bag of giblets and a neck, remove them now, and either discard or use for another purpose.

Place your duck on a rack in a roasting tray and bring a kettle of water to the boil. Pour half of the boiling water on top of the duck before flipping it over (tongs are this girl's best friend) and pouring the rest over its backside. Carefully lift the rack out of the roasting tray and pour away the water. Tip up the duck and pour out any water from inside its cavity as well.

When your duck is cool enough to touch, dry it inside and out with paper towels. Go crazy. You really want it as dry as you can get it. Prick your dry duck all over with either a sharp knife or skewer, making sure you pierce only the fat and do not penetrate through to the duck flesh. Next, score the duck with a sharp knife, criss-crossing the fatty skin, once again making sure you cut only through the fat and not down to the flesh.

Use your hands to pat the dry rub all over the duck. Use it all up. Cover the bird. And make sure you toss some inside the bird's cavity as well.

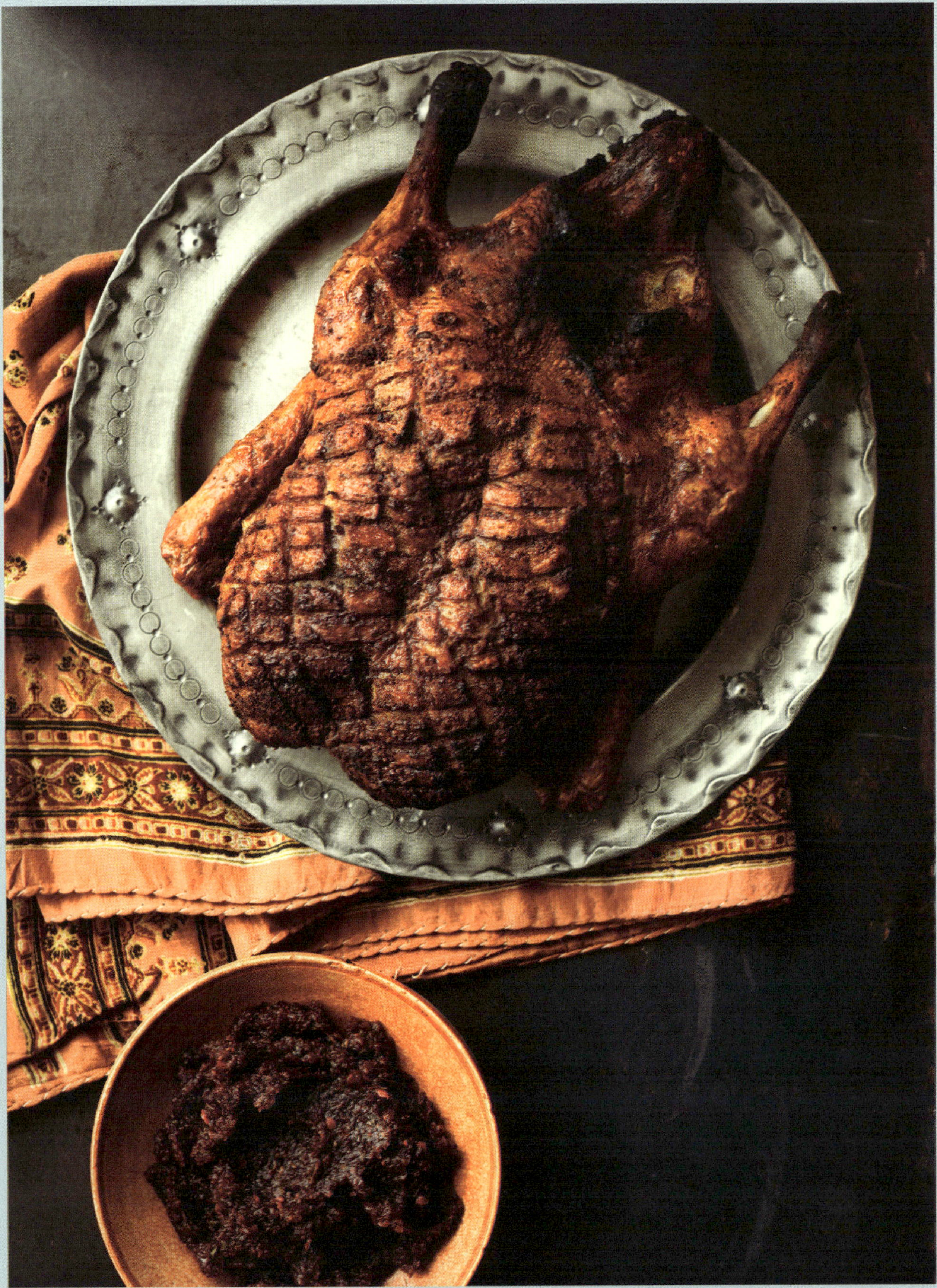

Place your duck, uncovered and breast-side up, on its rack and in its tray, and put it in the refrigerator for 12–48 hours. The longer your ducks chills out in the refrigerator, the drier it will be when it goes into the oven – and the drier the duck, the crispier the skin.

A few hours before you want to eat, bring your duck out of the refrigerator and up to room temperature, and preheat your oven to 220°C (200°C fan/425°F/Gas 7).

Loosely place a small piece of foil over the duck's breast. Once the oven is at temperature, pop your duck into the oven and roast it for 30 minutes.

After 30 minutes, remove the duck from the oven, discard the foil, and carefully flip the duck over so the breast faces down. Return your upside-down duck to the oven and roast for 30 minutes more.

Remove the duck from the oven again, flip it over again, then return it to the oven and roast, breast-side up, for a final 30 minutes, or until a thermometer inserted into the breast reads 75°C (167°F). If at this point, your skin isn't as crispy as you would like, you can crisp it up a bit under the grill (or not – I'm the only one in my family and household who likes crispy duck skin; maybe no one in yours does).

While the duck is roasting, soak the cranberries for the *tkemali* in a bowl of boiling water for 20 minutes, then drain and set aside.

When your duck is cooked, remove it from the oven, tip out and discard any and all cavity juices, and let your bird rest for 15 minutes while you make your *tkemali*.

Combine all the *tkemali* ingredients in a food processor or blender, and blend to a paste. Taste and season to your liking with more salt, herbs, spices, molasses – you name it. If my quantities and proportions are not your cup of tea, that's OK; make it yours.

Carve your duck. Enjoy your duck. Eat it with some cranberry *tkemali*.

According to my dad, this is "probably Tashkent because it has sidewalks and it was a very important and well-financed Soviet city and sidewalks were expensive". Probably Tashkent, Uzbekistan. October 1978.

JUJEH BRICK CHICKEN THIGHS

Serves 4–6

August 18, 2008. Marlow and Sons. "Dinner with Michael" – so says my calendar. People had been raving about the "chicken under a brick" served at the cosy farm-to-table-esque restaurant nestled under Brooklyn's Williamsburg Bridge. Michael, a dear friend since childhood and fellow Michigander-in-NYC, had convinced me to join him for dinner, raving about this chicken, telling me I would love it and that we would have oysters too, and that I could tell him about my first day of law school and my mother's recent cancer diagnosis. And so we did, and so I did. Many times over the years that followed. With and without Mike.

While it seemed revolutionary at the time in its simplicity (in New York City dining circles, at least), it turns out that Marlow and Sons' chicken, though exceptional, was nothing special. I didn't know it then, but Italians have a dish like this – *pollo al mattone*. And guess what? So do Azeris, Uzbeks, and Georgians – *tabaka* – and they have for centuries. Chicken is spatchcocked and then fried on a cast-iron or heavy metal pan while being flattened and weighted down by something very heavy. In Iran, meanwhile, they have one of my favourite dishes ever – *jujeh* kebab, a luscious, saffrony, buttery chicken, typically grilled over the barbecue.

This is my brick chicken. This is my *jujeh* chicken. A chicken *tabaka*, a *pollo al mattone*. An ode to friendship and to simplicity – and it is incredible.

Enjoy with a crisp white wine, freshly shucked oysters, wilted greens, rice, a crumpled linen napkin, and a circa-2010 indie-rock playlist. Imagine you're in Brooklyn, by way of Iran, Georgia, and Azerbaijan. It's a lovely place to be.

You will need two bricks for this recipe. (Yes, you read that right: regular house bricks. Preferably clean.)

PS RIP Marlow and Sons. We miss you.

1kg (2¼lb) chicken thighs, skin-on and bone-in

3 tbsp olive oil

50g (1¾oz) unsalted butter

For the marinade

0.5g saffron, ground with ¼ tsp granulated sugar using a mortar and pestle, and then brewed with 1 tbsp rose water and 3 tbsp hot water

250g (9oz) plain yogurt

120ml (½ cup/4fl oz) olive oil

12 garlic cloves, grated

zest of 2 limes, juice of 4

3 tbsp fine sea salt

1 tbsp coarsely ground black pepper

Combine all the marinade ingredients in a large non-reactive mixing bowl.

Add the chicken thighs to the bowl and mix well to coat, then cover and leave to marinate in the refrigerator for a minimum of 4 hours, but preferably overnight.

When you are nearly ready for your meal, remove the chicken thighs from their saffrony tub. Scrape most of the marinade off the chicken and discard the remainder.

Heat the oil in a large sauté pan over a medium–high heat. Once the oil is hot, add your chicken thighs to the pan, skin-side down. Plop a second pan on top of the chicken, making sure the bottom is spick-and-span clean. Alternatively, cover your chicken thighs with a bit of baking parchment before setting the pan down on them. Then, place your bricks in the upper pan. Step back and wait for the magic to happen.

Let the chicken cook, undisturbed, under the weight of a pan and two bricks, for 10–13 minutes, or until

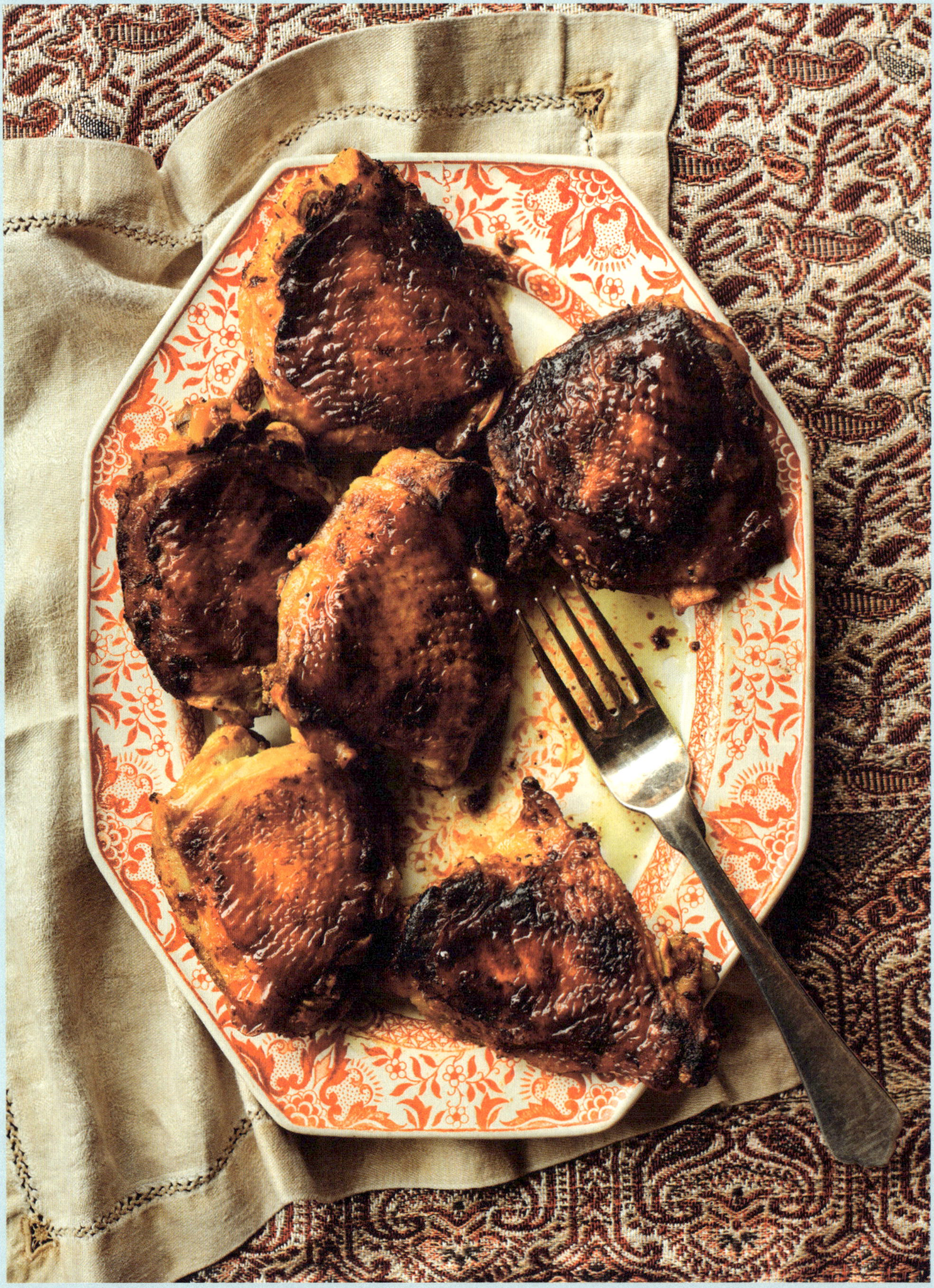

the internal temperature of your chicken reaches 68°C (155°F). Depending on what type of meat thermometer you use, you may need to carefully remove the bricks and pan to take the chicken's temperature.

Once the chicken hits 68°C (155°F), remove the bricks and top pan and turn the chicken over. Add the butter to the pan and watch it melt. Use a spoon to baste the chicken a couple of times with the melted butter. Take a look at that glorious, golden, browned, buttery, glistening skin. It's only minutes now before you get to eat it. Be patient. Get excited.

Return the pan and bricks to the top of your golden skin-side up chicken, and cook the chicken for another 2 minutes under their weight.

Once again, carefully remove the bricks and upper pan before transferring your chicken thighs to a platter to briefly rest – before you eat them and they blow your mind.

My sister Maria, some cousins and a flock of fat-tailed sheep.
Iran, sometime in the mid-1970s.

UYGHUR LAMB CHOPS

Serves 2–4

The ubiquity and popularity of Uyghur lamb kebabs – typically sold street-side in China, by men fanning glowing charcoal embers and cooking 10, 15, 20 skewers at a time – suggests that, like so many foods once belonging to a minority group, they – *kawap* in Uyghur, *yangrou chuan* in Mandarin – have become firmly entrenched in the modern food culture of the Han Chinese majority. You can see them in every city in China. And they are always delicious.

However, instead of approximating the skewers found in China, I give you a recipe for Uyghur-style lamb chops, simply because I love a lamb chop, and I've given you a skewered meat recipe elsewhere (see p132). And though I haven't strayed too far from the seasoning you'll find both in Xinjiang and elsewhere in China, I do encourage you to play around with the spices a bit. If you don't like chilli, don't use as much as I have. If you don't like the numbing nature of Sichuan peppercorns, leave them out. If you don't like cumin, though, you are out of luck, as the only suggestion I'd give for cumin is that there's never going to be too much, so be generous.

Note: If you don't have a barbecue, you can cook the chops on a hot griddle pan on the stove.

---

2 tsp sesame seeds, toasted

2 tbsp fennel seeds, toasted

2½ tbsp cumin seeds toasted

1 tsp Sichuan peppercorns, toasted

1½ tsp ground cumin

3 tsp Kashmiri chilli powder

¾ tsp MSG

½ tsp caster or granulated sugar

3 tsp fine sea salt

500g (1lb 2oz) lamb or mutton chops

2 tbsp Shaoxing wine

freshly chopped coriander, to serve

Tip the toasted sesame, fennel, and cumin seeds and Sichuan peppercorns into a large mixing bowl, then add the ground cumin, chilli powder, MSG, sugar, and salt. Add your lamb chops and toss them in the spice rub to coat. Drizzle the Shaoxing wine over the top and toss again to evenly coat your meat.

Leave your lamb chops to hang out in their rub and wine for a minimum of 20 minutes, but preferably a few hours (keep them in the refrigerator if marinating for more than 20–30 minutes).

While your lamb is absorbing all those incredible flavours, fire up the barbecue. If using a gas barbecue, you want it at medium–high heat, and if using charcoal, you want the coals to be hot, ashed over, and glowing. When you're ready to grill, place the lamb chops on the grill, directly over the glowing charcoals, in the hot zone.

Cook your lamb chops for 4–5 minutes per side, or until the meat reaches your desired level of doneness. An internal temperature of 65–70°C (149–158°F) will give you a medium chop, but 60–65°C (140–149°F) will give you the sweet spot medium-rare that this cut of meat cries out for. Anything over 70°C (158°F) will give you disappointment.

The flavours of your spice mix, combined with the meat itself – the char from the grill, the melted fat – should all come together for a juicy, lamby, Uyghur umami party in your mouth. Top your chops with any leftover spice-rub mix and a hefty handful of chopped coriander. Dig in. Use your hands. Grab a cold beer and enjoy.

UYGHUR ROAST LAMB

Serves 4–6

It was a rare occasion when I ate this dish, but, my goodness, was it memorable. Every time. The leg would arrive on the table and we would ooh and ahh, and we would dig in. Meaty. Lamby. Cuminy. Spicy. Goodness. Exceptional, tender, juicy Uyghur roast leg of lamb. And, in the midst of eating it, someone would undoubtedly remark, "We need to get this more often. We need to do this more often." Because the Uyghur restaurant in Shanghai's Xujiahui district required a one-week lead time for their *kao yang tui*, and we were in our twenties and no one was planning dinners a week in advance. Here I am, decades later, looking at a calendar and planning dinners and lunches months out – and making sure that calendar includes this roast with decent frequency.

- 1.5–2.5kg (3lb 3oz–5½lb) lamb leg or shoulder
- 750ml (3 cups/1¼ pints) lamb stock or water
- 2 tbsp dark soy sauce
- 3 spring onions, coarsely chopped
- 3 star anise
- 2.5cm (1in) piece of fresh ginger
- 4 tbsp olive oil
- fresh coriander leaves, to serve

For the spice rub

- 3 tsp fine sea salt
- 2 tbsp ground cumin
- 1 tbsp ground Sichuan peppercorns
- 1–2 tsp chilli powder (or more, depending on your mood and heat tolerance)
- 1 tsp ground white pepper
- 2 tbsp soft dark brown sugar
- 2 garlic cloves, minced
- 2.5cm (1in) piece of fresh ginger, minced

Score your meat diagonally three times on each side, then place the lamb in a roasting pan or oven-safe dish such as a large casserole pot.

Mix all your spice-rub ingredients together in a small mixing bowl, and then use your hands to scoop up the mixture and press it into the lamb. Try to cover the meat as best you can, both sides and edges, and make sure you get some into the slits you scored earlier.

Place your rubbed lamb, covered with foil or your pot's lid, into the refrigerator and let the magic happen – ideally overnight, but at minimum for 4 hours.

Remove your lamb from the refrigerator 45 minutes–1 hour before you intend to put it in the oven, and preheat your oven to 150°C (130°C fan/300°F/Gas 2).

Lift your lamb out from its cooking vessel and discard any excess spice rub from the pan. Add the lamb stock, soy sauce, spring onions, star anise, and ginger to the pan, then place your lamb back into the pan, making sure it is fat-side up. Drizzle the olive oil on the top of the meat, cover with a double layer of foil or the pot's lid, and slide that baby into the middle of your preheated oven.

Cook for 5–6 hours, basting every 1½–2 hours, until the meat is well and truly falling off the bone. Lamb shoulder will cook quicker than lamb leg, but either way the roast will most likely take at least 5 hours.

Once it's done, remove the lamb from the oven and allow it to rest for 15–30 minutes.

Shred your lamb on to a platter, top with a heaping pile of coriander leaves, and serve.

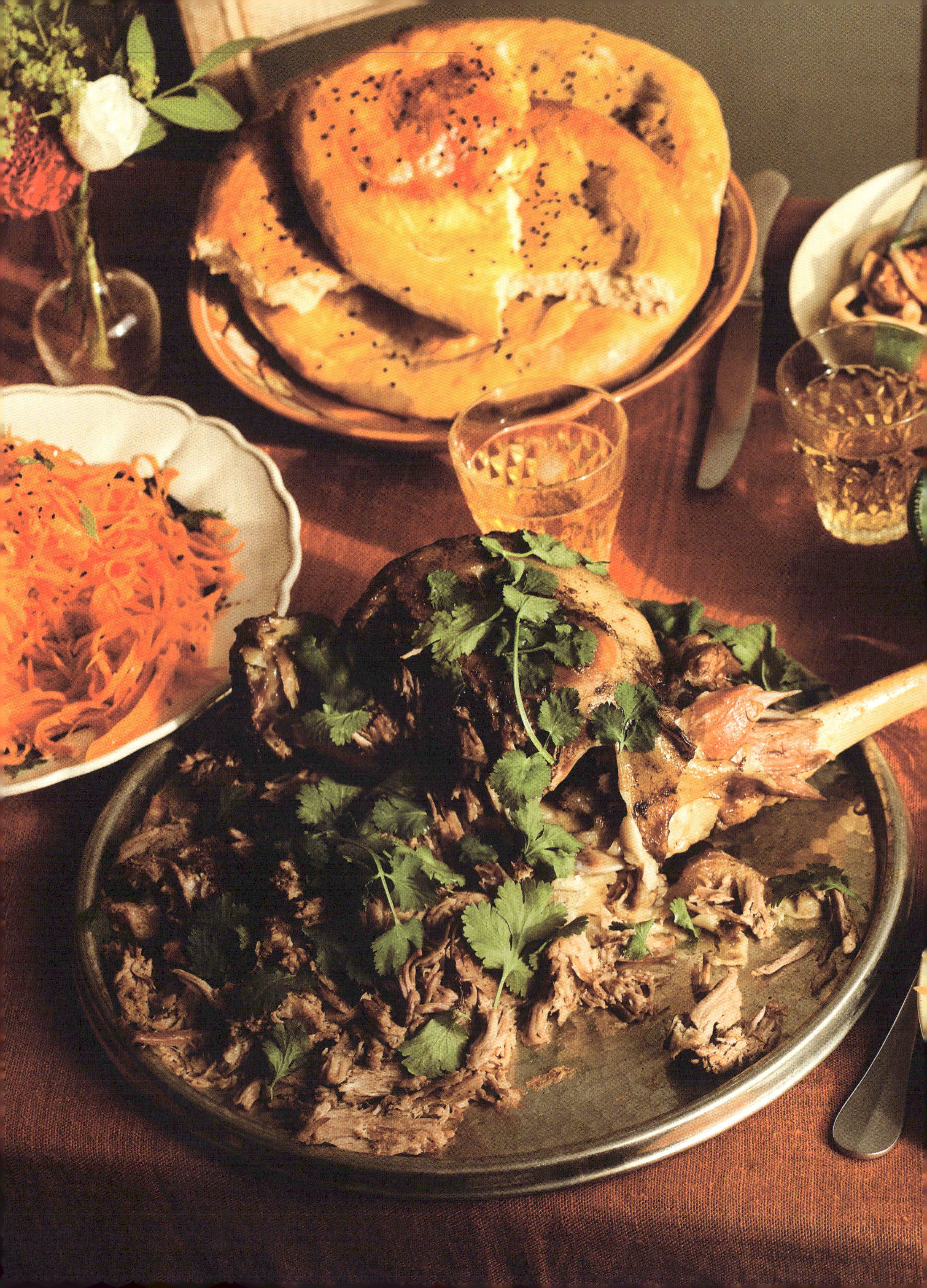

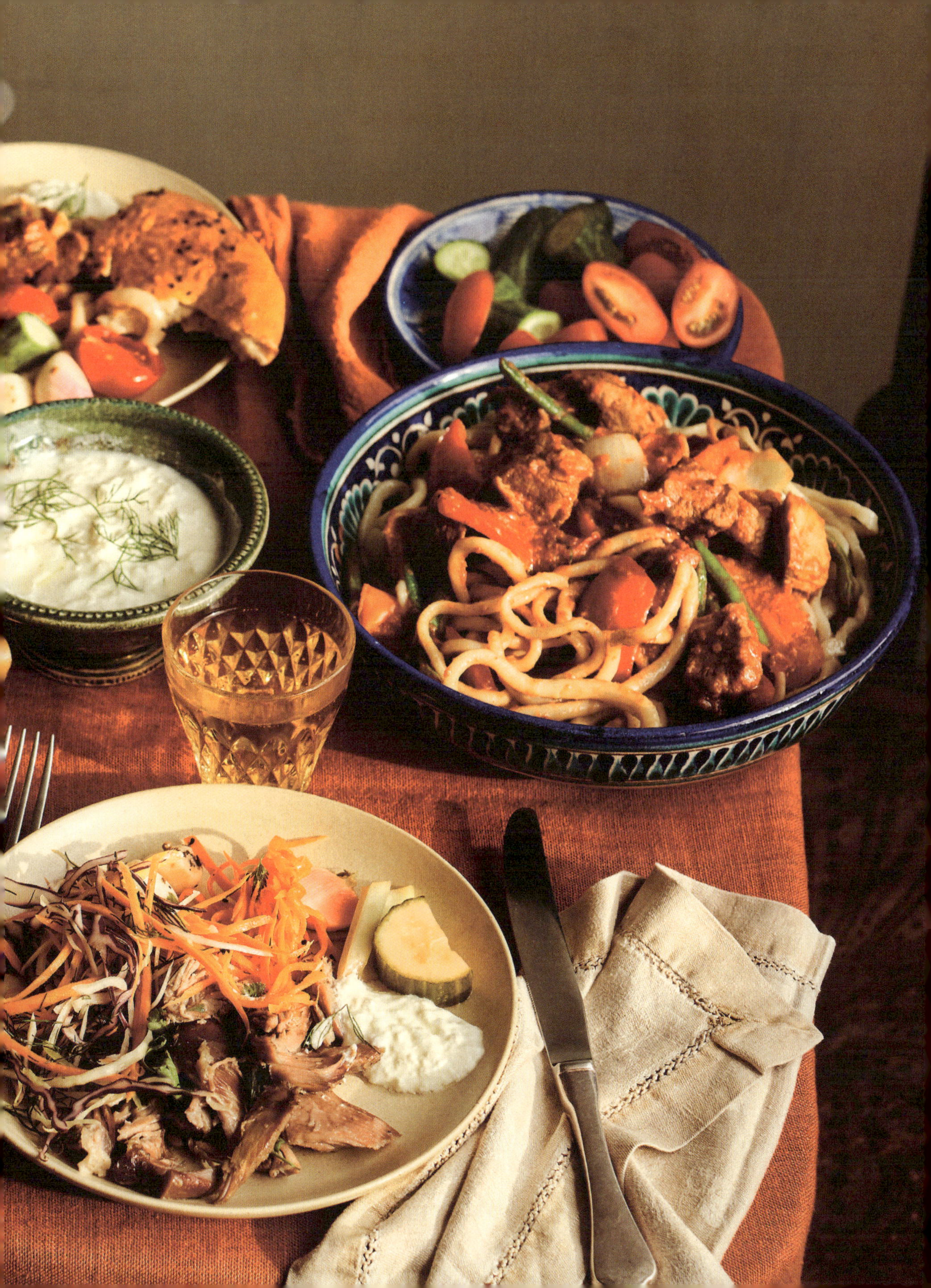

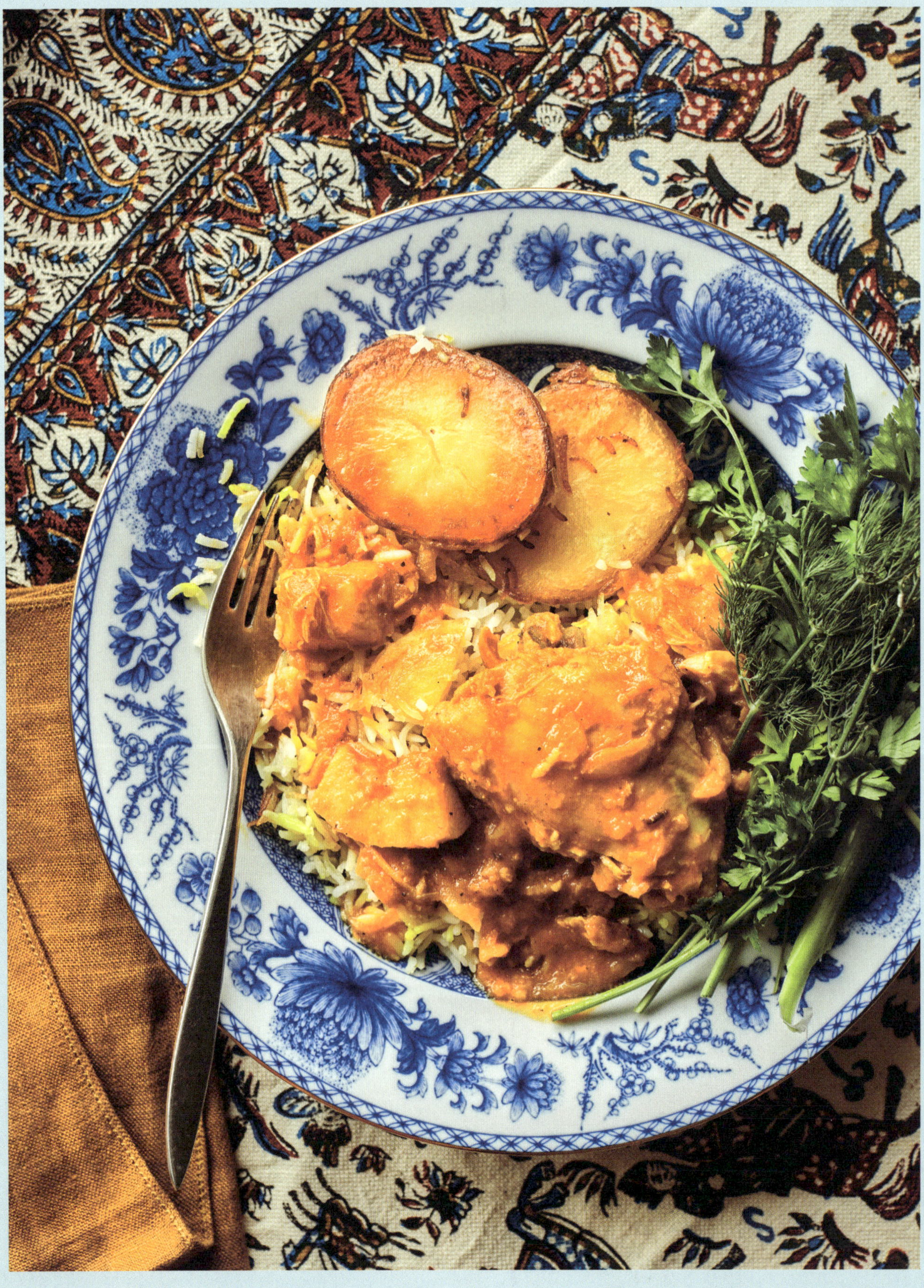

QUINCE KHORESH

Iranian Quince & Chicken Braise

Serves 4–6

Originally native to the ancient Hyrcanian forests near the Caspian Sea, the quince, like so many other foodstuffs, spread across the globe via the trade routes of antiquity, and has featured in mythology and superstition for centuries. Some believe the mythic golden apple that sparked the Trojan War was actually a quince. Others claim the golden peaches of Samarkand, the inspiration for this very book, were quinces. Further west, some Europeans in the Middle Ages believed eating quinces could stave off the Black Death, while others, including Britain's "Bloody" Tudor Queen Mary, believed the fruit to be an aphrodisiac.

In the UK these days, people are familiar with quince primarily in the form of *membrillo*, a concentrated, sugary jelly paste of Spanish origin that pairs perfectly with a slice of Manchego cheese. Every year, without fail, someone in my neighbourhood Facebook group posts something along the lines of: "Hey guys! I have so many quinces on my tree! What do I do with all of these? What can I make other than *membrillo*?"

When I tell my father of the British quince glut, his eyes grow wide in shock and envy. We don't have a lot of quinces in America, you see. "You are so lucky," he tells me. And I am, for many reasons, least of which is my ability to cook this sweet and sour *khoresh* on a pretty regular basis during the autumn quince season. Quince and chicken, a duo even more perfect than jelly and cheese, if you ask me.

- 1kg (2¼lb) skinless chicken thighs or legs
- 2 tsp fine sea salt, plus extra to taste
- 6 tbsp olive oil
- 2 onions, sliced into half-moons
- ½ tsp freshly ground black pepper
- 1 tsp Advieh (see p50)
- ½ tsp ground turmeric
- 2 tbsp tomato purée
- 75g (2½oz) dried yellow split peas
- 100g (3½oz) dried apricots
- 700g (1lb 9oz) quinces, peeled, cored, and cut into 2.5cm (1in) chunks
- 0.25g saffron, ground with ⅛ tsp granulated sugar using a mortar and pestle, and then brewed with 1 tbsp orange blossom water and 1 tbsp hot water
- soft light brown sugar, to taste
- apple cider vinegar, to taste
- cooked rice, to serve

Season your chicken with 1 teaspoon of the salt, then set aside.

In a large casserole pot or saucepan for which you have a lid, heat 3 tablespoons of the oil over a high heat. Once the oil is shimmering, reduce the heat to low and add the onions. Sauté for 5–7 minutes, or until they are soft and golden, then add the remaining 1 teaspoon of salt, along with the black pepper, *advieh*, turmeric, tomato purée, split peas, and apricots. Stir to mix.

Add the chicken to the pot. Stir everything together, then add 600ml (2½ cups/1 pint) water.

Reduce the heat to the lowest it will go, then cover and cook on a quiet simmer for 1 hour, stirring occasionally.

Meanwhile, heat the remaining 3 tablespoons oil in a medium sauté pan over a medium heat. Add the quince pieces and cook, stirring occasionally, for 5–7 minutes, or until the fruit begins to brown at its edges. Set aside.

When the hour of simmering is up, add the browned quince to the pot with the chicken, using a slotted spoon to do so if you don't want any additional oil in your finished *khoresh*. Stir in the brewed saffron.

What a dish! Just take a look at it now. Smell it. The colours. The delicate fragrance. You're almost there! Stir everything together, put the lid back on, and cook for another 20 minutes. (You may want to add an additional 120ml (½ cup/4fl oz) water to the pot if it looks overly dry. You want your end product to be served over rice on a plate – you are not making a soup that goes in a bowl – so only add more liquid if you think it really needs it.)

After 20 minutes, add sugar and vinegar to taste, starting with ½ teaspoon of each. The *khoresh* should be a nice balance of sweet and sour, so adjust accordingly. For me, it's usually ½ teaspoon of sugar and 1½ teaspoons of vinegar, but it really depends on the tartness of the quinces, and every one is different. Add additional salt now if you so desire.

Stir everything together and cook for a final 10 minutes. Serve with rice, and never wonder what to do with quince again.

Look! It's 17-year-old me. Down near the Bund in Shanghai. February 1999.

TUSHONKA

Soviet Stewed Beef Short Ribs

Serves 4

While relatively recent in the long, historical scheme of this region, the Soviet influence on its former republics cannot be overlooked – whether politically, environmentally, religiously, culturally, linguistically, or culinarily. *Tushonka* – a Soviet dish of stewed meat preserved in its own fat and canned – is one of a number of lingering effects of the United Soviet Socialist Republics on the region's cuisine, but one whose roots, oddly enough, lie (like mine) in the American Midwest.

During World War II, the Soviet Union was starving. To help alleviate hunger and strengthen the forces keeping Hitler at bay, the United States sent its then-ally military rations, including cases of Spam, the infamous American canned pork product. The Soviet response was to send a recipe back to America with a request for a different canned, preserved meat product. Enter: *tushonka*, the first supply of which was produced at meatpacking plants in Ohio and Iowa. Exit: hungry Red Army (and, eventually, Nazis from the Eastern Front).

Once World War II ended, US–USSR relations took a chilly turn and the Cold War began. The fact that America no longer supplied the Soviets with *tushonka* was perhaps an unexpected blessing for the USSR, as formalized factory production of the meat product both helped buoy the country's meatpacking industry and economy, and also provided a shelf-stable, protein-heavy foodstuff for its large population. Most Soviet *tushonka* was made of pork and beef scraps, preserved in lard, and frankly does not sound at all delicious. The *tushonka* I ate one evening in Baku, announced not-so-enticingly on the menu in English as "stewed meat with bay leaf and black pepper", however, was delicious. And, of course, mine is too.

Like the one I had in Baku, my *tushonka* is modestly seasoned and made from beef short ribs. Though not totally traditional, I love this piled on top of a bowl of soft polenta, and enjoyed with a simple green salad or a side of steamed greens.

1kg (2¼lb) beef short ribs

1 tbsp fine sea salt

2 tsp coarsely ground black pepper

1 tbsp neutral oil

1 onion, quartered

6 bay leaves

1 tbsp black peppercorns

1 garlic clove

Season your ribs on all sides with the salt and ground pepper. Cover and leave in the refrigerator for at least 4 hours, but preferably overnight.

When you are ready to begin cooking, remove the ribs from the refrigerator. Use a knife to scrape off the visible salt and pepper, then pat the ribs dry with paper towels and preheat your oven to 120°C (100°C fan/250°F/Gas ½).

Grab a casserole pot or similar ovenproof dish for which you have a lid and in which your ribs will fit cosily. Add the oil to the pot and heat it over a medium–high heat. Once the oil is shimmering, add the ribs. Sear and brown the sides of the ribs until they develop a dark brown, caramelized crust. For me, this takes 4–6 minutes per side. Once nicely browned, remove the ribs from the pan and set them aside on a plate.

Add your quartered onion to the pot. Cook, stirring occasionally and turning it from side to side, for 3–5 minutes, or until it is seared and browned on all sides. Don't worry when the onion quarters start to fall apart.

Return your ribs to the pan, along with any juices released. Add 100ml (6½ tbsp/3½fl oz) water and use a wooden spoon to deglaze the bottom of the pot. Add the bay leaves, black peppercorns, and garlic, then cover the pot and place it in the oven.

Cook for 6 hours, checking every 2 hours to make sure the liquid has not all evaporated, and adding 1–2 tablespoons of water if it has. After 6 hours, the meat should have fully fallen off the bone and collapsed into itself and the onion in a dark brown pile of peppery deliciousness.

Remove and discard the bones, then stir to mix the meat together. Taste and season further if you so desire. Enjoy.

PORK MTSVADI

Georgian BBQ Pork

Serves 4–6

Because of Islam and its proscription against swine, kebab and shashlik in the Middle East and Central Asia tend to be made with lamb. Sometimes it's beef, sometimes it's chicken, but 99 per cent of the time, it is lamb you will find skewered and cooked over charcoal, wood, and occasionally gas grills. Never pork. Never.

Though my father is not a practising Muslim, I did not grow up eating pork, and I never really cared for it. Not until I went to Georgia. Not until I sat under a grape arbour at a home winery in Kakheti and ate a pork kebab while the sun set over the Caucasus mountains and mosquitos attacked my ankles.

The pork in question was a simple kebab – a *mtsvadi* – salted and peppered and cooked on a barbecue, then served topped with pickled red onions and pomegranate arils. Beautiful. Simple. Easy. Almost basic. However, the sauce accompanying the *mtsvadi* was anything but pedestrian. A smooth purée of strawberries, pomegranate, chilli, and tarragon that astonished. A perfect marriage of flavours. A bright revelation and a game-changer for me vis-à-vis both barbecue and pork. However, rather than offer you a sauce recipe to go with a barbecued pork skewer, instead I give you a marinade to end all marinades, and a resulting pork *mtsvadi* that will haunt your dreams, as it does mine, in the very best way.

You'll need skewers for this recipe. Long, flat metal skewers are best, but I've also made this with both thin wooden and metal ones. Note that if you're using wooden skewers you will want to soak them in water for at least 20 minutes prior to using so that they don't burn when on the grill.

1.5kg (3lb 3oz) pork fillet/loin, diced

unsalted butter, for basting

For the marinade

1 onion, grated

200ml (scant 1 cup/7fl oz) pomegranate juice

25g (scant 1oz) fresh tarragon, chopped, plus extra to serve

2–3 red chillies, minced

100g (3½oz) strawberries, diced

1 tsp fine sea salt

½ tsp coarsely ground black pepper

To serve

flatbreads

pickled red onions

pomegranate arils

Combine all the marinade ingredients in a large non-reactive bowl. Add the pork and use your hands to mix everything together well; you want every surface of the meat nicely coated. Cover your bowl and place it in the refrigerator to marinate for at least 4 hours, but preferably overnight.

When you're ready to cook, fire up your barbecue. If using a gas barbecue, you want it at medium–high heat, and if using charcoal, you want the coals to be hot, ashed over, and glowing.

Remove your pork from its marinade and arrange the pieces on the skewers close to one another, nice and cosy, not spread out along the skewer as you may have done (or seen done) in other kebab preparations.

Melt the butter in the microwave or in a small saucepan over a low heat and have it next to you at the grill, with a basting brush at the ready.

Place the skewers on the grill, baste with the butter, and turn every 2 minutes or so. You want some char, but not too much, and you want your pork appropriately and safely cooked, but not dried out, so take its temperature after the 5-minute mark and keep checking until you hit 65°C (149°F). If you don't have a meat thermometer, this is likely to take about 12–15 minutes in total (and also, you really should get a thermometer).

Serve your *mtsvadi* with flatbreads, pickled red onions, pomegranate arils, and fresh tarragon. Be amazed at this flavour combination. I certainly was, and still am.

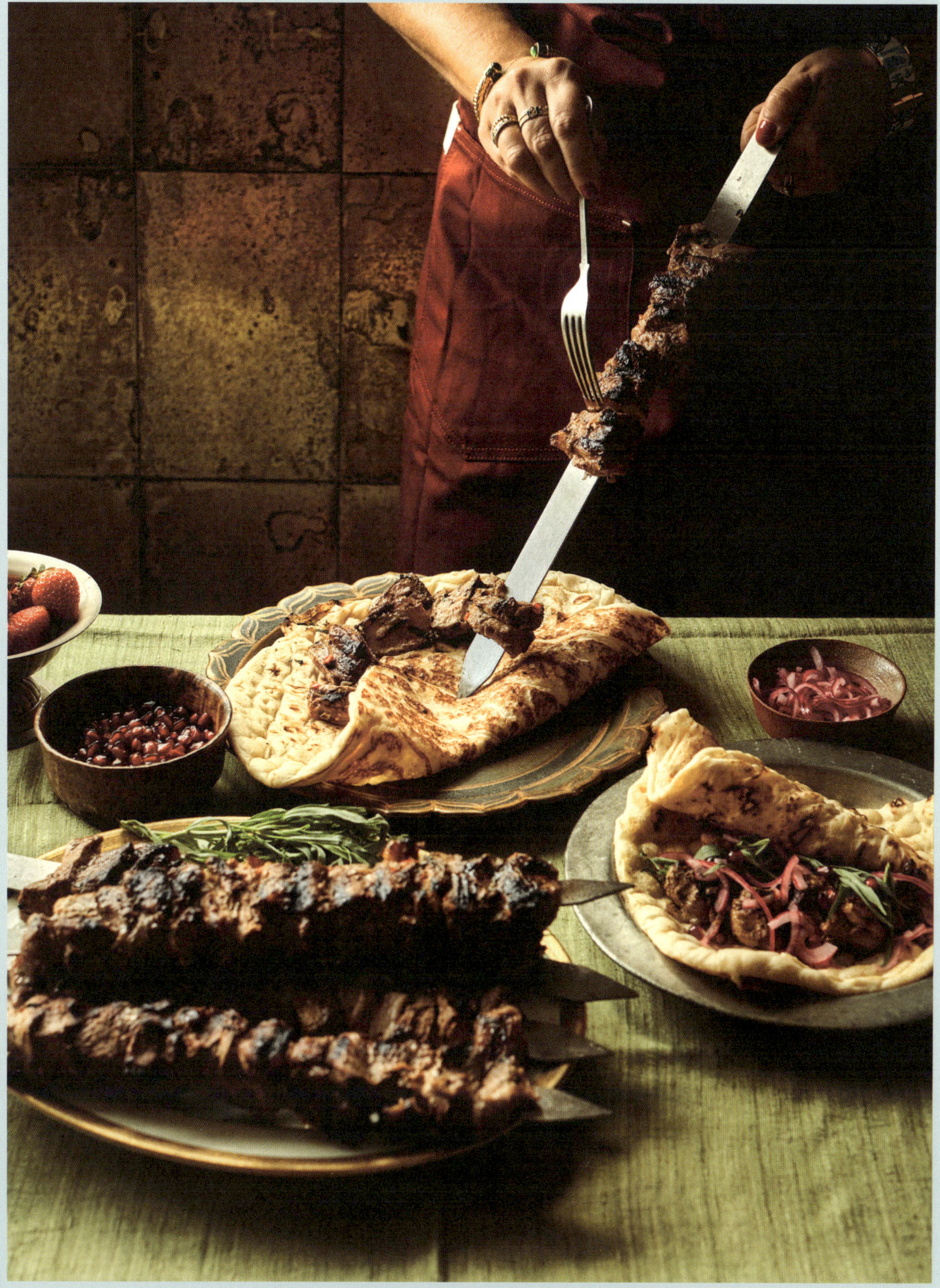

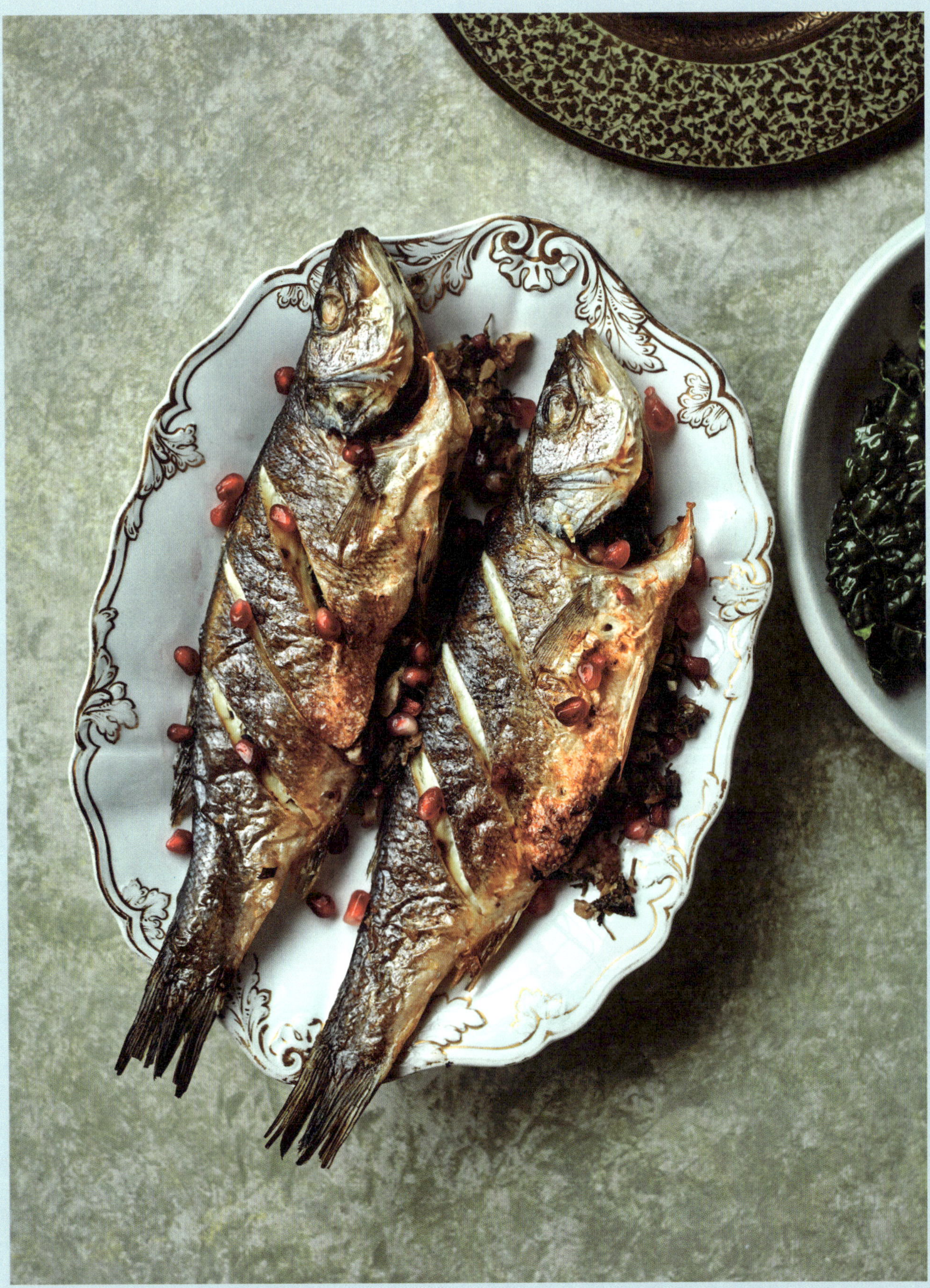

SILK ROADS STUFFED FISH

Serves 2–3

The moniker "Silk Roads" doesn't exactly conjure up images of fish. Camels, deserts, noodles, dumplings, fat-tailed sheep: sure. But not fish, not really. And yet, here we are, with a Silk Roads stuffed fish because there are indeed myriad fish-eating traditions between Baku and Beijing.

Among other species, the Caspian Sea teems with sturgeon, beloved not only for their eggs (hello, Grade 1 caviar!), but for their flesh, which Azeris grill and roast. And then there are the carp- and trout-filled rivers and lakes of Central Asia from which people have been fishing and eating for thousands of years.

Of course, things are changing, and bodies of water – such as the once-magnificent Aral Sea at the Uzbek-Kazakh border (in its heyday the fourth-largest lake in the world) and Lake Urmia, near my father's hometown (once the largest lake in the Middle East) – are drying up and dying, collateral damage from foolhardy government policies. I digress …

Azeris love to stuff fish with a variety of herbs, walnuts, and sour plums or plum paste, especially for Noruz, the new year. Bukharan Jews begin their Friday Shabbat meals with fried fish fillets topped with tangy coriander-and-garlic paste. I have combined these two traditions to give you this: a garlicky, walnutty, coriandery stuffed fish (with lemon and pomegranate too), a happy combo of flavours and food cultures that just so happens to also taste amazing. Serve your fish with simple boiled or roasted potatoes and some wilted leafy greens.

---

2 tbsp olive oil, plus extra for drizzling and serving

100g (3½oz) fresh coriander (stems included), chopped, plus extra to serve

4 spring onions, chopped, plus extra to serve

6 garlic cloves, minced

100g (3½oz) walnuts, coarsely chopped

juice of 1 lemon

5–6 tablespoons pomegranate arils, plus extra to serve

1 tbsp pomegranate molasses

1kg (2¼lb) whole white fish, scaled and gutted (sea bass, red snapper, meagre, and sea bream will all work)

fine sea salt and freshly ground black pepper

Preheat your oven to 250°C (230°C fan/480°F/Gas 10) and line a baking tray with baking parchment or a non-stick silicone baking sheet.

Heat the oil in a sauté pan over a medium heat. Add the coriander, spring onions, garlic, walnuts, and a large pinch of sea salt. Cook, stirring frequently, for 5 minutes, or until the coriander and spring onions are fragrant but not burnt.

Remove the pan from the heat and add the lemon juice, pomegranate arils, and molasses. Stir to evenly combine, and set aside.

Pat your fish dry with paper towels, checking for and discarding any errant scales as you do, then place it on your lined baking tray. Cut three diagonal slits on either side of the fish's body, each about 2.5cm (1in) apart. Don't cut too deeply; you just want a little penetration.

Generously season both the inside and outside of the fish with salt and pepper, then use your hands to pack all the filling into the fish's body cavity. Seal the little dude(s) up, either by tying the fish closed with kitchen twine or by pinning it/them shut with wooden cocktail sticks placed 4cm (1¾in) apart.

Drizzle the fish with a bit more olive oil and roast for 25 minutes, or until the fish feels firm and flaky to the touch.

Move your fish to a serving platter and release it from its bondage. Drizzle with additional pomegranate molasses and olive oil, and sprinkle with any extra spring onions and/or coriander you may have, then serve.

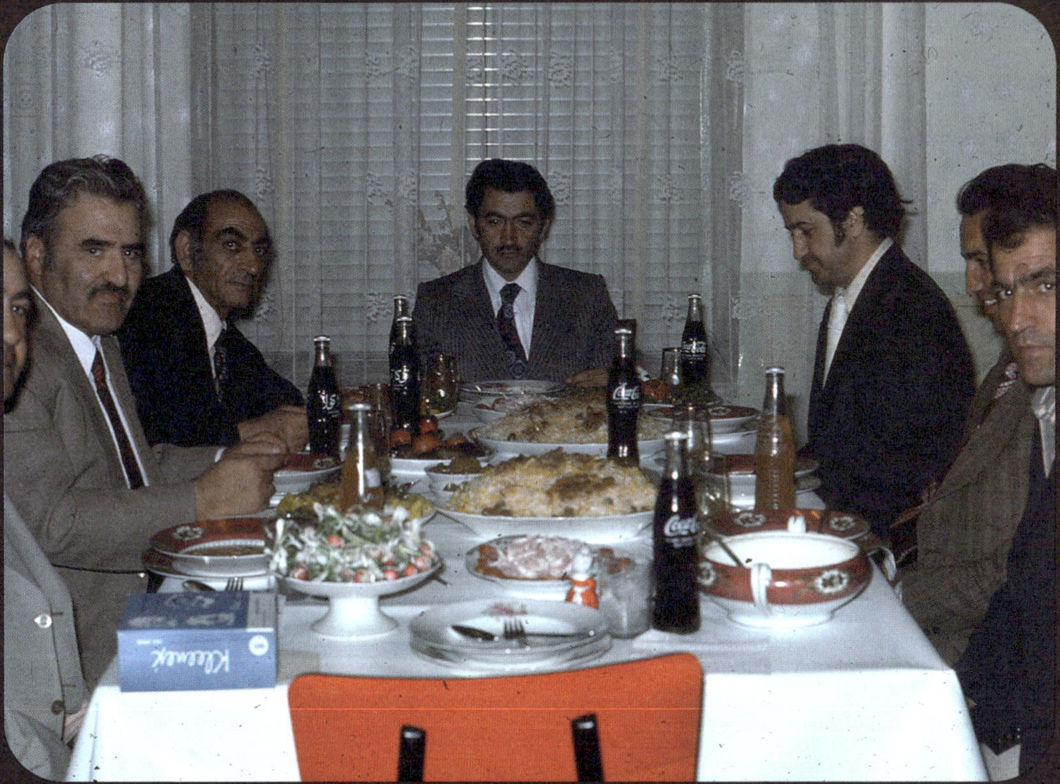
Coca-Cola
Kleenex

RICE

RICE IS LIFE
138

**A PERFECT POT OF IRANIAN RICE
(WITH POTATOES)**
143

SHAH PLOV
Azeri King/Crown Rice
145

AN UZBEK PLOV
149

TACHIN
Iranian Chicken & Rice Cake
151

RISOTTO ALLA BUKHARESE
154

TURKMEN FISH RICE
157

SHILA PLAVI
Georgian Mushroom "Risotto"
158

RICE IS LIFE

Rice: the grain that is humans' second most-consumed food crop, the grain that has fed more humans over a longer period than any other, the grain that is the staple food for over half the world's population, the grain that is my favourite food, my first food, my son's first food, and probably yours as well. Rice, or *Oryza sativa*, if we are being technical, is life. And it has been for millennia.

Archaeobotanical studies suggest two separate, distinct origins of rice cultivation and eventual domestication. The first and oldest evidence dates to 10,000 BCE in the lower Yangtze River valley of China, where rice remains have been found in both modern-day Jiangxi and Zhejiang Provinces. However, cultivation does not equal domestication – it took a while for China's wild *Oryza rufipogon* to become its domesticated *Oryza japonica*. A long while – approximately 4,000 years, in fact. And around 1,000 years after the Chinese domesticated rice, further south in India's Ganges River valley, Indians began cultivating their native *Oryza rufipogon*, as well as a second variety, *Oryza nivara*. Fast-forward another few millennia, and *Oryza japonica* had arrived in India from China, possibly/probably brought in seed form via travellers and traders who braved and crossed the deadly Himalayas to get from one land of antiquity to the other. The immigrant *japonica* strain hybridized with the local rice cultivars, and India's domestication of rice, of *Oryza indica*, was complete.

Now, hear me out. There are a lot of scholarly articles on the history of rice; I've read many of them, too many of them. No one really agrees on anything. The origin story I've just given you is generally, but not 100 per cent, accepted. Some guy a few decades back suggested that all rice originated from the ancient supercontinent of Gondwana, whose eventual split into today's continental land masses accounts for the presence of ancient wild rice in Asia (as *Oryza rufipogon* and *nivara*) as well as Africa's native red rice (*Oryza glaberrima*). Just as no one takes that supercontinent rice origin theory seriously anymore, it is possible that current, more accepted theories of rice origin will also eventually be debunked, modified, or proven. Science continues to advance. Scientists and historians continue to hypothesize. Good for them. I'm not one of them, and chances are you aren't either. So we are just going to leave this little, really old, maybe-or-maybe-not-entirely-correct origin story here, and move along.

In addition to traversing the Himalayas, domesticated *japonica* rice from China also made its way to both Korea and Japan. If you hadn't guessed it by now, *japonica* rice is the short, round rice typically associated with East Asian cuisines, while *indica* rice is the long-grained one associated with – and now I *know* you've guessed it – Indian, Iranian, and South East Asian cuisines. Jasmine rice, basmati rice: *indica*. Sushi rice, Korean rice, Chinese rice: all *japonica*. In Central Asia today, the rice one encounters in *plovs* is a medium-grained one, a pseudo-hybrid of rice from both India and China. And in Iran and Azerbaijan, you cannot have a great *polo* without great basmati rice, an *indica* strain, which made its way to the Middle East either via Alexander the Great's troops returning from India in the 3rd century BCE or centuries later from coastal trade routes.

> **RICE, OR *ORYZA SATIVA*, IF WE ARE BEING TECHNICAL, IS LIFE. AND IT HAS BEEN FOR MILLENNIA.**

Top: Me at the Longji Rice Terraces. Guilin Province, China. July 2006.

Bottom: A massive *kazan* of *plov* ready to be dished out. Samarkand, Uzbekistan. March 2024.

There are not a lot of historical sources and scientific data, archaeobotanical, written, or otherwise, to support any meaningful theory as to the definitive origin of long-grained rice in Iran, the Middle East, and the Mediterranean. There's so little that there's nothing for scientists and historians to argue about, even. But it got there – a long time ago. We know that for certain. Pliny the Elder writes about rice. Apicus writes about rice. Egyptian papyrus logbooks reference rice. And, by the time Khusrow I becomes ruler of Sasanian Iran in 531 CE, rice is important enough as a foodstuff, a crop, and a commodity that Iranian taxes are based upon it and celebratory Noruz feasts include it.

Even today, you cannot have a Noruz celebration in Iran without rice – without *sabzi polo*. *Sabzi* means "herbs" in Farsi, and herbs are an integral part of the new year's table, signifying growth, rebirth, spring, and life. *Sabzi polo* is chock-a-block with herbs – coriander, parsley, and dill, to name a few. So many herbs go into the dish that the white rice grains themselves nearly disappear. It is a beautiful, fresh, elegant, fragrant, and beloved preparation; and it's the reason for my initial interest in the Bukharan Jewish rice dish, *bakhash*.

We didn't plan on taking a cooking course in Bukhara. And yet, there we were. In the courtyard of a hotel down the lane from ours, next door to the synagogue and kitty corner from a Hebrew school – the only one, I was told, in all of Central Asia. A long wooden table was laden with ingredients for the evening's class – a massive mountain of chopped green and purple herbs, diced onions, cubes of fat, meat and liver, bowls of unnamed spices and ingredients (including, I would later learn, MSG – which was described to me as "Korean salt"), and rice soaking in a basin. There was also a bottle of Irish whiskey, a pack of cigarettes, an ashtray, two boxes of matches, and a small, lame cat prowling about.

PLINY THE ELDER WRITES ABOUT RICE. APICUS WRITES ABOUT RICE. EGYPTIAN PAPYRUS TRADE LOGBOOKS REFERENCE RICE.

The cigarettes and whiskey, we would discover, belonged to a rotund Russian man in his forties, dressed, like so many of his countrymen we encountered in Uzbekistan that trip, from head to toe in a matching synthetic tracksuit. His two female companions sat at the table, scrolling on their phones for the entirety of the class, barely looking up and certainly not saying a thing. An American man completed our group, a 50-some-year-old from New Jersey, a solo traveller who, like us, had signed up for the class as a result of seeing signage on the lane – "Bukhara Jewish *Plov* Cooking Class Here" – and who, unlike us, had never heard of this dish. Nor was he a Gentile. We would later learn that the New Jerseyan, whose name we never caught and with whom we were grouped because of our shared native tongue, was Jewish, as was the Russian man; the New Jerseyan told us as much, while the Russian's faith was gleaned from his donning a yarmulke at the dinner table. Two Jewish men, two silent women, and us, the only two students who had any idea what dish they were about to eat and cook: *bakhash*, a dish that, to me, epitomizes so much of what the Silk Roads were about, so much of what this book is about.

When they fled east from Iran to Central Asia in the middle of the 6th century, like so many who leave their native lands for new ones, Jews took with them their culinary heritage, practices, and flavours. As it was originally a sabbath dish, Bukharan Jews traditionally cooked *bakhash* in a special cloth bag, boiling everything together overnight so as to not break Shabbat rules against work. I was obviously not going to give you a recipe for a dish that involves a bag you will never be able to find, so, at home in London, with Noruz around the corner, my initial version of *bakhash* was based upon *sabzi polo* – I essentially just added beef to a dish I already knew and loved. And it was delicious. It is delicious. And it is not in this book. Why? Because of a cooking class in Bukhara I took by chance with my husband, a lame cat, a New Jerseyan, and a Russian man in a yarmulke and polyester tracksuit. Because in that cooking class, I learned to pour water into the rice – not *sabzi polo*'s basmati, by the way, but a medium-grain rice, one akin to the Italian arborio or *carnaroli* – and let everything cook slowly, not in a bag but on a stovetop, the grains leisurely absorbing the liquid, the herbs infiltrating the dish minute by drawn-out minute, and I realized what I would give you: a *bakhash*, cooked risotto-style, but *sans* liver and cubes of fat. It's excellent, of course, as delicious as my Iranian-inspired *bakhash* was, but with the added bonus of: 1) being based on a real-life experience; and 2) being a risotto! And I'll give you one more little smidge of delightful history before unleashing you into this chapter.

Risotto alla Milanese. The near neon saffron-infused risotto from Northern Italy. Get this: Arabs brought rice to Sicily in the 10th and 11th centuries. It went north, eventually into the Po River valley, where it was cultivated and became arborio rice. Arabs also took rice to Spain, where it was cultivated and became *bomba* and *calasparra* – rices for paella. Arabs also took saffron from Iran to Spain … and then the Spanish took it to Milan when they ruled the duchy in the 16th and 17th centuries. And the Milanese started using saffron in their cooking. And they started using rice in their cooking. And *risotto alla milanese* was eventually born – out of ingredients that had no right to be there, no reason to be where they were used, beloved, and embraced, where they became part of the culinary lexicon, part of culture, part of identity, other than that these ingredients, from China, from India, from Iran, were carried there by foreigners, were traded, imported, integrated, and, of course, eaten. Which is what I am going to do now: eat. And you should, too – there are seven life-affirming rice dishes that beckon.

> WHEN THEY FLED EAST FROM IRAN TO CENTRAL ASIA IN THE MIDDLE OF THE 6TH CENTURY, LIKE SO MANY WHO LEAVE THEIR NATIVE LANDS FOR NEW ONES, JEWS TOOK WITH THEM THEIR CULINARY HERITAGE, PRACTICES AND FLAVOURS.

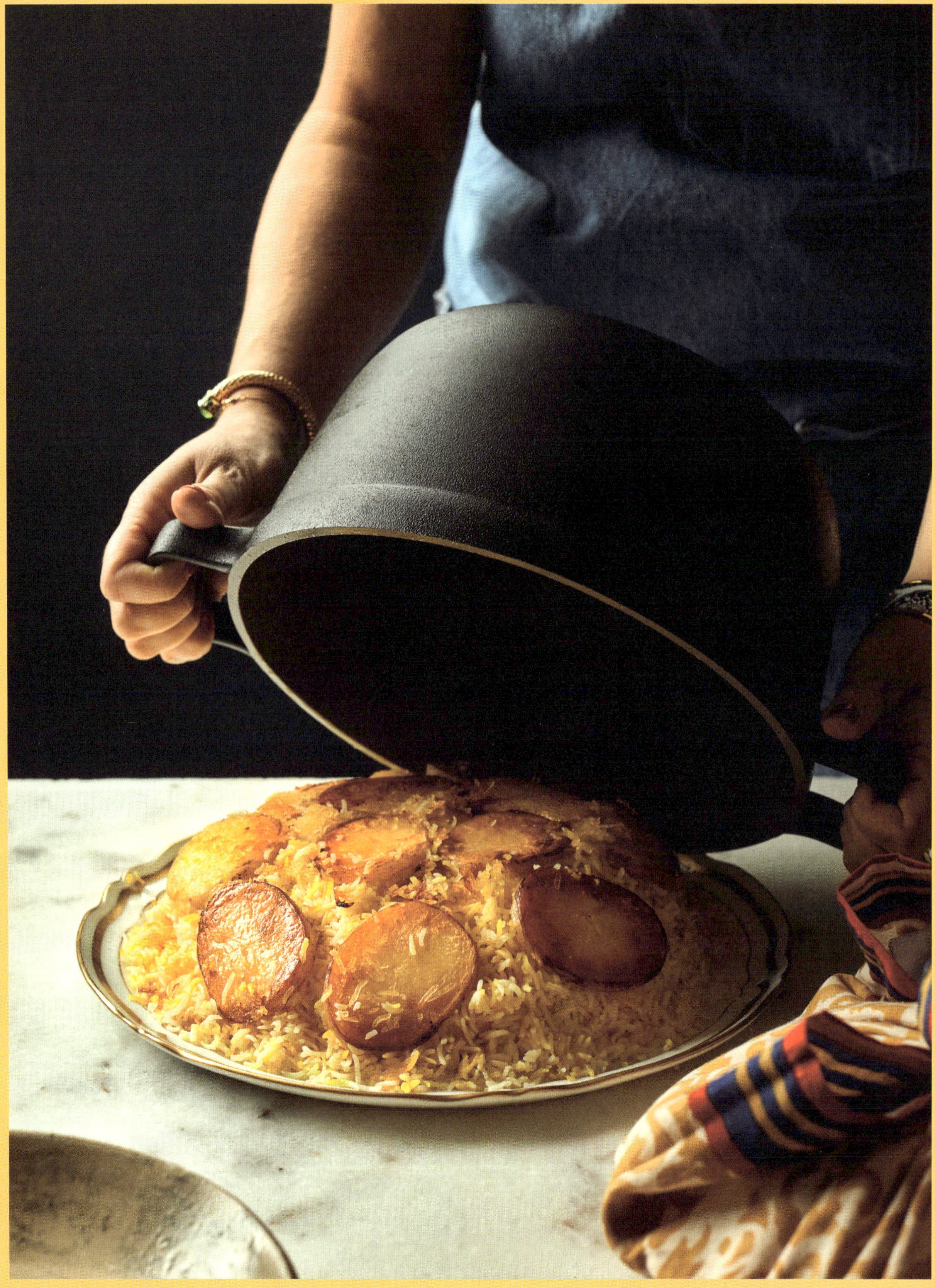

A PERFECT POT OF IRANIAN RICE (WITH POTATOES)

Serves 4–8

For a grain eaten by so many around the world, rice can be tricky to cook. You can end up with indigestible hard grains if you don't use enough water, or a bowl of mush if you use too much. You can easily scorch your rice. You can easily undercook it. Tricky. Tricky. Tricky. And, if you're trying to make Iranian rice, with a gorgeous, golden crust that effortlessly releases from the bottom of the pot when you flip it over, "tricky" doesn't even come close to describing the process. But I'm going to help you out. I'm going to help you make a pot of rice so good, so perfect, you may feel the need to call someone after you've cooked it, just to tell them of your achievement. Plus, there's something super magical at the bottom of this pot of rice: a potato *gazmakh* – that coveted, crispy rice layer also known as *tahdig*. I'm so excited for you.

- 400–500g (14oz–1lb 2oz) basmati rice
- 2 tbsp fine sea salt
- 3½ tbsp olive oil or melted unsalted butter
- 250g (9oz) potatoes, cut into 1cm (½in) rounds
- 50g (1¾oz) unsalted butter, cut into 10g (¼oz) pieces
- 0.5g saffron, ground with ¼ tsp granulated sugar using a mortar and pestle, and then brewed with 1 tbsp rose water and 3 tbsp hot water

---

Parboil the rice according to the instructions overleaf, then set aside.

Rinse the pot you used to boil your rice with cold water, then add the olive oil or melted butter, along with 3½ tablespoons water, and swirl to coat the bottom of the pot. Arrange the potato slices across the bottom of the pot, making sure to cosy them up tight to one another without overlapping.

Return to your colander of rice. Give it a good shake, then take a large spoonful of rice and spread it across the top of your layer of potatoes, pressing it down gently – you want the rice to fill in the small gaps between the potatoes. This way, you'll get some delicious golden crispy rice alongside your delicious golden crispy potatoes!

After the first spoonful of rice has been layered across the bottom of the pot, spoon the rest of the rice in, fluffing it with a fork and forming it into a pyramid-like mound as you go. Once all your rice is in and you have what looks more like a mound than a pyramid (no matter how hard you tried) take the end of a wooden spoon and poke 5–7 holes in the top of the mound. Place your pieces of butter over and around the holes in the rice. Drizzle the brewed saffron and its water over top.

Wrap the lid of the pot in a clean tea towel, making sure to secure the towel on top of the pot so that it doesn't catch fire if you are using a gas burner (I use a rubber band tied around the gathered corners of the towel). Place the towelled lid back on the pan.

If you have a gas stove and a heat diffuser, this is the perfect time to pop that diffuser on your burner. Cook your pot of rice over a medium heat for 8 minutes, then reduce the heat to the lowest possible setting and cook for a further 45–60 minutes, or until your rice is fluffy and tender.

Fill your sink with 2.5cm (1in) cold water and place your pot in the sink for 10–15 seconds – the cold water will help release the *gazmakh* from the pot.

Find a platter that fits over the top of your pot. Carefully remove the pot from the sink, take off the lid, and place the platter on top. Then, using both hands, flip the pot over in one quick fluid motion. Take a deep breath, lift the pot from the platter, and see if you've done it. You very well may have a perfectly intact, perfectly golden, presentation-worthy round of crispy rice-and-potatoes on your platter. And you may not. If you don't, join the club. It's not very exclusive, but it's pretty awesome and very delicious all the same. I'm in it – check out that not-quite-perfect version of this dish in the photo on page 142. The flip that day did not go as planned, but the taste and flavour certainly did! In any case, don't worry – I never said you'd have perfect *gazmakh*, just perfect rice – and that, I am certain, you have.

Alternatively, you can just do what my mom always did with *gazmakh* (and, frankly, I prefer this method, though it doesn't quite have the same showstopping impact or grandeur). Simply scoop the rice out of the pot (leaving the potatoes at the bottom undisturbed and making sure to reserve 2–3 tablespoons of saffron rice from the top for a garnish) and place it on to a platter in as lovely a mound as a mound of rice can ever be. Then attend to your layer of potatoes. Extricate those and place them around the outer edges of your rice, before spooning the reserved saffrony rice across the top of your platter of rice.

There you have it. A perfect pot of rice. And some potatoes, too. This one's for you, Katharine Herskovic.

HOW TO PARBOIL RICE

Rinse the rice 3–4 times in cold water, then tip into a large bowl of cold water, add 1 tablespoon of salt, and leave to soak for at least 1 hour. Once the soaking time is up, drain and rinse the rice in cold water once more. Pour 3 litres (12⅔ cups/5¼ pints) water into a large saucepan for which you have a lid. Add 1 tablespoon of salt, and bring to a rolling boil over a high heat. Once the water is boiling, add your rice to the pot and stand at attention. Check the rice after 3 minutes by grabbing a grain and squishing it between your fingers. If you feel a hard centre but soft outer bits, you've done it. You only want the grains to be halfway cooked; you really do not want to overcook your rice at this stage. You kind of can't really come back from that.

When the rice is appropriately parboiled, immediately turn off the heat and quickly drain the rice in a fine colander over the sink. Quickly rinse the parboiled rice with cold water to stop the cooking process. If you have a tap with a nozzle, use it now; it really comes into its own here. Set the colander aside until needed; your best bet is to leave it in the sink to let any excess water continue to drain.

SHAH PLOV

Azeri King/Crown Rice

Serves 4–8

Azerbaijan has over 200 different *plovs*. And, as in Uzbekistan and Iran, rice is respected and revered – no celebration is complete without *plov*. For some, no meal is complete without *plov*. Raftara, a woman I met in southern Azerbaijan, an entrepreneurial citrus farmer whose kumquat jam is the stuff of which dreams are made, told me how, as a child, her father became angry with her mother if he found that, upon returning home after working elsewhere for a few days, she and her siblings had had no *plov* while he was away.

Her mother fed them well, Raftara stressed, as she relayed this story to me under the midday Lankaran sun, pouring another cup of tea with a smile. "But my father, he thought if we were not eating *plov*, his kids must have been going hungry! He would yell at my mother," she said, still all smiles. "'You didn't feed my kids when I was away! Why did you not give them any *plov*?!' That is what he would say to her. That is how important *plov* is to Azeris."

And this *plov* – *shah plov* – this is the king of Azeri *plovs*. The crown *plov*. Literally. There are countless gorgeous recipes in this book. Countless dishes you will proudly bring to the table not only because of their exceptional taste, but also because of their beauty. But they all pale in comparison to this one. There is simply nothing like it. This is a showstopper of a dish – certainly in terms of flavour, but also in terms of presentation. And, despite its opulent look, it is relatively simple to make. When you come at the king, you best not miss – and you won't with this recipe.

100g (3½oz) barberries or cranberries

1kg (2¼lb) skinless, boneless chicken thighs

1¾ tsp fine sea salt, plus extra to taste

¼ tsp freshly ground black pepper, plus extra to taste

4 tbsp ghee or olive oil

2 onions, thinly sliced into half-moons

180g (6oz) cooked chestnuts

1 tsp ground cumin

¾ tsp ground coriander

0.5g saffron, ground with ¼ tsp granulated sugar using a mortar and pestle, and then brewed with 1 tbsp rose water and 3 tbsp hot water

2 tablespoons ghee, or 30g (1oz) unsalted butter

150g (5½oz) dried apricots and/or prunes, chopped into 2–3cm (¾–1¼in) pieces, plus extra to serve

1 tsp ground cinnamon

nuts, to garnish (optional; I like flaked almonds and pistachio nibs)

For the rice

500g (1lb 2oz) basmati rice

1 tbsp fine sea salt

250g (9oz) unsalted butter, melted

enough flatbread/tortilla rounds to cover the bottom and sides of your pot, all but two cut in half

---

Soak the barberries or cranberries in a bowl of warm water for 20 minutes, then drain and set aside. Season your chicken with ½ teaspoon of the fine sea salt and the black pepper, then set aside.

In a large sauté pan for which you have a lid, heat 3 tablespoons of the ghee or oil over a medium heat. Add the sliced onions and ⅛ teaspoon of the salt. Cook your onions, stirring frequently, for 10–12 minutes, or until they are soft and golden.

Add the chicken to the pan, along with the remaining 1 tablespoon ghee or oil. Cook for 2 minutes on each side to brown, then add the chestnuts, cumin, and coriander, along with an additional teaspoon of salt. Stir to mix well and cook for 2 minutes more.

Now, pour 250ml (1 cup plus 1 tbsp/9fl oz) water into the pan. Drizzle 1 tablespoon of the saffron and its brewing water over the top of the chicken. Cover the pan with its lid and increase the heat to bring the mixture to the boil. Once boiling, reduce the heat to low and cook for 25 minutes.

While your braise is a-braising, melt the 2 tablespoons butter or ghee in a separate medium sauté pan over a medium heat. Once melted, reduce the heat to low and add the chopped apricots and/or prunes, along with the cinnamon and the final ⅛ teaspoon of fine sea salt. Stir to coat the fruit in the seasoning, and sauté for 2 minutes.

Add the drained barberries or cranberries to the pan and sauté for 1 minute more, stirring near constantly to make sure the berries don't burn. Remove the fruit from the heat, and set aside until your chicken is ready to welcome it.

After the chicken has been cooking for 25 minutes, remove the lid and increase the heat to medium–high. Cook the chicken for a further 10 minutes to reduce and thicken the sauce, then taste and season to your liking with additional fine sea salt and/or black pepper. Add your cooked fruit to the pan, mix everything together well, then take off the heat and set aside while you attend to your rice.

Preheat the oven to 180°C (160°C fan/350°F/Gas 4).

Parboil your rice according to the instructions on page 144.

Pour 50 ml (3 tbsp) melted butter into a large, ovenproof casserole pot, swirling to coat the bottom of the pot. Place one tortilla/flatbread round on top of the butter. Then, use a pastry brush to brush more melted butter over the top of the bread, and all the way up the sides of the pot. Layer your flatbread/tortilla halves vertically along the sides of the pot, overlapping them with each other, brushing them generously with melted butter as you go, and making sure there is a bit of overhang at the top – you will be folding them down and in when you close up the *plov*. Brush the sides of the pot with more butter along the way as needed, as it will drizzle downwards.

Return to your colander of parboiled rice. Give it a good shake, then add a few spoonfuls of the rice to the bottom of the bread-lined pot. Use the back of a spoon to smooth it down evenly, then drizzle 1 tablespoon of the brewed saffron and its water across the rice. Spoon in half of your chicken-and-fruit filling on top, spreading it across the rice as evenly as you can. Layer in half of the remaining rice on top of the meat and fruit. Follow with another 1 tablespoon drizzle of saffron water and then the rest of the meat. Top with the remaining rice, ending with a final 1 tablespoon drizzle of saffron.

Take the final tortilla/flatbread round and place it across the top of your saffron-laced rice. Brush the bread with more melted butter. Now, gently fold each of the overhanging vertical pieces of bread in toward the middle. You are sealing up the most incredible package; Santa's got nothing on you!

Once all the bread has been folded in, brush everything down with the last of the melted butter. I bet you didn't think you would use it all, did you? But you did. There are many reasons this is an occasional dish, and the amount of butter used in it is one of them.

Place the lid on top of your pot and slide it into your preheated oven. Cook for 1–2 hours, or until the top is golden brown.

Carefully remove the pot from the oven, take off the lid and let the *plov* cool for 5 minutes. Then, find a platter that fits over the top of your pot, place it on top and, using both hands, quickly flip the pot over in one fluid motion. Take a deep breath, remove the pot from the platter and see if you've done it. I bet you have; if you've used enough butter, I'm sure you have, and what an incredible sight it is. Congratulations.

Decorate the top of your *plov* with more dried fruit and perhaps some dried nuts too. To serve, carve into the *plov* like it's a cake. Let its insides tumble out. Marvel at its beauty. Then spoon some onto your plate, and marvel at its taste as well.

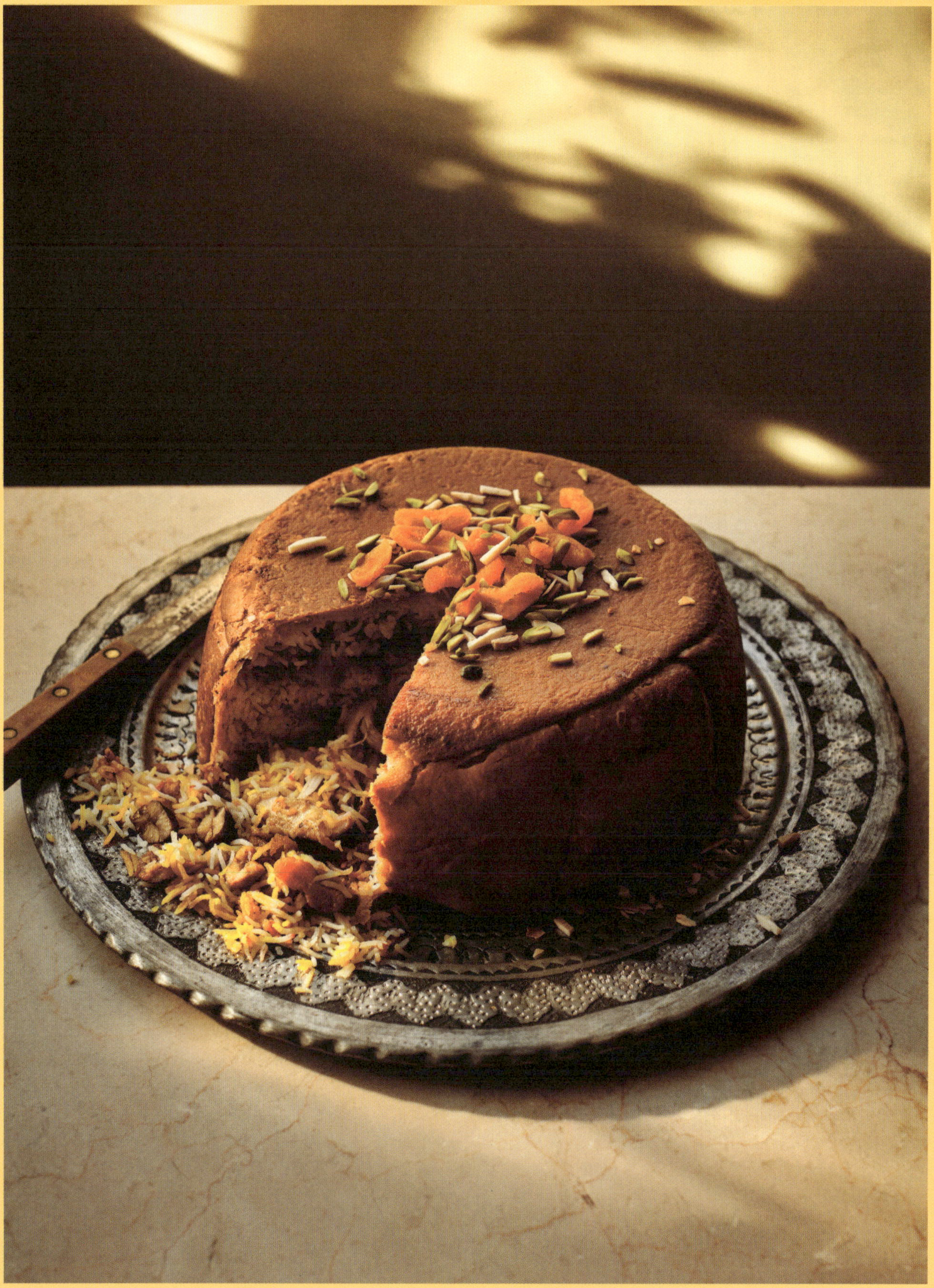

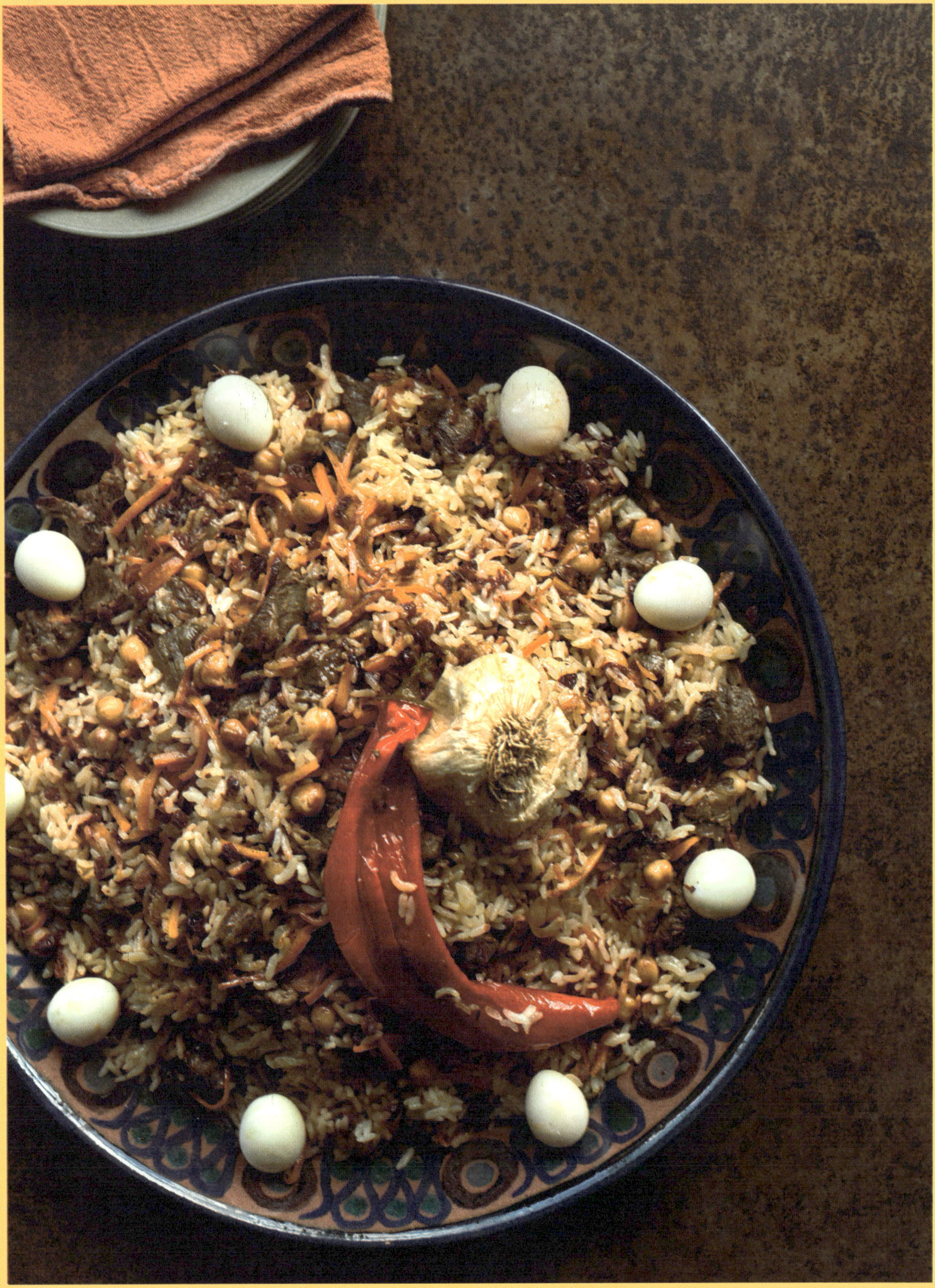

AN UZBEK PLOV

Serves 4–8

There is no definitive "Uzbek *plov*". There is no singular preparation, set of ingredients, method, flavour. Some cooks, some families, some areas, use lamb, others beef. Some add chilli or barberries, apricots or chestnuts, chickpeas or quince. Some layer the ingredients, others mix them all together. One opulent recipe I came across calls for minced lamb-stuffed quails, while a friend in Bukhara tells me his city's *plov* is healthier and less oily than elsewhere, because the last Bukharan emir, Sayid Mir Muhammad Alim Khan, had a sensitive stomach. However, no matter their additions or cooking methods, all *plovs* must contain five key ingredients: oil, onion, meat, carrots, and rice.

The dish, in all its variations, is beloved across Uzbekistan. It is a part of life, a part of culture, of history, and even of religion. I am told by my friend in Samarkand that *plov* is meant for Thursday evenings: the rice dish strengthens the man so that he and his wife can make love before he bathes himself and goes to the mosque on Friday. Go figure. Some say Alexander the Great was the OG *plov* master, coming up with the dish to easily feed his troops after having conquered Samarkand in 329 BCE. Centuries later, in 1402 CE, Tamerlane too is said to have made sure his troops were full of *plov* prior to attacking Ankara, believing the dish would give them nourishment as well as strength and courage. (Side note: had I been an advisor to the infamous Timurid emperor, I would have voted against a heavy rice dish before battle, but that's just me – this dish is delicious, but it is filling.) And then there is the tale involving Ibn Sina, the Persian thinker and astronomer, born in Bukhara and known as Avicenna in the Western world. According to the story, this so-called "father of medicine" advised a prince, frail and weak with heartsickness, to eat *plov* to regain his strength. Avicenna also supposedly then helped bring the prince and his erstwhile star-crossed lover together; everyone lived happily ever after, and Avicenna wrote down the very first "recipe" for *plov*.

I've read and tried countless recipes. And they're basically all good, because what's not to love in an Uzbek *plov*? No – actually, I take that back: they're basically all *great*. And I think mine is, too – I hope you will agree.

Note: Ideally, you would use a medium-grain Uzbek rice, but that is pretty impossible to come by outside of Central Asia, so I have written this with basmati, as it's easily accessible. If you are able to find Turkish/*baldo* rice, give it a go with that. Same thing goes for the oil: unless you have a secret supplier of unrefined Uzbek cottonseed and/or melon seed oil, use ghee or whatever neutral oil you have. To make this vegetarian, leave out the meat and add an additional can of chickpeas.

- 500g (1lb 2oz) basmati rice
- 3 tbsp fine sea salt
- 400–500g (14oz–1lb 2oz) diced lamb shoulder or beef chuck
- 1 tsp freshly ground black pepper
- 150ml (5fl oz/scant ⅔ cup) ghee or neutral oil
- 2 onions, thinly sliced into half-moons
- 3–4 carrots (about 400g/14oz), peeled and cut into 3–6cm (1¼–2½in) matchsticks
- 400g (14oz) can chickpeas, drained and rinsed
- 100g (3½oz) barberries, raisins, or chopped dried apricots
- 2 tbsp cumin seeds, toasted
- 1 garlic bulb, top 1cm (½in) cut off so you can just make out the raw cloves
- 1 long, thin red or green chilli
- hard-boiled quail eggs, to serve

Rinse the rice 3–4 times in cold water, then tip into a large bowl of cold water, add 1 tablespoon of the salt and leave to soak for at least 1 hour.

Season your meat with 1 teaspoon each of the fine sea salt and black pepper.

In a medium saucepan for which you have a lid, heat the ghee or oil over a medium–high heat. Once it is hot and glistening, reduce the heat to medium and add the onions, along with ½ teaspoon of the salt. Cook, stirring occasionally, for 8–10 minutes, or until golden.

Add the meat and cook for 2–3 minutes, stirring occasionally, until it is no longer pink on the outside. Add the carrots and 1 teaspoon water, then cook for another 5 minutes, stirring frequently.

Drain your soaking rice in a fine colander over the sink. Rinse the rice with cold water to remove most of the salt in which it's been soaking.

Return your attention to the pan. Pick up a carrot. Is it limp? Yes? If so, you're ready for the next step. Reduce the heat to medium–low, then layer in the chickpeas and dried fruit. Don't mix them together, just use the back of a wooden spoon to smooth everything out across the pan. Sprinkle over 1 tablespoon of your toasted cumin seeds and ½ tablespoon of the salt, distributing them as evenly as you can across the top.

Now, add the rice to the pan, again using a wooden spoon to spread it across the top in an even layer, gently pressing down as needed. Sprinkle over the remaining cumin seeds, along with another 1 tablespoon salt, again distributing them as evenly as you can.

Carefully pour in 700ml (2¾ cups/generous 1 pint) water, drizzling it around, or pouring it in at an angle at the edge of the pot so as to not to disturb the rice. Plop your garlic bulb into the middle of the pan, cut-side down. Gently push the garlic down into the rice until it's just below the surface of the water. Plop your raw chilli next to the garlic and push it under in the same way.

Increase the heat to medium, then cover the pan with a lid and cook for 25 minutes.

Now wrap the lid of the pan in a clean tea towel and put the towelled lid back on the pan. Turn the heat off and let your rice sit, towelled and undisturbed, for 25 minutes.

Dish the *plov* out on to a platter. Mix together all the constituent parts and enjoy your trip to Uzbek rice heaven.

My father and grandmother in front of Detroit's skyline. Along with icons like Cobo Hall and the Penobscot Building, the eagle-eyed can spy a real piece of Detroit history in this pic – a Boblo Boat! Windsor, Canada. Mid-1960s.

TACHIN

Iranian Chicken & Rice Cake

Serves 4–6

Maybe it's morbid, but I occasionally find myself thinking about my final meal, a death-row dinner, a last supper. What to have for one's last bite on this earth? What would I have? What would I want? Every time this macabre (but, I believe, commonplace – come on, everybody does this, right?) hypothetical pops into my head, I end up back at the same answer. Right here. Right on this page. *Tachin*. My always and forever last supper. My love.

Chicken and rice: a simple combination adored across the world, made even more satisfying here with the addition of yogurt, saffron, and onions. Serve it turned upside down, golden *gazmakh* and barberries glistening, pistachio nibs beckoning, the whole glorious Iranian dish begging you to cut large cake-like slices for yourself and all those lucky enough to be at your table. Hopefully not your last supper, but decidedly a most memorable one.

- 650g (1lb 7oz) skinless, boneless chicken breasts or thighs
- 1 tbsp plus 2 tsp fine sea salt
- 1¼ tsp coarsely ground black pepper
- 3 tbsp olive oil
- 2 large onions, thinly sliced into half-moons
- ½ tsp Advieh (see p50)

- 2 garlic cloves, finely minced
- 0.5g saffron, ground with ¼ tsp granulated sugar using a mortar and pestle, and then brewed with 1 tbsp rose water and 3 tbsp hot water
- zest of 1 lemon
- 500g (1lb 2oz) full-fat plain yogurt
- 3 egg yolks

- 500g (1lb 2oz) basmati rice
- 3 tablespoons neutral oil or melted unsalted butter

To serve

- Candied Barberry Topping (see overleaf)
- 1 tbsp pistachio nibs

Season your chicken breasts with 1 teaspoon of the fine sea salt and ½ teaspoon of the coarsely ground black pepper. Set aside.

In a medium sauté pan for which you have a lid, heat the oil over a high heat. Once the oil is shimmering, reduce the heat to medium and add the onions, along with ½ teaspoon of the salt, ½ teaspoon of the black pepper, and the *advieh*. Stir to combine and then cook, stirring occasionally to stop any threat of burning onions, for 10–15 minutes, or until golden brown. If, during this time, your onions do seem like they may burn, add a tablespoon of water to the pan.

Add the garlic and cook for 30 seconds, or until fragrant, then place your seasoned chicken on top of the onions and garlic. Evenly pour 1 tablespoon of the saffron water over the top of the chicken, then scatter over the lemon zest.

Add 200ml (scant 1 cup/7fl oz) water to the pan (around, not over, the chicken) before covering it with its lid and cooking for 20 minutes, flipping the chicken over halfway through.

Meanwhile, in a large mixing bowl, combine the yogurt and egg yolks, along with the remaining ½ teaspoon of salt and ¼ teaspoon of black pepper. Add the rest of the saffron water and mix well, then set aside.

Preheat your oven to 180°C (160°C fan/350°F/Gas 4).

Parboil your rice according to the instructions on page 144. Once drained, add your parboiled rice to the yogurt and egg yolk bowl. Gently but assuredly mix the rice into the yogurt – you want everything coated. The bowl should look like it's full of uncooked rice pudding.

Once your chicken is cooked, remove the meat to a plate to cool. As for the onions, don't take them out of the pan – they're not done yet. Give them a good stir and continue cooking, uncovered and still at a medium heat, for 10–15 minutes, or until nearly all

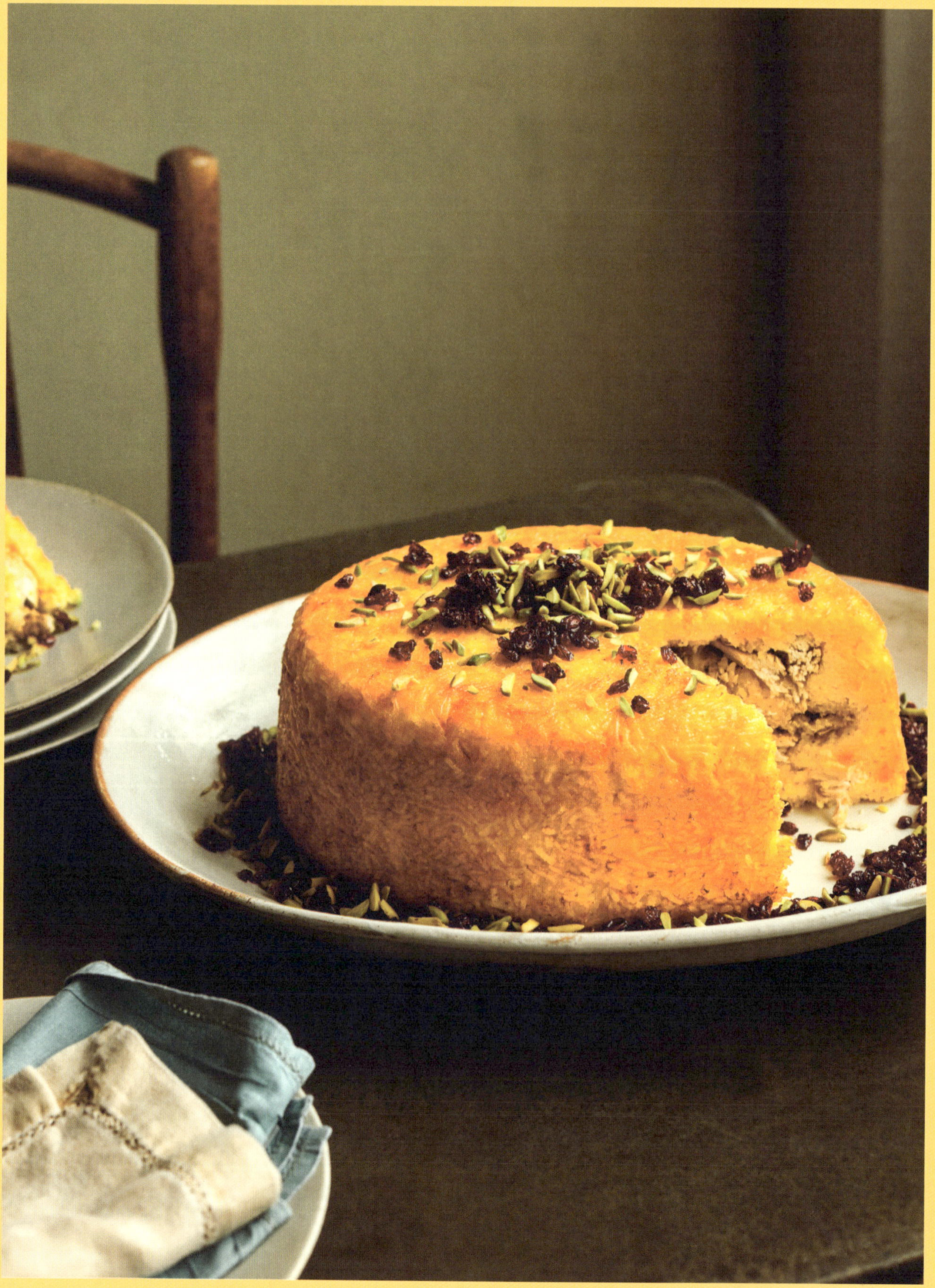

the liquid in the pan is gone. Transfer the onions to a mixing bowl, using a slotted spoon to do so if an overabundance of liquid remains.

When the chicken is cool, use your hands to tear it into 5 × 2cm (2 × ¾in) pieces. Place your torn chicken into the bowl with the onions and mix them together.

Now, prep your cooking pot. Cut a piece of baking parchment to fit the bottom of a medium-sized ovenproof casserole pot. Use a pastry brush to brush the bottom of the pot with the oil or melted butter, then add the baking parchment and brush that with oil or butter too. Finally, brush the sides of the pot with more oil or butter.

Take a large spoonful of the yogurt rice and spread it across the bottom of the pot, on top of the baking parchment. Press it down with the back of your spoon. You want the first layer to be about 1cm (½in) deep. Spoon half the chicken-and-onion mixture on top, spread it across the rice, but make sure to leave a 2.5cm (1in) buffer around the circumference of the pot. You do not want your chicken and onions to touch the sides of your pot. For this dish to work, only the yogurt rice should touch the sides of the pot.

Top the chicken and onions with half of the remaining yogurty rice. Press it down and across the pot; it needs to fully fill in that 2.5cm (1in) border, to get all the way to the sides of the pot. Repeat this layering process with the remaining chicken mixture and yogurt rice. Cover with a lid, put your *tachin* in the oven, and cook for 1½ hours.

When it's time, remove your *tachin* from the oven and let it cool, uncovered, for 5 minutes. Then take a knife and gently run it around the circumference of your *tachin*, ensuring that nothing sticks to the side of the pot.

Grab a large platter, place it on top of your pot, and get your hands protected. Grab the platter and the pot and, in one fast and fluid movement, flip it. Your *tachin* should release easily onto the platter.

Top with candied barberries and pistachio nibs, and serve.

CANDIED BARBERRY TOPPING

Makes enough for one Tachin or Risotto alla Bukharese (see p154).

Ingredients
40g (scant 1½oz) dried barberries
1 tbsp olive oil
1 tbsp soft light brown sugar or date molasses

Method
Soak your berries for 10 minutes in a bowl of warm water.

Once they've finished their soak, drain using a fine mesh sieve.

Add the drained barberries to a small sauté pan, along with the oil and your sweetener of choice. Cook over a medium heat for 2 minutes, stirring frequently so that the berries do not burn, and so that the sugar, if that's what you are using, dissolves.

Remove the pan from the heat and immediately transfer the sweetened berries to a heatproof plate to cool.

RISOTTO ALLA BUKHARESE

Here it is. You're welcome.

Serves 4–6

500g (1lb 2oz) beef chuck, cut into 1cm (½in) cubes

1 tsp fine sea salt

½ tsp coarsely ground black pepper

200g (7oz) mix of fresh parsley, mint leaves, dill, spring onions, and coriander, finely chopped

7 tbsp olive oil

2 onions, diced

4 garlic cloves, minced

2 litres (8½ cups/3½ pints) beef or chicken stock

300g (10oz) risotto rice

To serve (optional)

Candied Barberry Topping (see p153)

ground cinnamon, for sprinkling

toasted flaked almonds

extra fresh herbs

Place your meat in a bowl, and season with ¼ teaspoon of the fine sea salt and the black pepper. Stir to coat, then set aside.

Add the chopped herbs and spring onions to a separate large bowl and gently mix them together with your hands. Try to somewhat evenly distribute the different types of greens throughout the bowl.

In a large sauté pan for which you have a lid, heat 4 tablespoons of the oil over a medium–high heat. Add half the diced onion, along with ¼ teaspoon of the salt. Cook, stirring occasionally, for 5–7 minutes, or until the onion is golden brown, then add another tablespoon of oil to the pan, along with your meat. Cook, turning and stirring near constantly, for 60–90 seconds, or until the pink of the meat is just about gone.

Stir in the garlic and cook for about 30 seconds, or until fragrant, then add half of your bowl of mixed and chopped herbs to the pan. Stir to mix well and cook for 1 minute.

Now add 500ml (2 cups plus 2 tablespoons/16fl oz) water to the pan and stir everything together. Increase the heat to high and bring the mixture to the boil. Once boiling, cover the pan with its lid, reduce the heat to low, and cook for 30 minutes.

After 30 minutes, remove the lid and continue to let your herby beef cook, uncovered, stirring occasionally, for up to an additional 30 minutes, or until most if not all the liquid has evaporated from the pan.

Meanwhile, turn your attention to your rice. Bring your stock to a simmer in a saucepan over a medium–high heat. Reduce the heat to low, cover, and keep the broth hot until you need it.

Heat the remaining 2 tablespoons of oil in a wide saucepan over a medium heat. Add the rest of your diced onion, along with ½ teaspoon of salt, and sauté for 3–5 minutes, or until soft. Add the rest of your chopped herbs to the pan, stir to mix, and sauté them for 60–90 seconds, or until wilted and fragrant. Now add the rice to the pan and cook, stirring constantly, for 1 minute to lightly toast the rice grains.

Add a ladleful of your simmering stock to the rice pan. Cook, stirring near constantly with a wooden spoon, until the rice has absorbed nearly all the liquid. Repeat this process, one ladleful of stock at a time, for 20–25 minutes, stirring near constantly, until your rice is just tender but retains a slight bite, and the entire mixture is creamy but neither stodgy nor soupy. Taste and add salt and/or black pepper to taste.

To serve, ladle your herby risotto into shallow bowls or plates, then spoon some of the beef mixture on top. If you like, sprinkle some candied barberries, ground cinnamon, toasted flaked almonds, and/or extra herbs over each serving. Or not. Your call.

RICE

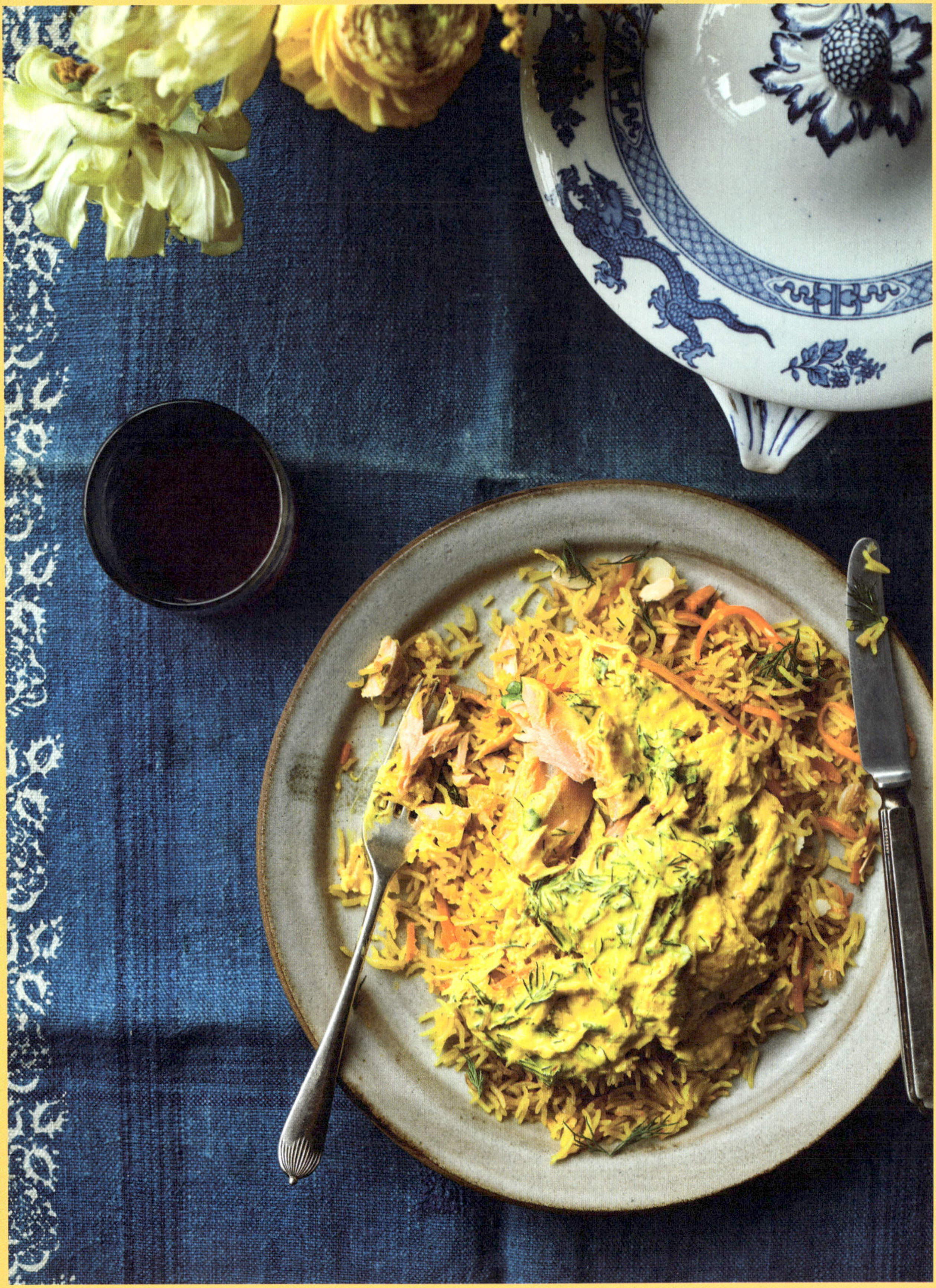

TURKMEN FISH RICE

Serves 4–6

This dish comes to us from Turkmenistan's Caspian coastline, where it is typically made with sturgeon, the whiskered grey fish responsible for the dear Beluga caviar. I don't like sturgeon, so I'm not sorry that I can't get it in the UK or the US, and that I can't recommend you use it for this recipe. Salmon works perfectly here, but any firm-fleshed fish (e.g., cod, halibut, or trout) will do – and I suppose if you do have some sturgeon on hand, you could use it, if you must.

- 500g (1lb 2oz) basmati rice
- 2 tbsp plus 2 tsp fine sea salt
- 4 fish fillets (see above)
- 200g (7oz) parsley root or celeriac, peeled and grated
- 20g (¾oz) fresh dill, chopped, plus extra to serve
- 25g (scant 1oz) fresh mint, stems included
- ½ tbsp black peppercorns
- 1 bay leaf
- 4 garlic cloves, 1 whole, 3 minced
- 2 onions, 1 finely diced, 1 quartered
- 120ml (½ cup/4fl oz) sesame oil
- 200g (7oz) carrots, peeled and cut into matchsticks
- 1 tsp fennel seeds
- 1 tsp cumin seeds
- 1g saffron, ground with ¼ tsp granulated sugar using a mortar and pestle, and then brewed with 4 tbsp hot water
- 15g (½oz) fresh flat-leaf parsley, chopped, plus extra to serve
- 2 tsp freshly ground black pepper
- ½ tsp dried chilli flakes
- ½ tsp ground cumin
- ¼ tsp ground coriander
- 1½ tsp cornflour
- 2 egg yolks
- 500g (1lb 2oz) full-fat Greek yogurt, at room temperature
- 1 tbsp pomegranate molasses
- toasted flaked almonds, to serve (optional)

Rinse the rice 3–4 times in cold water, then tip into a large bowl of cold water, add 1 tablespoon of the salt, and leave to soak for at least 1 hour.

Pat your fish dry with paper towels, season it with salt and pepper, and set it aside.

Pour 800ml (generous 3 cups/generous 1¼ pints) water into a medium straight-sided sauté pan for which you have a lid. Add half the grated parsley root or celeriac and half the dill, along with the mint, black peppercorns, bay leaf, the whole garlic clove, and the quartered onion. Cover and bring to the boil, then reduce the heat to medium–low and simmer for 5 minutes. After this, reduce the heat further – to the lowest possible setting. Slide your fish fillets into their liquid bathtub and poach, uncovered, for 2 minutes. You do not want to fully cook the fish here. (Is par-poaching a term? It is now. You only want to PAR-poach the fillets before removing them from the pan and setting them aside on a plate.)

Using a colander, strain the fish-poaching liquid into a bowl. You will use the aromatic broth shortly, so don't throw it away! Go ahead and discard those solid bits, though; you won't need them again.

In a medium saucepan for which you have a lid, heat the sesame oil over a medium–high heat. Add the diced onion, then reduce the heat to medium and cook for 5–7 minutes, or until the onion starts to turn golden brown. Add the minced garlic, carrots, and fennel and cumin seeds, and stir everything together. Cook for a further 5–7 minutes, stirring occasionally, or until the carrots have softened slightly.

Use this time to drain your rice and rinse it in clean cold water.

Add the rice and 1 tablespoon of the salt to the pan with the onion mixture. Stir everything together well before using your cooking implement of choice to spread everything out in an even layer, gently pressing it down as needed.

The rice needs to be cooked in 800ml (generous 3 cups/generous 1¼ pints) of liquid – a combination of the fish-poaching broth and water. Measure how much broth you have reserved, and top up that amount with water until you have the right quantity. Carefully pour this liquid in the pan, drizzling it around, or pouring it in at an angle at the edge of the pot so as to not disturb the rice. Drizzle in half of the saffron and its water too. Increase the heat to medium, cover, and cook for 25 minutes.

Now, wrap the lid of the pan in a clean tea towel and put the towelled lid back on the pan. Turn off the heat and let your rice sit, towelled and undisturbed, for 25 minutes.

In the same pan you used to par-poach your fish, combine the remaining dill and grated parsley root or celeriac. Add the rest of the saffron water and 2 teaspoons of the salt, then stir in the chopped parsley, black pepper, chilli flakes, ground cumin and coriander, cornflour, egg yolks, and yogurt. Stir everything together to mix well.

Warm this mixture slowly over a low heat. Be gentle with it, watching closely and frequently stirring. You don't want it to curdle (not just yet, at least), and ostensibly, this low-and-slow method (along with the cornflour) should prevent that. Once the yogurt is warm, use a spatula to carefully add the fish. Warm your fish through in the yogurt sauce, still over a low heat, until it is fully cooked, about 7–10 minutes. (Oh, and by now it will likely have curdled. No getting around that. But it'll still be delicious – and beautiful.)

Serve your fish on a platter with some of the yogurt sauce. Top with additional parsley and/or dill. Dish up your rice, fluffing it nicely with a fork as you remove it from the pot, and serve alongside the fish, drizzled with the pomegranate molasses. Toss some dill fronds on for good measure, and scatter over some toasted flaked almonds too.

Eat the fish and rice together, marvelling at how extraordinarily well all these flavours work.

SHILA PLAVI

Georgian Mushroom "Risotto"

Serves 4–6

Unlike in neighbouring Azerbaijan (not to mention Iran, Uzbekistan, and, frankly, most of Asia – Central, East, South, and South East), rice plays a very limited role in Georgian cuisine. Indeed, this dish – *shila plavi* – is little known outside the country, as it is most often seen and served at funerals. While typically made with lamb, mushrooms may be substituted for the ovine, as I have done here – a choice born from my desire to feed my vegetarian mother and sister, and all the other vegetarians I know and don't know. Plus, as a rule, mushroom risotto is delicious, and *shila plavi* is essentially a delicious spiced Georgian mushroom risotto.

Shila plavi is also essentially a way of saying goodbye. Most Georgian meals, most *supras*, are informal affairs, with diners, guests, and plates of food lingering for hours. Courses are not part of the Georgian mealtime lexicon. Among other things, breads and cheeses from the start of the meal remain on the table until is it cleared at the end of the night, enabling diners to return to salty snacks even after sweets and tea have been served; a savoury bite of *sulguni* cheese makes a perfect accompaniment to the seventh or tenth of many toasts. However, this casual *longueur* is not how funeral *supras* work. The arrival of *shila plavi* at a funeral is the bereaved family's polite way of telling their guests it's time to leave. Enjoy some rice and then leave us to our grief, *shila plavi* says; leave us to our loss, leave us to our tears and memories, but do please leave us now. Stop all the clocks and cut off the toasts. It is time to say goodbye … in an exceptionally delicious, risotto-y manner.

- 80g (3oz) dried mushrooms
- 4 tbsp olive oil
- 60g (2oz) unsalted butter
- 1 onion, diced
- 1¾ tsp fine sea salt
- 2 garlic cloves, minced
- 400g (14oz) mushrooms, roughly diced (I like ceps, oysters, and/or chanterelles for this, as they are all native to Georgia)
- 1 tbsp cumin seeds
- 2 tsp whole black peppercorns
- 300g (10oz) risotto rice
- 240ml (1 cup/8fl oz) dry amber, orange or white wine

To serve (optional)
- truffle oil
- grated Pecorino or halloumi cheese
- shaved truffles

Add your dried mushrooms to a medium saucepan and pour in 2.5 litres (10½ cups/4½ pints) water. Bring to the boil over a high heat, then reduce the heat to low and simmer for 30 minutes. After 30 minutes, strain into a bowl, reserving the mushroom solids (you can roughly dice these, or leave them whole if they are already tiny). Set aside the mushroom stock and the solids.

Meanwhile, heat the oil and butter in a large sauté pan over a medium heat. Once the butter melts, add the diced onion and ¼ teaspoon of the salt. Cook, stirring occasionally, for 5–7 minutes, or until the onion turns a light golden brown. Stir in the garlic and cook for another 30 seconds until fragrant, then add both the fresh and rehydrated mushrooms to the pan, along with a further ½ teaspoon of the salt. Cook, stirring occasionally, for 8–10 minutes, or until most of the water the mushrooms release has evaporated and the fungi have turned a lovely golden brown.

Meanwhile, using a mortar and pestle, roughly grind together the cumin seeds and peppercorns, then set aside.

Add your rice to the mushroom pan and cook, stirring constantly, for 1 minute to lightly toast the grains. Add the ground cumin and peppercorns, as well as a final teaspoon of salt, and stir to mix well.

Next up: add your wine and cook, stirring frequently, until the liquid has nearly evaporated and the alcohol has cooked off.

Pour the mushroom stock back into the saucepan you used earlier and bring it to a simmer over a low heat.

Add a ladleful of your simmering stock to the rice pan. Cook, stirring near constantly with a wooden spoon, until the rice has absorbed nearly all the liquid. Repeat this process, one ladleful of stock at a time, for 20–25 minutes, stirring near constantly, until your rice is just tender but retains a slight bite, and the entire mixture is creamy but neither stodgy nor soupy. Taste and add more salt and/or black pepper to taste. If you have extra mushroom broth left over, freeze that umami gold and save it for later!

To serve, ladle your *shila plavi* into shallow bowls or plates. If you like, top with a drizzle of truffle oil, and some grated Pecorino or halloumi – or, if you're feeling super flush, shave some fresh truffle over the top.

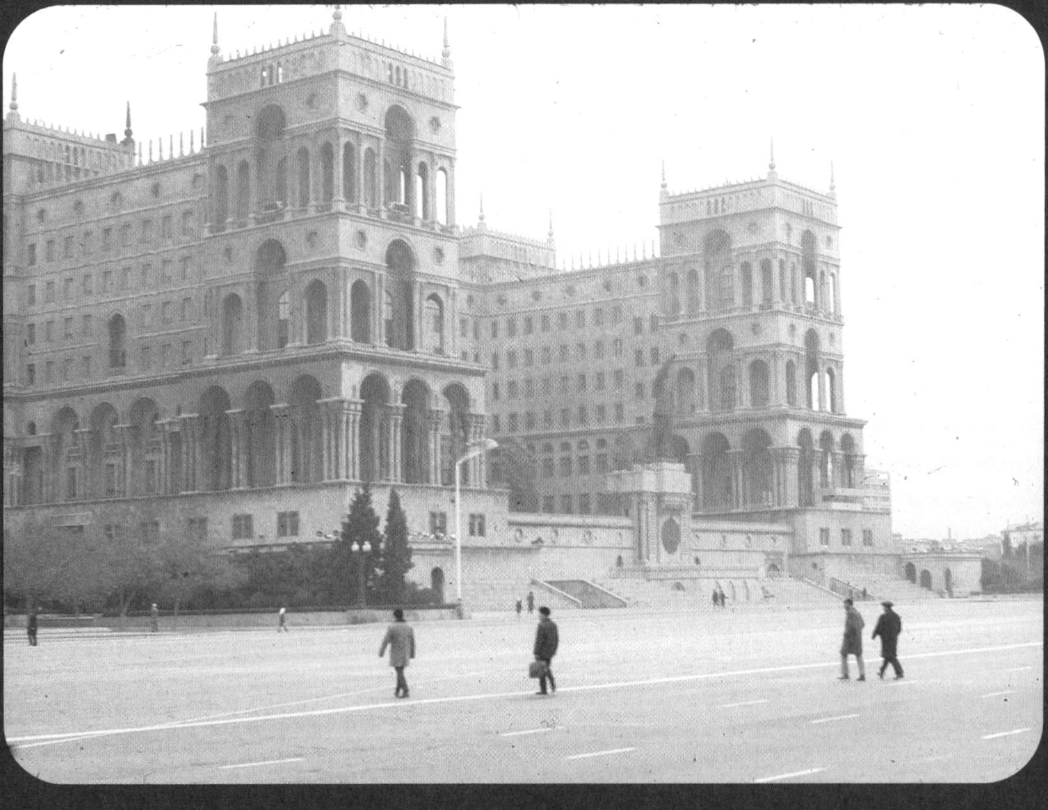

NOODLES

LES PÂTES DES ROUTES DE LA SOIE
162

BESHBARMAK
"Five Fingers" Noodles with Beef
167

KHINGAL
Azeri Noodles with Crispy Minced Lamb
168

A MEMORY OF LAMIAN
Uyghur Lamb Noodles
171

SHIVIT OSHI
Khivan Green Noodles with Beef Stew
173

COLD SESAME NOODLES
177

CHEESEBURGER MAKARONI
178

FUNCHOZA
Uyghur Vermicelli with Minced Meat
181

LES PÂTES DES ROUTES DE LA SOIE

I first learned to make *laghman*, the iconic Central Asian noodle dish beloved and claimed by Uzbeks, Kazakhs, Uyghurs, and Krygyz alike, and whose name is a derivative loanword from the Chinese *la mian* ("pulled noodles"), at Barchinoy's plastic-covered table in a village 45 minutes outside of Samarkand.

Barchinoy was strikingly beautiful, with an impish smile and a laugh that suggested a youthful soul and spirit, even though she was at least as old as me. Fluent in both French and Russian, on top of Uzbek, of course, Barchinoy knew only a smattering of English – which is how I ended up taking my first *laghman* instruction in the language of Voltaire. Maybe you're thinking, as I did: *How romantic, how charming, but how totally bizarre for an American to learn how to make Central Asian noodles in French, in a village in Uzbekistan some 5,000 kilometres from the Arc de Triomphe. But I bet you're not thinking: Of course, she's learning* laghman *in French – go fucking figure, how hilariously full-circle*. Because that's what I was thinking.

My French lessons began at age five, at a Montessori school in Monroe, Michigan, a small town near the Ohio border, where my mother was born and raised, and where my father's medical clinic was located. My French teacher, Farimah, was an Iranian immigrant whose presence in Michigan was the result of my father's employment of her gastroenterologist husband, Akbar, in his clinic. The daughter of one of Iran's top endocrinologists, Farimah – unlike my father, whose hometown was a mid-sized one – grew up in the big city of Tabriz. We forget sometimes how Western and how cosmopolitan pre-Islamic Revolution Iran was – "the Paris of the Middle East" is how so many described Tehran in the 1960s and 1970s. And in the Paris of the Middle East, as well as its provincial capitals such as Tabriz, there were French schools.

From a young age, Farimah's entire education was conducted in French and taught by Lazarist Catholic nuns at Tabriz's all-female St Vincent de Paul School. From the mid-20th century onwards, a French education was relatively commonplace, not only for the daughters of Iran's wealthy elite, but also for those of educated, professional, upper-middle-class families such as Farimah's. This meant that when Farimah and Akbar emigrated to the United States, Farimah brought with her both unsurpassable Iranian cooking skills (her party spreads were epic) and French language fluency. And so, like her, I learned French from a young age. While my speaking ability has lapsed over the years, my comprehension is more than passable – and sufficiently *biao jun*, as they'd say in Mandarin – for me to follow Barchinoy's *laghman* instructions on a spring day in a village in Uzbekistan.

As the midday sun poured into her kitchen, Barchinoy told me: *"D'abord, vous vous huilez les mains, puis vous roulez la pâte. Rapidement. Ton mari doit nous aider aussi!"* So, as requested and required by our French-speaking Uzbek teacher, I roped in my *mari* Ed, asking him to join us in oiling our hands and rolling out the dough, very quickly – as *rapidement* as possible – grinning inwardly and

> WE FORGET SOMETIMES HOW WESTERN AND HOW COSMOPOLITAN PRE-ISLAMIC REVOLUTION IRAN WAS – "THE PARIS OF THE MIDDLE EAST" IS HOW SO MANY DESCRIBED TEHRAN IN THE 1960S AND 1970S.

Top: Prepping to make some *biang biang* noodles. Xian, China. April 2024.

Bottom: A peek into the Aminov family's kitchen in Kokand, Uzbekistan. March 2024.

outwardly, the irony of the situation not lost upon me. Here I was, the daughter of a Turkic man who had not taught me his language – a language that, although not identical to Barchinoy's native Uzbek, was so closely related that had I known it, I may have had an entirely different, Turkic-language based *laghman* class. Instead, I was able to understand my noodle teacher because I'd once had an Azeri-Iranian French teacher whose presence in my life and education was indirectly my father's doing. What a world. What a life.

My dad hates noodles. He claims he and my mother didn't want to take us to Italy when we were children because they thought it was unsafe; I think it's because he didn't want to visit a country whose cuisine and culture is so noodle-heavy. The only time I recall having pasta growing up was either in the form of pre-packaged spinach-and-cheese tortellini from the refrigerated section of a Kroger, or fettucine alfredo at a rare meal out at The Olive Garden. And then everything changed, and 15-year-old me went to China.

July 23, 1997. They gave me a massive bowl of noodles. On the second floor of a two-storey restaurant in the Yu Yuan Garden area of Shanghai. Gu Laoshi told me I couldn't break the noodles – that I needed to slurp them up whole, long. I had learned how to wield chopsticks only a week prior, at my first ever meal in China, which I vividly recall included opaque and chewy-looking white-ish rings of jellyfish that I refused to sample. The whole experience was challenging – the chopsticks, the jellyfish, the snakes curled and cured and soaking in the large glass jars on a neighbouring table. So, to now be told not only that I must eat my 16th-birthday noodles with chopsticks, but also that I could not break them or I would risk a year of bad luck (and I couldn't do that: I had college to apply to!), was a lot of pressure. I definitely broke the noodles and, though I did not get into Georgetown as I wanted, I was accepted at Barnard, so my 16th year on this earth worked out pretty well, if you ask me. Had I got into Georgetown, maybe I would not have taken a year off to return to China, to go to Beijing and to eat *another* bowl of noodles – the one that changed my life (see p13). Broken noodles, be damned!

I didn't know it then, but when I had that oh-so-memorable bowl of Uyghur noodles in that alleyway in Beijing's Ganjiakou neighbourhood, I was eating a microcosm of history. I was eating millennia worth of influences, traditions, stories, memories, connections, and culture. I was eating a story of trade, of travel, of homesickness, of assimilation, of belonging, of everything, everywhere, all at once. And 25 years later, in a village in Uzbekistan, a woman with whom I had perhaps little in common save our love of noodles and familiarity with a Romance language, taught me to make those noodles – or some variety of them, anyways.

I share that knowledge here with you, along with other noodle dishes of the Silk Roads, all related through either flavour, method, history, or culture, and, like everything in this book, all delicious. Feel free to play around with the recipes, to create and establish your own noodle dishes, to experiment with combinations and methods, to do what is right for your table, for your palate, for you. As for me, I love them all, and hope you will too.

> **I HAD LEARNED HOW TO WIELD CHOPSTICKS ONLY A WEEK PRIOR, AT MY FIRST EVER MEAL IN CHINA.**

Left: Prepping to make some *laghman*. Kokand, Uzbekistan. March 2024.

Bottom: Barchinoy dishing up our *laghman*. Outside Samarkand, Uzbekistan. March 2024.

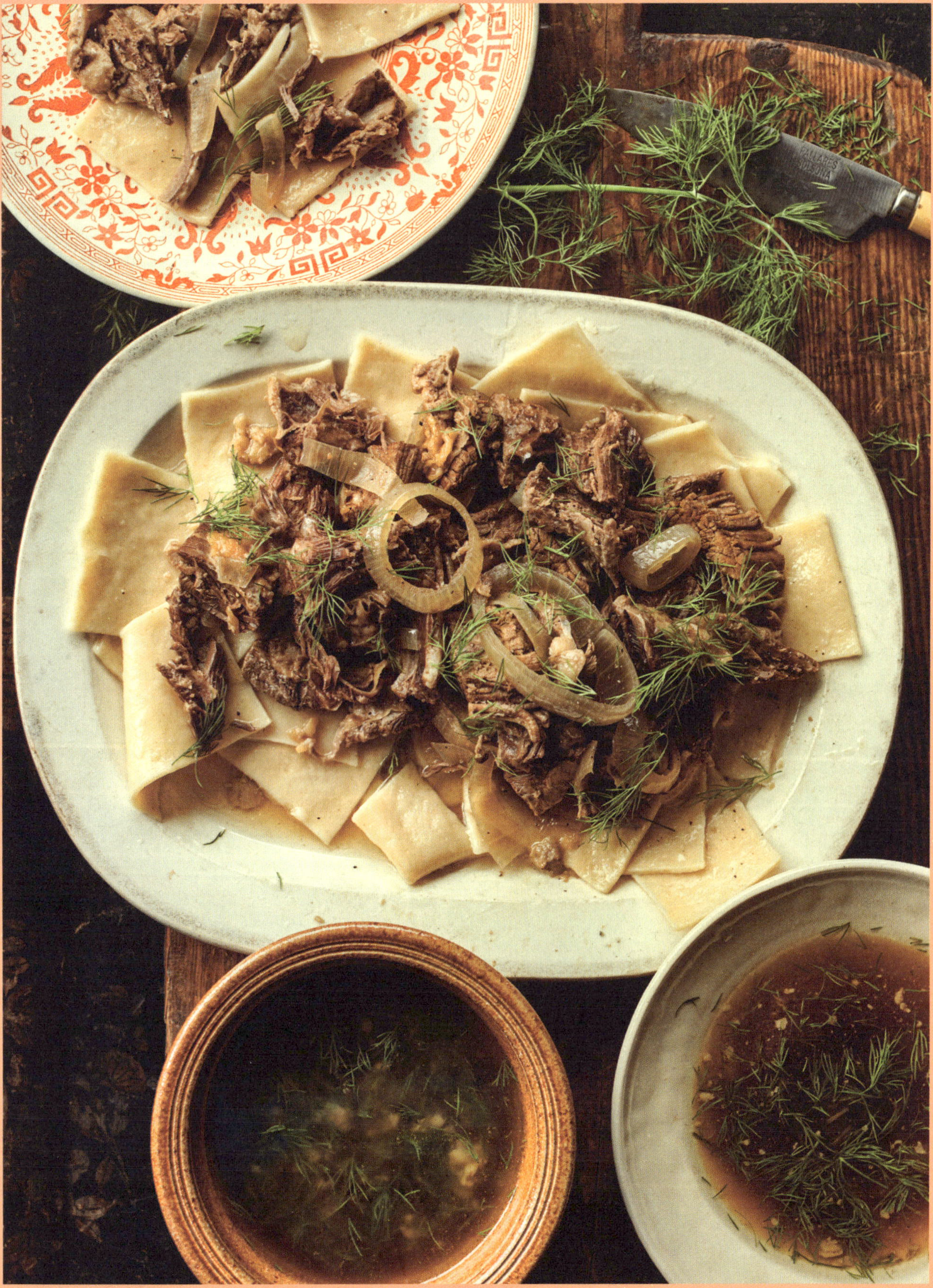

BESHBARMAK

"Five Fingers" Noodles with Beef

Serves 4–6

Claimed by both Kazakhstan and Kyrgyzstan as each country's emblematic "national" dish, *beshbarmak* is a simple preparation of noodles, boiled meat, and onions. The word *beshbarmak* itself means "five fingers", a reference to the fact that it was traditionally eaten by hand. I ate it in Uzbekistan, where the dish goes by the name *naryn*, and definitely used a knife and fork to do so. Traditionally, *beshbarmak* is also made with horsemeat; my recipe calls for beef short ribs. Sometimes tradition is great; other times, less so.

- 2kg (4½lb) beef short ribs
- 3 litres (12⅔ cups/5¼ pints) water or beef stock
- 1 onion, halved
- 1 tsp black peppercorns
- 25g (scant 1oz) fresh flat-leaf parsley, stems included
- 2 red onions, sliced into rings
- 10g (¼oz) fresh dill, roughly chopped, plus extra to serve
- flaky sea salt and freshly ground black pepper

For the noodles
- 1 egg
- 300g (10oz) plain flour (or '00' flour, if you've got it), plus extra for dusting
- ½ tsp fine sea salt, plus extra for cooking

To a large stockpot for which you have a lid, add the meat, water or stock, onion, peppercorns, and parsley. Cover and bring to the boil over a high heat. Once boiling, remove the lid and skim off any foam that has risen to the top. Reduce the heat to low and simmer, uncovered, for 2–3 hours, occasionally skimming off any foam from the surface.

Meanwhile, make your noodles. In a bowl, use a fork to whisk together the egg and 100ml (6½ tbsp/3½fl oz) room-temperature water.

Sift the flour and salt together into the bowl of a stand mixer fitted with a dough hook. Mix them together at a low speed, then, with the mixer still running, slowly pour in the egg and water mixture. Increase the mixer's speed to medium and let it work its magic, pausing occasionally to ensure the flour from the sides of the bowl is being well incorporated, and using a spatula to scrape those sides down if it's not. After 5–7 minutes, you should have a pliable dough that is tacky to the touch but does not stick to your hands.

Form the dough into a ball and leave it in its bowl, covered with a tea towel or cling film, to rest for 30 minutes.

When your dough has finished resting, lightly dust a baking tray with flour and generously dust your work surface with flour. Cut your dough in two, returning one piece to the covered bowl. Take the other piece and roll it out into a large rectangle about 3mm (⅛in) thick, either by hand, or by using a pasta attachment for your stand mixer or a stand-alone pasta maker if you have one in your kitchen arsenal.

With a sharp knife, cut the rolled-out dough into 5cm (2in) diamonds or squares, then transfer your cut noodles to the floured baking tray and dust them with some additional flour so that they don't stick to one another. Repeat for your second piece of dough, then set your noodles aside until I tell you otherwise.

After 2–3 hours, your beef should be well-cooked and falling off the bone. Turn off the heat and, with tongs or a spider, remove the cooked meat from the pot to a plate. Retain the liquid in the pot; you will use it later.

Once it's cool enough to handle, pull the soft beef off the bones into 2–3cm (¾–1¼in) pieces with your hands. Using our five fingers here is a symbolic, respectful nod to the dish's name, beauty, simplicity, and ritual.

When you've finished, set aside the hand-pulled beef. Either discard the bones, save them to make stock, or give them to your dog.

Turn your attention to your broth. Using a fine mesh sieve, strain the liquid from your stock pot into a large bowl. Then, return your strained broth to the pot, along with the sliced red onions and hand-torn beef. Place over a low heat and simmer for 10 minutes.

Meanwhile, to cook your noodles, bring a large pot of well-salted water to a boil. Once boiling, gently lower your noodles into the pot and cook them for 2–3 minutes. Then, using a slotted spoon or spider, gently lift your noodles out and give them a little shimmy over the sink to shake off any excess water.

Place the noodles on a platter and spoon a small amount of broth over them. Now grab that slotted spoon or spider again. Use it to extricate the beef and onions from the broth, plopping them right on top of the noodles, along with a handful of dill fronds, some flaky sea salt, and a good grind of black pepper.

Add the rest of your dill to the pot of broth. Ladle up and serve the dilly broth in individual bowls alongside the platter of beef and noodles. Dig in. With your five fingers, if you want.

KHINGAL

Azeri Noodles with Crispy Minced Lamb

Serves 4–6

"**He's KGB. He's KBG. He's KGB.** I don't know him. That one's KGB too. Not that guy over there, though." My dad quietly shared these bits of knowledge with me, along with a few (relatively) discreet head nods in the direction of each of the men in question. It was January 2016, and we were in the process of being seated in a small, windowless private dining room in Baku, KGB and non-KGB folk alike. Implicit in my father's description of our fellow diners, of course, was the prefix "ex", as these men, though supposedly once part of the long-dismantled Soviet intelligence community, were now upstanding businessmen and industry leaders in the free-since-1991 independent Republic of Azerbaijan. I don't know what their names were, but I can probably dig out their business cards if pushed. I was the only woman in the room. Naturally.

Soon enough, the table was heaving with food. Pomegranates. Pickles. Cheese. Platters of olives, tomatoes, herbs, cucumbers. Baskets of bread. Bowls of yogurt. Wine glasses filled with fresh pomegranate juice. Small shot glasses filled with vodka, and then filled again, and again, and again. Where was the main meal, I wondered, as I not-so-slowly-but-most-assuredly became quite drunk. Everyone was. Even my generally teetotalling dad.

And then the *khingal* appeared. One by one, the waiters gave us each our own massive platter, covered with broad, flat, thin pasta. The noodles looked like a cross between sheets of lasagne and ribbons of pappardelle, while also being their own entirely distinctive selves. Dollops of caramelized onions were dotted across the noodles. A waiter made the rounds, spooning crispy minced lamb over the top. Another server followed, offering lashes of what looked like sour cream. I didn't know what was going on. I was drunk with my dad and a bunch of ex-KGB dudes in a windowless dining room in Azerbaijan in the middle of winter, and I had definitely not been expecting pasta for dinner. And I know my father, an avowed hater of noodles, had not either. But there we were, and there was the *khingal* – and it was everything.

I fell in love that night. With *khingal*, that is. With a noodle dish that was simultaneously novel and familiar. It reminded me of a deconstructed *pierogi* – but it had flavours that danced on my tongue in a way nothing at my beloved Polish haunts in Greenpoint, Brooklyn ever had. Cha cha cha. It was totally new and hearty and satisfying and exceptional. But maybe that was the vodka talking. I don't think so, though; try this recipe and you be the judge.

For the noodles

1 egg

300g (10oz) plain flour (or '00' flour, if you've got it), plus extra for dusting

½ tsp fine sea salt, plus extra for cooking

For the caramelized onions

40g (scant 1½oz) unsalted butter

4 tbsp olive oil

3 onions, thinly sliced into half-moons

1 tsp fine sea salt

1 tsp red wine vinegar

For the lamb topping

1 tbsp olive oil

30g (1oz) unsalted butter or 3 tbsp ghee

500g (1lb 2oz) minced lamb

1 tsp fine sea salt

½ tsp coarsely ground black pepper

0.25g saffron, ground with ⅛ tsp granulated sugar using a mortar and pestle, and then brewed with 2 tbsp hot water

For the yogurt topping

500g (1lb 2oz) plain yogurt

4 garlic cloves, grated

To serve

60g (2oz) unsalted butter, melted (optional)

We begin with our noodles. In a bowl, use a fork to whisk together the egg and 100ml (6½ tbsp/3½fl oz) room-temperature water.

Sift the flour and salt together into the bowl of a stand mixer fitted with a dough hook. Mix them together at a low speed, then, with the mixer still running, slowly pour in the egg and water mixture. Increase the mixer's speed to medium and let it work its magic, pausing occasionally at the start to ensure the flour from the sides of the bowl is being well incorporated, and using a spatula to scrape those sides down if it's not. After 5–7 minutes, you should have a pliable dough that is tacky to the touch but does not stick to your hands.

Form the dough into a ball and leave it in its bowl, covered with a tea towel or cling film, to rest for 30 minutes.

While you wait, get to near-caramelizing your onions. Heat the butter and oil in a large sauté pan over a medium heat. Once the butter has melted, add the sliced onions and salt. Stir, and reduce the heat to its lowest setting. Cook the onions for 25–30 minutes, or until they turn not-quite-caramelized: you want some to be dark brown and others to be lighter in colour. You will need to check in on and stir the onions occasionally to make sure they are neither burning nor sticking to the pan; if they threaten to do either, add a tablespoon of water.

Once your onions are near-caramelized, stir the vinegar through them. Remove the onions from the pan, set them aside and return to your dough.

When your dough has finished resting, lightly dust a baking tray with flour and generously dust your work surface with flour. Cut your dough in two, returning one piece to the covered bowl. Take the other piece and roll it out into a large rectangle about 3mm (⅛in) thick, either by hand, or by using a pasta attachment for your stand mixer or a stand-alone pasta maker if you have one in your kitchen arsenal.

With a sharp knife, cut the rolled-out dough into 5cm (2in) diamonds or squares, then transfer your cut noodles to the floured baking tray, and dust them with some additional flour so that they don't stick to one another. Repeat for your second piece of dough, then set your noodles aside until I tell you otherwise.

Now for your lamb topping! Heat the oil and butter or ghee in a large sauté pan (the same one you used for the onions, if you like) over a medium–high heat. Add the lamb, salt, and pepper. Use a wooden spoon to break up and cook the mince for 10 minutes, or until its pinkness is entirely gone, and it's also nearly crisping up, with some of the fat having cooked off. The pan may start sputtering hot oil, so prepare yourself accordingly. Tip the saffron and its water into the pan and stir through the meat. Remove the pan from the heat and set it aside.

As for the garlicky yogurt, simply mix the grated garlic through the yogurt.

To cook your noodles, bring a large pot of well-salted water to the boil. Once boiling, lower your noodle diamonds into the water. Cook for 2–3 minutes then, using a slotted spoon or spider, gently lift your noodles out and give them a little shimmy over the sink to shake off any excess water.

Though I generally favour serving crowd-friendly meals on a massive platter, I find *khingal* is best served and plated individually. Accordingly, place a portion of cooked noodles on each diner's plate. If you like, drizzle a bit of melted butter over each portion of noodles. Follow the butter with a spoonful of the lamb topping, a few dollops of garlicky yogurt, and some caramelized onions.

Vodka time? Vodka time.

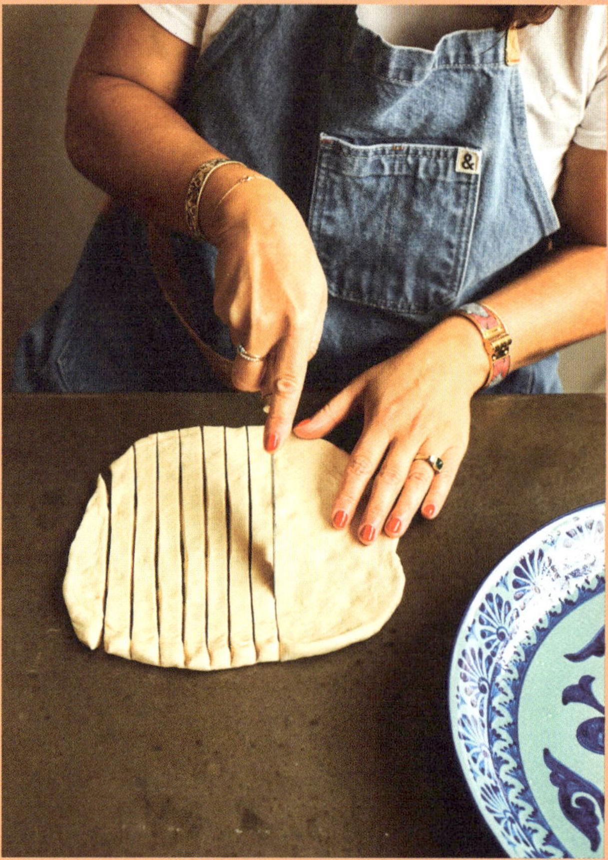
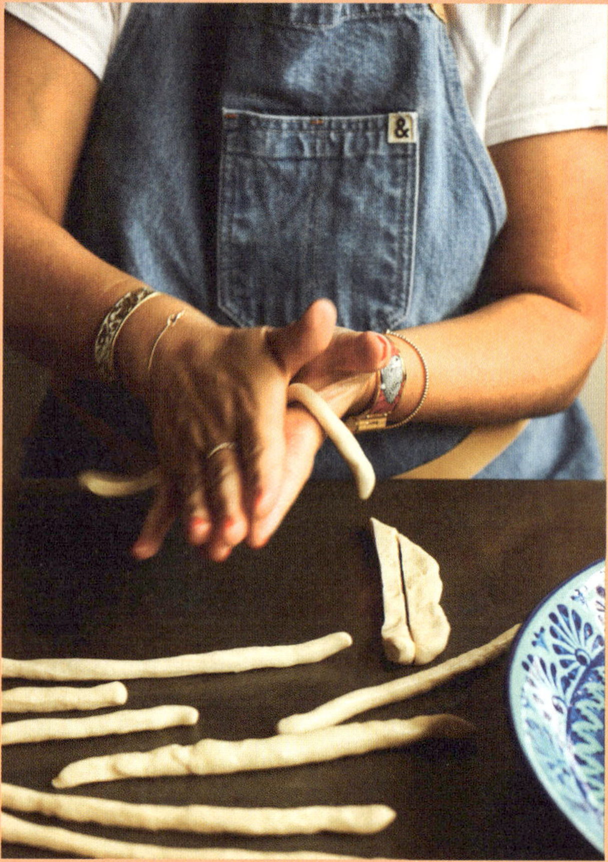
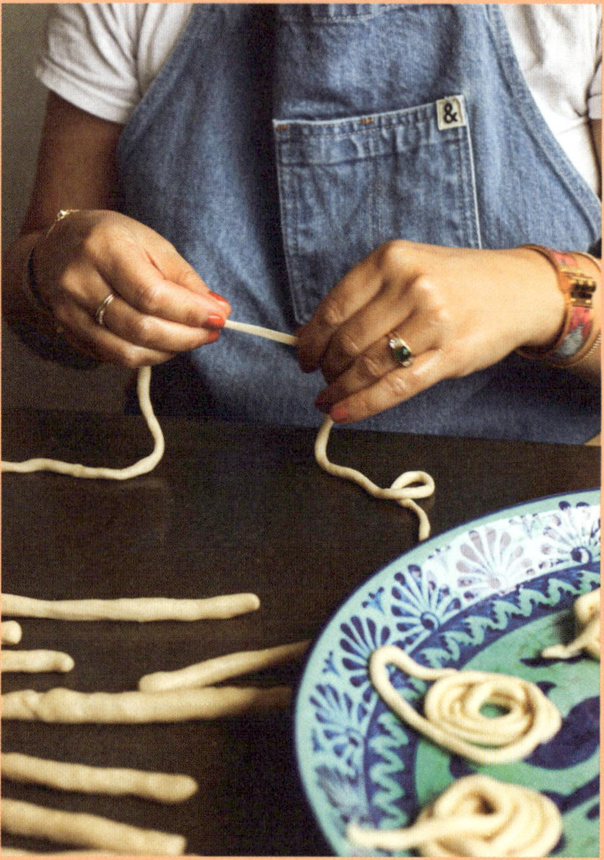
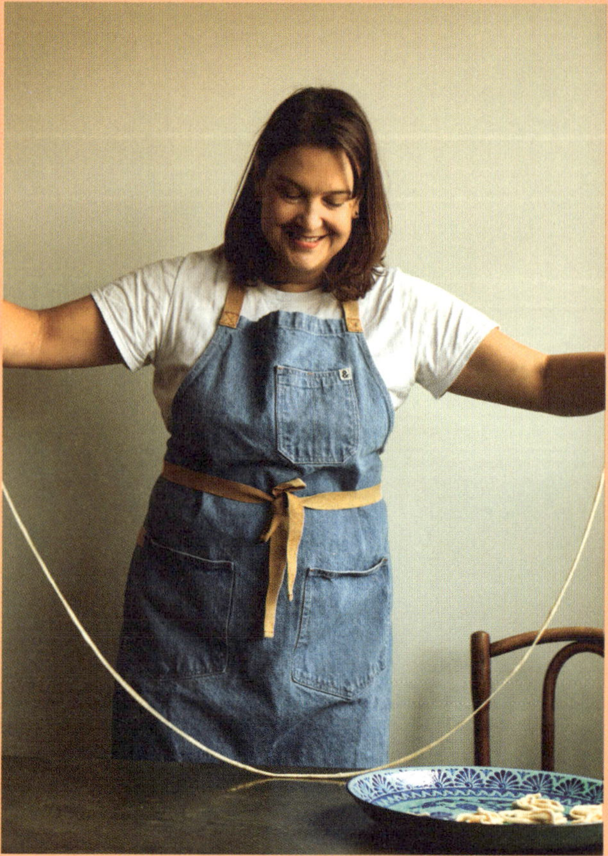

A MEMORY OF LAMIAN

Uyghur Lamb Noodles

Serves 4–6

This dish is a translation of a memory. It is as close to that early September day in 1998 (see p13) as I will ever – can ever – get. And that's OK. It's life. We cannot go back. I learned that right around then as well, while reading my forever favourite book, Paul Bowles' *The Sheltering Sky*, for the first time.

I have tried, since then, as did the novel's main character, to be a traveller – not a tourist – when I leave home, to confront both myself and my native culture, to reevaluate my values, assumptions, and worldviews based on experiences, sights, scenes, smells, tastes, conversations, and feelings encountered when I travel. Paul Bowles gave teenage me that. And he also gave me this, a maxim to live by, a reminder to cherish the present, to relish in the now – because you can't go back, ever: "One never took the time to savour the details; one said: another day, but always with the hidden knowledge that each day was unique and fatal, that there never would be a return, another time." He also gave Kit the fuzzy end of the proverbial lollipop, if you ask me, but that's neither here nor there.

In any event, I can't go back to that alleyway in Beijing, no matter how I sometimes wish I could. I will never have the mind-blowing epiphany of a teenage girl from Michigan, tasting her first bowl of Uyghur *lamian*; but at least I can have this, and at least I can give it to you.

I've also given you a recipe and method for making hand-pulled noodles, just like Barchinoy taught me that day in the outskirts of Samarkand (see p162), but feel free to use pre-packaged noodles. There are so many great ones available at Asian supermarkets these days that I only pull my own noodles when I'm really feeling nostalgic. And, while you can easily use lamb here, I urge you to use mutton instead, as the more mature meat lends the dish a much-deserved deeper, richer flavour.

- 325g (11½oz) mutton or lamb rump, cut into 3 × 3 × 1cm (1¼ × 1¼ × ½in) pieces
- 3 tbsp neutral oil
- ½ onion, cut into 3cm (1¼in) chunks
- 1 pepper (colour of your choosing), cut into 3cm (1¼in) chunks
- 2 finger chillies (optional)
- 200g (7oz) tomatoes, cut into 1–3cm (½–1¼in) wedges
- 3 fat garlic cloves, minced
- 2 tsp ground cumin
- ½ tsp cumin seeds, toasted
- 75g (2½oz) green beans (or Chinese long beans if you can find them), trimmed and cut into 5cm (2in) pieces
- 325g (11½oz) tomato passata
- 4 tbsp stock (preferably lamb)

For the marinade

- 1½ tsp ground Sichuan peppercorns
- 1 tsp fine sea salt
- ½ tsp ground white pepper
- 1 tsp ground cumin
- ⅛ tsp MSG
- ½ tsp cumin seeds, toasted
- 1 tbsp Shaoxing wine
- ½ tbsp sesame oil

For the noodles

- 200g (7oz) plain flour
- 1 tsp fine sea salt, plus extra for cooking
- olive oil

Add your marinade ingredients to a medium mixing bowl, along with your meat. Stir to coat and set aside for 15–20 minutes.

Heat the oil in a wok (or a large sauté pan) over a medium–high heat, swirling the oil around to coat the base of the wok. When the oil shimmers, add the onion, pepper, and chillies (if using). Tip in your bowl of marinated lamb. Stir to combine, then cook, stirring occasionally, for 2–3 minutes, or until your meat is not too pink on the outside. Now add the tomatoes, garlic, cumin, cumin seeds, and green beans. Stir to mix and coat, and cook for 1 minute more.

Finally, add the tomato passata and stock. Stir to mix, and cook for 3 minutes, or until the sauce has reduced slightly. Turn off the heat and set aside while you make the noodles.

In a mixing bowl, using your (clean) hands, mix together the flour, salt, and 100ml (6½ tablespoons/ 3½fl oz) water. Once the mixture comes together into a dough, knead it for 2 minutes. Still in the mixing bowl, form your dough into a small ball and either spritz or brush the dough ball with oil, coating it on all sides before covering the bowl with a tea towel and leaving it to rest for 15 minutes.

Remove your dough from its resting place and, on a clean unfloured work surface, use the heel of your hand to press the dough down into a circle 25–28cm (10–11in) in diameter. Now use your knuckles to punch the dough down even further, puckering its surface in the process. With a sharp knife, cut your dough circle into strips 2cm (¾in) wide.

Lightly oil a large platter, and your hands as well. Get ready to make some noodles.

Working with one dough strip at a time, roll it out into a long cylindrical skein. Do this by either rolling the dough between the palms of your hands, or on your work surface, or a combination of the two. Leave each rolled-out noodle on your work surface until you have finished with all your dough strips and your kitchen looks like it's covered in long, skinny, noodley worms … that are about to get even longer.

Bring a large, well-salted pot of water to the boil. Have it at the ready.

Re-oil your hands. Then, take the first of your rolled-out noodles and use your fingertips to further thin and lengthen it, gently twisting and pulling the dough to do so, and loosely coiling the oiled noodle onto the oiled platter. Repeat with the rest.

Now stand up (if you've been sitting down). Grab one noodle coil. Hold an end in each hand. Gently move your hands further and further from one another until your arms are shoulder width apart and a skinny noodle hangs between them.

Quickly smack that skinny noodle down on to the table/workspace in front of you, continuing to hold onto its ends with your two hands. Gently move your arms wider as you lift the noodle up from the table, pulling it ever thinner and longer as you do so. Repeat this a couple times. (Or not, because your noodle will likely break, because, like me, you are not a noodle master. It's still fun to try, though, and it's still going to taste great!)

Drop the noodle into the boiling water, quickly returning to smack and pull another noodle and repeat the process until you have a mass of fresh noodles boiling in your pot. Barchinoy would be proud of you; I certainly am.

The noodles will be ready in 2–3 minutes; use this time to reheat the lamb. Strain the noodles from the pot and top them with lamby, tomatoey goodness.

SHIVIT OSHI

Khivan Green Noodles with Beef Stew

Serves 4–6

This and the Jujeh Brick Chicken Thighs (see p121) are my son's favourite dishes in this book. He is six years old, and not infrequently asks me to make him "green noodles". I usually yield to his request, in part because my husband and I also love *shivit oshi* and in part because I find it so delightfully charming that Theo loves beef stew-topped, dill-infused noodles from a (relatively) remote part of Uzbekistan: Khiva, in the country's western Khorezm region.

The noodles are actually quite easy, and the beef stew, reminiscent of a goulash, is straightforward as well. What is not easy, and what I have been unable to uncover, is the origin of this dish. Why dill? Why only in Khorezm, in Khiva? I'm stumped. Everyone I've asked – in and outside of Khiva – had a matter-of-fact answer that went nowhere beyond the perfunctory. "*Shivit oshi*? It is from Khiva. From Khorezm. It is an old dish." That's all I got; and that's not much. I can tell you this, though. Nearly 3,000 miles west of Khiva, in Xian (and nowhere else in China), you can find another bright green noodle dish. The noodles in the old Chinese dynastic capital, the old terminus/starting point of the Silk Roads, are made from spinach – but they weren't always. As local folklore would have it, during the early Tang Dynasty, courtiers and royalty were served green noodles that had been infused with leaves from pagoda trees. Plebs, eager to imitate culinary fashions of the court, began to make their own green noodles, but using spinach – which had recently been introduced to China via Nepal. Fast forward 2,100 years, and I'm slinging back a lukewarm, watery beer and slurping egg-and-tomato-topped spinach noodles on a sidewalk in Xian, two weeks after I learned to make *shivit oshi* in Khiva.

Now, I'm not saying there's a connection between the two noodle preparations, but there definitely *could* be. Right? Whatever *shivit oshi*'s origin, it's delicious. Plus, some say the English word "dill" comes from the Norse word *dylla*, which means "to soothe," and these dill noodles most definitely soothe me, my husband, and my son. I hope they will do the same for you.

For the green noodles

75g (2½oz) dill, plus extra to serve

1 egg

300g (10oz) plain flour (use '00' flour if you've got it), plus extra for dusting

½ tsp fine sea salt, plus extra for cooking

For the topping

500g (1lb 2oz) beef shin, diced

1½ tsp fine sea salt

1 tsp freshly ground black pepper

4 tbsp ghee or olive oil

1 onion, thinly sliced into half-moons

2 garlic cloves, minced

200g (7oz) peppers (colour of your choosing), cut into 2cm (¾in) pieces

1–2 spicy chillies (e.g. jalapeños), seeded and minced (optional, but highly recommended)

½ tsp hot or sweet smoked paprika

½ tsp ground cumin

2 tbsp tomato purée

250ml (1 cup plus 1 tbsp/9fl oz) milk

200g (7oz) tomatoes, roughly diced

300g (10oz) waxy potatoes, well washed or peeled and cut into 2cm (¾in) pieces

200g (7oz) carrots, peeled and cut into 2cm (¾in) pieces

plain yogurt, to serve

In a blender, blitz the dill for the noodles with 200ml (scant 1 cup/7fl oz) water. Once fully mixed, set your dilly water aside for at least 1 hour while you get started on the topping; this will give the dill time to infuse the water with colour and flavour.

Pat your meat dry with paper towels and season it on all sides with 1 teaspoon of the salt and the black pepper.

In a large sauté pan for which you have a lid, heat 1 tablespoon of the ghee or oil over a high heat. Once hot, add the meat, making sure you don't overcrowd the pan. Brown the meat on one side before turning it over and browning the other side; you'll know it's ready when it easily releases from the pan. For me, this process takes about 1 minute per side. Once browned, remove your beef from the pan and set it aside on a plate.

Reduce the heat to medium, and add the remaining 3 tablespoons of ghee or oil, along with your onion. Cook for 5–7 minutes, stirring occasionally, until softened and just starting to brown. Add the garlic, peppers, and chilli(es) (if using), along with the final ½ teaspoon of salt. Stir in the paprika and the cumin, then add the tomato purée. Stir again to coat and mix everything together well.

Return the meat to the pan, along with any juices released. Stir to combine. Deglaze the pan with the milk and leave everything to simmer for 13–15 minutes, still over a medium heat, or until the milk has almost completely evaporated and the sauce has turned a dark sienna in colour. Add 750ml (3 cups/1¼ pints) water, then reduce the heat to low and leave to simmer, with the lid on but slightly ajar, for 1½ hours. Set a timer so you don't forget.

Meanwhile, once the dill's infusion time is up, use a fine mesh sieve to strain the liquid into a bowl. Discard the dill and measure your water. It should be a shocking green. You will need only 100ml (6½ tbsp/3½fl oz) of the bright green water, or about half of what you've got. Discard the excess dilly water (or save it and make more noodles tomorrow!).

Use a fork to whisk the egg and dill water together in a bowl or jug with a pouring spout.

Sift the flour and salt together in the bowl of a stand mixer fitted with a dough hook. Mix at a low speed, then, with the mixer still running, slowly pour in the egg and dill water mixture. Increase the mixer's speed to medium and let it work its magic, pausing occasionally to ensure the flour from the sides of the bowl is being well incorporated, and using a spatula to scrape those sides down if it's not. After 5–7 minutes, you should have a pliable, semi-hard dough. Form the dough into a ball, then leave it in its bowl, covered with a tea towel or cling film, to rest for 1 hour.

When your dough has finished resting, lightly dust a baking tray with flour and generously dust your work surface with flour. Cut your dough in four, returning three pieces to the covered bowl. Take the other piece and roll it out into a rectangle about 1.5mm (1/16in) thick, either by hand, or by using a pasta attachment for your stand mixer or a stand-alone pasta maker if you have one in your kitchen arsenal. If rolling out by hand, rotate the dough as you work – this helps you achieve a more even thickness, and also ostensibly prevents the dough from sticking to your work surface.

Lightly dust the top of your thinly rolled out dough rectangle, then use your hands to roll it up lengthways into a log, starting with the edge closest to you. Your goal is a tight-ish log; keep in mind that the tighter you roll, the more likely it is that your dough will stick to itself, and you don't want that, but you also don't want an overly loose dough log that won't yield enough noodles.

Use a sharp knife to cut your dough log into rounds. If you prefer a wider noodle, cut your log into 2.5cm (1in) slices. If, like me, you prefer your noodles a bit thinner, cut your log into 6mm (¼in) slices. However wide you cut them, unfurl the strips as you go, gently shaking them out on to the prepared baking tray. Dust some flour on top of your unfurled noodles so that they don't stick to one another. Repeat with the rest of the dough, re-flouring your workspace before rolling out each piece.

At some point during this process (unless you are a super-speedy noodle-maker) your 1½-hour beef-topping timer will go off. When that happens, add the tomatoes and a further 250ml (1 cup plus 1 tbsp/9fl oz) water to your sauté pan. Stir, cover your pan once more, and leave to cook for another hour.

Once that hour is up, add your potatoes and carrots to the sauté pan, stir to combine and cook for a final 30 minutes, or until your meat is falling apart and your potatoes and carrots are fork tender.

When your topping is ready and your noodles are too, bring a large saucepan of well-salted water to the boil. Grab a handful of noodles, shake off any excess flour, and add them to the boiling water; repeat until all your noodles are in the pan. Cook for 2–3 minutes then, using a slotted spoon or spider, lift them out and give them a little shimmy over the sink to shake off any excess water.

Serve your noodles immediately, with a portion of topping ladled over them, a dollop of yogurt, and some dill fronds on top for good measure. Don't you love them? They're so green, and you made them from scratch! Smile. Good on you!

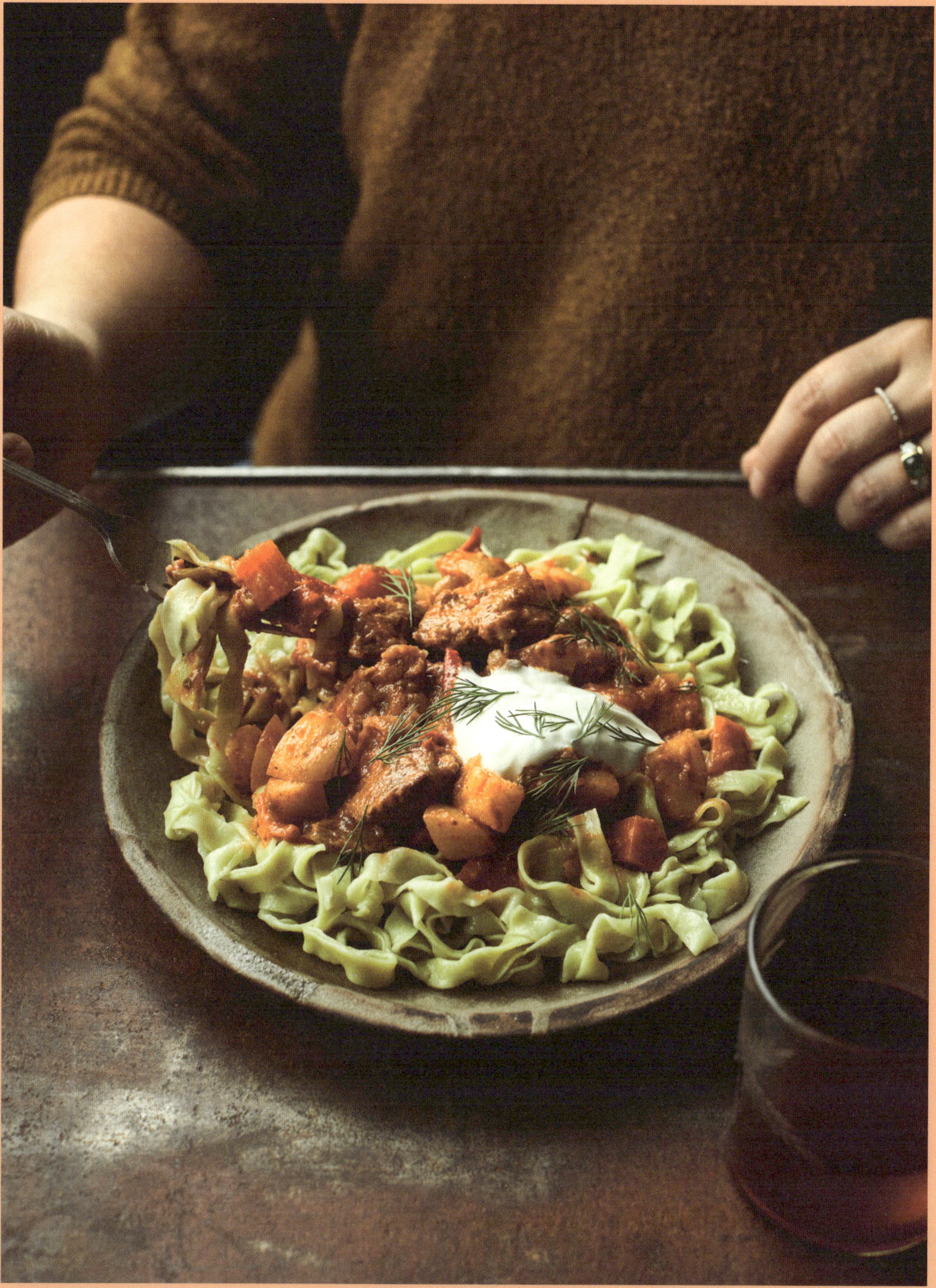

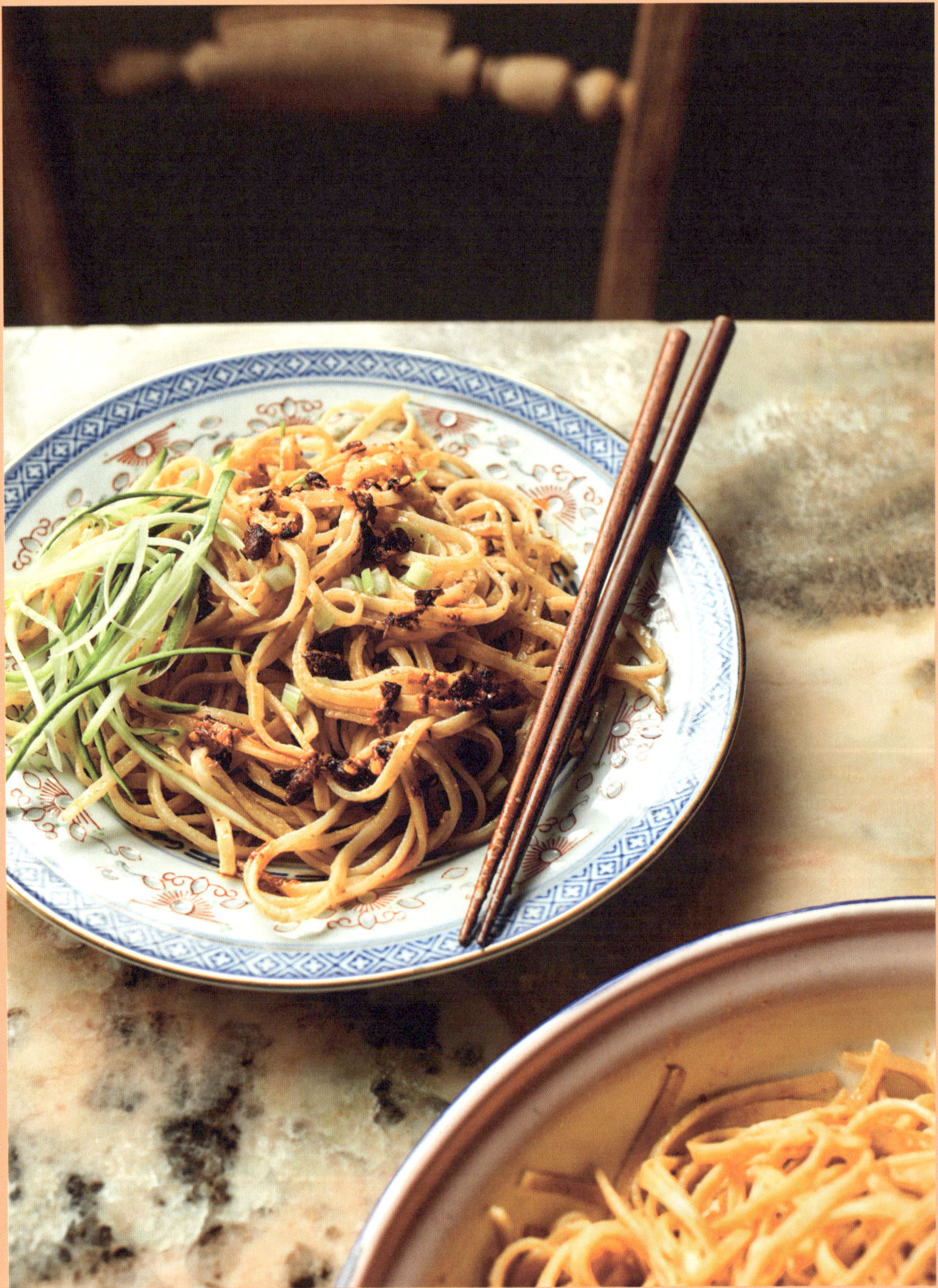

COLD SESAME NOODLES

Serves 3–4

Cold sesame noodles are a mainstay at Chinese-American restaurants, and have been since the 1970s when a wave of new immigrants from China set up shop in lower Manhattan and started cooking Chinese dishes that seeped into the cultural fabric of New York City. According to Sam Sifton at the *New York Times*, this new Chinese food, which included a cold noodle dish coated in a peanut butter and sesame sauce that was simultaneously spicy, sweet, and silky, became "as much a part of 1970s Manhattan as cocaine and disco". I wasn't around back in the '70s to speak to Mr Sifton's assertion, but cold sesame noodles became as much a part of my early 2000s Manhattan as The Strokes and lukewarm cans of Pabst Blue Ribbon did. And, frankly, they were not particularly special or delicious. In fact, they were often (and presumably still are) gloopy, heavy, and predominantly made from sweetened, highly-processed peanut butters. But I ate them and loved them, and they still remind me of Ollie's at 116th and Broadway.

These are not those noodles, though. I haven't eaten those in years. These are the noodles I learned to make in Xian, the erstwhile Silk Roads metropolis, and a city that today brags about being home to over 100 different types of noodle dishes. They simultaneously remind me of the sesame noodles of my New York young adulthood and transport me to a plastic fold-up street-side table near Xian's Bell Tower. They are evocative. They are simple. They are exceptional. And they are as much a part of my 2020s London as rain and motherhood; I hope they become part of your "now" too.

400g (14oz) pack of dried noodles (use whatever noodles you like – I use rice noodles or ramen, or whatever I happen to have in my pantry)

For the sauce

⅛ tsp fine sea salt

¼ tsp MSG

⅛ tsp caster or granulated sugar

¾ tsp ground Sichuan peppercorns

2 tsp light soy sauce

1 tbsp Chinese sesame paste

2 tsp crispy chilli oil, plus (a lot) more to serve

2 tsp sesame oil

2 garlic cloves, minced

To serve

julienned cucumber

chopped spring onions

Prepare your noodles according to the instructions on the packet, then drain and set aside.

Combine the sauce ingredients in a bowl with 4 tablespoons water. Mix well and give it a taste. See if you want a little more of anything – for me, this combination is perfect and immediately takes me to a sunny spring afternoon in Shaanxi Province, but if you prefer a slightly different flavour profile, by all means go for it.

Toss your noodles with your well-mixed sauce before serving in individual bowls topped with more crispy chilli oil, cucumber, and/or a sprinkling of spring onions. Slurp's up!

CHEESEBURGER MAKARONI

Serves 4–6

"You put that recipe in the book, guaranteed years of hate mail." That was my older half-brother's response when I shared my plan for this dish on our sibling group chat. He is full Iranian, you see, one of two children from my father's first (arranged) marriage to a fellow Iranian; I'm only half-Iranian because my mother is full American, all the way back to the *Mayflower*. And for my brother, to Americanize Iranian *makaroni* the way I have here is sacrilege. Which is ironic, because the dish itself is an Iranicization of spaghetti with *ragù alla bolognese*.

Makaroni is a classic Iranian comfort food, typically made with meat, spices, and seasonings commonly found in the Iranian larder – namely, lamb, turmeric, rose petals, cumin, cardamom, and coriander – and cooked somewhat similarly to Iranian rice. *Makaroni* even comes with a crispy layer at the bottom of the pot à la *gazmakh*.

The thing is: I've had *makaroni*. I don't love it. I find the traditional Iranian dish to be an acquired taste, beloved by Iranians probably because it reminds them of childhood, and I didn't eat it as a kid. With an American mother and a pasta-hating Iranian father, there was no way *makaroni* was ever going to land on our dinner table. What also never appeared on our table was the popular packaged pasta-and-seasoning-in-a-box product called "Hamburger Helper", one flavour of which was "Cheeseburger Macaroni".

This recipe is a nod to the cheeseburger macaroni I never had in my American childhood, and to the Iranian *makaroni* I never had in my Iranian-American childhood, as well as to my favourite cheeseburger of all time – the Gruyère-covered beef patty of my dreams – from the sadly shuttered Dumont in Williamsburg, Brooklyn.

There's a great line in Gabrielle Zevin's novel *Tomorrow and Tomorrow and Tomorrow* that resonates with (and occasionally breaks) me: "As any mixed-race person will tell you, to be half of two things is to be whole of nothing." Well, let me tell you something: my mixed-race cheeseburger *makaroni* is half of two things and whole of EVERYTHING. It is a confluence of flavours, preparations, and memories, and I'm hoping that by putting this recipe in the book, I'm guaranteeing myself years of *fan* mail.

Note: Feel free to use turkey or veal mince, but for that real Hamburger Helper feel, beef is the way to go. The sauce can be made ahead of time, doubled, and/or frozen, just like your favourite bolognese.

- 30g (1oz) unsalted butter
- 5 tbsp olive oil
- 1 onion, finely diced
- 1¼ tsp fine sea salt, plus extra for cooking the pasta
- ¾ tsp freshly ground black pepper
- 4 garlic cloves, minced
- 500g (1lb 2oz) minced beef
- 1 tsp hot or sweet smoked paprika
- 240ml (1 cup/8fl oz) milk
- 2 tbsp tomato purée
- 2 tbsp Worcestershire sauce
- 1 tbsp *colatura* or fish sauce
- 400g (14oz) can whole tomatoes (preferably San Marzano), with their juices
- 750ml (3 cups/1¼ pints) beef stock
- 1 bay leaf
- 200g (7oz) Gruyère cheese, grated
- 50g (1¾oz) Parmesan cheese, grated
- 500g (1lb 2oz) dried spaghetti

In a large sauté pan for which you have a lid, heat the butter and 1 tablespoon of the oil over a medium heat. Once the butter has melted, add the onion and ¼ teaspoon each of the salt and pepper. Cook, stirring frequently, for 8–10 minutes, or until the onion begins to turn a light golden brown.

Reduce the heat to medium–low and stir in the garlic. Cook for 30 seconds, or until fragrant. Then add the beef to the pan, along with the paprika and the remaining 1 teaspoon of salt, and ½ teaspoon of black pepper.

Use a wooden spoon to break up the meat and stir everything together. Cook for 3–5 minutes, or until nearly all the pink in the mince is gone. Add the milk and stir to mix. Cook for about 10 minutes until the milk has nearly all evaporated. Just like a bolognese, right?

Add the tomato purée and stir again to mix. Now it's umami time! Add the Worcestershire sauce and *colatura* or fish sauce, and mix together. Finally, add the tomatoes, stock, and bay leaf. Stir to combine, then cover the pan with a lid and increase the heat to high. Bring the mixture to the boil, then reduce the heat to the lowest possible setting and simmer your sauce, with the lid ajar now, until it reaches the consistency of your favourite bolognese – for me, this takes 1 hour and 20 minutes, as I prefer my sauce less saucy and more meaty. Adjust according to your preferences.

When your sauce is nearing perfection, bring a large, well-salted pot of water to the boil. Meanwhile, mix your grated cheeses together in a medium bowl.

Break your dried spaghetti in half before adding it to the boiling water. I know – this goes against everything you have ever been told, but it really does make eating the end product much easier. Cook your broken spaghetti until almost al dente, or for 1 minute less than instructed on the packet. Drain in a colander and rinse with cold water. Try to time your pasta cooking with your sauce; you don't want to leave your cooked pasta in a colander or bowl to congeal while you wait for your sauce.

When both your sauce and your pasta are ready, pour the remaining 4 tablespoons oil into a large saucepan or pot for which you have a lid. Use a pastry brush to get some of the oil up the sides of the pot as well.

In a large bowl, combine two-thirds of the al dente spaghetti with two-thirds of the sauce. Mix, then set aside.

Add the unsauced spaghetti to the bottom of your well-oiled pot, pressing it down with a wooden spoon to even it out into a thick layer. Now spoon the unmixed sauce on top of the pasta in the pot, again using your spoon to smooth and even it out into a nice layer. Sprinkle a third of the cheese across the top.

Take half of the combined pasta and sauce, and place it into the pot – again, smoothing it into a nice even layer. Top with half the remaining cheese. Repeat with your final bits of sauced spaghetti and cheese, making sure that everything is smoothed out evenly. Unlike Iranian rice dishes that call for layering into a mound or pyramid, we want a flat top here.

Place your pasta-filled pot over a medium heat. Cover and cook for 10 minutes.

Wrap the lid of the pot in a clean tea towel, making sure to secure the towel on top of the pot so that it doesn't catch fire if you are using a gas burner (I use a rubber band tied around the gathered corners of the towel). Place the towelled lid back on the pan. Reduce the heat to the lowest setting and cook for a further 45–50 minutes.

When it's ready fill your sink with 2.5cm (1in) water, then place your pot in the sink for 10–15 seconds – the cold water will help release the *gazmakh*-style pasta from the bottom. Find a platter that fits over the top of your pot, remove the lid, and place the platter on top of the pot. Then, using both hands, flip your pot of *makaroni* over in one quick, fluid motion.

Cheeseburger *makaroni* in paradise.

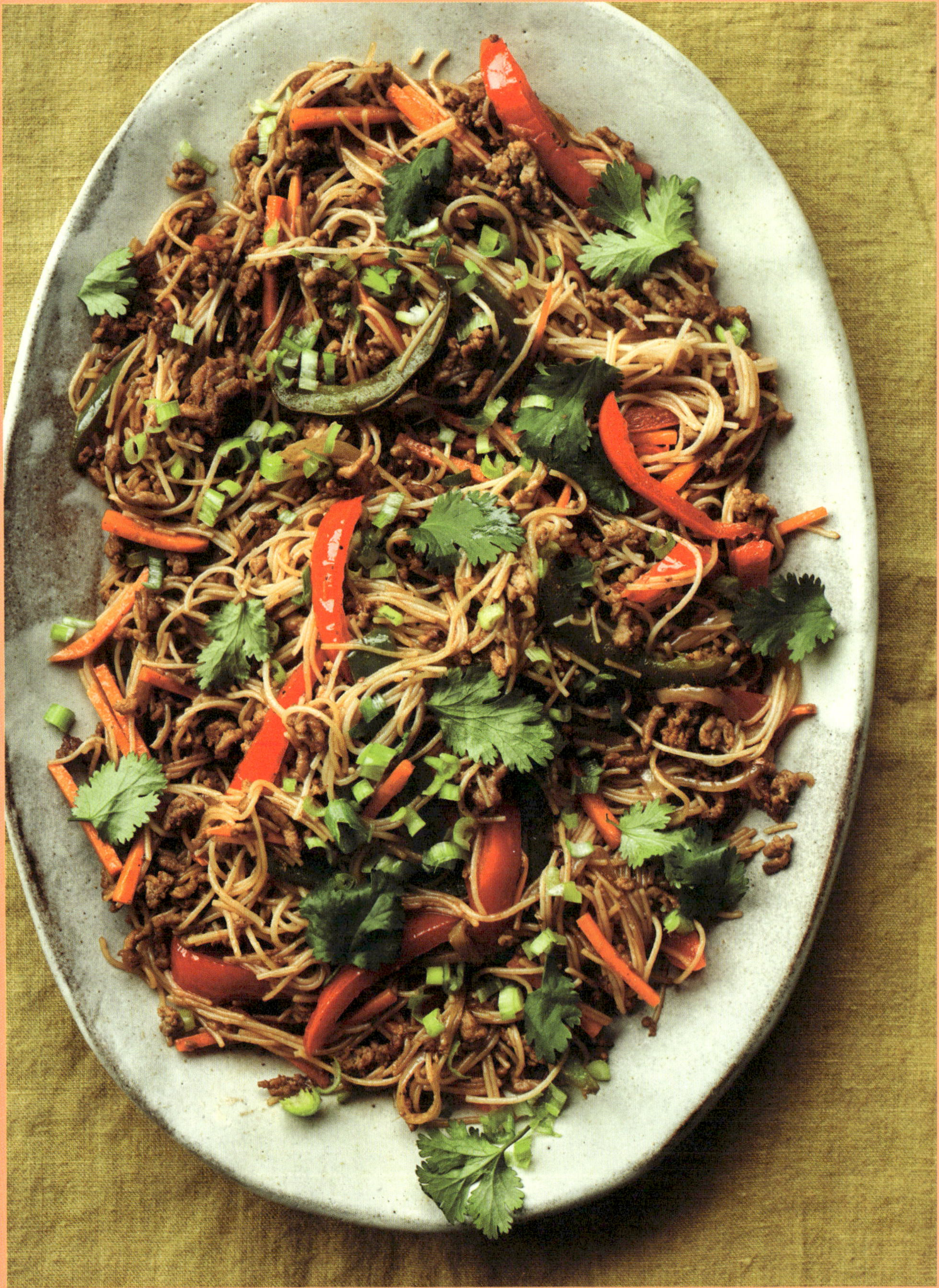

FUNCHOZA

Uyghur Vermicelli with Minced Meat

Serves 3–4

Funchoza, an addictive Uyghur noodle dish notably reminiscent of both Korean *japchae* and Sichuan *mayi shang shu* ("ants climbing a tree"), gets its name from *fentiao*, the Mandarin word for "noodle strip". Various iterations of this dish are found across Central Asia and Russia, with different characteristics and ingredients depending on locale. This *funchoza* highlights flavour constants of Uyghur food – lamb, pepper, cumin, coriander – while holding on to its Chinese linguistic roots through its inclusion of soy sauces, Chinkiang vinegar, and Sichuan peppercorns.

- 100g (3½oz) dried vermicelli (mung bean, sweet potato, or rice)
- 3 tbsp neutral oil
- 1 onion, thinly sliced into half-moons
- 2cm (¾in) piece of fresh ginger, minced
- 2 fat garlic cloves, minced
- 500g (1lb 2oz) minced lamb
- ½ tsp chilli powder
- 1 tsp ground cumin
- ½ tsp ground white pepper
- 2½ tsp ground Sichuan peppercorns
- 1 tsp fine sea salt
- ½ tsp MSG
- 2 peppers (colour of your choosing), thinly sliced
- 2 carrots, peeled and cut into thin, 2.5cm (1in) long matchsticks
- 2 tsp dark soy sauce
- 3 tsp light soy sauce
- 2 tbsp Chinkiang vinegar
- 2 spring onions, chopped
- handful of coriander leaves

Prepare your noodles of choice according to the packet instructions, then drain and set aside until the dish is nearly finished.

In a wok or a large sauté pan for which you have a lid, heat the oil over a medium–high heat, swirling the oil around to coat the base of the wok or pan. When the oil shimmers, add the onion and cook for 1 minute, then add the ginger and garlic, and stir for a few moments until fragrant.

Add the meat, along with the chilli powder, cumin, white pepper, and ground Sichuan peppercorns. Break up the mince with a wooden spoon, and cook for 2 minutes, or until just a hint of pink remains. Now add the salt and MSG, followed by the peppers and carrots. Stir in 4 tablespoons water, then cover with a lid and cook for 5 minutes, or until the carrots and peppers are soft and floppy.

Meanwhile, cut up your drained noodles with kitchen shears. I do this haphazardly and randomly, Edward Scissorhands-style; feel free to do the same. He made masterpieces and so too will you!

Uncover your wok/pan, and turn the heat to high to cook off any excess liquid. Once this is done, reduce the heat to the lowest setting, and add your noodles and both soy sauces. Stir to coat and combine everything well before turning off the heat and drizzling the vinegar over the top.

Toss the *funchoza* to combine, then transfer to a serving bowl or platter, and garnish with the spring onions and coriander to serve.

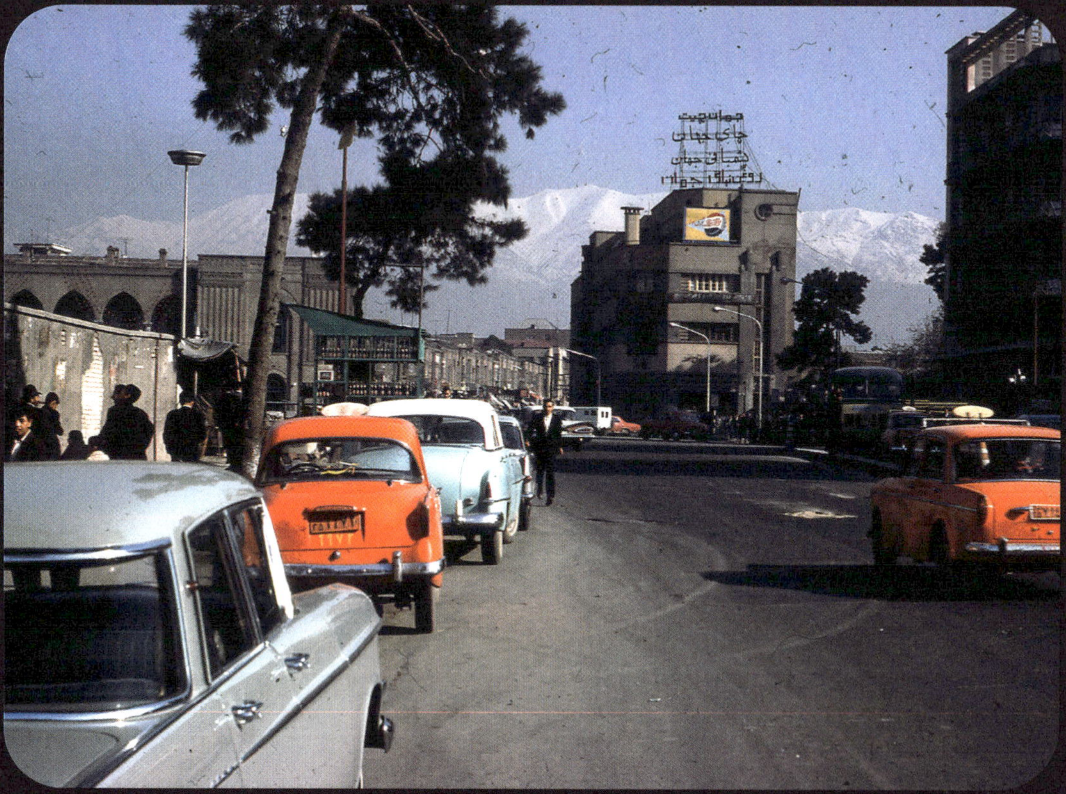
جهان چیت
چای جهان

DUMPLINGS & BREADS

HOT POCKETS
184

SILK ROADS DUMPLING DOUGH
188

A XANADU OF DUMPLING FILLINGS
188

MANTI
Central Asian Dumplings
192

OROMO
Kyrgyz Rolled Dumplings
195

DUSHBARA & CHOCHURE
A Duo of Dumplings en Brodo
197

KAO BAOZI/SAMSA
Roast Lamb Dumplings
200

SPINACH & TOFU BAOZI
203

A CENTRAL ASIAN BREAD
205

CHVISHTARI
Cheesy Georgian Cornbread
209

LAYERED & FRIED FLATBREADS
211

GUTAB
Azeri "Quesadillas"
212

HOT POCKETS

We lived on the 31st floor of a 34-floor apartment block. One of three communist-style buildings, differentiated only by the strip of colour that ran down the outside of the elevator shaft. We were in the yellow one, a block east of Shanghai's Xujiahui Park and kitty corner from a ground-floor hole-in-the-wall dumpling restaurant. Too poor to hit up M on the Bund, the newly-opened Jean Georges, or even Maoming Lu's Blue Frog on our (very meagre) English teaching salaries, my boyfriend and I ate dumplings at the Jianguo Lu *jiaozi guan* at least three times a week. For a year. The only foreigners ever present at the eight-table spot, where we could pay 4 RMB for six dumplings (in 2003, 4 RMB was equivalent to 50 US cents or 30 pence), we ordered plate after plate of boiled, northern Chinese-style dumplings. Pork and cabbage. Pork and leek. Lamb and coriander. More pork and cabbage. We inhaled dumpling after dumpling after dumpling, dipping each into black vinegar mixed with hot chilli oil, until we were full and ready to return home to watch a bootleg DVD.

"I think about that dumpling place all the time," Joe tells me in 2024.

"How so?," I ask him.

"It's really hard for me to pay eight dollars for eight dumplings at Vanessa's Dumpling House," he replies. "I think about it that way."

I don't tell him that I think about that dumpling place all the time too, but not as a price comparison to *jiaozi* in London. No, I think about that dumpling place all the time because it's the first place I remember eating and loving dumplings.

When I was a teenager in Beijing, I would *bao* – wrap – *jiaozi* with my host family on a pretty regular basis. My host mother would bring out a vat of soft raw mince speckled with spring onions, a pile of pre-rolled-out dough wrappers, and a few sets of chopsticks. She and I and my host sister would sit around our dining table, chatting about who-knows-what, using our chopsticks to place a dollop of meat into a wrapper, then using our hands to fold and seal the wrappers, and placing our filled and finished dumplings on a tray from whence they would eventually make their way into a pot of boiling water and our hungry bellies. It sounds cute, right? A scene you might see in study-abroad brochures or on exchange-programme websites as an example of deep cultural immersion, personal growth, and fulfilment. A meaningful family bonding session. A cultural and culinary bridge between disparate women. An inadvertent dumpling diplomacy. I absolutely hated it. I hated *bao*-ing *jiaozi*. And I hated *jiaozi*. Passionately. And I don't know why. And I don't know what happened between 1998 and 2003 that made me change my mind and my culinary preferences, but change they did, and by the time I was living my not-so-best post-collegiate life in Shanghai, I was not just a dumpling convert, but a devoted disciple.

I adore dumplings. Any and all varieties. Steamed. Fried. Boiled. Deep-fried. Thick-skinned. Thin-skinned. *Jiaozi. Manti. Baozi. Gurza. Pelmeni.* Should I go on? *Tuhum barak. Vareneki. Khinkali. Gyoza. Xiao long bao.* I love any stuffed dough product, more or less, from Baku to

BY THE TIME I WAS LIVING MY NOT-SO-BEST POST-COLLEGIATE LIFE IN SHANGHAI, I WAS NOT JUST A DUMPLING CONVERT, BUT A DEVOTED DISCIPLE.

My host mother (top) and sister (bottom), and a whole lot of *jiaozi*. Beijing, China. 1998.

Beijing – and beyond. Stuffed with pork. Lamb. Leek. Tofu. Prawns. Coriander. Egg. Cheese. Carrot. Cabbage. Mushrooms. OK, I take that back – I don't like mushroom dumplings (other than those made with my mushroom filling on page 190), but you get the picture. Winter, spring, summer, or fall, all you have to do is … give me a dumpling, and I will be there.

Writing nearly 2,000 years ago during China's Western Jin Dynasty, the poet Shu Xi provides us with some of the earliest references to the ancient bready preparation known as *bing*. While *bing* today in Mandarin refers to flat pancake-like breads, the word initially referenced several different types of dough preparations, including flat, stuffed, and fried breads, noodles, and dumplings.

Among the myriad things Shu tells us about *bing* is when to eat different types. Stuffed breads, like the modern *baozi*, are for springtime. Summer calls for thin pancakes. Autumn is leavened bread time, while winter is for steaming bowls of noodles. To every *bing* there is a season. Except for dumplings. Unlike other *bing*, *laowan*, a meat-filled stuffed dough ball (aka dumpling), can, Shu declares "always be served all year round, / and in all four seasons freely used, / in no respect unsuitable". A *bing* for all seasons. I can get behind that. Oh, and the name of Shu Xi's prose-poem is "Rhapsody on *Bing*". A literal rhapsody on bread and dumplings. I can *definitely* get behind that.

Noticeable in Shu Xi's rhapsody is the inference that wheat both existed in and was commonplace to the Chinese diet by the 3rd century CE, as well as the idea that some *bing* were not originally native to China; he specifically says that "some of the methods come from alien lands". Wheat, too, came from alien lands, though archaeobotanical studies debate the precise time and manner of the grain's importation into and domestication within China. We do know that the earliest bread remnants have been found in Jordan and date to 12,400 BCE, and that einkorn wheat in the Fertile Crescent of modern-day Turkey and Syria was the first domesticated wheat (8000 BCE). We also know that (probably naturally) hybridized wheat spread eastward from Turkey to Iran and across Central Asia, ending up in China by 2000 BCE at the latest, and that the earliest Chinese wheat remains have been discovered in Gansu Province's Hexi Corridor – that all-important strip of traversable land linking China's central plains to Central Asia, that key Silk Roads passageway.

> COMPARED TO NOODLES AND DUMPLINGS, CHINESE BREADS ARE FAR LESSER KNOWN AROUND THE WORLD, BUT EVERY BIT AS DELICIOUS AS THEIR MORE CELEBRATED COUSINS.

Compared to noodles and dumplings, Chinese breads are far lesser known around the world, but every bit as delicious as their more celebrated cousins. But today's Chinese breads are not the *bing* rhapsodized about by Shu Xi. Rather, many are the descendants of Tang Dynasty steamed and/or fried "cakes", sold and introduced by the Turkic and Persian denizens of multicultural, multinational 8th-century Chang'an, for whom bread, much more so than rice, was life.

In his introduction to his translation of the Mongol-era cookbook *The Soup for the Qan*, American anthropologist Paul D. Buell tells us that "the diet of the ordinary peasant in the early Middle East, as in remote parts of Iran and Central Asia today, was bread, leavened or not, yogurt or cheese, and whatever wild or cultivated greens and herbs were available". Absence of fruit notwithstanding, Buell may as well have been describing my father's diet today. Indeed, when I was growing up, bread reigned supreme in our household. But not just any bread.

We drove to Canada to buy bread. To Toronto, where there was a sizable Iranian expatriate population and accompanying stores selling Iranian foodstuffs and sundries. We drove to Toronto, stocked up on bread and rice and saffron and rose petals, and stayed the night before returning home and filling our freezer with thin *sangak* and fluffy *barbari* breads, as well as round wholemeal rolls that were not Iranian at all, but beloved and sourced from Canada all the same.

The industrialized and chemical-filled sliced bread found in Michigan grocery stores, no matter how artisan or fresh the packaging claimed, was a far cry from the bread with which my father had grown up in Iran. When he was a child, two women bread-makers came to his house on a monthly basis. One was in charge of making the dough, the other of forming the breads and baking them. They didn't make *barbari*, my father tells me. Rather, the ladies made piece after piece of thin flatbread – *lavash* – which they stacked one upon another in a large wooden storage box, where it would not only keep, but also, slowly but surely, dry out over the course of the month. "It was not a problem, though – the dried-out bread," my father says. "I would pick one bread whenever I wanted it, and if it was dry, I would sprinkle some water on both sides and then eat it. Usually with *ab goosht*," he remembers.

The thin bread with which my father grew up does indeed keep well, and is similar to the breads carried and eaten for millennia by Central Asian steppe dwellers and nomads. Though once a mainstay of Silk Roads caravan cuisine because of their staying power, unleavened flatbreads are associated far more closely today with Levantine cuisine than with Central Asia, whose most recognizable breads are clay-oven-baked, patterned-pricked rounds, glistening and often topped with sesame or nigella seeds.

I haven't given you a plain flatbread recipe here, but worry not. You'll find a fabulous bread round recipe, as well as a template for a fried and layered bread, and a stuffed flatbread too. There's a fluffy *baozi*, a cornbread (I know! I'm surprised too, but Georgians love cornbread and so do I!) – and dumplings. Dumplings galore. Because what is that Laozi said? "Give a man a dumpling and you feed him for a day. Teach him how to make dumplings and you feed him for a lifetime." That was it, wasn't it?

> THE LADIES MADE PIECE AFTER PIECE OF THIN FLATBREAD – *LAVASH* – WHICH THEY STACKED ONE UPON ANOTHER IN A LARGE WOODEN STORAGE BOX, WHERE IT WOULD NOT ONLY KEEP, BUT ALSO, SLOWLY BUT SURELY, DRY OUT OVER THE COURSE OF THE MONTH.

SILK ROADS DUMPLING DOUGH

For use with **Manti (see p192)** and Oromo (see p195). This is a generous recipe. Generous and delicious, and one day you will thank me for the abundance of dumplings in your freezer.

Makes enough for 30–32 *manti* or 2 *oromo*

1 egg, lightly beaten
300g (10oz) plain flour (or use '00' if you've got it)
¼ tsp fine sea salt

Use a fork to whisk together the egg and 130ml (generous ½ cup/4½fl oz) room-temperature water in a bowl.

Sift the flour and salt together in the bowl of a stand mixer fitted with a dough hook. Mix them together at a low speed, then, with the mixer still running, slowly pour in the egg and water mixture. Increase the mixer's speed to medium and let it work its magic, pausing occasionally to ensure the flour from the sides of the bowl is being well incorporated, and using a spatula to scrape those sides down if it's not.

After 3–5 minutes, you should have a soft, pliable dough that is tacky to the touch but does not stick to your hands. Form the dough into a ball, then leave it in a bowl covered with a tea towel or cling film, and let it rest for 30 minutes.

Follow further directions for Manti on page 192 and Oromo on page 195.

A XANADU OF DUMPLING FILLINGS

These fillings I give you are not imagined. They are not opulent. They are not going to break the bank or alienate you. They are going to fill you with love and comfort and joy and serious deliciousness. Come to think of it, maybe I should have dubbed them a "rosebud" of dumpling fillings. Hmm …

If someone can call a plurality of crows a "murder", then I give myself leave to hereby declare that these six recipes for dumpling fillings — three of which are vegetarian — are a Xanadu. Someone has to come up with collective noun names, after all.

Xanadu, that summer capital of Kublai Khan, located 230 miles north of Beijing in China's present-day Inner Mongolian Autonomous Region, though described in great detail by Marco Polo, was forever cemented in the imagination of the Western world centuries later by the English Romantic poet, Samuel Taylor Coleridge, as an emblem of a paradisiacal dream, a vision. And then there's Charles Foster Kane …

MINCED LAMB & ONION FILLING

500g (1lb 2oz) minced lamb (the higher the fat content, the better)
½ onion, finely diced
1 tsp hot smoked paprika
½ tsp coarsely ground black pepper
½ tbsp fine sea salt

Combine all the ingredients in a large bowl. Use your hands to mash and mix everything together very well, until it's almost like a paste. You'll need to knead it for about 5 minutes until it gets to that point. Your filling is now ready to party.

BEEF & POTATO FILLING

3 tbsp ghee or olive oil
½ onion, finely diced
1½ tsp fine sea salt
250g (9oz) potatoes, peeled and cut into 1cm (½in) cubes
1 tsp ground cumin
1 tsp freshly ground black pepper
250g (9oz) minced beef (the higher the fat content, the better)

In a sauté pan for which you have a lid, heat the ghee or oil over a medium heat. Reduce the heat to low, then add the diced onion and 1 teaspoon of the salt. Cook, stirring occasionally, for 10–12 minutes, or until the onion softens and turns a lovely light golden colour.

Add the potato cubes, cumin, and black pepper to the pan. Stir well, then pour in 150ml (⅔ cup/ 5fl oz) water. Cover the pan and cook for 15 minutes to soften the potatoes. At this point, if your mixture is still quite watery, remove the lid, increase the heat to high, and cook for another 5 minutes, or until most of the water has evaporated.

Transfer the contents of the pan to a mixing bowl and leave to cool. Once cool, add the beef and remaining ½ teaspoon salt to the bowl. Gently mix everything together. Your filling is now ready.

BASIC MEAT FILLING

500g (1lb 2oz) minced lamb or beef (the higher the fat content, the better)
½ onion, finely diced
1 tsp freshly ground black pepper
3 tsp fine sea salt
50g (1¾oz) unsalted butter, chilled

Combine all the ingredients except the butter in a large bowl. Use your hands to mash and mix everything together well. That's it: that's the filling ready to go.

When the time comes to form your dumplings, plop a smidge of the cold butter on top of the meat filling before sealing each dumpling.

CARROT FILLING

4 tsp olive oil
20g (¾oz) unsalted butter
2 onions, thinly sliced into half-moons
1½ tsp fine sea salt
500g (1lb 2oz) carrots, peeled and finely diced
¾ tsp coarsely ground black pepper
1½ tsp ground cumin
100g (3½oz) fresh coriander and/or parsley, finely chopped

Heat the oil and butter in a medium sauté pan over a medium heat. Once the butter has melted, add the onions and ½ teaspoon of the salt. Stir to combine, then reduce the heat to its lowest setting. Cook for 25–30 minutes, or until the onions are not-quite-caramelized: you want some to be dark brown and others to be lighter in colour. You will need to check in on and stir them occasionally to make sure they are neither burning nor sticking to the pan; if they threaten to do either, add a tablespoon of water.

Increase the heat to medium and add the carrots and the remaining 1 teaspoon salt, along with the black pepper and cumin. Stir to mix everything together. Cook for 3–5 minutes, or until the carrots have softened slightly.

Add the fresh herbs, mix well, and cook for a further 2–4 minutes, stirring near constantly, until the herbs are fragrant and have wilted into near oblivion.

Remove the pan from the heat and allow to cool. Once cool, it's go time.

POTATO FILLING

3 tbsp ghee, or 40g (scant 1½oz) unsalted butter
½ onion, finely diced
1 tsp fine sea salt
500g (1lb 2oz) potatoes, (I suggest using all-rounders like Maris Pipers), well washed or peeled and cut into 1cm (½in) cubes
1 tsp ground cumin
1 tsp coarsely ground black pepper

100g (3½oz) spring onions, finely chopped

In a large sauté pan for which you have a lid, melt the ghee or butter over a medium heat. Reduce the heat to low, then add the diced onion and salt. Cook, stirring occasionally, for 10–12 minutes, or until the onion softens and turns a lovely light golden colour.

Add the potatoes, cumin, and pepper, and stir to mix everything together. Pour in 250ml (1 cup plus 1 tbsp/9fl oz) water, then cover the pan and cook for 15 minutes to soften your potatoes.

After 15 minutes, if your mixture is still quite watery, remove the lid, increase the heat to high and cook for another 5 minutes, or until most of the water has evaporated.

Remove the pan from the heat and stir through the spring onions, then transfer to a bowl to cool. Once cool, it's party time.

MUSHROOM & TOFU FILLING

3 tbsp ghee, or 40g (scant 1½oz) unsalted butter
250g (9oz) mushrooms, roughly diced
1 onion, thinly sliced into half-moons
1 tsp fine sea salt
1 tbsp apple cider vinegar
1 fat garlic clove, minced
25g (scant 1oz) flat-leaf parsley (stems included), chopped
¼ tsp dried chilli flakes
225g (8oz) firm tofu
freshly ground black pepper

Melt the ghee or butter in a medium sauté pan over a high heat. Add the mushrooms, onions, and salt, then reduce the heat to medium. Cook, stirring occasionally, for 20 minutes.

Reduce the heat to low, then add the vinegar and cook for another 20 minutes, stirring occasionally. If your onion and mushrooms are threatening to burn (and they just well might), add a splash of water to the pan.

After 20 minutes, add the garlic, parsley, and chilli flakes, along with a few grinds of black pepper. Cook for a final 3–5 minutes before transferring the mixture to a large mixing bowl.

Allow the mixture to cool for a few minutes before using your hands to crumble in the tofu. Stir to mix everything together. Your filling is now ready for its close-up.

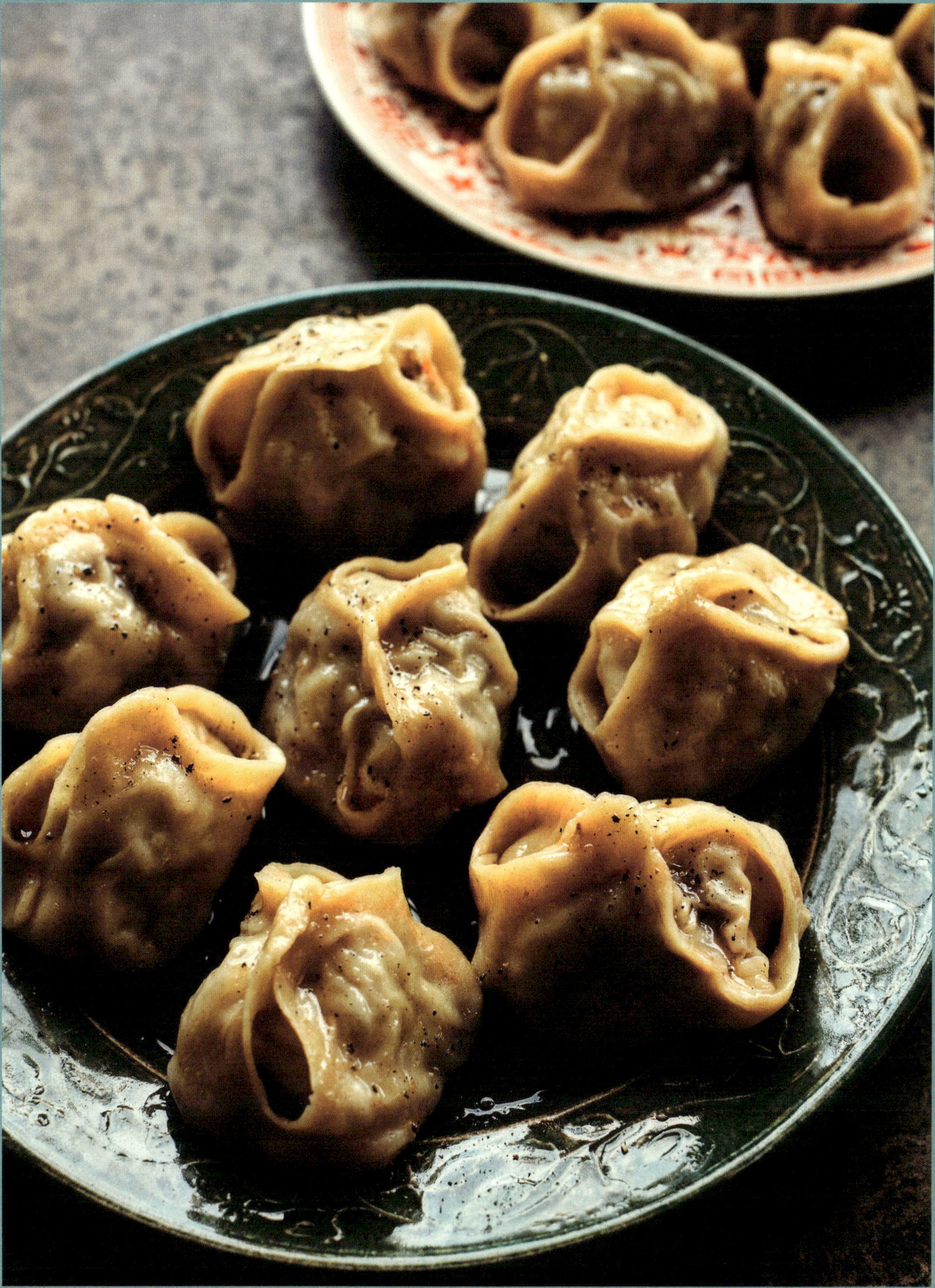

MANTI

Central Asian Dumplings

Makes 30–32 dumplings
(Serves 6–10)

Maybe one of the reasons I hated *bao*-ing *jiaozi* with my host family in the '90s so much was the difficulty I had stuffing, forming, and sealing the little half-moon-like dumplings. Some people are really good at it. I was not. I still *am* not. I found and continue to find *jiaozi*-making frustratingly difficult. Azerbaijani *gurza*, though elegant in their plaiting, I also find impossible to form. *Manti*, on the other hand – whether teeny, tiny ones from Turkey or heftier Uzbek ones – I can do. And I know you can, too. This is how.

Note: Once formed, you can either steam your *manti* straight away, or cover and refrigerate them until you want to eat them. Alternatively, you can freeze them. My move is generally to freeze the first batch I make and then cook and eat the second batch. To freeze, arrange in a single layer on a baking tray dusted with flour. Once frozen, transfer into a freezer-proof bag and freeze for up to 3 months. They will also keep in an airtight container in the refrigerator for up to 3 days.

---

1 portion Silk Roads Dumpling Dough (see p188)
plain flour, for dusting

2 portions dumpling filling of your choice
(see pp188–90)

Tip your dough out on to a well-floured work surface. Split the dough into two roughly equal balls. Return one to the bowl and cover with a tea towel while you roll out the other.

Roll your first dough ball into a large, thin rectangle about 2–3mm (⅛in) thick. Use a sharp knife to cut the rectangle into 8–10cm (3–4in) squares.

Take 1 tablespoon of your filling and plop it into the middle of each square. If you're using the Basic Meat Filling (see p189), now's the time to top each with a smidge of cold unsalted butter.

Time to get folding! Take two opposite corners of a dough square, then bring them together in the centre and pinch together to seal. Hold on to this centre pinch with your non-dominant hand, and use your dominant hand to bring the remaining two corners to the centre as well, forming a makeshift envelope-like pyramid. Pinch the four edges of the pyramid together to seal in your filling. If you like, you can stop right here. Alternatively, you can opt to join the neighbouring dough corners together and give your *manti* a shape for which I have no name … but they're cute, and I like doing this final pinch.

As you go, place each filled and formed *manti* on a baking tray lined with baking parchment, and keep them covered with a damp tea towel. Repeat with the remaining dough and filling.

Steam your dumplings for 20–30 minutes, using either a lined bamboo steamer basket or, if you've got one, a lightly greased metal steamer basket.

There are many ways to enjoy your dumplings – with a side of Suzma (see p77) or a generous dusting of freshly ground black pepper; drizzled with brown butter (see p17), caramelized onions, and/or garlicky yogurt (see Khingal, p168, for the latter two); dipped in spicy chilli oil or even – gasp! – ketchup. Listen: I'm a mom. We do what we got to do to get our little ones to eat. And, trust me, they (and you) will want to eat these little hot pockets of deliciousness all the time.

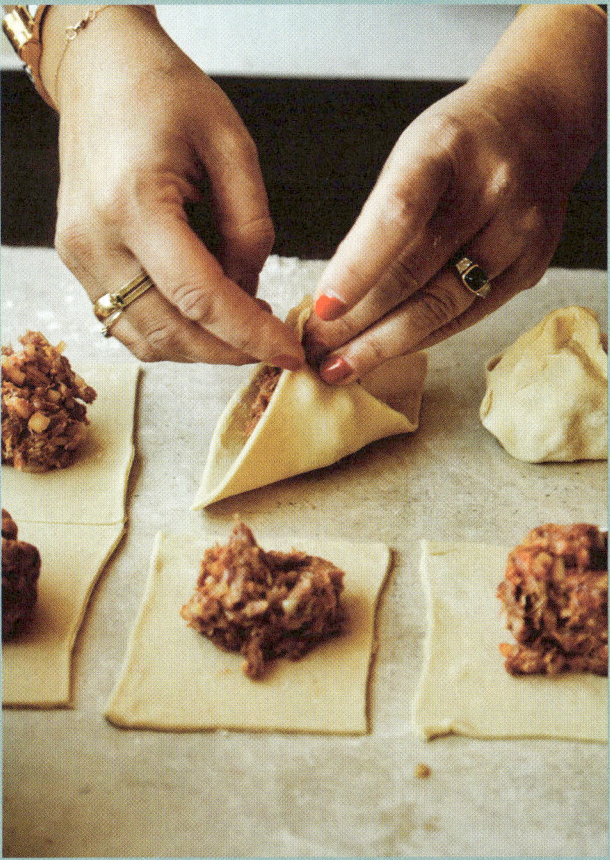
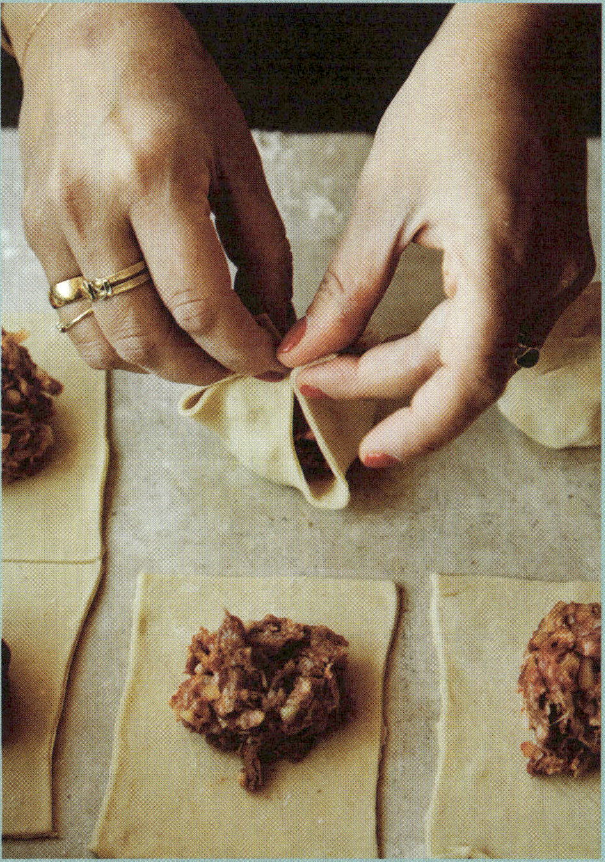
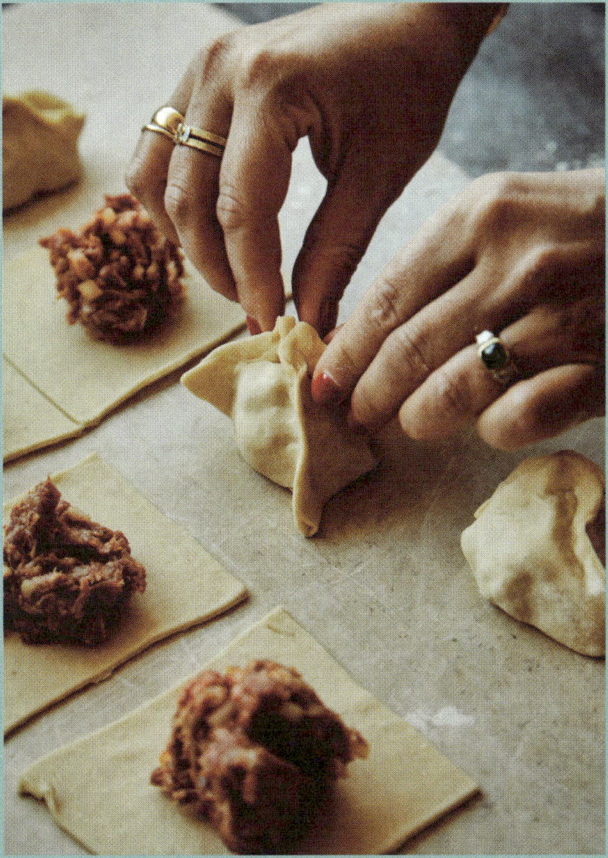
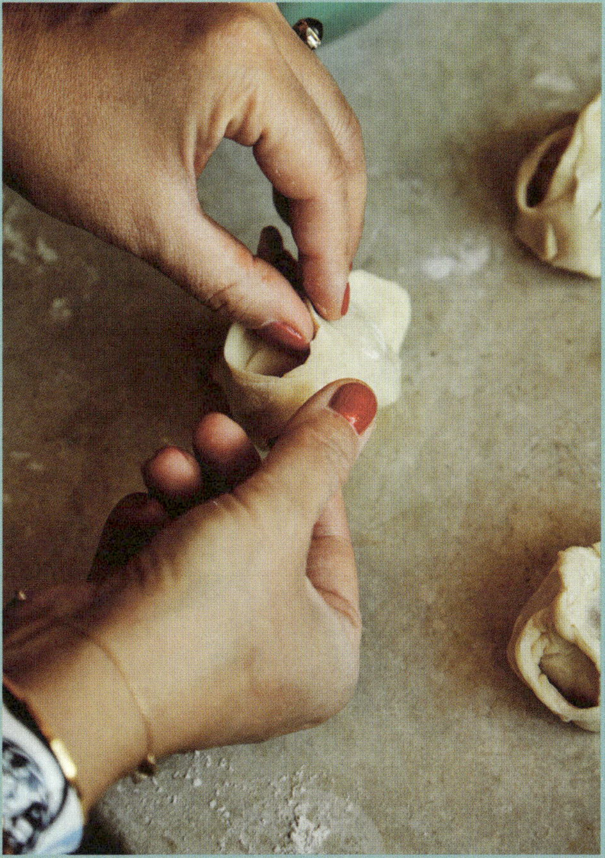

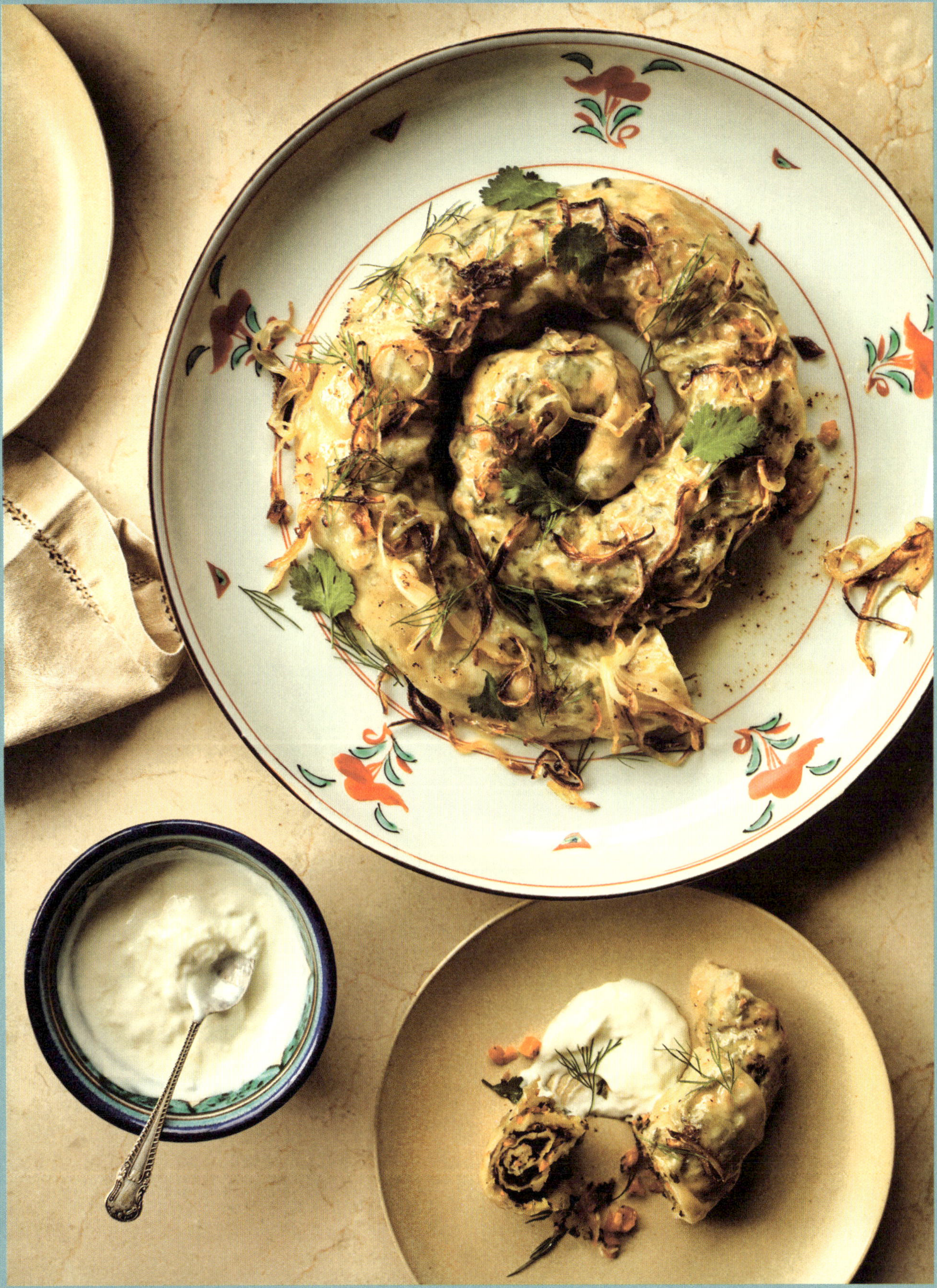

OROMO

Kyrgyz Rolled Dumplings

Makes 2 large dumplings (Serves 6–10)

Hailing from Kyrgyzstan, *oromo* can either be horseshoe-shaped or snail-shaped. Either way you choose to shape yours, add it to the (long) list of showstoppingly awesome dishes in this book.

plain flour, for dusting
1 portion Silk Roads Dumpling Dough (see p188)
neutral oil, as needed

2 portions dumpling filling of your choice (see pp188–90)

Tip your dough out on to a well-floured work surface. Split the dough into two roughly equal balls. Return one to the bowl and cover with a tea towel while you roll out the other.

Lightly dust the top of your dough ball with flour, then roll it out into a very thin 30 × 50cm (12 × 20in) rectangle. If you can't get the dough rolled into a perfect rectangle (and, let's face it, you probably can't; I certainly can't), use a knife to trim it to the proper size.

Arrange the dough rectangle in a landscape position and spray or lightly brush it with oil, then spread half of your filling on to it. You want to fill the dough rectangle with filling as evenly as you can, leaving a 1cm (½in) border across the long top edge and on both shorter sides.

Fold the two shorter dough borders in over the filling. Then, starting from the bottom (the edge with no border), gently but deftly roll up your dumpling into a massive, tight log, coiling the filling and dough into layers as you roll. Take care; you don't want to break the dumpling skin as you roll it up, but you also want it to be firmly and tightly rolled.

When you reach the empty dough border at the top, pull it down gently but tautly over the rolled dumpling log and press to seal.

Lightly grease a metal steamer basket or line a bamboo one with baking parchment, then carefully transfer your tube of a dumpling into it, placing it seam-side down. You can choose to either lay your *oromo* into the steamer in a circle or horseshoe shape, or you can tightly (or not-so-tightly, but always gently) coil the *oromo* into a snail snape – like a *pain au raisin*, but in Central-Asian-dumpling form. I find the latter to look more impressive, and the former to be easier to eat.

Repeat this process with the second dough ball and the rest of the filling, either placing the second filled *oromo* in a second, stacked steamer to cook, or wrapping it in cling film and chilling in the refrigerator to wait for your next meal, where it will keep for up to 3 days (or you can freeze it for up to 3 months).

Whether making one or two molluscan dumplings, steam your *oromo* for 20–30 minutes. Carefully lift each dumpling out of the steamer and enjoy. As with the *manti* on page 192, how you serve your *oromo* will depend on your choice of filling and personal (and family) flavour preferences.

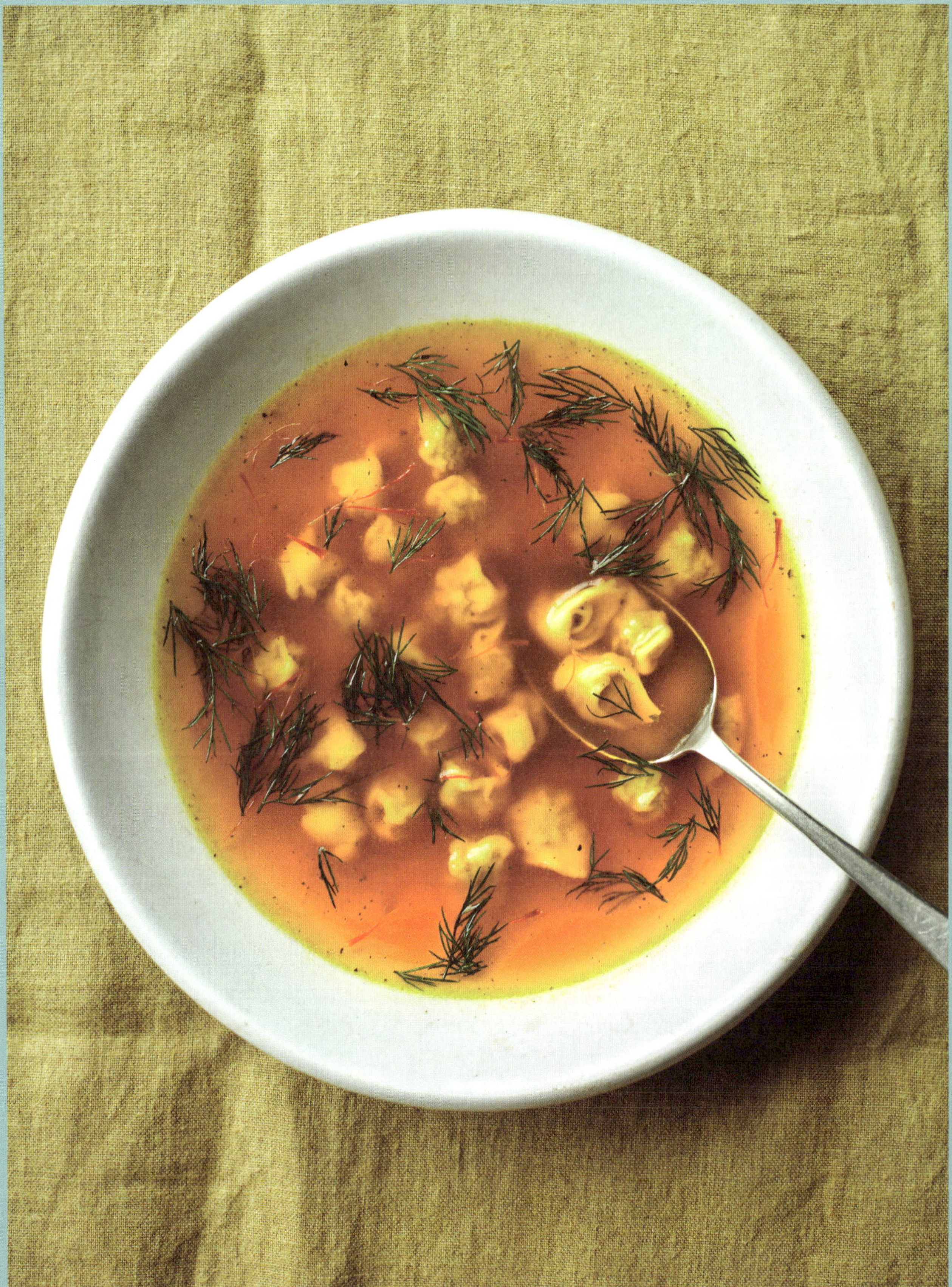

DUSHBARA & CHOCHURE

A Duo of Dumplings en Brodo

Serves 3–4

I first learned to make tortellini on a rooftop in Bologna, Italy – the supposed birthplace of the little hat-shaped pasta most typically stuffed with meat and cheese. I was studying international arbitration at the city's University of Law Faculty on a summer programme and, in addition to UNCITRAL rules, the programme taught pasta-making. Stuff. Fold. Pinch. Seal. Fold again.

The second time I learned to make a stuffed hat-shaped pasta was in a 12th-century caravanserai-turned-restaurant in Baku – *dushbara* this time, not tortellini. But the method was the same – stuff, fold, pinch, seal, fold again – and the end product looked the same. Well, almost.

Dushbara are small. Very small. If you're a good Azeri wife, you should be able to make your *dushbara* so small that you can fit 18–20 on one spoon. That's how small.

The word *dushbara* comes from the Persian *dush bareh*, which means an ear-shaped boiled piece of stuffed dough, and encompasses the little dumplings as well as a broth. *Dushbara* is a dumpling soup; it is an Azerbaijani *tortellini en brodo*, if you will. And my saffron *brodo* is amazing. And so are these little pieces of stuffed dough. And they don't have to be super tiny to be delicious. Are you a grand Azeri wife, or a mere mortal like me? It's OK. We are OK. We have no one to impress but our taste buds – and they, I can assure you, are delighted.

A bit bigger in size than *dushbara* and served in a more assertively flavoured broth, *chochure* are an Uyghur dumpling *en brodo*. I include a recipe for them here, alongside their Azeri cousin, to underscore the similarities in preparation between the two dishes. Though separated geographically by thousands of miles, *dushbara* and *chochure* (and *tortellini en brodo*, too) are forever linked. They are modern reminders of either a shared culinary genealogy shaped by centuries of trade and travels across Asia, or by the disparate, distinct compulsion of cooks long ago who made little bits of dough, stuffed them, folded them, pinched them, sealed them, folded them again, boiled them, and served them in a warm broth. Either way, whether *dushbara* or *chochure*, enjoy.

For the dough

1 egg

300g (10oz) plain flour (or use '00' if you've got it), plus extra for dusting

½ tsp fine sea salt, plus extra for cooking

For the *dushbara* filling

½ onion, peeled

1 garlic clove, minced

200g (7oz) minced beef or lamb, (the higher the fat content, the better)

½ tsp ground cumin

¼ tsp ground coriander

¼ tsp fine sea salt

For the *dushbara* broth

1 litre (4⅓ cups/1¾ pints) beef or lamb stock

1g saffron threads

25g (scant 1oz) dill fronds, chopped, plus extra to serve

sea salt and freshly ground black pepper

For the *chochure* filling

½ onion, peeled

1 garlic clove, grated

200g (7oz) minced beef or lamb (the higher the fat content, the better)

½ tsp ground cumin

¼ tsp ground white pepper

¼ tsp fine sea salt

For the *chochure* broth

1 litre (4⅓ cups/1¾ pints) beef or lamb stock

1 tbsp olive oil

½ onion, finely diced

1 pepper (colour of your choosing), finely diced

1 garlic clove, grated

2 tbsp tomato purée

25g (scant 1oz) coriander, chopped, plus extra to serve

3 tsp Chinkiang vinegar

1½ tsp dark soy sauce

sea salt and ground white pepper

Begin by making the dough. Use a fork to whisk together the egg and 100ml (6½ tbsp/3½fl oz) room-temperature water in a bowl.

Sift the flour and salt together in the bowl of a stand mixer fitted with a dough hook. Mix them together at a low speed, then, with the mixer still running, slowly pour in the egg and water mixture. Increase the mixer's speed to medium and let it work its magic, pausing occasionally to ensure the flour from the sides of the bowl is being well incorporated, and using a spatula to scrape those sides down if it's not.

After 5–7 minutes, you should have a pliable, semi-hard dough. Form the dough into a ball, then leave it in a bowl covered with a tea towel or cling film, and let it rest for 30 minutes.

Meanwhile, make your filling. The process is the same whether you are making *dushbara* or *chochure*, and it goes like this. Grate the onion into a bowl lined with a piece of muslin or cheesecloth. Gather up the cloth and squeeze the pouch with all your might; you're basically juicing an onion to get rid of as much onion juice as possible. When you can squeeze no more, you're done; discard the juice and tip the parched onion out of the cloth and back into the bowl. Add the minced or grated garlic, along with the minced meat, spices, and salt, and mix well, preferably with your hands.

Line two large baking trays with baking parchment, lightly dust them with flour, and wait for your timer to go off.

When your dough has rested for 30 minutes, transfer it to a well-floured work surface. Cut your dough in two, returning one piece to the covered bowl. Take the other piece and roll it out into a rectangle about 3mm (⅛in) thick, either by hand, or by using a pasta attachment for your stand mixer or a stand-alone pasta maker if you have one in your kitchen arsenal.

For *dushbara*, your goal is teeny-tiny dumplings. *Chochure* are a bit bigger. But honestly, you can make your dumplings any size you want.

Use a sharp knife to cut the dough into squares (2–2.5cm/ ¾–1in for *dushbara* and 2.5–3cm/1–1¼in for *chochure*).

Dollop some filling into the middle of each dough square; ⅛ teaspoon for *dushbara*, ½ teaspoon for *chochure*. And don't worry – it might look like there is no way you can form these little filling-topped squares into dumplings, but the dough is pliable and will stretch as you work.

To form your dumplings, fold your dough squares diagonally, stretching the dough a bit to bring the two opposite corners together in the middle. Look – you've got a cute little dough triangle! Pinch the top of the triangle to seal it and then make your way down both sides of it, pressing as you go to squeeze out any air and seal it up. If, at any point, the dough isn't sealing, wet your fingers a bit and try again.

Now this sounds tricky, but it's really not. Promise. Grab a chopstick. Trust me. Fold the two outer corners of the dough triangle around the chopstick, overlapping them slightly when they meet. Pinch the two ends together and slide the dumpling off your chopstick and on to the floured baking tray. Repeat with the other dough squares, then repeat all the above for your second piece of dough and the rest of the filling. And then give yourself a pat on the back. That took a while, didn't it? It'll be worth it, I swear.

Broth time! In a medium–large saucepan, bring your stock to the boil, then reduce the heat to low and let it simmer.

- **If you're making *dushbara*,** add the saffron and dill, and season to taste with salt and pepper.

- **If you're making *chochure*,** grab a sauté pan and heat your olive oil over a medium heat. Add your onion and pepper, and cook for 5 minutes, or until just starting to brown. Add the garlic and sauté for 30 seconds, or until fragrant. Stir in the tomato purée, and cook for a further 2 minutes. Tip the contents of your pan into the simmering stock. Add the coriander, vinegar, and soy sauce. Stir and season to taste with salt and white pepper.

To cook your dumplings, bring a separate pot of well-salted water to the boil. Once boiling, gently lower your dumplings in. Let them cook in the boiling water for 2–3 minutes, depending on their size (bigger ones will take longer).

Using a slotted spoon, lift out your cooked dumplings and add them to your pot of broth. You will need to do this in batches depending on the size of your pot as well as that of your dumplings.

Ladle your dumpling soup into bowls. Top *dushbara* with flaky sea salt and some more dill; for *chochure*, you will want more coriander leaves to finish. Enjoy.

Top: Freshly baked roadside *samsa* in Samarkand, Uzbekistan. March 2024.

Bottom: Freshly baked roadside *puri* on the road to Kakheti, Georgia. June 2024.

KAO BAOZI/ SAMSA

Roast Lamb Dumplings

Makes 8 "hot pockets"

I don't think I ever ate a "hot pocket" as a kid. More mass-processed, chemical-filled junk, according to my parents. Nope. I definitely never had one. But I remember the advertisements on TV. Every American so-called "geriatric millennial" does. And we all remember the jingle. It's deeply seared into our collective memory. Deeply.

Decades ago, at dinner at a beloved Uyghur restaurant in Shanghai, a platter of *kao baozi* – the Mandarin name for Uyghur roast and stuffed buns – appeared on the table. My friend Rindy, a New Jerseyan who had moved to China for the love of a charismatic Sichuanese girl, picked up one of the fresh-from-the-oven parcels, looked it over, and, before taking a bite, out came the jingle: "Hot pockets!" A melodious incantation which garnered a few giggles from the fellow Americans and nothing but a blank stare from Rindy's now-wife, Xianyi.

"What is 'hot pocket'?" she asked. We explained as best as we could. Meat. Cheese. Sauce. In bread – a pocket of bread. She didn't get it. Didn't see what we found funny. Didn't understand our shared reference and collective culinary memory. We couldn't explain what the tune meant to us, what the words "hot pocket" invoked beyond the surface level of their ingredients. You had to be there. Really. In America. In the 1980s and 1990s. And if you were, you knew. And if you weren't and you don't know, well, now you're in luck. Because this hot pocket right here, this *kao baozi*, this *samsa* (as this tasty little dude is called by Uyghurs and myriad Central Asian peoples alike) is so much more than any mass-produced, chemical-filled junk.

If you want a hot meal, without a big deal, see if you can still pick up a hot pocket at the grocery store. But if you want *samsa* without a flight to Asia, I've got you covered.

250g (9oz) strong white bread flour, plus extra for dusting

1 egg, gently beaten, for the egg wash

sesame, nigella, and/or cumin seeds (optional)

For the filling

250g (9oz) lamb shoulder, finely minced, preferably by hand

1¼ tsp fine sea salt

3 tsp ground cumin

1 tsp cumin seeds, lightly toasted

¼ tsp ground white pepper

2 tbsp sesame oil

1 onion, finely diced

½ tsp coarsely ground black pepper

To make the dough, sift the flour into the bowl of a stand mixer fitted with a dough hook. Mix at a low speed, then, with the mixer still running, slowly pour in 120ml (½ cup/4fl oz) cold water. Increase the mixer's speed to medium and let it work its magic, pausing occasionally to ensure the flour from the sides of the bowl is being well incorporated, and using a spatula to scrape those sides down if it's not.

After 5–6 minutes, you should have a stiff, hard dough. If you don't, you may need to add an extra tablespoon of water or flour depending on your particular flour – they're all different and come together differently.

Once you have that hard dough, use your (clean) hands to bring it together into a ball, then cover the bowl with a tea towel and leave to rest for 30 minutes.

Meanwhile, prepare the filling. In a medium mixing bowl, combine your hand-diced lamb with the salt, ground cumin, cumin seeds, white pepper, and sesame oil. Let the meat marinate for 15 minutes, soaking up all that goodness and flavour, before adding the diced onion and coarse black pepper to the bowl, and mixing to combine.

Preheat your oven to 220°C (200°C fan/425°F/Gas 7). If you have a baking stone, pop it in the oven to preheat; otherwise, grab a non-stick baking tray (or a regular one lined with a non-stick silicone baking sheet) and set aside.

Lightly dust your work surface with flour and, when the dough's 30-minute nap is over, divide it into eight relatively evenly sized dough balls. Roll them out one at a time, keeping the dough balls you aren't using under their tea towel blanket; they can nap some more, lucky ducks.

Roll each dough ball out into a 15–18cm (6–7in) circle, trying your best to make them thinner at the edges than at the centre. If you can't, don't worry. These guys are going to be awesome no matter how you roll out your dough, but if you can't get thinner edges and a thicker centre, you will likely need to bake them for a minute or two longer to make sure the dough fully cooks. No one wants a soggy bottom – I learned that from *The Great British Bake-Off*.

Place 2 tablespoons of the lamb-and-onion filling in the centre of each dough round. Brush a smidge of egg wash around the outside perimeter of your dough before you begin folding and sealing it.

Compared to other dumpling-folding methods, this is a walk in the park. Simply fold the top half of the round down over the filling, and then fold the bottom half up and over the top half. Easy! Then, fold one side into the centre before doing the same with the opposite side. You're basically making a meat-filled dough envelope. Press down gently with your fingertips on your soon-to-be hot pocket's seam to seal it up, and then paint the seam with a bit of egg wash for good measure.

Arrange your little bundles of joy seam-side down. Press down on the top of each with your palm to gently flatten it and even out the filling. Generously brush each dumpling with more egg wash and, if you like, sprinkle with some sesame, nigella, and/or cumin seeds.

Bake your *samsa* in the oven – either on the non-stick baking tray or on the preheated baking stone – for 18–20 minutes, or until the tops are golden brown and almost crispy when you knock on them gently.

Try these hot pockets – they're breathtaking.

A bazaar in Bukhara, Uzbekistan. October 1978.

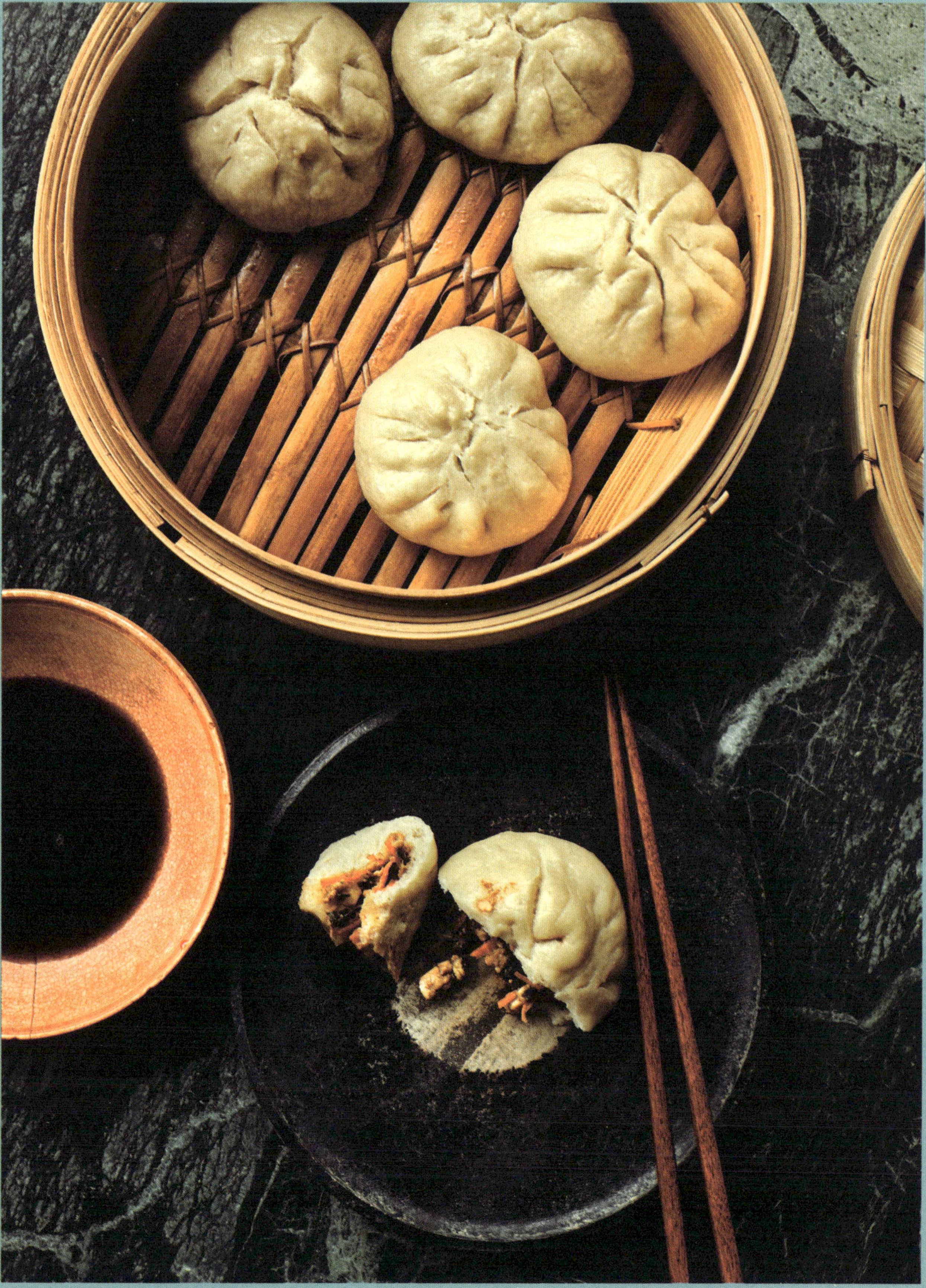

SPINACH & TOFU BAOZI

Makes 18 *baozi*

Ubiquitous in China, yet unfamiliar to most outside Asia, the *baozi* is the unsung hero of the dumpling world. Or, at least, of my dumpling world. I love them so much.

Baozi's soft, pillowy yeasted dough is increasingly known in the Western world because of the popular Taiwanese *gua bao*, a sandwich-like bun with a near-identical dough that typically houses melt-in-your-mouth braised pork belly. And *baozi* fillings, this one included, are generally near-identical to those of the boiled dumplings (*shui jiao*) found in Chinese restaurants the world over. *Baozi*: simultaneously unfamiliar and yet instantly recognizable at first bite.

But *baozi* are only *baozi* when they are stuffed. A steamed bun made from the same dough, yet unfilled, is called *mantou*, a word that sounds suspiciously like *manti* – the Turkic word used to describe dumplings from the shores of the Mediterranean to the mountains of Xinjiang. And this may be no coincidence. *Mantou* of yore, like *baozi* of today, were stuffed with meat and spices, and some scholars believe they criss-crossed Central Asia starting in the 13th century when the Pax Mongolica, that lauded time of peace and stability, resulted in a massive increase in usage of the overland trade routes known as … drumroll, please … the Silk Roads.

Could it be that stuffed *mantou* travelled these roads alongside Kublai Khan's soldiers, emissaries, and tradespeople? We can't be certain, but it is certain that these *baozi* are real, and they are spectacular. Enjoy your *baozi* plain, dipped in soy sauce mixed with some black vinegar, or smothered in crispy chilli oil.

For the dough

2 tsp granulated sugar

7g (¼oz) packet fast-action dried yeast

500g (1lb 2oz) plain flour, plus extra for dusting

100g (3½oz) cornflour

1 tsp fine sea salt

For the filling

225g (8oz) firm tofu

350g (12oz) frozen chopped spinach

1 carrot, peeled and julienned

5cm (2in) piece of fresh ginger, peeled and grated

1 tbsp cornflour or potato starch

½ tsp ground white pepper

¼ tsp Chinese five spice powder

1 tbsp fine sea salt

1 tsp MSG

5 tsp sesame oil

2 tsp dark soy sauce

In a small bowl, combine the sugar and yeast with 300ml (1¼ cups/10fl oz) lukewarm water. Mix and set aside for 5 minutes.

Sift the flour, cornflour, and salt into the bowl of a stand mixer fitted with a dough hook. With the mixer on low, briefly combine the dry ingredients, then, with the mixer still running, slowly pour in the sugar and yeast water. Set a timer for 9 minutes, turn the mixer to a medium speed, and let it work its modern magic.

After 9 minutes, the dough should be well-combined, smooth, and a bit stiff. Turn off your mixer and, using (clean) hands, knead the dough for 1 minute more, then shape it into a ball. Keep the dough in the bowl (or move it to another if you really want), cover it with a clean tea towel, and put it somewhere warm to rise for 1 hour.

While your dough is proofing, prep your filling, the first step of which is draining your tofu. Draining your tofu is vital when making *baozi*, because an overly wet filling will overwhelm the dough and it just won't be good. I promise. So remove the tofu from its packaging and drain the water into your sink, then place the tofu on a chopping board, top it with a paper towel, and then place another chopping board on top. Plop a super-heavy book on top of everything and let the tofu drain for 10–20 minutes.

Meanwhile, bring a medium saucepan of water to the boil and quickly blanch your spinach for 2 minutes, then drain in a fine mesh sieve. Using a wooden spoon, press down on the drained spinach to try and get as much moisture out of the spinach as possible.

Take your well-drained block of tofu and, using your hands or a fork, crumble it into a medium bowl. You want it to look like minced meat. Once you get the tofu to that texture, add all the other filling ingredients, including the spinach (once it's cool enough to handle), and mix everything together. Set aside and return to your dough.

Hopefully after 1 hour, your dough will have risen and doubled in size. If it hasn't, give it some more time, making sure to wait until it has doubled to bring it out for the next step.

Prepare a lightly floured surface and release your risen dough from its bowl on to that surface. Divide the dough into 18 pieces, each approximately 50g (1¾oz) in weight, and shape them into little balls.

Using the heel of your hand, press down on the first dough ball so that it becomes a thick, flat circle, then roll it out into a thin circle about 13cm (5¼in) in diameter. Rotate the dough as you roll it out, to get that circle as evenly rounded as possible. Do this for each ball and line them up in a row, ready for the filling.

In the middle of each dough circle, plop a heaping tablespoon of your filling. To pleat and seal your *baozi*, you have a couple of options. The simplest is to gather the edges of the circle, pull them up over the centre of the filling and pinch them together tightly to seal. If you opt for this method, flip your *baozi* over and steam them with the non-pinched side up.

The other option is only a bit more difficult once you get the hang of it, and yields a classic pleated dumpling pouch familiar across the globe. Use your non-dominant hand to keep the dough steady on your work surface, then use your other hand to pull up and pleat your dough, like a little accordion, all the way around the dough circle. When you come full-circle (literally), pinch the tops together to firmly seal them. You should end up with between 12 and 18 pleats. And you won't win a prize for the most pleats, so don't stress; your goal is to seal the *baozi*, and then steam and eat them. That's it.

Line up your beautifully filled and formed *baozi*, cover with a clean tea towel once again, and let rest for 15 minutes.

Once your *baozi* have rested, it's time to steam them. Arrange your *baozi* on a bamboo steamer lined with baking parchment, making sure to leave a 2cm (¾in) gap between each *baozi* and around the edges of the steamer. Depending on the size of your steamer, you will need to steam the *baozi* in batches.

Steam each batch for 15 minutes, then allow them to cool for another 5 minutes before serving (after all this work, you don't want to burn off the top of your mouth).

If you've made more than you can eat in one go, worry not: once cooled and nestled into an airtight container, the *baozi* will keep beautifully in your refrigerator for 3–4 days (or in your freezer for up to 3 months). Steam or microwave to reheat.

A CENTRAL ASIAN BREAD

Makes 2 bread rounds

Well, we are not in Central Asia now, are we? We are probably at home in the UK, the US, or maybe even somewhere glamourous like Canada. Hey – I'm not knocking the Canucks; I was born in Canada. It's awesome. Great health care. Gorgeous lakes. Ice hockey. I digress. But the point is, you are probably not going to be making this bread in a purpose-built oven in your backyard or front garden. If you are, I'm supremely jealous. The rest of us do not have the ovens of the Middle East, and Central and South Asia. And we are not making exactly the same kind of bread you would find in Urumqi, Khiva, or Ashgabat. We are making an approximation – a very, very tasty and satisfying approximation that asks to be torn off in chunks with your hands, dipped in Suzma (see p77), or covered in Gaymak (see p80) and honey. Save it for tomorrow's Dograma or Yangrou Paomo (see p54). Use it to sop up tonight's Da Pan Ji (see p117), or eat it with a bowl of Piti (see p59). Savour it. Enjoy it. Respect it.

7g (¼oz) packet fast-action dried yeast

400g (14oz) plain or strong white bread flour (I have used both successfully, so use whichever you have), plus extra for dusting

2 tsp fine sea salt

Glazes (optional)

1 egg yolk, beaten with 2 tbsp milk

olive oil

Toppings (optional)

sesame seeds

nigella seeds

Pour 260ml (1 cup plus 2 tablespoons/9¼fl oz) lukewarm water into a jug and add the yeast. Stir to dissolve, then set aside.

Sift the flour into the bowl of a stand mixer fitted with a dough hook. Add the salt. With the mixer on low, slowly add your yeasty water. Once all the water has been added, increase the speed to medium and let the mixer work its magic for 8–10 minutes. Your resulting dough should be soft, pliable, and a bit sticky, but not so sticky that it glues itself to your hands when you touch it.

Form the dough into a ball, then leave it in a bowl covered with a tea towel or cling film, and let it rest and rise in a warm place for 1½–2 hours, or until doubled in size.

Once he is risen, remove the cover and take out your aggression by punching the dough down in the bowl with your fist.

Generously flour your work surface and then, using a bench scraper or stiff silicone spatula, transfer your dough from its bowl to the work surface. Sprinkle a light dusting of flour on top of your dough, and then use your knuckles (I'm telling you, this recipe is really satisfying in its hands-on nature) to punch it out into a 20 × 25cm (8 × 10in) rectangle.

Fold the dough rectangle in half, from bottom to top. Punch the dough down again.

Now fold the dough rectangle in half again, this time from right to left. Punch it down again.

Fold the dough rectangle in half from left to right. Punch it down again.

Finally, fold the dough rectangle in half from top to bottom and punch it down a final time.

Split the dough into two equal portions and shape the portions into balls. Cover with a damp tea towel and leave to rest for 15 minutes.

Meanwhile, preheat your oven to its highest possible temperature. If you have a pizza stone, put it in the oven now to preheat.

After 15 minutes, take one rested dough ball, lightly dust its top with flour, and use the heel of your hand to flatten into a round pancake. Leave the other cosy under its damp towel.

Here's where things get funky. And fun! Your goal is to turn your little dough pancake into a circle 20–26cm (8–10¼in) in diameter, with the outer 3cm (1¼in) of its circumference twice as thick as the rest of it. Think of a pizza dough and its raised crust – you're basically going for the same thing.

To shape the dough, I like to pretend I'm a *pizzaiolo* like my next-door neighbour Huw – this means I lift the dough circle over my clenched fists and then open my fingers and stretch the dough in the air, turning my hands and the dough as I stretch. It takes some practice, but it's fun. If you prefer, you can just use a rolling pin, as long as your end result is a circle of dough with raised edges.

Use the tines of a fork or, if you're super special/lucky, a cool contraption known in Uzbekistan as a *chekich*, to generously pierce the inner circle of your dough all over, all the way through. You can even make patterns if you like. I try, but they never look how I want them to, so I consider random piercings the way to go.

If you like, now's the time to glaze your dough by brushing it with an egg wash or some olive oil. You can also sprinkle some nigella and/or sesame seeds over the top.

If you have a pizza peel, use it to transfer your dough to the preheated pizza stone in your oven. If you're not outfitted like a pizzeria, that's fine – carefully transfer your dough to a non-stick baking tray, and place it in your preheated oven, on the middle rack, to bake.

Key to our approximation of a Central Asian oven (and to the tastiness of this bread) is the introduction of some steam. To do this, you can spritz the bottom of your oven with water halfway through the baking process; I then continue to do this every 3 minutes until the bread is baked. Alternatively, you can also place some ice cubes in a tray and put it on the bottom rack of your oven when you first put your bread in. Work with what you've got, but definitely get some steam in there.

How long your bread will need to bake will depend on your oven's maximum temperature, but allow up to 15–18 minutes baking per round. My oven gets hot; my rounds take 9–12 minutes each. They take 18 minutes in my in-laws' oven.

Repeat with your second ball of dough.

Allow your bread to cool before eating.

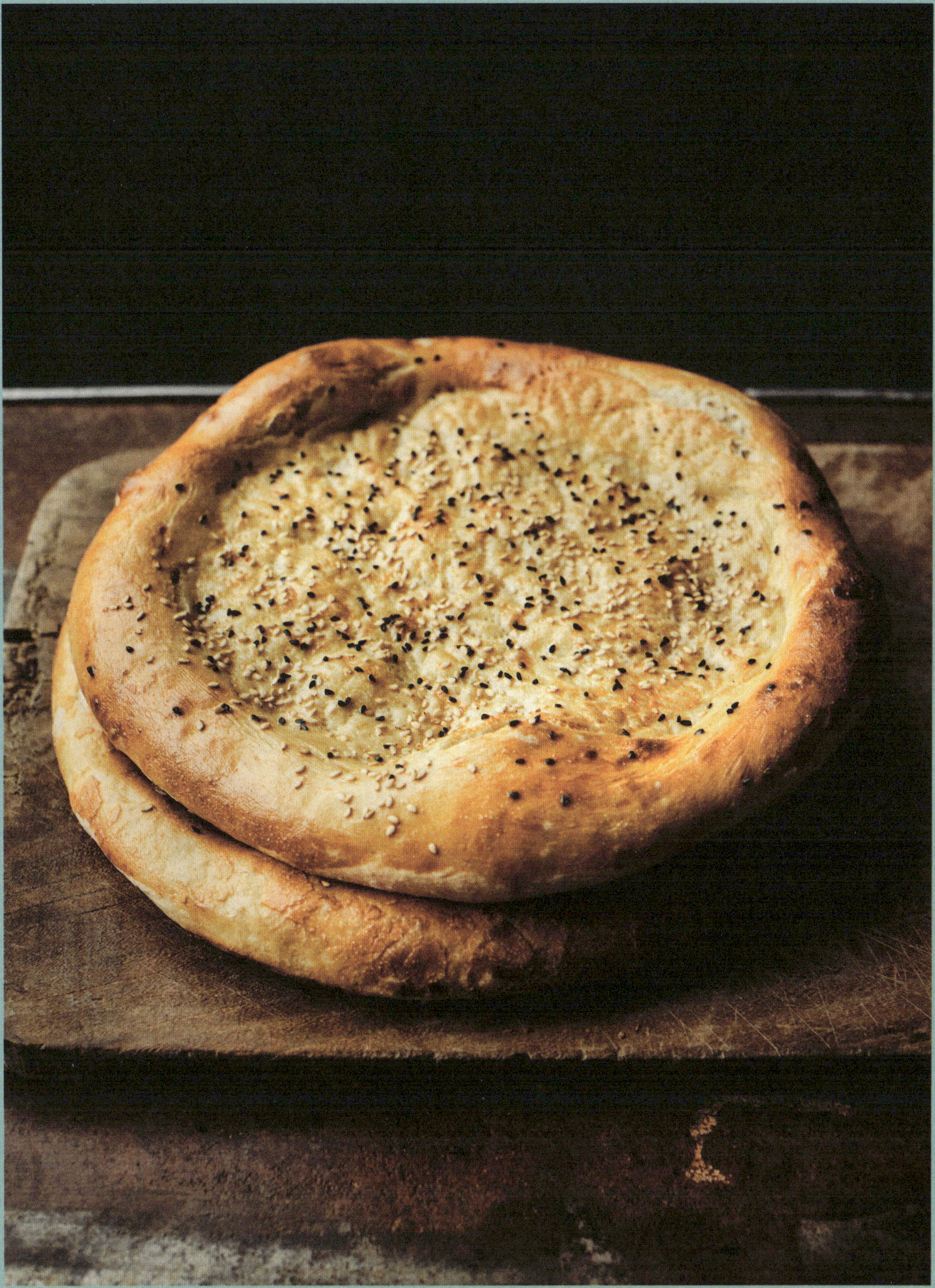

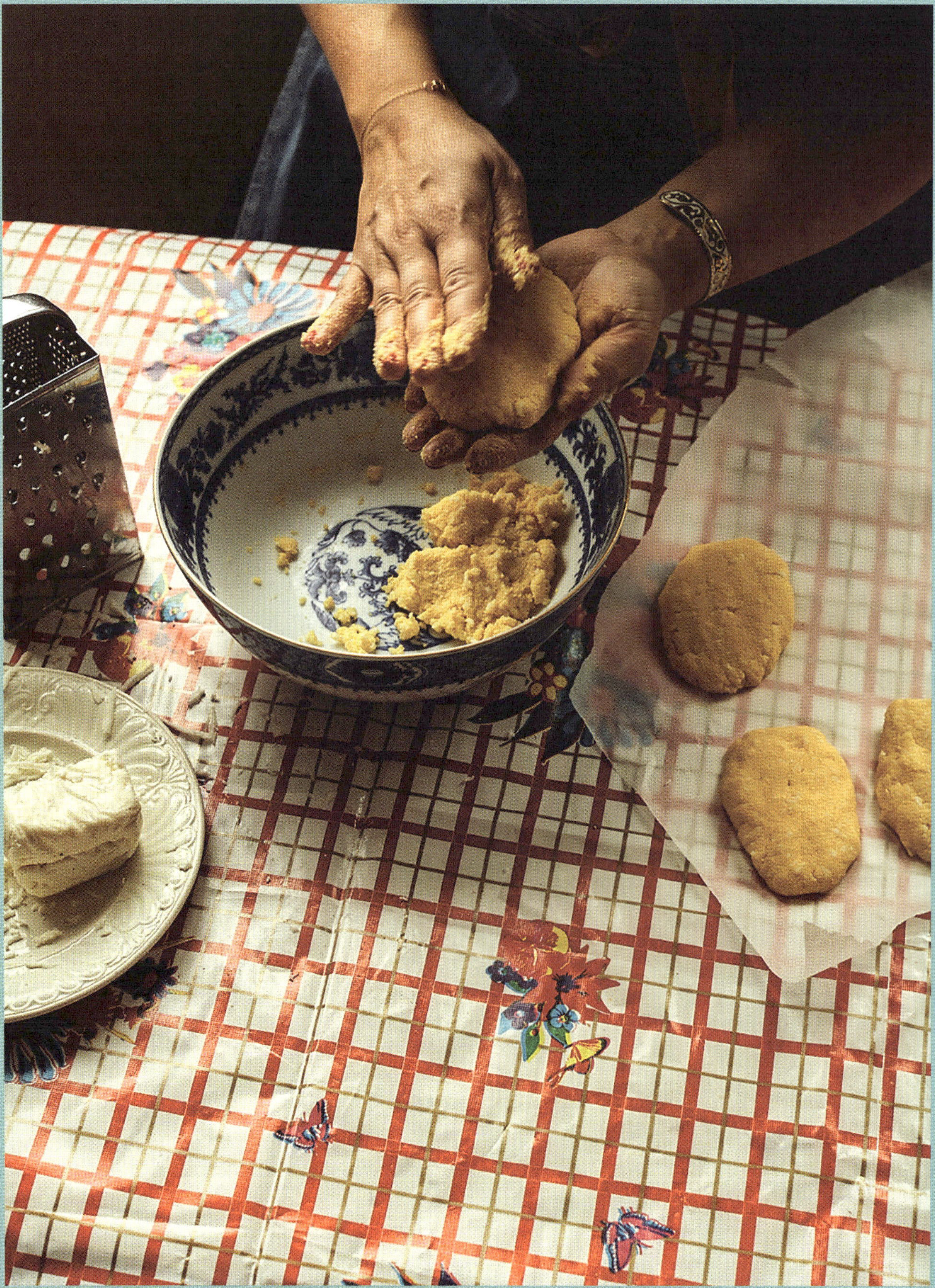

CHVISHTARI

Cheesy Georgian Cornbread

Makes 8–9 cakes

The USSR may have been ineffectual on many fronts, but it was skilled at dividing and compartmentalizing – at making sure that each republic's welfare depended on that of the union as a whole. Uzbekistan provided the USSR with its cotton, Azerbaijan with its oil, and Georgia with its citrus, tea, and wine. In return, the USSR provided its republics with "free" energy: gas for heating and cooking, electricity for lighting. Electricity, like that lighting the news stand my father noticed in Tashkent (see p6), that no one needed to turn off … until someone did.

Maka's aunt was getting ready to fry the *mchadi* when the gas supply was cut off. It was late November 1991 and the family had gathered in Tbilisi, both to welcome Maka's cousin home from Germany and to belatedly celebrate their country's independence, which had been declared some six months earlier. While the USSR wasn't formally dissolved until a month later, it was effectively dead in the water by November 1991, with Kazakhstan the only republic left in the collapsed union.

Initial joy and elation turned to despair and difficulty. Soon after the gas disappeared, so too did the electricity. Maybe freedom wasn't all it was cracked up to be, not when you only got electricity for two hours a day and couldn't even cook something as simple as cornbread. But Maka's family was resilient – they found an old gasoline-powered oven, scavenged some gasoline, and were able to feed themselves. Georgians in general are resilient, still fighting, still protesting, still resisting occupation, both physical and soft, by a northern neighbour greedy and eager to (re-)establish empire and regional supremacy.

Mchadi, the cornbread Maka's aunt was making when the Russians shut off the gas, is a simple preparation consisting of cornmeal (usually white), salt, and water, whereas *chvishtari* is a cheese-stuffed cornbread. I have given you a recipe for the latter here, but cooked *à la* johnnycakes/hoecakes, a fried bread beloved from America's New England to Jamaica, the history of which is intertwined with American indigenous peoples whose resilience in the face of empire and supremacy must also be applauded and remembered.

Best enjoyed with Lobio (see p65).

- 200g (7oz) cornmeal (white if you can find it)
- ¼ tsp fine sea salt
- 100g (3½oz) grated scamorza (or halloumi, if you can't find scamorza)
- 100g (3½oz) unsalted butter, plus extra if needed

Combine the cornmeal, salt, and grated cheese in a large mixing bowl. Slowly pour in up to 250ml (1 cup plus 1 tbsp/9fl oz) just-boiled water, mixing it in with a wooden spoon as you do so. The amount of water you need will depend on the type of cornmeal you use. Watch the texture – you want it firm enough so that you will be able to shape it into patties, but not so firm that it becomes stodgy.

Use your (clean) hands to shape the mixture into patties. While I make mine oval and palm-sized, and can cook about four at a time in my pan, you can make your cornmeal patties as large or small as you like. But unless you have an obscenely large pan or a massive flat-top griddle plate, you're going to need to cook your *chvishtari* in batches, adding more butter to the pan each time.

Melt some of the butter in a sauté pan over a medium–high heat. Reduce the heat to low, and plop your cornmeal patties into the buttery pan. Depending on their size, cook for 5–6 minutes on one side, then flip and cook for another 5–6 minutes on the other side. The goal is glistening and golden corn cakes, so adjust your cooking time accordingly. You may want to use a spatula to press down your *chvishtari* to an even thickness. Transfer to a plate to keep warm and repeat with the remaining butter and *chvishtari* mixture.

Get 'em while they're hot!

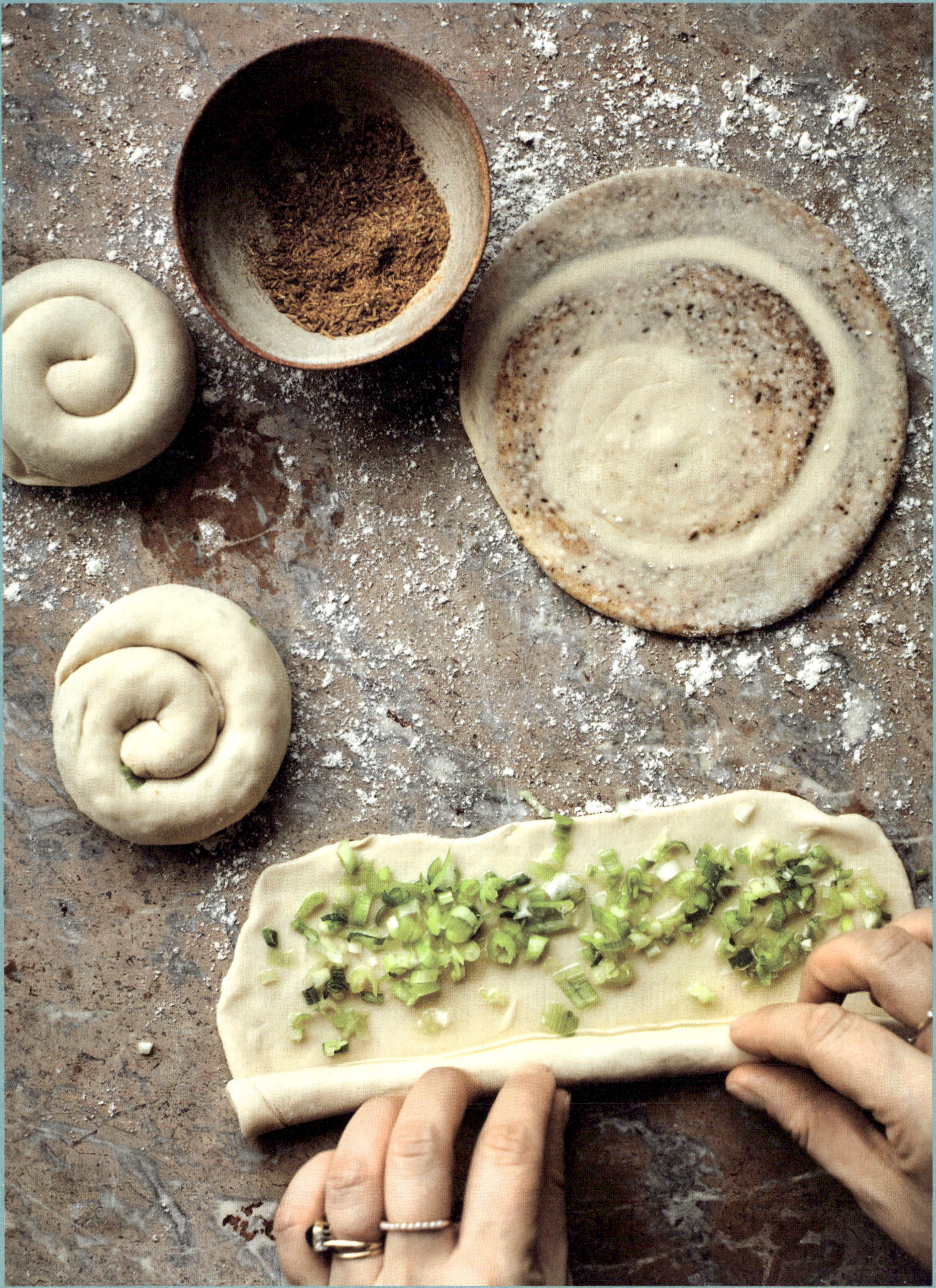

LAYERED & FRIED FLATBREADS

Makes 4 breads

The spiritual cousin of paratha and roti, this simple pan-fried flatbread, laminated with fat and often filled with herbs, spices, or meat, exists in various iterations across Asia. In China, one version is *cong youbing*, aka the beloved spring onion-filled pancake, while Tajikistan's *fatir*, and Azerbaijan's *feseli*, like China's lesser-known *laobing* and the Kyrgyz *katama*, are more modestly filled with nothing more than ghee – lots and lots of ghee. In Uzbekistan, the *katlama* takes things up a notch with a minced meat, ghee, and onion filling reminiscent in both name and composition of the Pakistani *keema katlama*, a deep-fried beef-filled bread with rumoured Turkic origins.

I've included here a base recipe for the flatbread, as well as some suggested fillings. Feel free to experiment with ingredients and flavours you enjoy – that's how I ended up with my favourite, the caramelized onion and feta filling I've shared with you overleaf.

250g (9oz) plain flour, plus extra for dusting

½ tsp fine sea salt

120ml (½ cup/4fl oz) cup olive oil, melted unsalted butter, or melted ghee

filling of your choice (optional; see suggestions on p212)

Sift the flour and salt together in the bowl of a stand mixer fitted with a dough hook. Mix them together at a low speed, then, with the mixer still running, slowly pour in 120ml (½ cup/4fl oz) warm water. Increase the mixer's speed to medium and let it work its magic, pausing occasionally to ensure the flour from the sides of the bowl is being well incorporated, and using a spatula to scrape those sides down if it's not.

After 5–6 minutes, you should have a pliable dough that is tacky to the touch but does not stick to your hands. If you don't, add a bit more flour and knead for a further minute. Form the dough into a ball, then leave it in a bowl covered with a tea towel or cling film, and let it rest for 45 minutes.

Pour your fat of choice into a small bowl and grab a pastry brush. This is what you will brush onto your breads to achieve their glorious layers of flaky dough. I like to use ghee when making the meat filling, but otherwise tend to stick to olive oil – though this is not the norm in these breads' countries of origin.

Tip your rested dough out of its bowl on to a well-floured surface and divide it into four equal pieces. Take one piece of dough and pat it into a small round, before lightly flouring its top and rolling it out into a thin 15 × 20cm (6 × 8in) rectangle.

Brush your dough rectangle with your fat of choice, covering it from edge to edge. This is no diet food, and if you're using enough fat, you should get through the entire 120ml (½ cup/4fl oz) by the time you're done with your four flatbreads.

If using, place a quarter of your filling evenly across the top of each oiled dough rectangle.

Starting with the long edge closest to you, carefully roll up the rectangle into a tight log. As it is a thin, delicate dough, you will need to be gentle.

Take one end of your dough log and curl it into itself, like a snail, coiled snake, or cinnamon roll. You get the picture. I hope. If not, look left. Tuck the tail end of the dough underneath and, using the heel and palm of your hand, press down into the centre to flatten the coiled dough into a puck. Gently roll it out into a 15cm (6in) circle and brush the top with your liquid fat of choice.

Heat a non-stick sauté pan over a medium heat. Place your flatbread, oiled-side down, onto the pan and cook for 2 minutes. Brush the non-oiled side with oil, then flip the bread and cook it on its other side for another 2 minutes. Set aside on a plate while you repeat this process with the other three pieces of dough, then serve.

CARAMELIZED ONION & FETA FILLING

5 tbsp olive oil
2 onions, thinly sliced into half-moons
80g (3oz) crumbled feta cheese
fine sea salt and freshly ground black pepper

Heat the oil in a sauté pan over a medium heat. Add the sliced onions and a generous pinch of salt, stir, and turn the heat to its lowest setting. Cook the onions for 25–30 minutes, or until they are soft and golden. You will need to check in on and stir them occasionally to make sure they are neither burning nor sticking to the pan; if they threaten to do either, add a tablespoon of water.

Remove the caramelized onions from the pan and cool them in a bowl. Season with a few grinds of black pepper, then stir in the feta cheese. Your filling is ready to go!

MINCED BEEF & ONION FILLING

3 tbsp ghee or olive oil
½ onion, finely diced
75g (2½oz) minced beef, (the higher the fat content, the better)
fine sea salt and freshly ground black pepper

Heat the ghee or olive oil in a sauté pan over a medium–high heat. Add the diced onion and cook for 5 minutes, or until soft and translucent. Transfer to a bowl. Add the beef, a generous pinch of salt and a few grinds of pepper. Mix well, and this filling is ready to party.

GUTAB

Azeri "Quesadillas"

Makes 5

I first tasted *gutab* in 2016 in Baku. At dinner one evening, my father's friend Ismail, our host and unofficial guide, restaurant-selector, and food-orderer that trip, surprised us with plate after plate of *gutab* – some filled with herbs, some with pumpkin, some with lamb – and I inhaled all of them. My dad took one from the platter, held it between his fingers, looked at me quizzically and said, "What is this? Some Mexican quesadilla?"

A couple of things: 1) He was so confused by the *gutab*, a dish with which he was entirely unfamiliar, that he sounded like Derek Zoolander asking Mugatu whether an architectural mock-up was a "building for ants", and, 2) at nearly eighty years old, having lived in North America for decades, my father assumed the half-moon filled flatbread in his hand was Mexican in origin rather than Azeri. Though born and raised only a few hundred miles south of the border of the country in which we were sitting, my dad equated the Azeri flatbread with something commonly eaten south of the American border.

"No," I told him, "It's not a quesadilla – but it's kind of like one, I guess – sort of. Just try it."

I'll say that to you as well – it's kind of like a quesadilla; just try it.

250g (9oz) plain flour, plus extra for dusting

¼ tsp fine sea salt

For the filling

500g (1lb 2oz) butternut squash, peeled and cut into 1cm (½in) dice

30g (1oz) unsalted butter, or 2 tbsp olive oil

1 onion, finely diced

1 tsp pomegranate molasses

For the topping (optional)

melted butter (salted or unsalted)

flaky sea salt

Sift the flour and salt together in the bowl of a stand mixer fitted with a dough hook. Mix them together at a low speed, then, with the mixer still running, slowly pour in 125ml (½ cup plus 1 teaspoon/4¼fl oz) lukewarm water. Increase the mixer's speed to medium and let it work its magic, pausing occasionally to ensure the flour from the sides of the bowl is being well incorporated, and using a spatula to scrape those sides down if it's not.

After 5–6 minutes, you should have a pliable dough that is tacky to the touch but does not stick to your hands. Form the dough into a ball, then leave it in a bowl covered with a tea towel or cling film, and let it rest for 30 minutes.

Meanwhile, make your filling.

Tip the diced squash into a medium saucepan and add enough water to the pan to just cover it. Simmer over a medium heat for 10–15 minutes until just tender. Drain and set aside.

Heat your butter or olive oil in a large sauté pan over a medium heat. Add the diced onion and cook for 5–7 minutes, or until soft and golden. Add the drained squash to the pan, and stir to mix. Cook the onion and squash together for a further 2–3 minutes.

Transfer the cooked mixture to a medium mixing bowl, then use a potato masher or fork to mash everything together. Drizzle in the pomegranate molasses and stir to mix. Set aside to cool and return to your dough.

Turn out your rested dough ball on to a well-floured work surface and divide it into five equal pieces. Shape each one into a ball. Return four of them to the covered bowl, and use a (clean) palm to flatten out the fifth dough ball on your work surface before rolling it into a thin circle 22–25cm (8½–10in) in diameter.

Take a fifth of your filling mix and spread it over half of the dough circle, leaving a 5mm (¼in) border at the edges. Fold the other half of the dough over to make a half-moon-shaped *gutab*. Use your palm to gently flatten the filling, then use your fingertips to press and seal the edges.

Repeat with the rest of your dough balls, while keeping your stuffed *gutab* waiting under yet another tea towel.

Heat a non-stick sauté pan over a high heat – you want it super-hot to start with – and then reduce the heat to medium. Place your filled *gutab* in the pan and cook for 2–3 minutes, or until the underside is freckled with brown spots. Flip the *gutab* and do the same on the other side, then set aside on a plate. Repeat with the other stuffed and waiting *gutabs*.

Serve the *gutabs* hot, warm, or even cold. They're always delicious. If you opt for the hot route, spread a bit of butter on top before serving, and add a sprinkling of flaky sea salt too – what a decadent quesadilla!

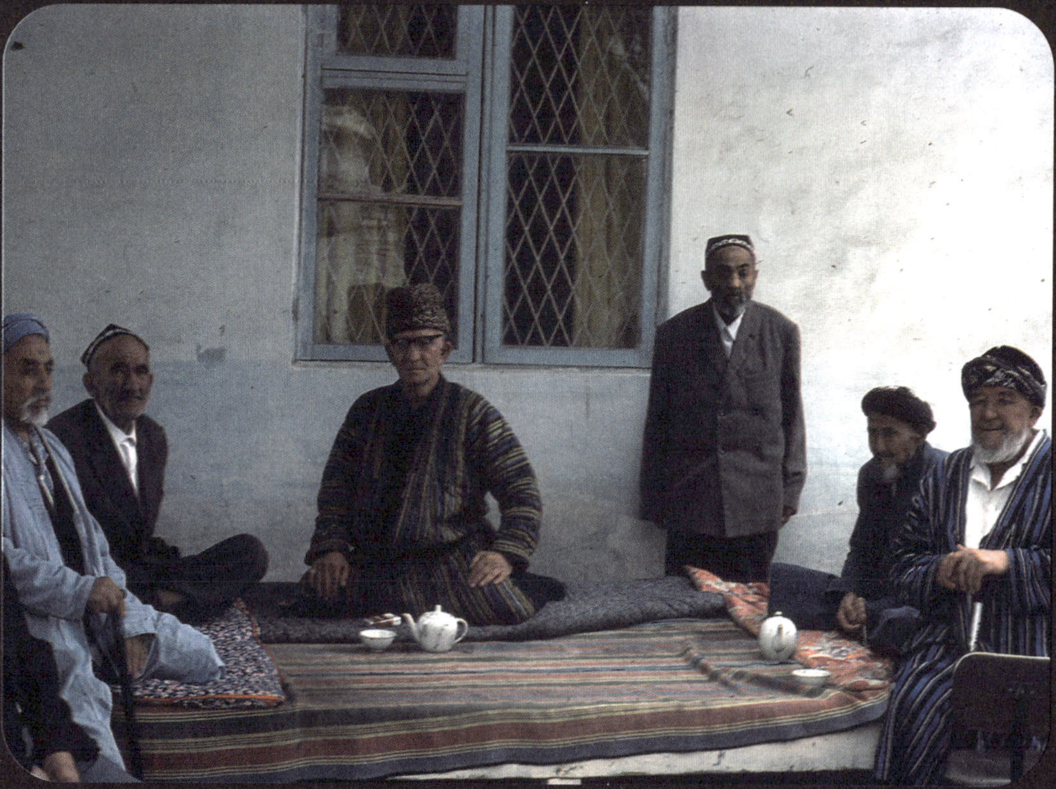

SWEET TREATS

FRUIT ROLL-UPS
& TEATIME
IN THE GOBI
216

APPLE (& QUINCE) PIE
221

TRES LECHES
RICE PUDDING
223

ALMOND BUNDT CAKE
227

SPICED WALNUT
BLONDIES
229

CHERRY KOMPOT
Uzbek Cherry "Punch"
231

NOT-YOUR-AVERAGE-
COUNTY-FAIR
FUNNEL CAKES
232

PEANUT &
POPCORN BRITTLE
234

TRIO OF SHARBATS
Iranian Fruit Syrups
235

TRIO OF JAMS
239

STICKY MAPLE
PERSIMMON PUDDING
241

SOUR CHERRY &
WALNUT SHORTBREAD
244

QUINCE BAKEWELL
PUDDING
246

LAVASHAK
*Fruit Roll-Ups
(with Actual Fruit)*
249

FRUIT ROLL-UPS & TEATIME IN THE GOBI

When I was a kid, my father was often away from home — either working at the hospital and his medical clinic in Michigan, or setting up medical clinics and hospitals in Iran. Before he headed overseas, we would fill up his suitcases with gifts for our family: party-sized bags of candy bars, Detroit Pistons jerseys, Air Jordans, and Nintendo Game Boys, along with clothes and toys we had outgrown. When my father returned, his suitcases were still bursting at the seams, but were now filled with saffron, dried chickpeas and mulberries, rolled-up carpets, the occasional piece of gold jewellery, inlaid tissue boxes and picture frames, and pounds and pounds of pistachios. We sent over America and we got Iran back.

(ASIDE: Oh — and there were sanction regimes in place. There still are. Rules to stop people like us sending America over to Iran and bringing Iran back to America. Sanctions were supposed to act as pressure on the *mullahs* in Iran, supposed to penalize them for taking Americans hostage in 1979, supposed to financially punish if not cripple the regime, to force it to fail, to fall. And yet, here we are, decades later, and not a lot has changed. I'm not going to say that all that the sanctions did/do was make it harder for millions of people to eat Hershey's Kisses, play video games, and eat the best pistachios in the world without worrying about when their freezer stash would run out, but I will say that sometimes it certainly seemed and continues to seem that way. I digress. Again.)

Back to the suitcases! The suitcases brimming with foodstuffs (and not-so-legally imported carpets, of course) that filled our American house with not only the taste of Iran, but the scent of it as well. And, as the smell of my father's erstwhile homeland permeated his adopted one, you could always find me devouring my favourite part of Iran — *lavashak*.

I can still hear it — the plastic wrap, ripping off the fruit paste. I can still feel it — the tacky stickiness. And, wow, I can still taste it. The apricot. The pomegranate. The grape. Flavour so intense, so concentrated that it almost overwhelmed your taste buds. I would tear a bit off and put it in my mouth. Chew it. And then suck on it, extracting as much tart sweetness from it as I could. Chew some more, swallow, and go back for another bit, another bite, unable to stop at just one little strip, addicted. They were like Fruit Roll-Ups, like the Yoyos my six-year-old eats now, but better, bigger, and bolder.

> I CAN STILL TASTE IT. THE APRICOT. THE POMEGRANATE. THE GRAPE. FLAVOUR SO INTENSE THAT IT ALMOST OVERWHELMED YOUR TASTE BUDS.

The fruit roll-ups you could buy at American grocery stores when I was a kid were massively popular and a commercial hit for the big manufacturers. I loved them, at least as much as Iranian *lavashak*, but my parents didn't love me eating them — too much sugar, too many chemicals, they said. Turns out Sue and Shapoor were right: fast-forward a few decades, and those manufacturers were sued for deceptive advertising because their fruit roll-ups didn't even contain fruit; go figure. That was in 2011, over a century after George Shalhoub, an immigrant to New York City, began selling snippets of imported sheets of apricot paste out of his Brooklyn grocery store, and thus catalyzing the history of fruit leather in America.

People have been making fruit roll-ups for centuries. Well, maybe they weren't making roll-ups, per se, but they were making fruit leather for certain. Stewing fruit over heat, turning it into a paste, straining out the pips, seeds, stones, and

Top: *Lavashak*, fruit, jams, pickles, and all sorts of deliciousness on the road to Sheki, Azerbaijan. May 2017.

Bottom: Teatime picnic in Iran. Sometime in the 1990s.

peel, then thinly spreading out the paste and drying it in the light and warmth of the sun, preserving summer goodness for the winter, creating long-lasting, portable fruit snacks: that's been going on for centuries. In Iran, from whence my father and *lavashak* hail, and in Syria, too, from whence George Shalhoub came.

At the start, George simply sold bits of *amardeen*, a sticky Syrian fruit paste he imported from his old country into his new. This went on for decades, an immigrant doling out pieces of home in the form of fruit leather. It was George's grandson, Louis, however, who had the idea to make a proprietary fruit leather by hand, right there in downtown Brooklyn, and package and sell it in individual rolls. And he did it. Louis sold the first commercial fruit roll-up in 1960. They were a success, so much so that big companies such as Sunkist and General Mills eventually took note, and started making their own – the ones that I grew up coveting and loving. Louis' company, Joray, still trades today, still based out of Brooklyn, and is run by George Shalhoub's great-grandson and his wife. Immigrants – we really do get the job done, don't we?!

I'm not going to lie – though I loved *lavashak*, I never really enjoyed the immigrant Iranian dessert spreads found at parties chez nous and at our family friends' houses. Saffron. Rose water. Honey. *Bamieh*. Brittle. Baklava. No, thank you. Not for me. They were not my favourite flavours. They were not my favourite desserts.

This remains more or less true today. It's not necessarily a continued dislike of the sweets and flavours of my father's heritage and the surrounding cultures and countries and traditions; it's more that I hold tightly to the sweets and dessert traditions of my mother's heritage, and of the country from which I hail.

I love American baked goods. I love a chewy chocolate-chip cookie. I love a brownie, a cherry pie, an apple cider doughnut, a banana split, a pecan sandie. I love them and I miss them. And, though I have come to embrace many British "puddings" in the last decade, my sweet tooth still gravitates to the New World, to the comforts of home and childhood.

With a few exceptions, though the recipes in this chapter highlight the flavours and ingredients of Iran, Azerbaijan, and Central Asia – the Silk Roads – and many are grounded in "traditional" preparations or approximations thereof, they are original creations that celebrate my own personal, cultural, and geographical experiences and flavour preferences. They are not "authentic", but they take me home. They take me back. They are comforting and soothing, while also tantalizing and inspiring. Most importantly, they are delicious. I hope you love them as much as I do.

In addition to edible sweet treats, I've also given you recipes for some drinkable ones. As with *lavashak*, *sharbats* and *kompots* are means of extending the life of fruits. *Sharbats* are, in the most basic terms, fruit-flavoured simple syrups, concentrated fruity sweetness meant to be enjoyed cold, over ice, and diluted with water, still or sparkling. Similar to but different from *sharbat*, *kompots* need no dilution, as fruit, water, and sweetener come together to form a refresher that is complete on its own. And, while no one will stop you from having a slice of cake, a nibble of blondie, or a bite of pudding with your fruity beverage, these drinks are not typically enjoyed alongside an additional sweet – that's where tea comes in.

Across the Middle East and Central Asia (as well as in the UK, now that I think of it) sweets tend to be enjoyed with a cup (or bowl or pot or *samovar*) of tea. For the most part, I encourage you to do the same with the recipes in this chapter. Black, unsweetened tea. Or maybe green tea, if that, like many across the Silk Roads, is your preferred cuppa. But, you know what goes well with black coffee? Some damn fine apple pie (see p221).

Left: Teatime next to the Khudafarin Bridge at the Azerbaijan–Iran border. The green mountains in the back are Iran. This is the closest I've ever been – so close that my phone sent me a "Welcome to Iran" message. April 2024.

Bottom: Me, Maria, my dad, and Sara in a field of poppies on the road to Quba, Azerbaijan. May 2017. Not pictured: A LOT more people stopping for blossomed-themed photo ops on a glorious spring day.

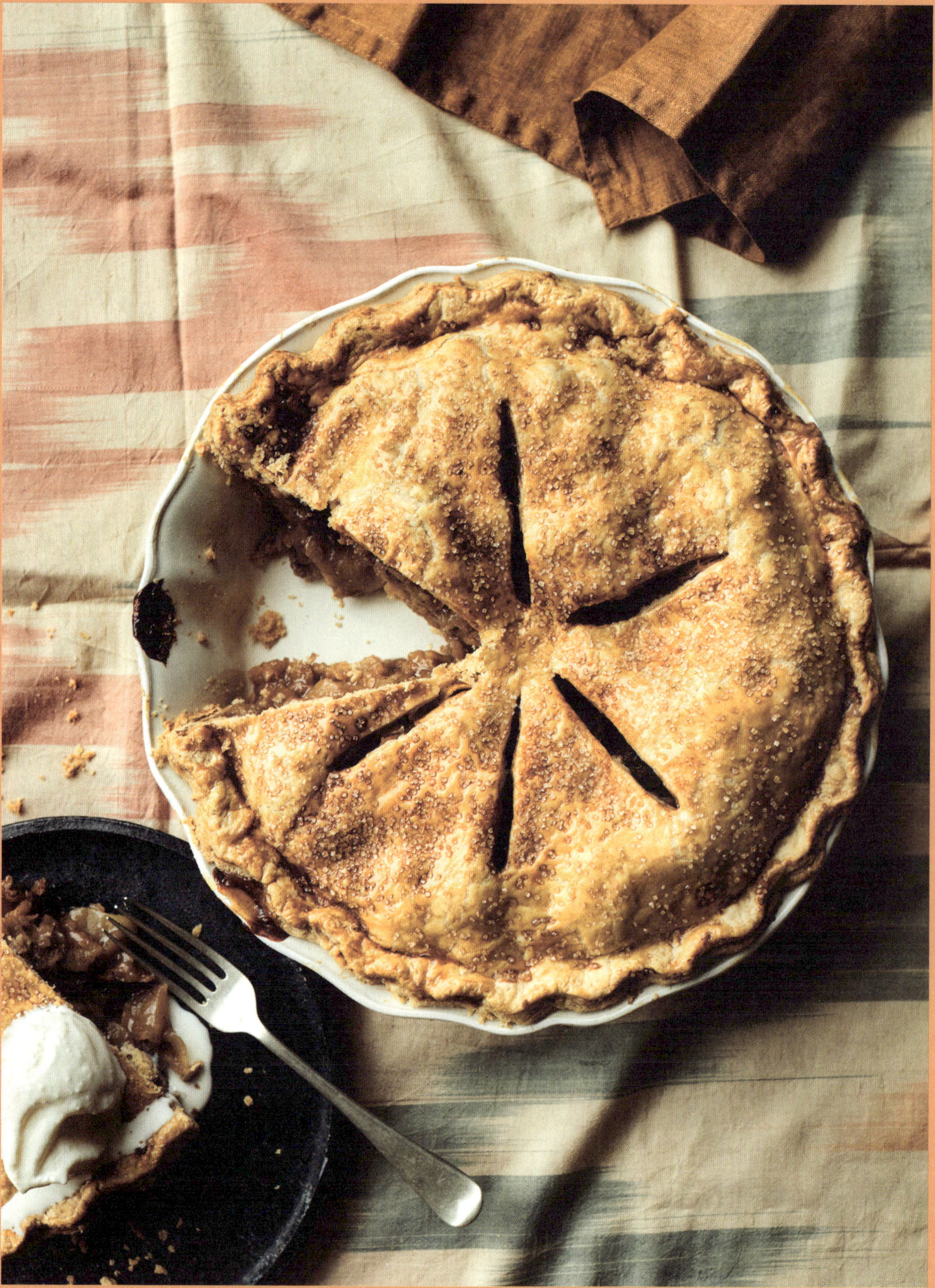

APPLE (& QUINCE) PIE

Serves 12

There are over 7,000 apple varieties grown in the world, of which nearly 3,000 are grown in the UK. Ditto the United States. Every single one of these apples – Pink Lady, Bramley, Walthamstow Wonder, Cox, unnamed garden apples, wild apples, lost apples, you name it – all of them originated in the very same place: an ancient forest in the Tianshan Mountains, somewhere near the China-Kazakhstan border. Right smack dab in the middle of Silk Roads territory, a veritable garden of Eden, an ancestral home, a *lao jia* from which apples spread across the globe.

Wild bears were the first Silk Roads apple tradesmen – or so some say. Gorging on the sweetest fruits in the forest, these bears unwittingly deposited apple seeds in a way, ahem, unfitting to discuss in a book about food. The seeds turned into saplings turned into fruit-bearing apple trees, and the process repeated itself, with bears eating and spreading apple progeny further and further from the initial forest. And man eventually tasted this fruit, loved it, planted it, harvested it, shared it, traded it, travelled with it. And baked it into a pie.

No fruit is more emblematic of Silk Roads trade and transmission of food, flavours, and ingredients than the humble apple. And no dessert is more associated with the United States than the humble apple pie. "As American as apple pie," they say. Well, I call shenanigans. The apple belongs to us all, the world over, and this pie celebrates not only the dessert traditions of my home country, but also the proverbial "old country", Central Asia: home of both the apple and the quince – of which I've included two in this recipe, and which lend this pie a pleasant tartness and further tether it to its Asian homeland.

Sweet and tart and warm and warming, serve your pie with cold vanilla ice cream (or – gasp! – a slice of sharp Cheddar) if you're American like me. Serve it with custard or cream if you're British like my husband. Serve with Gaymak (see p80) if you're Iranian like my dad. Apple pie: à la mode, à la Silk Roads.

Note: Once the dough has been mixed and formed into discs, it needs to spend at least 1 hour in the refrigerator, but it can also be frozen at that point and used whenever needed, so plan accordingly.

For the dough

300g (10oz) plain flour, plus extra for dusting

1 tsp fine sea salt

225g (8oz) unsalted butter, chilled and cut into 2cm (¾in) dice, plus extra for greasing

For the filling

1.9kg (4¼lb) apples, peeled, cored, and cut into thin, uniform slices

2 quinces, peeled and coarsely grated

¼ tsp fine sea salt

1 tbsp ground cinnamon

¼ tsp ground nutmeg

¼ tsp ground ginger

¼ tsp ground cloves

100g (3½oz) soft light brown sugar

100g (3½oz) granulated sugar

4 tbsp tapioca flour, or 4 tbsp plus 2 tsp plain flour

For the top

1 egg, lightly beaten

3–4 tbsp coarse demerara sugar (optional)

Combine the flour and salt in a food processor. Add the diced butter and pulse until the butter is nearly but not fully incorporated – you're after pea-sized chunks.

With the food processor running, drizzle in up to 4 tablespoons ice-cold water, ½ tablespoon at a time, until the dough just comes together. This should not take more than 30 seconds.

Don't overwork or over-hydrate your dough. It'll firm up and come together while it rests in the cool of the refrigerator.

Remove the dough from the food processor and divide it into two equal pieces. Place each dough half on a large piece of cling film and shape into a circular disc. Wrap the discs in their separate pieces of cling film and refrigerate for at least 1 hour while you prepare your filling.

With the exception of the tapioca or plain flour, combine all your filling ingredients in a very large bowl. Mix everything together as best you can, and let the mixture sit at room temperature for 2–4 hours.

When you're ready to assemble your pie, lightly grease a 24cm (9½in) pie dish.

Take one dough disc out of the refrigerator and, on a well-floured work surface, roll it out into an evenly thick circle with a diameter of 33cm (13in). Carefully transfer your rolled-out dough to the prepared pie dish, pressing it gently but firmly into the bottom and sides of the dish. Leaving a slight overhang, trim any excess dough from the edges. Place the dough-lined pie dish in the refrigerator for 15 minutes.

Add the tapioca or plain flour to the bowl of pie filling and toss to coat. Remove your dough-lined pie dish from the refrigerator and spoon in your apple filling, and then use your hands to form it into a large, relatively even mound. It may seem like there are a lot of apples. There are. That's the point. This is no dainty *tarte tatin*. This is an apple pie. An American pie. A big, tall, heaping, heaving, apple (and quince) pie.

Take your second dough disc out of the refrigerator and, on a well-floured surface, roll it out, aiming again for an even thickness and a diameter of 33cm (13in). Drape your rolled-out dough evenly over your hill of apples. Once again, trim any excess from the edges, and then fold the slight overhang from the lower crust up over the edge of the upper crust. Using your fingers or the tines of a fork, pinch and crimp the two together.

Cut four to six 7cm (2¾in) slits in the top of your pie (this will allow steam to escape while the pie bakes), and place the assembled pie in the refrigerator to chill for half an hour.

Meanwhile, preheat your oven to 200°C (180°C fan/400°F/Gas 6).

After 30 minutes, remove your pie from the refrigerator. Brush the top of it with the beaten egg, and sprinkle it with sugar, if using. Bake on the middle rack of the oven, and place a baking tray on the rack below to catch any drips that might bubble out of the pie. After 15 minutes, reduce the heat to 170°C (150°C fan/340°F/Gas 3½) and bake for an additional 1–1¼ hours, checking it after 35 minutes. If, at that time, the crust is browning faster than you want it to, cover your pie loosely with foil, and let it continue baking until it's ready – you'll know your pie is nearly ready when you see some of the filling bubbling through the vents you cut out of the upper crust; take it out 5 minutes after the bubbling begins.

Let your pie cool on a wire rack, uncovered, for a minimum of 2 hours or overnight.

Slice. Serve. Enjoy. Repeat.

TRES LECHES RICE PUDDING

Serves 6–8

I make *tres leches* cake whenever I want to be transported to coastal Mexico, where my dad's breakfast, on our father–daughter trips, usually consisted of grocery store-bought fruit and *tres leches* cake, shoved into the (emptied out) minibar refrigerator to stay cool, and eaten with a teaspoon on a balcony overlooking the Pacific Ocean.

A *tres leches* also takes me to my best friend Caroline's grandmother's home on Fishers Island, NY, where my sister Sara honed her peerless *tres leches* cake recipe over a three-day period on an oppressively hot Fourth of July weekend. The problem with Sara's cake, though, is that it takes a long time to make. And, frankly, it takes up a lot of space in the refrigerator. A *tres leches* rice pudding, on the other hand, does neither.

Rice puddings abound across myriad cultural and culinary traditions. In Mexico, it's *arroz con leche*. For the Swedes, Christmas wouldn't be Christmas without *risgrynsgröt*. China's *ba bao fan* is fruit-studded and auspicious, while Iran's *sholezard* is, unsurprisingly, fragrant and rich with saffron and rose. In America, we make our rice pudding on the stovetop; in Britain, where rice pudding is often baked, fights have been known to break out over the pudding's caramelized skin. It is India, though, that may hold the claim for the world's oldest rice pudding – or, at least, written evidence thereof.

Kheer, the Indian mixture of rice, sugar, and milk, makes an important appearance in the *Ramayana*, an epic Hindu depiction of the triumph of good over evil written between the 4th and 7th centuries BCE. The poem tells the story of Lord Rama, a human incarnation of the god Vishnu, and his victory over the demon Ravana, as well as Rama's devotion to and love for his wife, Sita. At the start of the epic, Rama's father, a son-less king, is gifted a bowl of *kheer* by a mystical emissary and encouraged to share it with his wives so that they may become pregnant with sons – sons who are incarnations of Vishnu, for only in human form can Vishnu defeat Ravana. Rama is the first born, an incarnation of a god and an epic hero. And, to think, it all started with rice pudding.

That is how good rice pudding is. Or can be. It is such a simple dish. Simple, comforting and life-affirming. A triumph of good over evil indeed. Rice. Sugar. Milk. Or, in this case, three milks: *tres leches*.

225g (8oz) pudding or risotto rice

½ tsp fine sea salt

1 cinnamon stick

450ml (scant 2 cups/15fl oz) whole milk

400ml (1¾ cups/14fl oz) sweetened condensed milk

170ml (scant ¾ cup/6fl oz) evaporated milk

10 good scrapes of nutmeg

1½ tsp vanilla extract

30g (1oz) salted butter

To serve

strawberries

whipped cream

Combine the rice, salt, and cinnamon stick in a medium saucepan for which you have a lid. Add 450ml (scant 2 cups/15fl oz) water and bring to the boil over a high heat, then cover, reduce the heat to low, and let the rice cook for 15–18 minutes, or until all the water has been absorbed.

Meanwhile, in a medium bowl, whisk together the three milks – ahem, *tres leches* – and nutmeg.

Once the rice is cooked, remove the cinnamon stick and pour in the *tres leches* mixture. Mix well to combine.

Cook your rice pudding uncovered over a low heat for 25–30 minutes, stirring frequently so that the mixture does not burn. You will know the rice is ready to come off the heat when nearly all the liquid has been absorbed. At that point, stir through the vanilla, along with the butter.

Set your pudding aside to cool slightly if you want to serve it warm. You can, of course, also let it cool completely, put it in the refrigerator and serve it cold. Either way, I recommend topping it with sliced strawberries and a dollop of whipped cream.

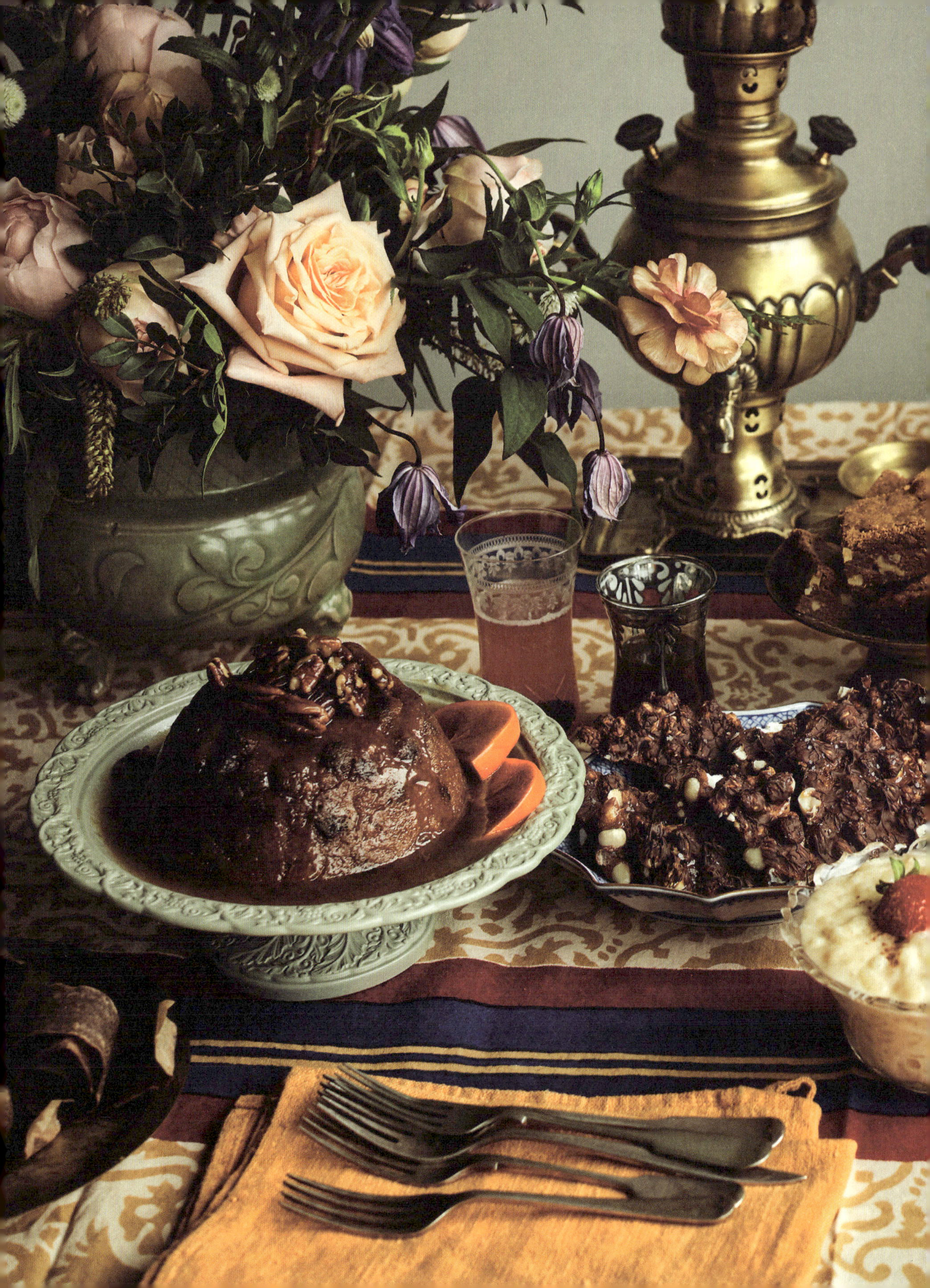

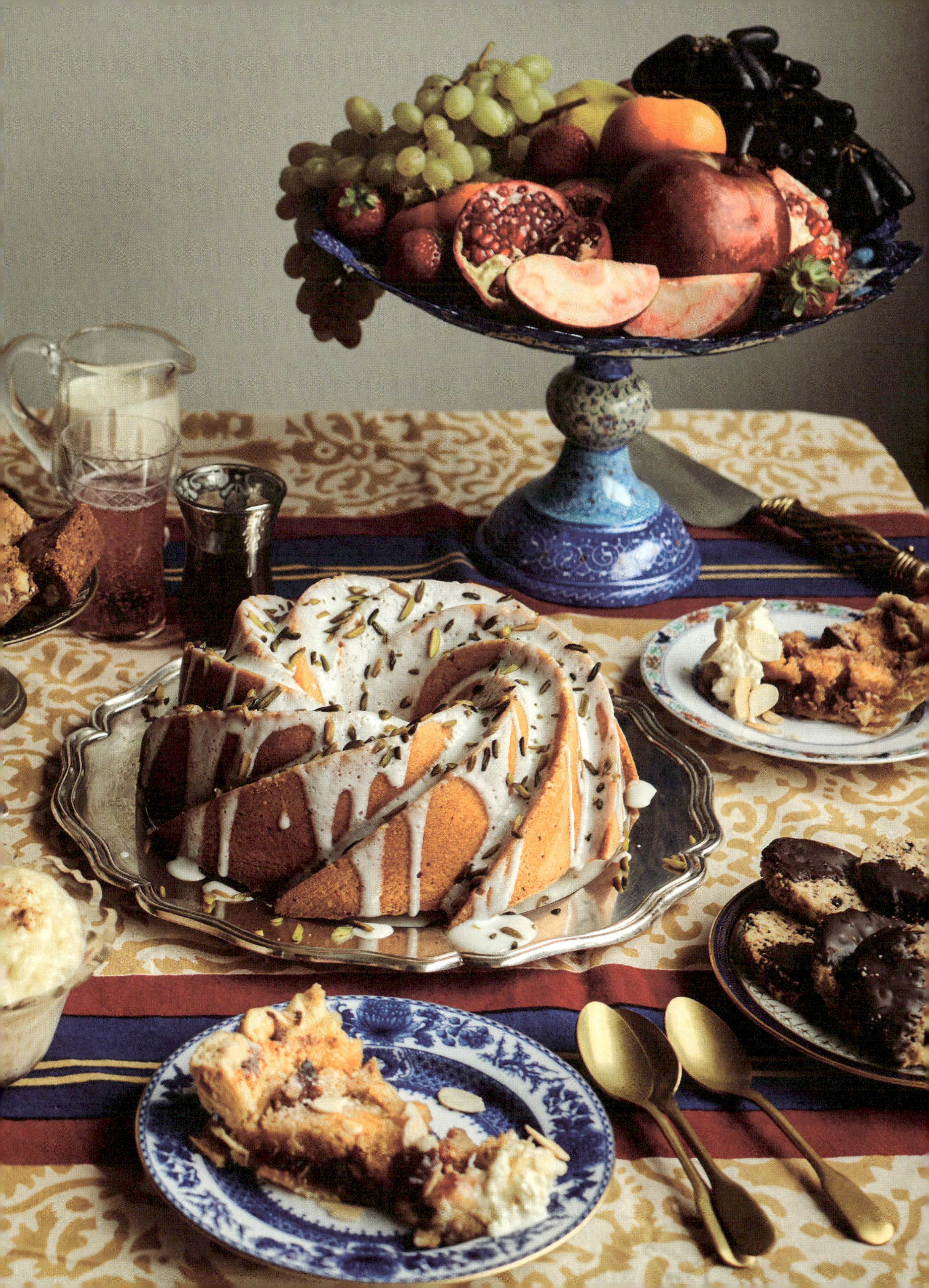

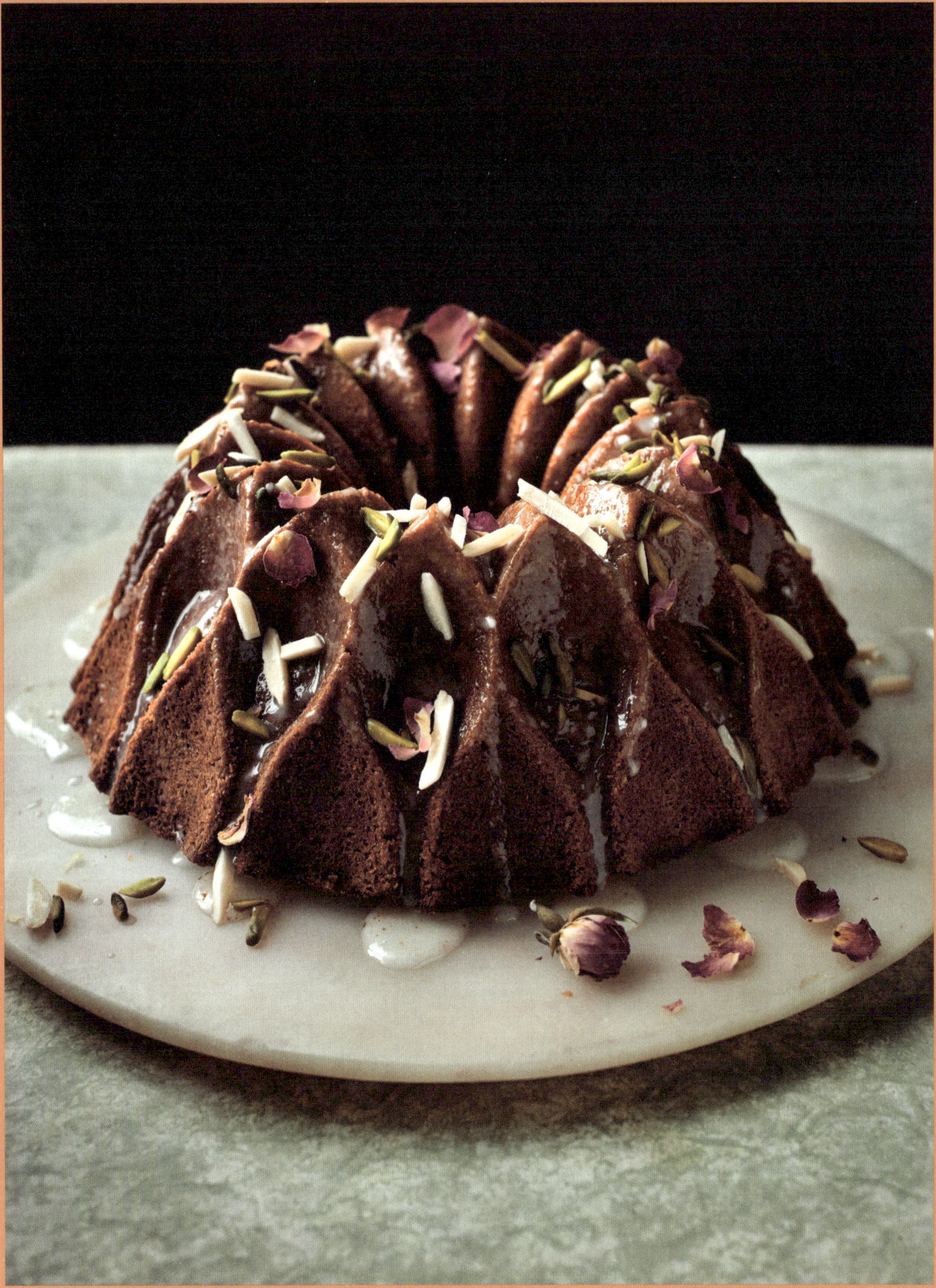

ALMOND BUNDT CAKE

Serves 10–12

Our family friend (and my French teacher – see p162) Farimah made the most incredible Iranian almond cookies: sweet, chewy, and perfectly crackled on top. I can still taste them. And I can still hear her telling my mother, in her accented English, "No, Sue. I cannot. I don't have recipe to give you. I don't know."

It was the late 1980s in suburban Detroit. You couldn't search online for "Iranian almond cookie recipe". You could barely find one in a cookbook because, well, in those days, there was approximately one Iranian cookbook on the American market. My mom tried that recipe multiple times with little success. "Something's missing," my dad would say.

The area we lived in had a lively but small Iranian (mostly medical) expatriate community. This meant we attended and hosted a lot of Iranian parties, and *this* meant that my Michigan-born-and-raised American mom, who had never been to Iran, needed a dessert suitable for a lot of Iranians – and it needed to be one that didn't taste like anything was missing. So she made an almond bundt cake, the recipe for which she found on the back of an industrially produced tin of "almond filling". Everyone loved it.

My recipe is based upon the one my mother made for years, for Iranian party after party after party, but with some updates (*adios*, corn syrup-based almond filling!) and additions (hello, yogurt icing and rose petals!). This cake is a testament to my mother's understanding of the Iranian palate, her ingenuity, and her dedication to good food and great hosting.

Note: The recipe below will make 540g (1lb 3½oz) of almond filling – 225g (8oz) more than you need for this recipe. But the leftover quantity just so happens to be the perfect amount needed for the Quince Bakewell Pudding (see p246).

225g (8oz) unsalted butter, plus extra for greasing

200g (7oz) caster or granulated sugar

3 eggs, at room temperature

280g (9¾oz) plain flour, plus extra for dusting

½ tsp fine sea salt

2 tsp baking powder

4 tbsp whole milk

For the almond filling
(makes 540g/1lb 3½oz)

150g (5½oz) unsalted butter, at room temperature

150g (5½oz) granulated sugar

3 eggs

¼ tsp vanilla extract

¼ tsp almond extract

150g (5½oz) ground almonds

For the glaze

165g (5¾oz) icing sugar

¾ tsp almond extract

110g (3¾oz) Greek yogurt

To decorate (optional)

edible rose petals

flaked almonds

pistachio nibs

sprinkles

Start by making the almond filling. In either a stand mixer fitted with a paddle attachment, or in a medium bowl and using a hand mixer, cream together the butter and sugar until light and fluffy, stopping to scrape down the sides of the bowl with a spatula when necessary. Add your eggs, one at a time, and mix well, scraping down the sides of the bowl between each addition. Add the vanilla and almond extracts and, once mixed in, add the ground almonds. Mix until fully combined and set aside. (The almond filling will keep for 2–3 days, covered tightly, in the refrigerator.)

Now on to the cake! Preheat your oven to 170°C (150°C fan/340°F/Gas 3½) Butter a 2.4 litre (10-cup) bundt or tube pan, and dust with flour. Be very, very generous. Get into every nook and cranny so that nothing sticks when you pull your cake out. Set the prepared pan aside.

In either a stand mixer fitted with a paddle attachment, or in a large bowl and using a hand mixer, cream together the butter and sugar. Scrape down the sides of the bowl and then add the eggs, one at a time, mixing well and scraping down the sides of the bowl between each addition. Add 315g (11¼ oz) of the almond filling and mix again until combined.

In a separate bowl, use a fork to combine the flour, salt, and baking powder.

Add your flour mixture to your wet ingredients a little at a time, adding a dash of the milk after each flour addition and mixing well. You want to alternate additions – dry ingredients, milk, dry ingredients, milk, etc. – and make sure to scrape down the sides of the bowl after each addition. Fully combine everything.

Pour your batter into the prepared bundt pan, using a spatula to spread it around as evenly as possible. Holding the pan on two sides, knock it gently but firmly on your work surface a couple of times to evenly distribute the batter in the pan.

Bake for 40–55 minutes, or until a cake tester inserted into the fattest part of the cake comes out clean. I start testing at 40 minutes and go from there. When your cake is ready, remove it from the oven and let it cool for 15 minutes in its pan on a wire rack. Then, cross your fingers, put your wire rack on top of your cake, turn it upside down, and pray for a quick and smooth cake release! Let your cake cool completely before icing and decorating.

To make the glaze, whisk together the sugar, almond extract, and yogurt in a bowl. Add more sugar or more yogurt to achieve your desired texture. I sometimes go crazy and add an extra smidge of almond extract.

Depending on the viscosity of your glaze, you will either drizzle it over your cooled cake or use a pastry brush to paint it on. If you like, decorate your cake further with dried edible rose petals, flaked almonds, and/or slivered pistachios. If you are my son, you will also cover it haphazardly with brightly coloured sprinkles. Whatever works. It is going to taste amazing, in any case.

Alfred Nobel made his fortune from Azeri oil, and so too did Isa Hajinski – the man responsible for the impressive building seen here on the left. On the other side of the boulevard and trees is the Caspian Sea. Photo taken from the base of the 12th-century Maiden Tower. Baku, Azerbaijan. 1975.

SPICED WALNUT BLONDIES

Makes 16–36 blondies, depending on size

Before you bake, I implore you to pay attention to what you are about to make. A blondie is a brownie, basically – a brownie that is blonde. A brownie that is made without chocolate (OK, you can have chocolate chips in blondies, but that's it). Like a brownie, a blondie should be gooey, chewy, fudgy, and dense. It should not be fluffy and airy. It is not a cake. It is not a sponge. A blondie is a blondie, and it is a mystery to me that it does not enjoy as much love as its chocolatey sibling receives.

Indeed, the blondie is the eldest child, the firstborn, around since at least 1896 (decades before the brownie made its written debut), when Fannie Farmer included a blondie recipe in her famous *Boston Cooking School Cookbook*. Butter. Sugar. "Porto Rico" molasses. Egg. Flour. Pecans. Six ingredients were all you needed to make a blondie in 19th-century America. Ten ingredients (and one-ish bowl) are all you need to make mine. And three of those ingredients – walnuts, cardamom, and nutmeg – are included as a nod to a beloved Iranian teatime treat.

Koloocheh is a round date-and-walnut-stuffed cookie flavoured with cinnamon, cardamom, and nutmeg, typically stamped with patterns, and enjoyed not only on holidays such as Purim, Easter, Ramadan, and Noruz, but also on an average day, with a cup of tea. And, while you can and should enjoy these blondies on an average day, with a cup of tea, I assure you they are in no way average.

- 170g (5¾oz) unsalted butter, melted and cooled until lukewarm, plus extra for greasing
- 210g (7¼oz) plain flour
- 1 tsp baking powder
- 1 tsp ground cardamom
- ½ tsp ground nutmeg
- 1 tsp fine sea salt
- 300g (10oz) soft light brown sugar (you could also use dark brown sugar for a more treacly treat, or a combination of both)
- 2 eggs, at room temperature
- 2 tsp vanilla extract
- 150g (5½oz) walnuts, lightly chopped (I have also used chopped hazelnuts on occasion – do with that information what you will)

Preheat your oven to 170°C (150°C fan/340°F/Gas 3½). Grease a 20–23cm (8–9in) square baking tin with butter, and line with baking parchment.

In a medium mixing bowl, sift together the flour, baking powder, cardamom, nutmeg, and salt. Set aside.

In either a stand mixer fitted with a paddle attachment, or in a large bowl and using a hand mixer, combine the melted lukewarm butter and sugar, and mix until smooth. Now add the eggs, one at a time, followed by the vanilla, mixing to combine after the addition of each ingredient.

Use a spatula to scrape down the sides of the bowl, and then use the same spatula to gently fold in the dry ingredients. Mix everything until just combined, but so that no white specks of flour can be seen.

Gently fold the walnuts into the batter, trying to distribute them evenly.

Pour the batter into your prepared tin, smoothing out the top as nicely as you can. Bake for 30–35 minutes, or until a tester inserted into the centre comes out clean, or nearly clean. The blondies will be gooey; that's OK. That's what you want. You just don't want them undercooked. If your tester has a few crumbs on it, that's OK – raw batter is not, though.

Let the blondies cool in their tin for 30 minutes before cutting them into 2.5 cm (1in) squares. They're delicious and gooey when warm, but frankly even better the next day, if you can wait that long. In theory they will keep in an airtight container at room temperature for 3–4 days, but they will be eaten long before then.

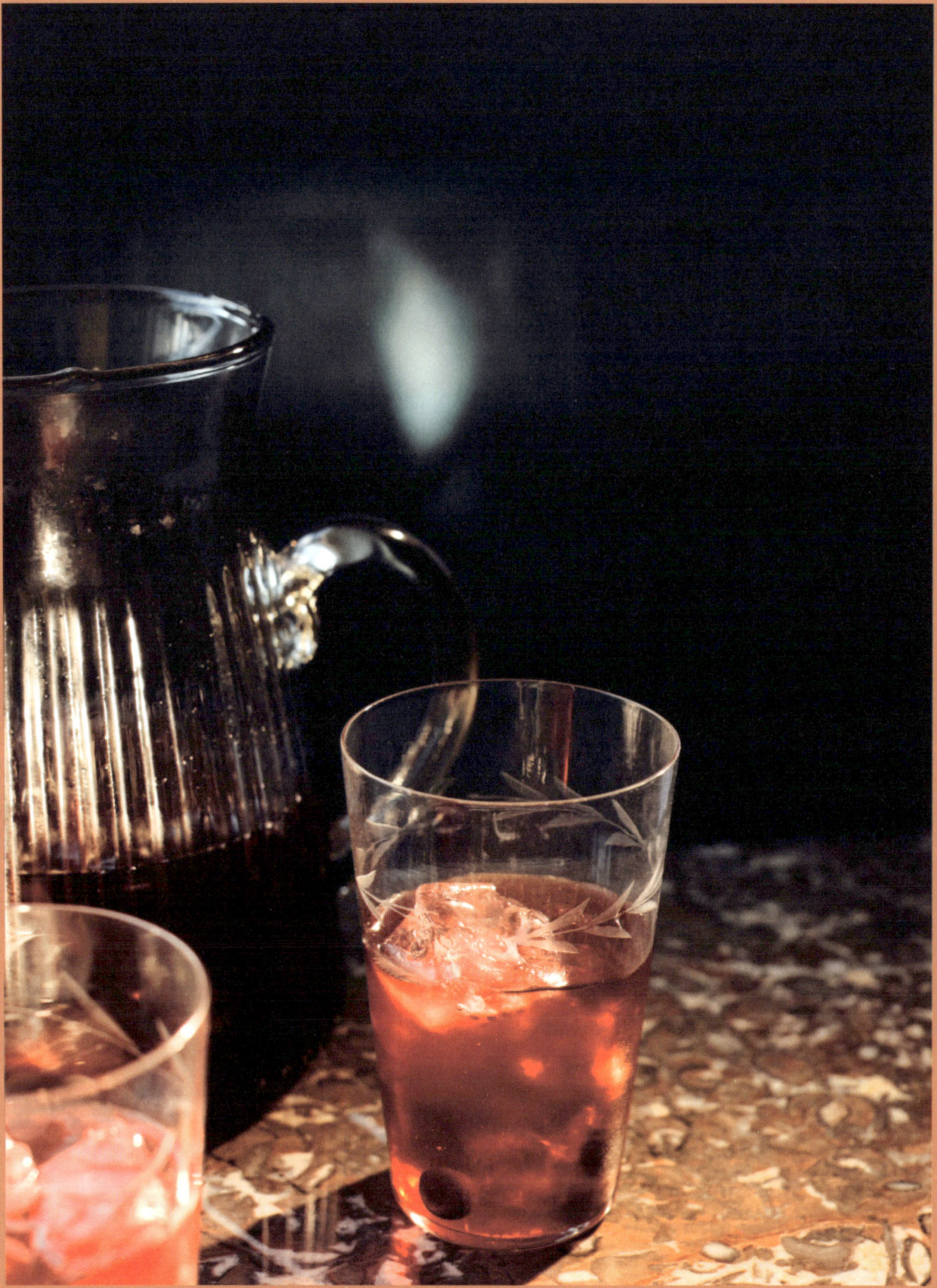

CHERRY KOMPOT

Uzbek Cherry "Punch"

Makes 2 litres (8½ cups/3½ pints)

This Central Asian way of extending the life and enjoyment of fruits, by boiling them with water and sugar, gives me a real fruit punch vibe. One of those 1980–90s, bright red, filled-with-who-knows-how-many-chemicals-but-you-know-there's-got-to-be-a-ton-of-them fruit punches. The kind named after America's 50th state. The one with the little red-headed cartoon mascot. You know what I'm talking about? It's OK if you don't. That's what I'm here for. A shockingly red, sugary drink, flavoured with orange, pineapple, passion fruit, and guava … *juices*? No: I don't dare say juices. I don't know what was in it. I just know that I wasn't allowed to have it as a kid. It was too processed, too full of sugar (or, more likely, corn syrup), too full of mystery chemicals and dyes. And you know what? My parents were probably right not to give it to me. I have good teeth, to this day, and I had good teeth as a kid too.

Like *sharbat* (see pp235–6 for my recipes), *lavashak* (see p249), and jam (see pp239–40), *kompot* is a time-honoured means of preserving fruit, of holding on to and extending the life of flavour and nutrient-giving produce whose consumption time is fleeting. This *kompot* not only reminds me of fruit punch, but also tastes like summer and brightness and youth and smiles. Here's the thing, though – even though there's nothing unnatural and processed about it, *kompot* does have a lot of sugar. And fruit, too, of course. And despite knowing what's in it, I'm not giving *kompot* to my kid any time soon. But I will probably figure out how to turn this into a "punch" for me and the other grown-up kid in my household – an old-fashioned rum punch, that is, akin to the ones British merchant sailors of yore drank on their ocean voyages – dental (and liver) decay be damned. Yo, ho, ho! (And a bottle of *kompot*).

400g (14oz) frozen pitted cherries

110g (3¾oz) granulated sugar

juice of 1 lemon or 2 limes (about 2 tbsp)

a sprig or 2 of tarragon, mint, or basil (optional)

In a large saucepan, bring 2 litres (8½ cups/3½ pints) of water to the boil over a high heat.

Carefully add the cherries to the boiling water. Reduce the heat to medium and cook, uncovered, for 7 minutes.

Add the sugar, citrus, and herbs, if using. Stir to dissolve the sugar. Simmer the *kompot* for a further 5 minutes before turning off the heat.

Let your *kompot* cool and then use a colander to strain out the solids.* Transfer your strained *kompot* to a pitcher and enjoy over ice. Any leftover *kompot* will keep in the refrigerator for 4–5 days.

* Psst: I'm not saying you absolutely *have* to use your leftover fruit to make Lavashak (see p249), but I am definitely saying I fully endorse that move.

NOT-YOUR-AVERAGE-COUNTY-FAIR FUNNEL CAKES

Makes 5 large funnel cakes

Nearly every culture has a version of fried dough. In "the West", we devour chocolate-dipped churros, sugar-glazed doughnuts, and icing sugar-dusted beignets. And if America runs on Dunkin', then Uzbekistan, Kazakhstan, and Tajikistan run on *chak-chak*, deep-fried and typically honey-smothered little pieces of dough. In Kazakhstan and Kyrgyzstan, you'll find *barusak* or *borsok* respectively, deep-fried puffed dough nuggets, enjoyed either as savoury treats to soak up sauces at mealtimes or as teatime sweets; Turkmen have a similar fried bread called *pishme*. And in China, never say no to a deep-fried *mantou* dipped into condensed milk.

Bamieh are an Iranian deep-fried choux pastry soaked in honey and rose water syrup. I've never met one I've liked. And the same goes for *zulbia* – another not-beloved-by-me Iranian deep-fried "treat" drenched in saffron, honey, and rose. I can taste their memory as I write this, and not in a pleasant way.

I can also taste the memory of funnel cakes at the Monroe County Fair, greedily enjoyed by my eight-year-old self while watching pot-bellied pig races, demolition derbies, and 4-H sheepherding trials. And that is a pleasant memory, indeed.

Here, I give you a combination of these memories, in the form of a honey, pistachio, and rose funnel cake, a beloved county fair staple for which we have 17th- and 18th-century Pennsylvanian Dutch (German) immigrants to thank. But this is very much NOT your average county fair funnel cake.

240g (8½oz) plain flour

1 tsp baking powder

½ tsp fine sea salt

240ml (1 cup/8fl oz) semi-skimmed milk

2 eggs, lightly beaten

½ tsp almond extract

1.5 litres (6¼ cups/2¾ pints) neutral oil, for deep-frying

honey, for drizzling

pistachio powder, for dusting (shop-bought, or make your own by grinding pistachio nibs in a food processor/spice grinder)

edible dried rose petals, for sprinkling

In a large bowl, vigorously whisk together the flour, baking powder, salt, milk, eggs, and almond extract until well mixed and completely smooth.

Carefully transfer your funnel cake batter into a squeeze bottle or pastry bag with a resealable tip. I do this with a funnel and a ladle.

Pour the oil into a medium straight-sided sauté pan over a medium heat. Heat the oil to 190°C (375°F). This heating-up process may take up to 10 minutes, but it's important; you do not want to fry in oil that is either too cool or too hot. Like Goldilocks, you want just the right temperature.

Once the oil is ready, use your squeeze bottle or pastry bag to drizzle the batter into the hot oil, swirling, overlapping, and criss-crossing it so that it won't fall to pieces when you take it out. Work quickly, stopping once you've created a two- to three-layer-deep circular lattice. This should take seconds.

Fry the cake for 2 minutes, or until light golden, then carefully flip and fry 1–2 minutes on the other side until similarly golden.

Remove the funnel cake from the oil and place it on a paper towel-lined plate to drain and cool for 30 seconds, before moving it to a serving plate. Immediately drizzle the cake generously with honey, give it a nice dusting of pistachio powder, and sprinkle it with a few dried rose petals. Repeat until you've used up all your batter.

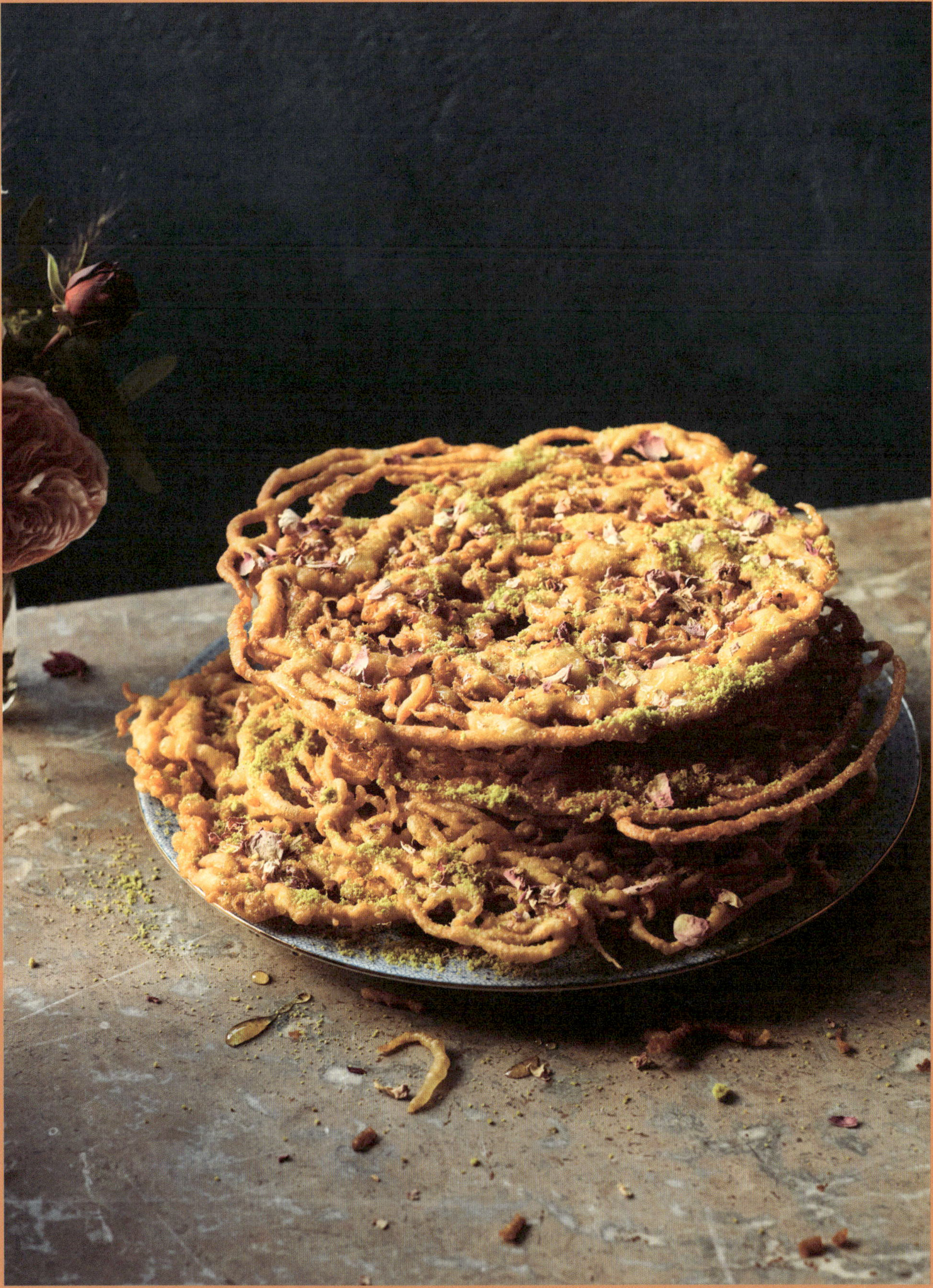

PEANUT & POPCORN BRITTLE

Makes 1 tray

Like fried dough, brittle and variants thereof are ubiquitous across Asia. In Iran, you will find *sohan*, a saffron, rose water, and pistachio candy visually reminiscent of American peanut brittle but entirely Iranian in flavour, as well as *shirini konjedi*, a saffron-sesame brittle, the flavour of which reminds me of childhood and, as with *bamieh* and *zulbia* (see p232) not in a delicious, pleasant way. China, too, has a tradition of candy brittle (*zhima tang*), often studded with peanuts, but in which sesame seeds play the starring (overpowering, if you ask me) flavour role. Uyghur brittle, *matang*, is more akin to nougat, with nuts and dried fruit bound together by honey or grape molasses to form a thick and dense confection that can be (and typically is) cut by knife and sold in chunks. I don't like any of them. I've tried. Over many years. I simply do not enjoy them. And I don't want to give you a recipe for something I dislike.

Instead, I give you a recipe that I love – an homage to both the brittle candies of Iranian, Chinese, and Uyghur traditions, as well as to America and my friend Becky, with whom I saw every one of a certain vampire movie series, and who opened my eyes to a concession stand combo that simply cannot be beat: peanut M&M's and popcorn. Sure, I'd had that combination before … but never Becky's way. She dumped the bag of candy into the popcorn, and then reached in to grab a handful. That was it. And it was everything. Simultaneously decadent and innocent, it's a salty-sweet flavour explosion that tastes amazing and is all I ever want at the movies forevermore.

And here it is for you, in brittle form. Not quite the type of brittle the Uyghurs and Chinese and Iranians eat; there is no saffron, no rose water, no sesame. No, no, no. This is my take on a sweet confectionery, one that transports me not to Kashgar, but instead to the Kips Bay theatre on Manhattan's East Side and Forks, Washington.

- 25g (scant 1oz) unsalted butter, plus extra for greasing
- 200g (7oz) soft light brown sugar
- 80g (3oz) honey or golden syrup
- 125g (4½oz) unsalted peanuts
- 2 handfuls plain popped popcorn
- ½ tsp bicarbonate of soda
- 40g (scant 1½oz) chocolate (I go for a nice 54 per cent dark chocolate, but, by all means, use whatever chocolate you like)
- flaky sea salt

Line a baking tray with baking parchment, then generously butter the parchment. If you have a non-stick silicone baking sheet, you can use that instead.

In a saucepan, combine 4 tablespoons water with the butter, sugar, and honey or syrup. Place over a medium–high heat and cook for 3–6 minutes, stirring near constantly, until it is golden and bubbling, and reaches 125°C (257°F) on a candy thermometer. Once it hits that temperature, up your stirring, and stir it constantly for another 2–4 minutes until it reaches 160°C (320°F). Your caramel candy (because that's what it is now, caramel candy) will be a dark golden colour.

Remove the pan from the heat and, moving quickly, add the peanuts, popcorn, and bicarbonate of soda. Stir together, then very quickly pour the brittle mixture on to your prepared tray. Spread it out with a knife or offset spatula, so that it is 5mm (¼in) thick, kernels of popcorn notwithstanding. Set aside.

If not already in pieces, break your chocolate into pieces and melt it, either in bursts in the microwave or in a heatproof bowl set over a pan of simmering water.

Use a pastry brush to paint the chocolate over your cooling brittle, then sprinkle some flaky sea salt on top and wait for your candy creation to fully cool and set.

TRIO OF SHARBATS
Iranian Fruit Syrups

Do you know where the word "sorbet" comes from? No? Well, I'll tell you: straight outta Iran, where *sharbats* – sweetened fruit- and floral-flavoured syrups, diluted with water – have been quenching thirsts for centuries.

As far back as 500 BCE, Persian Achaemenid kings enjoyed snow mixed with concentrated fruit juice as a cooling treat. And from around 400 BCE, Persians began building specialized ice canals and domed ice houses that held ice and snow so the royals' beloved sweetened snow could be enjoyed all year round. (These ancient Persian icy treats sound more like snow-cones to me than the iced beverages that are modern-day *sharbat*. But what do I know?)

The story then goes something like this, or at least we think it does: Arabs conquered Persia, then they went and conquered Sicily, taking Persian *sharbat* with them. *Sharbat* turned into *sorbetto* in Naples, *sorbetto* turned into sorbet, and, at some point, dairy got added, and after a few twists and turns we got gelato, ice cream, and sherbet. End of story. But it all started in Iran.

I've never been to Iran, and have never had a *sharbat* other than the tasty-but-perhaps-not- "authentic" ones I've made for myself. I give them to you here: three homemade second-generation attempts at bringing a taste of the proverbial "old country" into my new one. And into yours.

APPLE SHARBAT

Makes about 500ml (16fl oz)

This recipe is an ode to apple cider. American apple cider, that is. Apple cider in America is not the cider of the UK. It is a non-alcoholic preparation that involves pressing mountains of whole, unprocessed apples to release their juices. The fibrous pulp is discarded and the liquid that remains is the cider. At certain mills and in certain states, the cider stays as is, unpasteurized, and the natural yeasts slowly ferment, leading to a slight tang and fizz.

It is a joyous event when Michigan's cider mills open their doors each fall, and a bittersweet one when they shutter again in the spring. There are few things as perfect to me (and many fellow Michiganders) as a cold jug of fresh-pressed apple cider and a bag filled with hot-from-the-fryer apple cider doughnuts.

I can't always enjoy a cold cup of fresh-pressed Michigan apple cider, but at least I can have this – and now you can too.

3 apples, washed, cored, and halved
300g (10oz) caster or granulated sugar
juice of 1 lemon
½ tsp coriander seeds, toasted

In a heavy-duty blender or food processor, blend the apples and 2–3 tablespoons water into a pulp.

Position two layers of muslin or cheesecloth over a large bowl. Pour the apple pulp into the muslin/cloth, taking care to keep it over the bowl, as the juice will start draining through immediately.

Using your hands, squeeze the muslin/cloth as much as you can. Try to get all the liquid out. Every. Last. Drop. Then, discard the fibrous apple pulp. Depending on the size and juiciness of your apples, you should have about 150ml (⅔ cup/5fl oz) liquid in your bowl.

Pour 240ml (1 cup/8fl oz) water into a medium saucepan and add the sugar. Bring the mixture to the boil over a high heat, then add the apple liquid. Reduce the heat to medium and simmer for 30 minutes, stirring occasionally and making sure it does not simmer over. After 30 minutes, add the lemon juice and coriander seeds, then stir and simmer for a further 30 minutes.

Strain through a fine mesh sieve to remove the coriander seeds, then use a funnel to pour the syrup into a refrigerator-friendly container, and let cool.

Once cooled, your syrup is ready to party. Mix 1 part syrup with 3 parts cold water, still or sparkling. Mix it up. Pour over ice. Sit back and enjoy, with a doughnut if you have one.

MELON SHARBAT

Makes about 500ml (16fl oz)

We didn't come all this way for me not to include a melon recipe.

The thing about melons, though, is that they're never better than in their pure, unadulterated raw form. If they're good, that is. And that is key. So if you find yourself with a beautiful, sweet, juicy melon begging to be eaten as is, do it. Eat it. On the other hand, if you find yourself with a "not quality" melon, make this.

1 small cantaloupe or honeydew melon, peeled, deseeded, and cut into chunks
caster or granulated sugar, as needed

To serve
mint sprigs
lime slices

Put your melon in a small saucepan, along with 125ml (generous ½ cup/4fl oz) water. Cover and simmer over a low heat for 25 minutes, stirring and mashing the melon occasionally with a wooden spoon.

Remove the pan from the heat and use your spoon to turn what's left of the melon into a pile of mush (forgive me, I wish I had a more elegant turn of phrase for you, but, alas, mush it is).

Place a fine mesh strainer over a medium bowl. Pour in your melon mush, straining away and discarding the remaining melon solids. Measure the melony liquid in millilitres, then measure out the same amount of sugar in grams (so if you have 500ml liquid, you'll want 500g sugar).

Return the melon juice to the saucepan, along with the sugar. You're basically making a simple syrup, but substituting melon juice for water.

Reduce the heat to medium and stir to dissolve the sugar in the juice. Allow the mixture to simmer, uncovered, over a low heat, for 7 minutes to reduce slightly.

Remove the pan from the heat and allow your melon syrup to cool before using a funnel to pour it into a refrigerator-friendly container. Once cooled, your syrup is ready to party. Mix 1 part syrup with 3 parts cold water, still or sparkling, then pour over ice. Garnish with a mint spring and a slice of lime.

POMEGRANATE SHARBAT

When we went to restaurants when I was small, I always asked for a "Shirley Temple", the classic mocktail of grenadine, lemon-lime soda, and maraschino cherry. My teetotalling parents felt that such a beverage, despite being non-alcoholic, glamourized drinking, and wouldn't allow it. Alas, no Shirley Temples for me. Until now. Until I realized that grenadine is pomegranate *sharbat*. And that I can have a Shirley Temple anytime I want, by simply mixing 1 part pomegranate *sharbat* with 6 parts lemon-lime soda, then plopping in a maraschino cherry. Try it. And feel free to add 1 part vodka as well, if you're feeling a bit dirty.

I haven't given measurements here because you can make as much or as little as you like depending on how many pomegranates you have (or how many cocktails you are planning on making). I recently made it with two average-sized fruits and am up to my elbows in pomegranate *sharbat*. I would venture to say, however, that one pomegranate will yield approximately 250ml (9fl oz) *sharbat*.

pomegranates
caster or granulated sugar

Peel and deseed your pomegranates, and place the arils in a high-powered blender or food processor. Blend until the fruit has turned into a red mass of pulp and pips.

Line a bowl with a piece of muslin or cheesecloth, and pour in your blender contents. Gather the cloth around the pulp and squeeze to extract as much juice as possible into the bowl below.

Discard the leftover seeds and pulp, and measure your pomegranat juice in millilitres, then measure out the same amount of sugar in grams (so if you have 500ml liquid, you'll want 500g sugar).

Add the juice and sugar to a small saucepan, along with 125ml (generous ½ cup/4fl oz) water for every 100ml (6½ tbsp/3½fl oz) of pomegranate juice. Bring the mixture to the boil over a medium heat, stirring to dissolve the sugar. Reduce the heat to low and simmer for 10–15 minutes to reduce slightly.

Remove from the heat and allow your syrup to cool before using a funnel to pour it into a refrigerator-friendly container. Once cooled, your syrup is ready to party. Mix 1 part syrup with 3 parts cold water, still or sparkling, then pour over ice – or make a Shirley Temple.

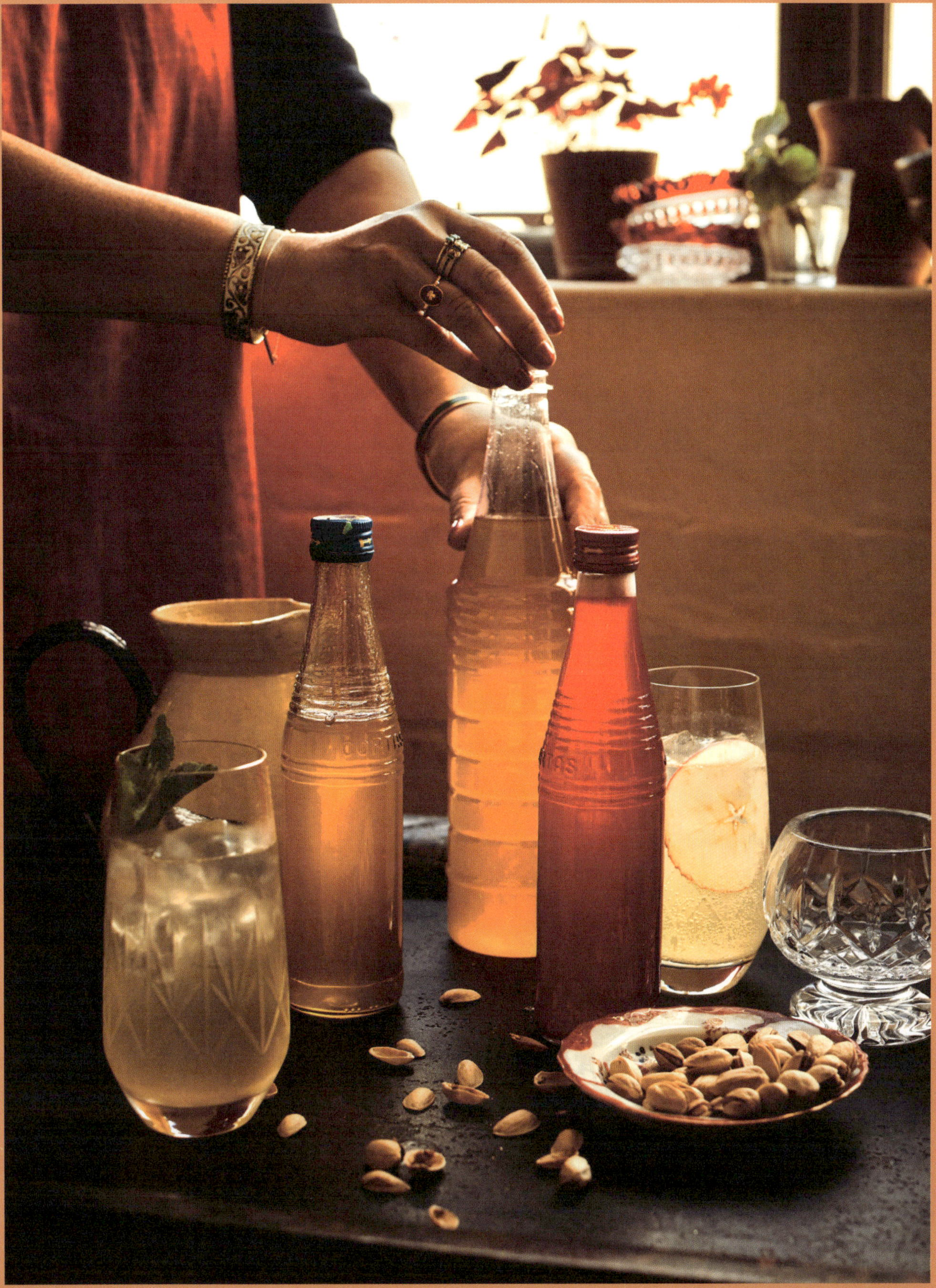

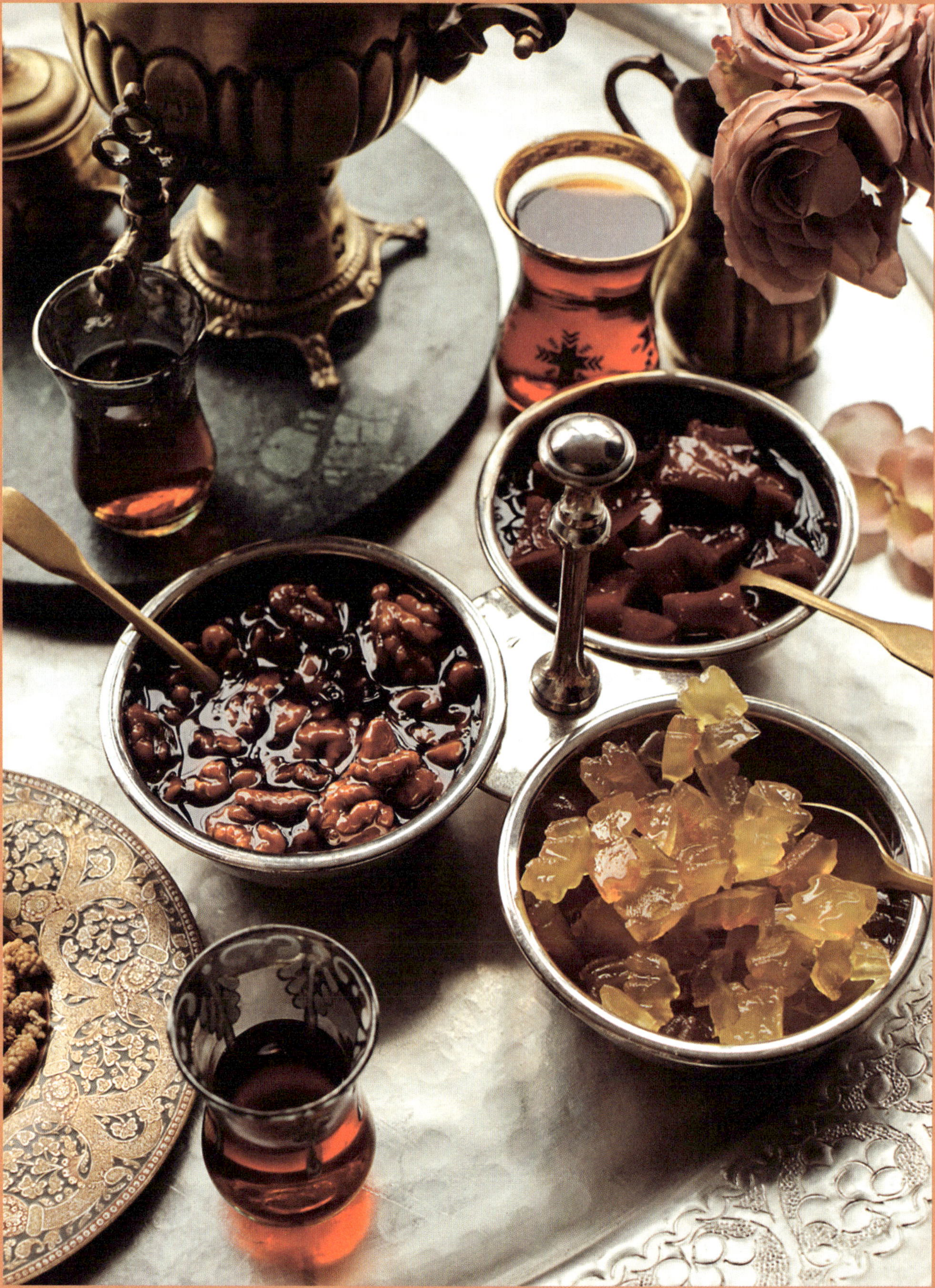

TRIO OF JAMS

I don't like jam. I've never liked jam. I don't like jelly either. Stewed saucy, spreadable fruits are not for me. Even as a kid, I rejected them all. PB & J? No, thank you. Nope. Pass. Beautiful French *confiture*? *Non, merci*. My mother-in-law's fresh-from-the-Scottish-garden raspberry and strawberry jams? Nae. But *these* jams are different. These jams I LOVE. These are something special.

Sure, you can spread them on a piece of warm bread and enjoy them with Gaymak (see p80) for breakfast. Nothing wrong with that. It'll be lovely. However, as one is made from melon rind and another from nuts, they are a bit chunky and not really spreadable in the way British-European-American jams are. So, while it may still be delicious, I don't totally advise you to make watermelon rind or walnut jam on toast your go-to morning treat. The quince, though? Go ahead – make your day.

What you *really* want to do, though, is get a cup of strong, unsweetened black tea and a little teaspoon. Take that teaspoon and spoon up some jam. Set it on your saucer. Have a sip of your tea. Then have a wee spoonful of the jam, while the warmth and flavour of the tea lingers in your mouth. And that's that. Tea with jam and bread: not one of my favourite things. Tea with watermelon, walnut, or quince jam: absolutely one of my favourite things.

WATERMELON RIND JAM

Makes about 370ml (13fl oz)

rind of 1 medium watermelon (peeling method below)
1 tsp bicarbonate of soda
peel and juice of 1 lemon
about 350g (12oz) granulated sugar
3–5 cloves
1 cinnamon stick

Remove all pink flesh from the melon. (But obviously don't discard it – eat it!) Use a sharp knife to fully remove the green skin from your fleshless rinds. You only want the white part of the melon rind, so trim accordingly.

Cut the white rind into 2–3cm (¾–1¼in) pieces. If you have a crinkle cutter, now's the time to break it out – this jam always seems to be crinkle-cut in Azerbaijan – but worry not, straight-knife cuts aren't going to change the jam's incredible taste, so use what you have.

Weigh the cut pieces and make a note of the weight you are working with. I've based this recipe on 350g (12oz) rind, but you may end up with a slightly different quantity, so jot it down.

Add the rind to a bowl and sprinkle over the bicarbonate of soda, then add the lemon juice. Pour over enough water to cover the rind, then set aside for 2 hours.

Drain the soaked rind in a colander and rinse thoroughly with clean water. Set aside.

Remember how I asked you to note the weight of your rind? This is why. The ratio we want is 1:1:1 – rind : water : sugar. So, if you ended up with 350g (12oz) rind, add the same quantity of sugar and 350ml (1½cups/12fl oz) water to a saucepan for which you have a lid. Add the lemon peel, too, then place the pan over a medium–high heat, and stir to begin dissolving the sugar. Once the mixture starts bubbling, add the melon rind, then stir again and reduce the heat to low.

Cook, partially covered, for 1–1½ hours, maintaining a gentle simmer and stirring occasionally. You're doing it! You're making jam! Out of watermelon rind!

Once your mixture reaches the consistency of runny honey, add the cloves and cinnamon, then turn off the heat, stir everything together and cover once more. Leave to set at room temperature for 45 minutes–1 hour. By now, the rind should be golden and translucent. The syrup should be syrupy but not crystalizing. Your erstwhile food waste will have been transformed, and when you try this jam, so too will you. Taste it now. Smile. Get excited for teatime. But first, spoon your cooked jam into a sterilized glass container (see p17), removing the cinnamon stick and cloves in the process, and let it cool. This will keep in the refrigerator for up to 2 weeks.

SWEET TREATS

QUINCE JAM

Your formula for this jam is a 1:1:1 ratio of cut and cored quinces to soft light brown sugar to water. It's that easy. If you can find quinces, of course. Once you find them, core and cut your quinces. That's basically all you have to do. Just don't be tempted to peel your fruit. Quince peel has a great deal of pectin in it, and you want that to help set your jam. I haven't given quantities here, but two large quinces will make about 1 × 370ml (13fl oz) jar.

quinces, well washed (not peeled), cored, and
   cut into 5cm (2in) chunks
soft light brown sugar
lemon juice (juice of 1 lemon per 2 whole quinces)
cardamom pods (optional; 1 pod for each whole quince)

Weigh your quinces, then measure out equal quantities of sugar and water.

Add the sugar, water, and lemon juice to a saucepan for which you have a lid. Stir to begin dissolving the sugar, then bring to the boil over a medium–high heat. Add the quinces and reduce the heat to low. Simmer, uncovered, for 45 minutes–1 hour, stirring occasionally. Then stir in the cardamom, if using, and turn off the heat. Wrap your saucepan's lid in a clean tea towel – just as you would if you were making rice (see p143) – and cover your pan.

After 30 minutes, take a peek. At this point, your quince chunks should be on the verge of total dissolution, but still maintaining some shape, and your syrup should be nearly as runny as runny honey, but not quite so. Not yet. If you added cardamom, fish it out now and discard. Or not– the longer you leave the cardamom in, the more cardamom-y your final jam will be. I like only a hint of cardamom, so this is where I say goodbye to mine.

Return the wrapped lid to the jammy quince-filled pan, and leave it to sit and set at room temperature for 12 hours, or overnight.

When you next open your pot, the quince should be deep red in colour and the syrup should be gloopy like runny honey. Spoon your jam into sterilized glass jars (see p17), in which it will keep for 2 weeks in the refrigerator, and put your kettle on. It's tea time.

WALNUT JAM

Makes about 370ml (13fl oz)

Nut jam. Who would have thought? The Azeris, that's who.

115g (4oz) walnuts
350g (12oz) granulated sugar
juice of 1 lemon
0.25g saffron, ground with ⅛ tsp granulated sugar
   using a mortar and pestle, and then dissolved in
   1 tbsp rose water and 1 tbsp hot water

Place the walnuts in a medium mixing bowl and pour over enough boiling water to cover the nuts. Set aside to soak for 1 hour. The water will soften the walnuts enough so that when you have a spoonful of your final product, the jam will be tender rather than crunchy.

Drain the soaked nuts in a colander and rinse them thoroughly with clean water, then set aside.

Combine the sugar and lemon juice with 350ml (1½ cups/12fl oz) water in a small saucepan for which you have a lid. Stir to begin dissolving the sugar, then bring the mixture to the boil over a medium–high heat. Once boiling, add the walnuts, stir, and reduce the heat to low. Cook, partially covered, for 45 minutes–1 hour, maintaining a gentle simmer and stirring occasionally. You want the syrup to have somewhat thickened and reduced, and for both the walnuts and syrup to have taken on a lovely golden hue. The bubbles will become thicker and darker as well.

Take the pan off the heat and add the saffron and its aromatic water. Stir everything together, then wrap your saucepan lid in a clean tea towel – just as you would if you were making rice (see p143) – place it back on your saucepan. Leave the jam to sit and set at room temperature for another 1–4 hours, or until the syrup reaches the consistency of runny honey.

Remove the lid. Behold! You made jam! Out of nuts! Nuts, I tell you. Nuts!

Spoon your cooked jam into a sterilized glass container (see p17) and let it cool, then store in the refrigerator for up to 2 weeks. It may seem weird to you – a walnut jam – but, trust me, as weird as it seems, it is even more wonderful than that.

STICKY MAPLE PERSIMMON PUDDING

Serves 4–6

There's something very American about this dessert. Maple syrup. Buttered pecans. Cinnamon. Heck, the English word "persimmon" even comes from the long-gone Powhatan language once spoken by indigenous Algonquin people on America's eastern seaboard, specifically in modern-day Virginia. Does the name Pocahontas ring any bells? She spoke Powhatan, though her descendants and those of her tribe no longer do. Plus, there is apparently a tradition of persimmon pudding-making in some parts of the States that I had never heard of before I started working on this book.

There's also something very British about it. To begin with, it's a steamed pudding, like the ones referred to in Dickensian tales and Christmas songs of yore, and seen perhaps but once a year on the British table (and never on the American), cooked according to a much-beloved family recipe … or simply purchased from a seasonal supermarket aisle. It is a distinctly British thing, the steamed pudding. And sticky toffee pudding – a major inspiration for this pudding, though typically not steamed – is, in my very humble immigrant opinion, not only the best British pudding, but one of the most delicious desserts ever. Full. Stop.

The essence of this dessert, though, is the persimmon. Not the steaming. Not the sticky maple sauce or buttery nuts. The persimmon – a deep orange fruit (a berry, actually) native to China, beloved in Iran and by my family, and first glimpsed and tasted by me on a chilly Beijing October morning in 1998 – is why we are here. We were told back then not to eat fruit unless it could be peeled or had a rind, otherwise we could get ill. Apples, peaches, and melons were fair game; strawberries and grapes were a no-go. I had neither heard of nor seen a persimmon until that autumn day, and I didn't know what to do with it. Could it be peeled like a pear? Or was it more akin to a plum, with a skin inseparable from its flesh and therefore *verboten*? As luck would have it, while you can eat persimmon skin, you don't have to, and that option meant I could try – and fall in love with – this sweet autumnal orb of delight. In fact, the preferred Iranian way of eating a persimmon is to slice off the top horizontally, spoon out the juicy ripe flesh, and discard the leftover skin. I enjoy a scooped-out persimmon as much as the next gal, but it's possible that this pudding is now my preferred way of eating this glorious fruit, and I expect it will soon be yours as well.

Note: You'll need a 1.4-litre (6-cup/2½-pint) pudding basin for this recipe.

3–4 soft, ripe persimmons

120g (4¼oz) plain flour

½ tsp baking powder

⅛ tsp fine sea salt

1 tsp ground cinnamon

125g (4½oz) unsalted butter, at room temperature, plus extra for greasing

125g (4½oz) soft light brown sugar

2 eggs, at room temperature

1 tsp vanilla extract

125g (4½oz) raisins

3 tbsp maple syrup

For the buttered pecans

50g (1¾oz) salted butter

100g (3½oz) pecan pieces

For the sauce

250ml (1 cup plus 1 tbsp/9fl oz) maple syrup

50g (1¾oz) salted butter

125ml (generous ½ cup/4fl oz) double cream

To serve

flaky sea salt

ice cream or custard (optional)

To make your permission purée, scoop out and blend the flesh of the very soft, very ripe persimmons in a food processor or blender. Set aside.

In a medium mixing bowl, mix together the flour, baking powder, salt, and cinnamon. Set aside.

In either a stand mixer fitted with a paddle attachment, or in a large bowl and using a hand mixer, cream together the butter and sugar, then add the eggs and vanilla, and mix again until combined.

Scrape down the sides of your bowl with a spatula before adding a third of your flour mixture. Mix to just combine. Scrape down the sides again and add half of the persimmon purée; mix to combine. Repeat this process – scrape, flour, mix; scrape, purée, mix; scrape, flour, mix – until you have added all the flour mixture and purée to your pudding batter. After a final scrape, fold in your raisins.

Set the bowl aside and prep your pudding cooking vessel. Cut a square of baking parchment that is slightly larger than the circumference of your pudding basin (mine is 15cm/6in). Fold it in half to crease the centre of the paper. Cut a square of foil that is slightly larger than your baking parchment square. Fold this in half as well to create a crease in the centre. Place the baking parchment on top of the foil – these will act as the lid to your pudding basin.

Generously butter the inside of the pudding basin, then add the maple syrup. Scoop your batter into the basin, making sure that you leave 3–5cm (1¼–2in) at the top for the pudding to rise as it cooks. Smooth out the top of the batter with the back of your spoon.

Place your paper "lid" on top of your pudding basin, parchment-side down. Using twine, securely tie the lid around the basin, just under its lip – you might need someone to help you. And when I say "securely", I mean it. Fold any excess foil over the twine.

I highly recommend tying on another piece of twine to use as a makeshift handle to help you lift your cooked pudding up and out of your pot later on.

Place a heatproof saucer upside down in the base of a large stockpot for which you have a lid and in which your pudding basin can fit comfortably. Place the stockpot on your stovetop, and then set your filled pudding basin foil-side up on the saucer. Pour enough just-boiled water into the stockpot to come halfway up the sides of your basin, but not any higher. Cover the stockpot with its lid, turn the heat to low and steam your pudding for 2½ hours, making sure to occasionally peek at the water level and top it up if needed.

Meanwhile, make your buttered pecans. Preheat the oven to 150°C (130°C fan/300°F/Gas 2) and line a baking tray with baking parchment. Melt the butter in a saucepan over a low heat, then remove the pan from the heat and add your pecans. Spread the buttery pecans in a single layer on the prepared baking tray and toast them in the oven for 15 minutes, or until you catch a whiff of their unmistakable fragrance. Remove from the oven and set aside to cool.

After 2½ hours, test to see if your pudding is done by inserting a skewer/cake tester into its top, piercing the foil and parchment paper in the process. If the skewer comes out clean, carefully lift out your pudding. If not, keep steaming and checking the pudding every 10 minutes until the skewer comes out clean.

Let your steamed pudding rest for 15 minutes before removing the twine, foil, and baking parchment.

While it's resting, make your sauce. Add the maple syrup to a small saucepan and bring it to a leisurely boil over a medium–high heat. Once boiling, reduce the heat to low and simmer, stirring frequently, for 8–10 minutes, or until the syrup has thickened and reduced by half.

Add the butter and stir to melt it before removing the pan from the heat. Then, add the cream and stir until combined. Set aside, covered, until needed.

Unwrap your pudding now, and let it rest for another 15 minutes, *sans* twine, foil, and parchment.

After 15 minutes, use a knife to gently loosen the pudding from the edges of its basin. It shouldn't stick like an oven-baked cake, but better safe than sorry. Place a plate or platter, serving-side down, on top of the pudding. You're going to flip this over, just like you do with *gazmakh*. Hold on to the edges of the plate and the bottom of the pudding basin and, in one movement, flip everything over, then slide the basin up and off the pudding.

Pour your maple sauce on top of the pudding, and then top it with some buttered pecans and a pinch of flaky sea salt. Serve with ice cream or custard, or whatever your heart desires.

You did it! A steamed pudding! Mrs Cratchit would be proud. And so am I.

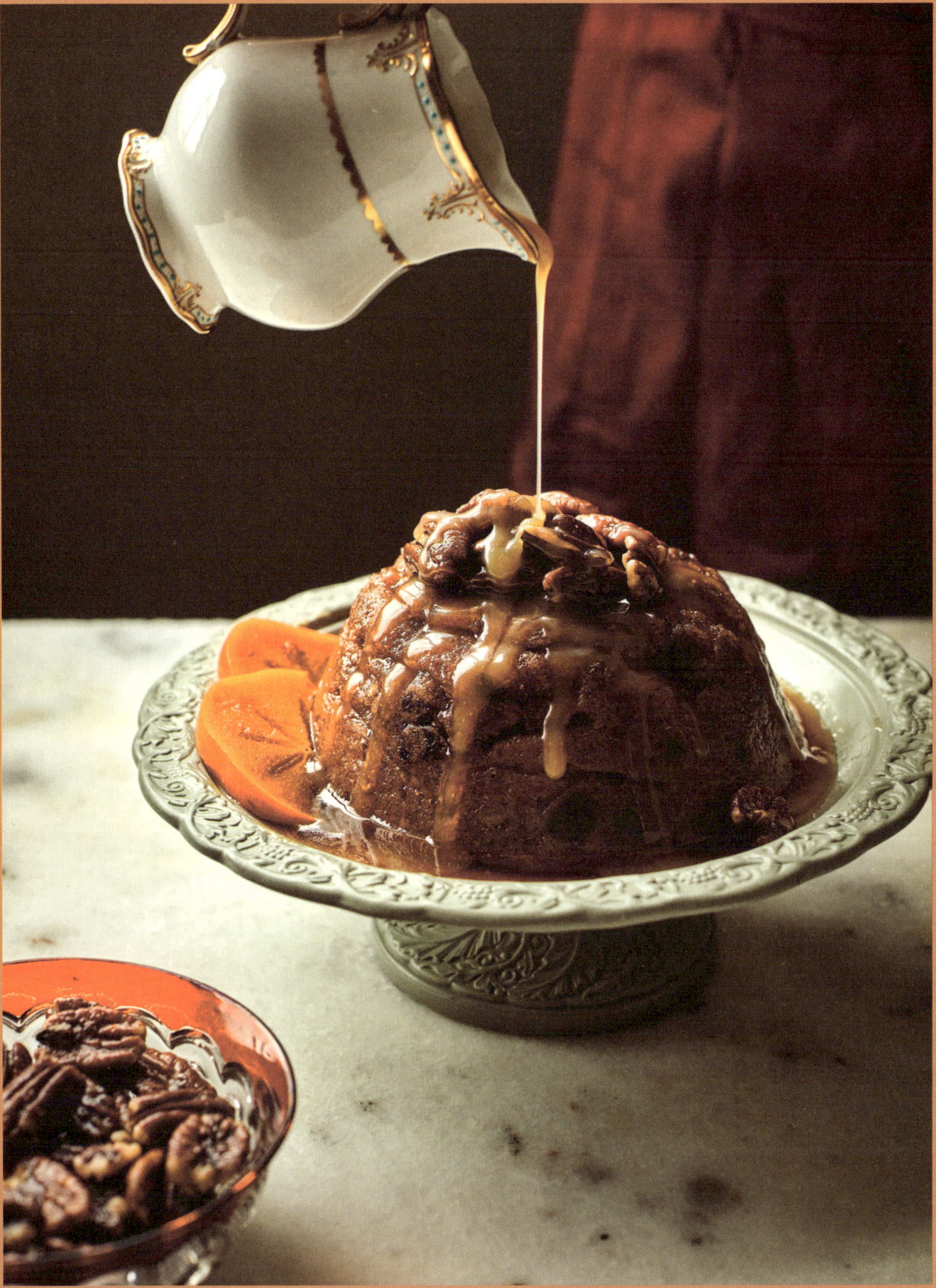

SOUR CHERRY & WALNUT SHORTBREAD

Makes 30–50, depending on size

Presumably introduced to China in the Han Dynasty via Silk Roads traders, walnuts were known initially as *hu tao*, or "foreign peach". Though not typically viewed by most in the West as a particularly "Chinese" culinary ingredient, the walnut enjoyed widespread popularity during the Tang Dynasty and continues to enjoy tremendous success in China, at least economically: China is the world's largest commercial producer of walnuts, accounting for more than 50 per cent of all global production.

In China today, you are most likely to encounter walnuts in a crispy, crumbly cookie called *hup toh soh*. I've never had one, myself, or at least not that I can recall. I'm told they are most frequently eaten around the Chinese New Year. Or, at least, they were "traditionally". Whatever that means. Across the world, in Scotland, where my husband and his family are from, the natives also "traditionally" ate a crumbly cookie around new year: shortbread.

This shortbread recipe comes from my Scottish mother-in-law and once belonged to her mother; it now belongs to us all. As homage to the "royal acorn of Jupiter", and its storied travels across the Silk Roads and into our collective cultural and culinary lexicon, I have added walnuts and, as a nod to a fruit beloved in both Iran and Michigan, dried sour cherries. I've also added the option of rolling your shortbread in sprinkles, sugar, or crushed walnuts, or half-dipping them in dark chocolate, a move which lends them an air of the iconic black and white cookies of NYC, my erstwhile home.

Note: Once you've formed the dough into logs, you can wrap them super tightly and bake them another day; your dough should last in the refrigerator for up to a week and in the freezer for up to a month.

100g (3½oz) walnuts

235g (8½oz) plain flour, plus extra for dusting

85g (3oz) cornflour

115g (4oz) caster sugar

100g (3½oz) dried sour cherries

225g (8oz) salted butter, chilled and cut into 2.5cm (1in) pieces

Optional (but highly recommended) upgrades

sprinkles, coarse demerara sugar, or crushed walnuts, for rolling

360g (12¾oz) dark chocolate (at least 54 per cent cocoa solids), for dipping

---

Preheat your oven to 190°C (170°C fan/375°F/Gas 5).

Spread your walnuts in a single layer on a baking tray and toast in the oven for 5–10 minutes, or until they just begin to turn dark brown and smell toasty. Alternatively, toast them in single layer in a dry sauté pan over a medium heat for 5 minutes, watching and stirring them frequently so that they do not burn.

Once toasted, move your walnuts to a plate to cool.

Add the flour, cornflour, and sugar to a food processor and pulse to combine. Add the toasted and cooled walnuts and process on low for 10 seconds, just long enough for the walnuts to devolve into grain-sized pieces. Add the cherries and pulse again for a few seconds. Finally, add the butter and blend on low until everything comes together to form a dough. For me, that takes 1–2 minutes.

Turn out your dough on to a lightly floured work surface and divide in half. Shape each half into a tight log about 4cm (1¾in) in diameter (or bigger, if you like – I enjoy my shortbread on the small side, but by all means feel free to diverge from my size directions from here on out, keeping in mind that the baking time will also diverge).

If you're going for one of the optional-but-highly-recommended upgrades, it's go time. Roll your dough logs in your sprinkles, sugar, crushed nuts, or – gasp – any combination thereof, pressing lightly with your hands to make sure the logs are well coated.

Wrap your plain or encrusted dough logs in either cling film or baking parchment, and place them in the refrigerator for at least 1 hour to firm up.

When you're nearly ready to bake, preheat your oven to 200°C (180°C fan/400°F/Gas 6), grab a baking tray or two, and remove one of your dough logs from the refrigerator.

Using a sharp knife, slice the chilled dough into rounds 1–2cm (½–¾in) thick (like I said, I like my shortbread tiny, so if you prefer yours a different size, go right ahead; just please pay attention to your cooking time). Because there are nuts and fruit in your dough, the rounds might not cut completely cleanly. That's OK – just use your hands to press in any pieces of nut or fruit that dislodge during the slicing process.

Place the dough rounds on a baking tray, roughly 2.5cm (1in) apart. Gently prick the tops of the dough rounds with the tines of a fork. "Docking" the shortbread like this both lends your finished biscuits a traditional Scottish look, and also helps them to bake properly.

Either bake your tray of shortbread immediately, or return it to the refrigerator while you repeat the above cutting steps for your second log of dough.

Bake your shortbread for 8–12 minutes, or until lightly golden, then carefully transfer your biscuits to a wire rack. Cool completely before trying to eat just one … or, if you're heading down the optional-but-highly-recommended chocolate upgrade path, read on.

If not already in pieces, break your chocolate into pieces and melt it, either in bursts in the microwave or in a heatproof bowl set over a pan of simmering water.

Dip a cooled biscuit halfway into the melted chocolate. Give it a little shake to get rid of any excess chocolate, and then place on a wire rack. Repeat.

Now all that's left is to wait for the chocolate to harden. You can either leave your shortbread on the counter and wait for who-knows-how-long for the chocolate to harden, or you could transfer your rack of chocolate-dipped biscuits to the refrigerator and wait only 15 minutes or so. Your call.

The unrestored facade of the 16th-century Abdullah Khan Madrasa. Bukhara, Uzbekistan. October 1978.

SWEET TREATS

QUINCE BAKEWELL PUDDING

Serves 6

If you have made the Almond Bundt Cake (see p227), you will have noticed that you have almond filling leftover – 225g (8oz) of it, to be precise. I tried adjusting the quantities, but the ratios just weren't right. This always irked me. I would squirrel away the leftover deliciousness in the refrigerator after baking the cake, unable to throw it away, but always ended up doing so because I didn't know what to do with it. Until one day, I did.

Bakewell pudding. It's a rather homely little dessert, looks-wise. Honestly, it's not much more than a little flabby golden pancake in its traditional, unadorned form. A pastry base topped with jam and an almondy-egg filling, and then baked – but the combination of the three come together to create something amazing, even if it's a bit unassuming visually.

This pudding is truly incredible when warm and topped with Gaymak (see p80), more jam, icing sugar, and toasted flaked almonds.

Note: If you don't have quince jam, use whatever you have. May I suggest cherry or sour cherry?

---

unsalted butter, for greasing

320g (10¾oz) sheet all-butter shop-bought puff pastry, at room temperature (I may make noodles, pie crust, and bread from scratch, but I draw the line at puff pastry; shop-bought is good enough for me and more than good enough for this pudding)

370g (13oz) Quince Jam (see p240), plus extra to serve

225g (8oz) prepared almond filling (see Almond Bundt Cake, p227)

To serve

icing sugar

toasted flaked almonds

Gaymak (see p80) or clotted cream

Preheat your oven to 190°C (170°C fan/375°F/Gas 5) and grease a 24cm (9½in) pie dish.

Unfold your puff pastry and lay it across the top of the dish. Press the pastry gently but firmly into the bottom and sides of the dish. There will most likely be a slight overhang; trim any excess dough from the edges or fold it up on itself to form a rounded pastry rim. Prick the bottom of the pastry all over with the tines of a fork.

Line the pastry with a sheet of baking parchment and fill it with baking beans. It's blind-baking time, so put the bean-filled pastry into the oven and bake for 15 minutes, or until the pastry edges are light golden.

Remove the dish from the oven, and then remove the beans and parchment from atop the pastry. Be careful – they will be hot! Return the bean-less dish to the oven and bake for another 5 minutes, or until the pastry crust is truly golden brown. Remove from the oven and let it cool for 10 minutes.

Spoon your jam into your cooled puff pastry crust and spread it around with a spoon or an offset spatula. You're going for a thin, even layer. Do the same with your almond filling – spread it on top of the jam in a thin, even layer; don't worry if some quince peeks through.

Return the dish to the oven and bake for a further 25–28 minutes, or until the almond filling on the top turns golden.

Let your pudding cool for 10 minutes before putting on its final touches.

Generously dust the top of the pudding with icing sugar, sprinkle over some toasted flaked almonds, plop a spoonful (or two or three) of *gaymak* or clotted cream on top, and finish it all off with a final dollop of quince jam. Wow.

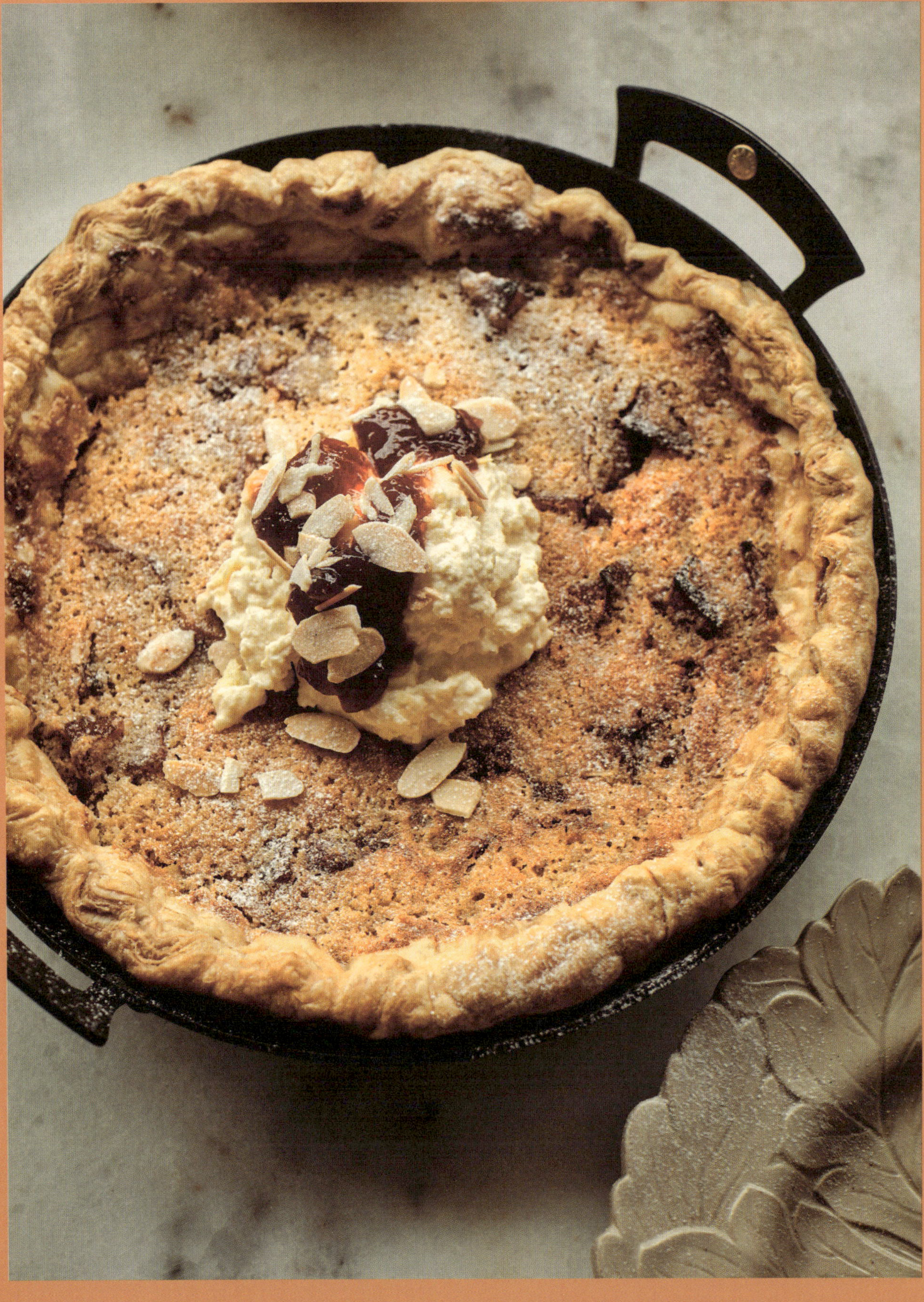

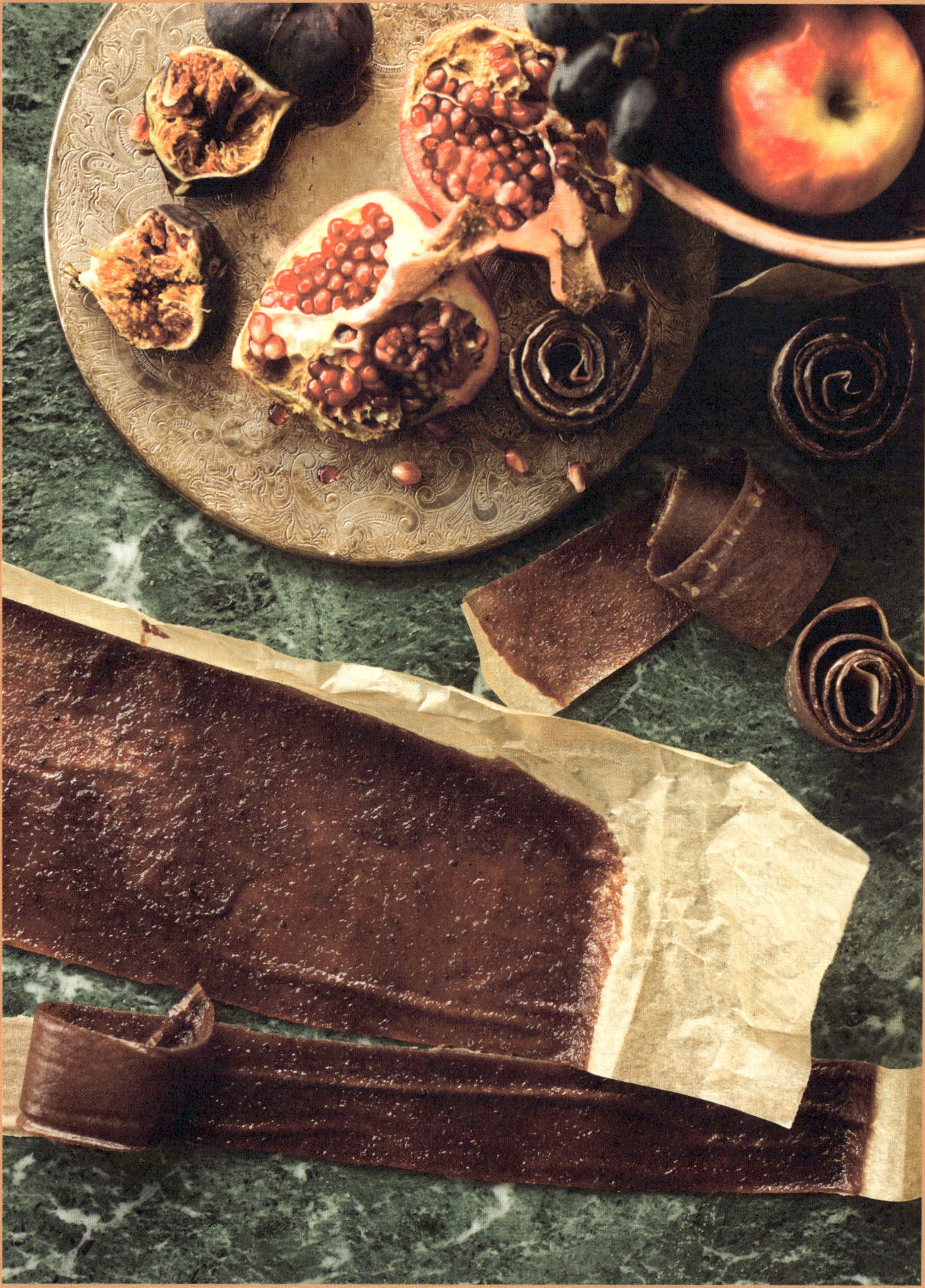

LAVASHAK

Fruit Roll-Ups (with Actual Fruit)

This is less a recipe than it is an outline for you: a roadmap to homemade, all natural, (usually) sugar-free fruit roll-ups. I haven't given quantities here; I've gone with ratios, using cups, so you can make as much or as little as you wish.

If you like, you can add some extra flavourings. For example, if I'm making apple *lavashak*, I add a pinch of cinnamon and some soft light brown sugar; it reminds me of fall in Michigan. If I'm dealing with a glut of my in-laws' sweet plums, I might not need to add anything. If I'm trying to use up not-so-delicious grocery-store grapes, I'll add a splash of pomegranate juice if I have some on hand. It all depends. On taste. On you.

---

fruit of your choosing, cleaned and prepped (deseeded, peeled, cored, pitted, etc.)

sugar and/or other flavour add-ins (optional; see above)

Measure your fruit in cups, then add to a saucepan. Add ½ cup water for every 4 cups of fruit. Place the pan over a medium heat and simmer, uncovered, for 20 minutes.

Take the pan off the heat and use a fork, potato masher, or wooden spoon to mash the fruit until it has a chunky consistency. Taste it. Think about what you want your end product to taste like and adjust accordingly, adding a pinch or a dash of whatever you feel it needs.

In any case, once you've (maybe/probably) zhuzhed up your fruit, place the pan over a low heat and let it simmer for another 5–15 minutes. Different fruits take different times to reach the desired heavy and thick consistency we want, so keep an eye on your mixture.

While your fruit continues to cook, grab a baking tray (or two, depending on how much fruit you are processing) and line it with baking parchment, leaving a bit of an overhang at either end of the tray. This is a crucial, not-to-be-missed step.

Once your stewed fruit is heavy and thick, transfer it to a blender and purée until silky smooth.

Pour the fruit purée onto your lined baking tray(s). Use a spatula to smooth it out into a thin layer (but not so thin that you can see through the purée to the paper underneath). You want the layer to be as even as you can get it; the spatula helps, but I find tilting the baking tray a bit to do so is also useful. Pop your trays into the oven. No preheating necessary; just turn the oven to its lowest setting, close the door, and wait.

Leave your fruit to dry out in the oven overnight or for up to 18 hours. Keep in mind that the thicker the purée, the longer it will take to set. You will know your *lavashak* is ready when your fingers don't stick to it when you touch it; obviously, it'll be *sticky* but you don't want to stick *to it*.

Once it's ready, remove the tray from the oven and, using the overhanging baking parchment, lift the *lavashak* from the tray.

Let your *lavashak* cool on your work surface, and then use kitchen shears to cut it (and the baking parchment it's stuck to) into strips as wide and as long as you like. Roll up your strips and store them in an airtight container at room temperature, where they will keep for 2–3 weeks. To eat, simply peel off the parchment.

ACKNOWLEDGMENTS

Well, it's Thanksgiving Day 2024 – what better time to write this than on the morning of my absolute favourite holiday? As a child at Meadow Montessori School, we broke up for Thanksgiving at midday the day before – but only after Stone Soup Day finished. For this, we read aloud from Marcia Brown's 1947 book *Stone Soup: An Old Tale* every year, dressed up in old-timey costumes, and each of us brought in a single vegetable from home for Miss Meg to use to make a soup for our lunch. In both the original folk tale and the book we would read, it is the coming together of the myriad individual ingredients that lends the dish its eventual deliciousness and nourishes all who eat it.

Never mind that there's trickery involved to get those ingredients into the communal pot; the fable and the half-day at Montessori not only taught me about the importance of sharing, but also what is possible to accomplish together as a group. *Stone Soup* is a tale about food and hunger, as well as collaboration, community, and thanksgiving – in its purest form. There are no Pilgrims. No Native Americans or turkeys. It's just a simple parable, as is the Thanksgiving holiday itself, holding space and time for inclusion and gratitude in all its forms, for friendship, family, opportunity, nature, abundance, kindness, sharing, and, of course, food. That sounds like what goes into making a cookbook, doesn't it? Indeed, that this book exists is due to a panoply of people, all of whom deserve more thanks than this space allows me to give them. But I'll try my best, all the same.

I'll start at the beginning. Kind of. Thank you to the teachers and professors who have inspired, encouraged and supported me. Catharine Calder. Winnifred Antonio. John McLaughlin. Gary "H" Hendrickson. Max Moerman. Helen Siu. Jonathan Spence. My education is the foundation upon which everything I am, this book included, is built. Meadow Montessori. Cranbrook Kingswood. School Year Abroad. Barnard. Columbia. Yale. Thank you.

Now for the actual book! A massive, monumental thank you to Cara Armstrong, Lucy Sienkowska, and Jordan Lambley at DK. You have done so much for me, for this book, that I barely have words to express my gratitude. Thank you. You brought Tara O'Sullivan, copy editor extraordinaire, the masterful photographer Laura Edwards, and the peerless designer Dave Brown into my life and on to these pages. And then there are the crazy-talented food stylists Sam Dixon and Kristine Jakobsson, and uber-chic prop stylist Charlie Phillips. Thank you. Beyond measure.

And Emma Bal – thank you. How'd I get so lucky as to have you as my agent? How'd that happen? Oh yeah! Don Sloan happened – the Yan-Kit So Award and Jane Grigson Trust Award happened. Thanks, Don – always a bridesmaid, never a bride, eh? But, hey, at least I was invited to the party. And what a party it has been.

To Mark, Jorge, and the team at Swaledale Butchers: thank you for providing me with SO much meat for recipe-testing and the photoshoots. Truly, thank you for your support, generosity, and enthusiasm before and since this book.

Thank you to everyone in Asia who helped make researching this book in situ an incredible experience. Maka Shengelia, Kristo Talakhadze, Dan Perez, and Paul Rimple in Georgia. Laman Alieyva, Salhat Abbasova, Shafag Mehraliyeva, and Jeyran Asgarova in Azerbaijan. Bu Ren, Miguel Payano and Luc Logan in China. Erin Levi, Farkhod Kadirov, Madina Abdullayeva, Sophie Ibbutson, Barchinoy, Sunnat, and the Aminov Family in Uzbekistan. What a trip! What a bunch of trips!

My recipe-testers – Eli Kagan. Caitlyn McCormick. Nicola Baines. Angela Rouse. Laura Biron. Zia Tyjebee. Beverly Scofield. Meghanne Barker. Emma Baker. Carolina Bolado. Nandini Sur. My mother-in-law Anne. My brother-in-law Mark. My sister Sara. Thank you all so very much.

I am also beyond fortunate to have incredible women around me who support me and hold me up. To the few but mighty I know in food – Georgia Freedman, Helen Goh, Olia Hercules, Rukmini Iyer, Megan Krigbaum, Jenny Lau, Marie Mitchell, and Meera Sodha – and to those whose might is elsewhere but no less formidable – Caroline, Priscilla, Becky and all of Babefest, Brigid, Karen and Rosie, Marina, Ang, Alex, Vic, Val, Sheelagh, Meghanne, Nicola, Nicole, Allie, Nandini, Katie, and Charlotte. Thank you: my life would be weak and dim without your love, support, and light. As it would be sans my boys – Garth, Tyler, Joe P. and K., Dan, Eli, Mike Robinson, Coley, Ben, Greg, and Will.

And then there's my family. This book wouldn't exist without my parents (for many obvious reasons), but it also wouldn't be here without the support, love, and encouragement of my sisters, Sara and Maria, and of my parents-in-law, Anne and Charlie. Thank you as well to my cousin, Shahpar, for the stories and insights, and to my niece Rania for your love and support. And thank you, Azizeh, for everything.

Last but the very opposite of least: my Ed and my Theo. My loves. My champions. My joys. My life. There is nothing I can say to thank Edward enough other than: thank fucking God I met you, because I would have lost it without you and have nothing without you, and thank God we had Theodore, because nothing is better than this. Nothing is beyond what we have. I love you and thank you for everything good in my life, including this book.

Writing this book has been a beacon of goodness in my life when there is often so much darkness. Like the stone soup of my Thanksgiving memories, it is a physical testament to not only what can be achieved when all those named and sorry-if-I-forgot-you-I-have-a-turkey-in-the-oven unnamed above work together, but also to the beauty and goodness of what comes from sharing across borders, generations, languages, and time, to the beauty of routes, both real and imagined, and to the Silk Roads of the past, present, and future.

ABOUT THE AUTHOR

Anna Ansari has a background in Asian studies, with a BA from Barnard College, Columbia University, and an MA from Yale University. Her writing focuses on the intersection of food, family, and history, with special attention to the immigrant experience, as well to foods of the Asian continent. She is particularly interested in the ways flavour, ingredients, and dishes move across borders, carried in the memories and pockets of travellers and transplants. You can find more of her writing in *Pit Magazine*, *Eaten Magazine*, and *Fillerzine*. An Iranian-American from Detroit and former international customs and trade attorney, Anna lives in London with her husband, son, and cat.

Photo by Kristin Perers

INDEX

ab goosht (Iranian lamb & chickpea stew) 44–46, 49–50
a Central Asian bread 205–06
a Central Asian slaw 35
achichuk (Uzbek tomato & onion salad) 24
advieh 50
  ab goosht (Iranian lamb & chickpea stew) 49–50
  quince khoresh (Iranian quince & chicken braise) 129–30
  roast duck with cranberry tkemali 118–20
  tachin (Iranian chicken & rice cake) 151–53
Afghanistan 44, 92, 187
a Georgian summer salad 36
Alexander the Great 13, 138, 149
almonds
  almond bundt cake 227–28
  quince Bakewell pudding 246
  risotto alla Bukharese 154
  rovoch salat (Uzbek rhubarb & radish salad) 39
  shah plov (Azeri king/crown rice) 145–46
  Turkmen fish rice 157–58
an Azeri tomato salad 32
An Lushan 14, 54
an Uzbek plov 149–50
apples 221
  apple (& quince) pie 221–22
  apple sharbat 235
  dimlama (Uzbek harvest stew) 51–52
apricots 216
  an Uzbek plov 149–50
  quince khoresh (Iranian quince & chicken braise) 129–30
  shah plov (Azeri king/crown rice) 145–46
Aral Sea 102, 135
A Ride to Khiva (Burnaby) 9, 115
Armenia 31, 72, 77
Ashoka 90
aubergines
  aubergine frites 107
  di si xian (four earthly treasures) 103–04
Avicenna (Ibn Sina) 149
Azerbaijan 14, 17, 21, 22, 32, 44, 45, 59–60, 63, 75, 77, 78, 94, 97, 98, 113, 118, 121, 138, 145–46, 168–69, 192, 197, 209, 211, 212–13, 217, 219, 228, 239

Babur 8–9
baijiu, paocai (Chinese fermented pearl onions) 87
bakhash 140–41
Baku 21, 22, 75, 115, 131, 135, 168, 197, 212, 228
bamieh 218, 232
baozi 186
  kao baozi (roast lamb dumplings) 200–201
  spinach & tofu baozi 203–04
barberries
  an Uzbek plov 149–50
  candied barberry topping 153
  risotto alla Bukharese 154
  shah plov (Azeri king/crown rice) 145–46
  tachin (Iranian chicken & rice cake) 151–53
barusak 232
basil, a Georgian summer salad 36
beans see also chickpeas
  lobio (Georgian bean stew) 65–66
  (mung) bean & rice soup 58
beef
  an Uzbek plov 149–50
  beef & potato dumpling filling 189
  beshbarmak ("five fingers" noodles with beef) 167–68
  cheeseburger makaroni 178–79
  chochure (dumplings en brodo) 197–98

dimlama (Uzbek harvest stew) 51–52
dushbara (dumplings en brodo) 197–98
layered & fried flatbreads + minced beef & onion filling 211–12
risotto alla Bukharese 154
shivit oshi (Khivan green noodles with beef stew) 173–74
tushonka (Soviet stewed beef short ribs) 131
beetroot
  no-waste beetroot borani (Iranian yogurt dip) 84
  torshi (Iranian pickled vegetables) 83
Beijing 12–13, 15, 90, 103, 135, 164, 171, 184, 185, 241
beshbarmak ("five fingers" noodles with beef) 167–68
blondies, spiced walnut 229
bocai 94
borani laboo (Iranian beetroot yogurt dip) 84
borsok 232
Bowles, Paul 171
bread 186–87
  a Central Asian bread 205–06
  bing 186
  chvishtari (cheesy Georgian cornbread) 209
  dograma (torn-bread-and-lamb soup) 54–55
  gutab (Azeri "quesadillas") 212–13
  layered & fried flatbreads 211–12
  qurutob (Tajik bread salad) 31
  yangrou paomo (torn-bread-and-lamb soup) 54–55
brittle, peanut & popcorn 234
broccoli, cruciferous kuku (Iranian broccoli frittata) 96
Buddhism 90–92, 103
Buell, Paul D. 186–87
Bukhara 8, 10, 23, 52, 115, 135, 140–41, 149, 201, 245
Burnaby, Frederick 9, 115
butter, browning 17
butternut squash, gutab (Azeri "quesadillas") 212–13

cabbage
  a Central Asian slaw 35
  dimlama (Uzbek harvest stew) 51–52
  torshi (Iranian pickled vegetables) 83
Cable, Mildred 23, 115
cakes, almond bundt cake 227–28
candied barberry topping 153
  risotto alla Bukharese 154
  tachin (Iranian chicken & rice cake) 151–53
capers, a Georgian summer salad 36
Carasso, Isaac 74
carrots 28
  a Central Asian slaw 35
  an Uzbek plov 149–50
  carrot dumpling filling 189
  dimlama (Uzbek harvest stew) 51–52
  funchoza (Uyghur vermicelli with minced meat) 181
  morkovcha (Korean-style carrot salad) 27
  (mung) bean & rice soup 58
  nokot (Uyghur chickpea & carrot salad) 28
  shivit oshi (Khivan green noodles with beef stew) 173–74
  spinach & tofu baozi 203–04
  spinach, carrot, & egg braise 101–02
  Turkmen fish rice 157–58
Caspian Sea 118, 129, 135, 157, 228
cauliflower, torshi (Iranian pickled vegetables) 83
celeriac, Turkmen fish rice 157–58
celery, torshi (Iranian pickled vegetables) 83
chak-chak 232

Chang'an 8, 14, 54, 92, 186
charlop 63
cheese 22, 72, 73, 158, 186
  cheeseburger makaroni 178–79
  chvishtari (cheesy Georgian cornbread) 209
  layered & fried flatbreads + caramelized onion & feta filling 211–12
  shila plavi (Georgian mushroom "risotto") 158–59
cherries
  cherry kompot (Uzbek cherry "punch") 231
  sour cherry & walnut shortbread 244–45
chestnuts
  piti (Azeri lamb, chickpea & chestnut stew) 59–60
  shah plov (Azeri king/crown rice) 145–46
chicken
  chicken chigirtma (Azeri saffron chicken & eggs) 98
  da pan ji (Uyghur "big plate chicken") 117
  jujeh brick chicken thighs 121–23
  quince khoresh (Iranian quince & chicken braise) 129–30
  shah plov (Azeri king/crown rice) 145–46
  tachin (Iranian chicken & rice cake) 151–53
chickpeas 44, 47
  ab goosht (Iranian lamb & chickpea stew) 49–50
  an Uzbek plov 149–50
  dovga (Azeri warm yogurt soup) 63
  nokot (Uyghur chickpea & carrot salad) 28
  piti (Azeri lamb, chickpea & chestnut stew) 59–60
China 8, 11, 12–13, 15, 46, 54, 60, 90, 91, 103, 104, 107, 112, 117, 124, 125, 130, 135, 139, 163, 164, 171, 173, 177, 184, 185, 188, 200, 203, 211, 223, 234, 241
Chinese long beans 46
a memory of lamian (Uyghur lamb noodles) 171–72
chochure (dumplings en brodo) 197–98
chocolate
  peanut & popcorn brittle 234
  sour cherry & walnut shortbread 244–45
chortan 31
Chun Wang (Du Fu) 54
chvishtari (cheesy Georgian cornbread) 209
Coleridge, Samuel Taylor 188
Columbian Exchange 103
Colombosian, Rosa and Sarkis 72
condensed milk, tres leches rice pudding 223
cong youbing 211
cornmeal, chvishtari (cheesy Georgian cornbread) 209
cranberries
  roast duck with cranberry tkemali 118–20
  shah plov (Azeri king/crown rice) 145–46
cream, gaymak (a clotted cream by any other name) 80
crème fraîche, rovoch salat (Uzbek rhubarb & radish salad) 39
cruciferous kuku (Iranian broccoli frittata) 96
cucumber
  doogh (Iranian yogurt spritzer) 78
  qurutob (Tajik bread salad) 31
  rovoch salat (Uzbek rhubarb & radish salad) 39
  torshi (Iranian pickled vegetables) 83
cumin 12
  advieh 50
  a memory of lamian (Uyghur lamb noodles) 171–72
  an Uzbek plov 149–50
  aubergine frites 107
  beef & potato dumpling filling 189

252

carrot dumpling filling 189
chochure (dumplings en brodo) 197–98
dimlama (Uzbek harvest stew) 51–52
dushbara (dumplings en brodo) 197–98
funchoza (Uyghur vermicelli with minced meat) 181
kao baozi (roast lamb dumplings) 200–201
(mung) bean & rice soup 58
potato dumpling filling 190
samsa (roast lamb dumplings) 200–201
shah plov (Azeri king/crown rice) 145–46
shila plavi (Georgian mushroom "risotto") 158–59
shivit oshi (Khivan green noodles with beef stew) 173–74
Turkmen fish rice 157–58
Uyghur lamb chops 124
Uyghur roast lamb 125
ziran doufu (Uyghur cumin tofu) 108
da pan ji (Uyghur "big plate chicken") 117
date molasses
    aubergine frites 107
    candied barberry topping 153
de Clavijo, Ruy Gonzalez 9, 39
Detroit 20, 22, 23, 72, 74, 150, 227
dill
    a Central Asian slaw 35
    beshbarmak ("five fingers" noodles with beef) 167–68
    dushbara (dumplings en brodo) 197–98
    shivit oshi (Khivan green noodles with beef stew) 173–74
    Turkmen fish rice 157–58
dimlama (Uzbek harvest stew) 51–52
Dioscorides, Pedanius 39
di si xian (four earthly treasures) 103–04
dograma (torn-bread-and-lamb soup) 54–55
doogh (Iranian yogurt spritzer) 78
dopu 59
doubanjiang, di si xian (four earthly treasures) 103–04
dovga (Azeri warm yogurt soup) 63
drinks
    apple sharbat 235
    cherry kompot (Uzbek cherry "punch") 231
    doogh (Iranian yogurt spritzer) 78
    melon sharbat 236
    pomegranate sharbat 236
    tea 218, 239
    vodka 168–69, 236
    wine 121, 209
duck, roast duck with cranberry tkemali 118–20
Du Fu 54
dumplings 184–86, 187
    chochure (dumplings en brodo) 197–98
    dushbara (dumplings en brodo) 197–98
    kao baozi (roast lamb dumplings) 200–201
    manti (Central Asian dumplings) 192
    oromo (Kyrgyz rolled dumplings) 195
    samsa (roast lamb dumplings) 200–201
    Silk Roads dumpling dough 188
    Xanadu of dumpling fillings 188–90
Dunhuang 92–93
dushbara (dumplings en brodo) 197–98

Eastern Market, Detroit 20, 72
eggs
    an Uzbek plov 149–50
    chicken chigirtma (Azeri saffron chicken & eggs) 98
    cruciferous kuku (Iranian broccoli frittata) 96
    dovga (Azeri warm yogurt soup) 63
    pomidor yumurta (Azeri eggs & tomatoes) 97
    spinach, carrot, & egg braise 101–02

spinach chigirtma (Azeri spinach & eggs) 94
tachin (Iranian chicken & rice cake) 151–53
Turkmen fish rice 157–58
evaporated milk, tres leches rice pudding 223
Farmer, Fannie 229
fatir 211
feseli 211
fish 113
    Silk Roads stuffed fish 135
    Turkmen fish rice 157–58
French, Francesca 23, 115
fruit see also specific fruits
    lavashak (fruit roll-ups (with actual fruit)) 249
funchoza (Uyghur vermicelli with minced meat) 181
funnel cakes, not-your-average-county-fair 232

Gansu Province 14, 39, 77, 186
gatyk 77
gaymak (a clotted cream by any other name) 80
gazmakh 13, 144, 178
Genghis Khan 31, 114
Georgia 12, 14, 36, 65–67, 73, 74, 77, 113, 118, 121, 132, 158–59, 187, 199, 209
Gobi Desert 15, 92
Greektown, Detroit 22, 72
green beans
    a memory of lamian (Uyghur lamb noodles) 171–72
    torshi (Iranian pickled vegetables) 83
Grigson, Jane 28
Guilin Province 139
gurza 192
gutab (Azeri "quesadillas") 212–13

halva 59
Han Dynasty 14, 92, 244
Hexi Corridor 14, 92, 186
honey 218
    a Central Asian slaw 35
    aubergine frites 107
    nokot (Uyghur chickpea & carrot salad) 28
    not-your-average-county-fair funnel cakes 232
    peanut & popcorn brittle 234
Hulegu Khan 114
hup toh soh 244
Ibn al-'awwām 94
Ibn Battuta 10, 78
Ibn Hawqal, Muhammad Abu al-Qasim 8
Ibn Sina (Avicenna) 149
ice cream 80
India 9, 14, 44, 90, 92, 138, 223
Iran 11, 15, 32, 45, 49–50, 58, 72, 78, 83, 84, 101, 114, 121, 123, 129–30, 138–40, 141, 143–44, 149–50, 151–53, 162, 178, 186, 187, 216–18, 219, 223, 227, 234, 235–36, 241
Islam 13, 23, 92, 114, 132

jiaozi 184, 185, 192
jonjoli 36
Judaism 135, 140–41
jujeh brick chicken thighs 121–23

kao baozi (roast lamb dumplings) 200–201
kao yang tui (Uyghur roast lamb leg) 125
kashk 31
katama 211
katlama 211
katyk 77
kawap Uyghur lamb chops 124
kaymak 80
Kazakhstan 14, 58, 167–68, 232
keema katlama 211
kheer 223

khingal (Azeri noodles with crispy minced lamb) 168–69
Khiva 9, 35, 173
khoresh 20, 47
khoresh havij 101
quince khoresh (Iranian quince & chicken braise) 129–30
Khorezm 9, 10, 173
kohlrabi, torshi (Iranian pickled vegetables) 83
koloocheh 229
kompot 218, 231
Kublai Khan 14, 114, 188, 203
kuku 96
kumis/kumiss/kumiz 78
kurut 31
Kushan Empire 92
Kyrgyzstan 27, 32, 167–68, 195, 211, 232

laghman 162–64, 165
lamb 114–15
    ab goosht (Iranian lamb & chickpea stew) 49–50
    a memory of lamian (Uyghur lamb noodles) 171–72
    an Uzbek plov 149–50
    basic meat dumpling filling 189
    chochure (dumplings en brodo) 197–98
    dograma (torn-bread-and-lamb soup) 54–55
    dushbara (dumplings en brodo) 197–98
    funchoza (Uyghur vermicelli with minced meat) 181
    kao baozi (roast lamb dumplings) 200–201
    khingal (Azeri noodles with crispy minced lamb) 168–69
    minced lamb & onion dumpling filling 188
    piti (Azeri lamb, chickpea & chestnut stew) 59–60
    roast lamb dumplings 200–201
    samsa (roast lamb dumplings) 200–201
    Uyghur lamb chops 124
    Uyghur roast lamb 125
    yangrou paomo (torn-bread-and-lamb soup) 54–55
lamian, a memory of lamian (Uyghur lamb noodles) 171–72
Lankaran 113, 145
laobing 211
laowan 186
Laozi 187
Lau, Jenny 35
lavashak (fruit roll-ups (with actual fruit)) 216–18, 249
Legend of the Camel Bell 11
lemons
    a Central Asian slaw 35
    apple sharbat 235
    cherry kompot (Uzbek cherry "punch") 231
    chicken chigirtma (Azeri saffron chicken & eggs) 98
    quince jam 240
    rovoch salat (Uzbek rhubarb & radish salad) 39
    Silk Roads stuffed fish 135
    tachin (Iranian chicken & rice cake) 151–53
    walnut jam 241
    watermelon rind jam 239
lettuce, qurutob (Tajik bread salad) 31
limes
    ab goosht (Iranian lamb & chickpea stew) 49–50
    cherry kompot (Uzbek cherry "punch") 231
    cruciferous kuku (Iranian broccoli frittata) 96
    jujeh brick chicken thighs 121–23
    melon sharbat 236
    no-waste beetroot borani (Iranian yogurt dip) 84
    spinach, carrot, & egg braise 101–02

limes, dried, *ab goosht* (Iranian lamb & chickpea stew) 49–50
lobio (Georgian bean stew) 65–66
Luoyang 92

makaroni 178–79
manti (Central Asian dumplings) 192
mantou 203, 232
Marlow and Sons 121
mastoni 77
matsun 72, 77
mchadi 209
melons 6–10
   melon *sharbat* 236
   watermelon rind jam 239
Michigan 6, 13, 20, 39, 46, 162, 187, 216, 244, 249
milk
   aubergine frites 107
   cheeseburger *makaroni* 178–79
   gaymak (a clotted cream by any other name) 80
   shivit oshi (Khivan green noodles with beef stew) 173–74
   tres leches rice pudding 223
mint
   doogh (Iranian yogurt spritzer) 78
   no-waste beetroot *borani* (Iranian yogurt dip) 84
   Turkmen fish rice 157–58
Mongols 9, 14, 15, 78, 92, 114, 186, 203
morkovcha (Korean-style carrot salad) 27
MSG 16, 140
   a memory of *lamian* (Uyghur lamb noodles) 171–72
   cold sesame noodles 177
   funchoza (Uyghur vermicelli with minced meat) 181
   spinach & tofu *baozi* 203–04
   Uyghur lamb chops 124
   ziran doufu (Uyghur cumin tofu) 108
mtsvadi, pork *mtsvadi* (Georgian BBQ pork) 132
(mung) bean & rice soup 58
mushrooms
   mushroom & tofu dumpling filling 190
   shila plavi (Georgian mushroom "risotto") 158–59
mutton 115
   a memory of *lamian* (Uyghur lamb noodles) 171–72
   Uyghur lamb chops 124
Myrdal, Jan 35

nargessi esfenaj 101
Nepal 90, 94, 173
nokot (Uyghur chickpea & carrot salad) 28
noodles 162–64
   a memory of *lamian* (Uyghur lamb noodles) 171–72
   beshbarmak ("five fingers" noodles with beef) 167–68
   cheeseburger *makaroni* 178–79
   cold sesame noodles 177
   funchoza (Uyghur vermicelli with minced meat) 181
   khingal (Azeri noodles with crispy minced lamb) 168–69
   shivit oshi (Khivan green noodles with beef stew) 173–74
   yangrou paomo (torn-bread-and-lamb soup) 54–55
not-your-average-county-fair funnel cakes 232
no-waste beetroot *borani* (Iranian yogurt dip) 84

Oghuz Khan 78
onions
   ab goosht (Iranian lamb & chickpea stew) 49–50
   achichuk (Uzbek tomato & onion salad) 24
   a memory of *lamian* (Uyghur lamb noodles) 171–72
   an Uzbek *plov* 149–50
   beshbarmak ("five fingers" noodles with beef) 167–68
   chicken *chigirtma* (Azeri saffron chicken & eggs) 98
   chochure (dumplings en brodo) 197–98
   cruciferous *kuku* (Iranian broccoli frittata) 96
   dimlama (Uzbek harvest stew) 51–52
   dograma (torn-bread-and-lamb soup) 54–55
   dushbara (dumplings en brodo) 197–98
   funchoza (Uyghur vermicelli with minced meat) 181
   gutab (Azeri "quesadillas") 212–13
   kao baozi (roast lamb dumplings) 200–201
   khingal (Azeri noodles with crispy minced lamb) 168–69
   layered & fried flatbreads + caramelized onion & feta filling 211–12
   layered & fried flatbreads + minced beef & onion filling 211–12
   lobio (Georgian bean stew) 65–66
   morkovcha (Korean-style carrot salad) 27
   (mung) bean & rice soup 58
   no-waste beetroot *borani* (Iranian yogurt dip) 84
   paocai (Chinese fermented pearl onions) 87
   pork *mtsvadi* (Georgian BBQ pork) 132
   quince *khoresh* (Iranian quince & chicken braise) 129–30
   qurutob (Tajik bread salad) 31
   risotto alla Bukharese 154
   samsa (roast lamb dumplings) 200–201
   shah plov (Azeri king/crown rice) 145–46
   shila plavi (Georgian mushroom "risotto") 158–59
   shivit oshi (Khivan green noodles with beef stew) 173–74
   spinach, carrot, & egg braise 101–02
   spinach *chigirtma* (Azeri spinach & eggs) 94
   tachin (Iranian chicken & rice cake) 151–53
   Turkmen fish rice 157–58
   tushonka (Soviet stewed beef short ribs) 131
   Xanadu of dumpling fillings 188–90
   ziran doufu (Uyghur cumin tofu) 108
orange blossom water, quince *khoresh* (Iranian quince & chicken braise) 129–30
oranges, spinach, carrot, & egg braise 101–02
oromo (Kyrgyz rolled dumplings) 195
ox cheek, *dimlama* (Uzbek harvest stew) 51–52

paocai (Chinese fermented pearl onions) 87
parsley root, Turkmen fish rice 157–58
peaches 8, 129
peanut & popcorn brittle 234
pecans, sticky maple persimmon pudding 241–42
peppers 28
   a Central Asian slaw 35
   a memory of *lamian* (Uyghur lamb noodles) 171–72
   chicken *chigirtma* (Azeri saffron chicken & eggs) 98
   chochure (dumplings en brodo) 197–98
   da pan ji (Uyghur "big plate chicken") 117
   dimlama (Uzbek harvest stew) 51–52
   di si xian (four earthly treasures) 103–04
   funchoza (Uyghur vermicelli with minced meat) 181

shivit oshi (Khivan green noodles with beef stew) 173–74
torshi (Iranian pickled vegetables) 83
persimmons, sticky maple persimmon pudding 241–42
pickles 73
paocai (Chinese fermented pearl onions) 87
torshi (Iranian pickled vegetables) 83
pies, apple (& quince) pie 221–22
pishme 232
pistachios 216
   almond bundt cake 227–28
   not-your-average-county-fair funnel cakes 232
   no-waste beetroot *borani* (Iranian yogurt dip) 84
   rovoch salat (Uzbek rhubarb & radish salad) 39
   shah plov (Azeri king/crown rice) 145–46
   tachin (Iranian chicken & rice cake) 151–53
piti (Azeri lamb, chickpea & chestnut stew) 59–60
plov 138, 139
   an Uzbek *plov* 149–50
   shah plov (Azeri king/crown rice) 145–46
plums, *piti* (Azeri lamb, chickpea & chestnut stew) 59–60
Polo, Marco 8–9, 14, 31, 39, 78, 188
pomegranate 216
   an Azeri tomato salad 32
   pomegranate *sharbat* 236
   Silk Roads stuffed fish 135
pomegranate juice
   an Azeri tomato salad 32
   pork *mtsvadi* (Georgian BBQ pork) 132
pomegranate molasses
   an Azeri tomato salad 32
   gutab (Azeri "quesadillas") 212–13
   roast duck with cranberry *tkemali* 118–20
   Silk Roads stuffed fish 135
   Turkmen fish rice 157–58
pomidor yumurta (Azeri eggs & tomatoes) 97
popcorn, peanut & popcorn brittle 234
pork, pork *mtsvadi* (Georgian BBQ pork) 132
potatoes
   ab goosht (Iranian lamb & chickpea stew) 49–50
   a perfect pot of Iranian rice (with potatoes) 143–44
   beef & potato dumpling filling 189
   da pan ji (Uyghur "big plate chicken") 117
   dimlama (Uzbek harvest stew) 51–52
   di si xian (four earthly treasures) 103–04
   (mung) bean & rice soup 58
   potato dumpling filling 189
   shivit oshi (Khivan green noodles with beef stew) 173–74
prunes
   as alternative ingredient 59–60
   shah plov (Azeri king/crown rice) 145–46
   spinach, carrot, & egg braise 101–02
Puck, Wolfgang 35

Qashqai 114
qatiq 77
qovunxona 9
quails eggs, an Uzbek *plov* 149–50
quince 129
   apple (& quince) pie 221–22
   dimlama (Uzbek harvest stew) 51–52
   piti (Azeri lamb, chickpea & chestnut stew) 59–60
   quince Bakewell pudding 246
   quince jam 240
   quince *khoresh* (Iranian quince & chicken braise) 129–30

qurut 31, 75
qurutob (Tajik bread salad) 31

radishes
   rovoch salat (Uzbek rhubarb & radish salad) 39
   shalgam (Kazakh radish salad) 28
   torshi (Iranian pickled vegetables) 83
raisins
   an Uzbek plov 149–50
   sticky maple persimmon pudding 241–42
Ramayana 223
rhubarb, rovoch salat (Uzbek rhubarb & radish salad) 39
rice 138–41
   an Uzbek plov 149–50
   a perfect pot of Iranian rice (with potatoes) 143–44
   dovga (Azeri warm yogurt soup) 63
   (mung) bean & rice soup 58
   parboiling 144
   risotto alla Bukharese 154
   shah plov (Azeri king/crown rice) 145–46
   shila plavi (Georgian mushroom "risotto") 158–59
   tachin (Iranian chicken & rice cake) 151–53
   tres leches rice pudding 223
   Turkmen fish rice 157–58
rose petals
   advieh 50
   almond bundt cake 227–28
   not-your-average-county-fair funnel cakes 232
rose water 218, 232, 234
   a perfect pot of Iranian rice (with potatoes) 143–44
   jujeh brick chicken thighs 121–23
   shah plov (Azeri king/crown rice) 145–46
   tachin (Iranian chicken & rice cake) 151–53
   walnut jam 240
rovoch salat (Uzbek rhubarb & radish salad) 39

sabzi polo 140
saffron 16–17, 141
   a perfect pot of Iranian rice (with potatoes) 143–44
   chicken chigirtma (Azeri saffron chicken & eggs) 98
   dushbara (dumplings en brodo) 197–98
   jujeh brick chicken thighs 121–23
   khingal (Azeri noodles with crispy minced lamb) 168–69
   piti (Azeri lamb, chickpea & chestnut stew) 59–60
   quince khoresh (Iranian quince & chicken braise) 129–30
   shah plov (Azeri king/crown rice) 145–46
   spinach, carrot, & egg braise 101–02
   tachin (Iranian chicken & rice cake) 151–53
   Turkmen fish rice 157–58
   walnut jam 241
salads
   a Central Asian slaw 35
   achichuk (Uzbek tomato & onion salad) 24
   a Georgian summer salad 36
   an Azeri tomato salad 32
   morkovcha (Korean-style carrot salad) 27
   nokot (Uyghur chickpea & carrot salad) 28
   qurutob (Tajik bread salad) 31
   rovoch salat (Uzbek rhubarb & radish salad) 39
   shalgam (Kazakh radish salad) 28
Samarkand 6, 8, 9, 10, 13, 21, 23, 39, 44, 75, 91, 129, 139, 149, 162, 165, 171, 199
samsa (roast lamb dumplings) 200–201
scamorza, chvishtari (cheesy Georgian cornbread) 209
Schafer, Edward H. 8

shah plov (Azeri king/crown rice) 145–46
Shahrisabz 23
shalgam (Kazakh radish salad) 28
Shalhoub, George 216, 218
Shanghai 107, 112, 125, 130, 164, 184, 200
sharbat (Iranian fruit syrups) 218, 235–36
Sheki 44, 59, 217
shila plavi (Georgian mushroom "risotto") 158–59
shivit oshi (Khivan green noodles with beef stew) 173–74
shortbread, sour cherry & walnut 244–45
Shu Xi 186
Sichuan Province 22, 117
Sichuan peppercorns
   a memory of lamian (Uyghur lamb noodles) 171–72
   cold sesame noodles 177
   da pan ji (Uyghur "big plate chicken") 117
   funchoza (Uyghur vermicelli with minced meat) 181
   paocai (Chinese fermented pearl onions) 87
   Uyghur lamb chops 124
   Uyghur roast lamb 125
   yangrou paomo (torn-bread-and-lamb soup) 54–55
   ziran doufu (Uyghur cumin tofu) 108
Sifton, Sam 177
Silk Roads dumpling dough 188
Silk Roads stuffed fish 135
Siyob Bazaar 21, 75, 91
Songdians 13–14, 54
Song Dynasty 90
soups
   chochure (dumplings en brodo) 197–98
   dograma (torn-bread-and-lamb soup) 54–55
   dovga (Azeri warm yogurt soup) 63
   dushbara (dumplings en brodo) 197–98
   (mung) bean & rice soup 58
   yangrou paomo (torn-bread-and-lamb soup) 54–55
sour cherry & walnut shortbread 244–45
spices, toasting 16
spinach 94, 173
   dovga (Azeri warm yogurt soup) 63
   spinach & tofu baozi 203–04
   spinach, carrot, & egg braise 101–02
   spinach chigirtma (Azeri spinach & eggs) 94
split peas, quince khoresh (Iranian quince & chicken braise) 129–30
spring onions
   da pan ji (Uyghur "big plate chicken") 117
   di si xian (four earthly treasures) 103–04
   funchoza (Uyghur vermicelli with minced meat) 181
   rovoch salat (Uzbek rhubarb & radish salad) 39
   Silk Roads stuffed fish 135
   yangrou paomo (torn-bread-and-lamb soup) 54–55
Stein, Marc Aurel 92–93
sticky maple persimmon pudding 241–42
strawberries
   a Georgian summer salad 36
   pork mtsvadi (Georgian BBQ pork) 132
   tres leches rice pudding 223
sumac, piti (Azeri lamb, chickpea & chestnut stew) 59–60
sunflower oil 73
sunflower seeds, a Georgian summer salad 36
suzma (Uzbek strained yogurt) 77
sweetcorn, a Central Asian slaw 35
sweets
   almond bundt cake 227–28
   apple (& quince) pie 221–22
   cherry kompot (Uzbek cherry "punch") 231

lavashak (fruit roll-ups (with actual fruit)) 249
not-your-average-county-fair funnel cakes 232
peanut & popcorn brittle 234
quince Bakewell pudding 246
sour cherry & walnut shortbread 244–45
spiced walnut blondies 229
sticky maple persimmon pudding 241–42
tres leches rice pudding 223
trio of jams 239–40
trio of sharbats 235–36

Tabriz 162
tachin (Iranian chicken & rice cake) 151–53
tahdig see gazmakh
Tajikistan 10, 31, 77, 187, 211, 232
Tamerlane 9, 114, 149
Tang Dynasty 8, 13, 14, 54, 92, 94, 173, 186, 244
tarragon, a Georgian summer salad 36
Tashkent 6, 7, 23, 120
Tbilisi 36, 67, 209
tea 218, 239
Tehran 15, 162
Telavi 73, 113
Teze Bazaar 21, 22
The Baburnama 9
The Book of Dede Korkut 78
The Gobi Desert (Cable & French) 115
The Golden Peaches of Samarkand (Schafer) 8
The Sheltering Sky (Bowles) 171
Timurid Dynasty 9, 149
tkemali 118–20
tofu 12, 90, 92, 93
   di si xian (four earthly treasures) 103–04
   mushroom & tofu dumpling filling 190
   spinach & tofu baozi 203–04
   ziran doufu (Uyghur cumin tofu) 108
tomatoes 24
   ab goosht (Iranian lamb & chickpea stew) 49–50
   achichuk (Uzbek tomato & onion salad) 24
   a Georgian summer salad 36
   a memory of lamian (Uyghur lamb noodles) 171–72
   an Azeri tomato salad 32
   cheeseburger makaroni 178–79
   dimlama (Uzbek harvest stew) 51–52
   dograma (torn-bread-and-lamb soup) 54–55
   pomidor yumurta (Azeri eggs & tomatoes) 97
   qurutob (Tajik bread salad) 31
   shivit oshi (Khivan green noodles with beef stew) 173–74
   torshi (Iranian pickled vegetables) 83
tomato passata, a memory of lamian (Uyghur lamb noodles) 171–72
tomato purée
   cheeseburger makaroni 178–79
   chicken chigirtma (Azeri saffron chicken & eggs) 98
   chochure (dumplings en brodo) 197–98
   da pan ji (Uyghur "big plate chicken") 117
   quince khoresh (Iranian quince & chicken braise) 129–30
   shivit oshi (Khivan green noodles with beef stew) 173–74
Toronto 188
torshi (Iranian pickled vegetables) 83
tres leches rice pudding 223
Turkmen fish rice 157–58
Turkmenistan 10, 31, 54, 58, 77, 157–58, 187, 232
turnips, torshi (Iranian pickled vegetables) 83
tushonka (Soviet stewed beef short ribs) 131

Uyghurs 12, 13, 28, 90, 107, 108, 117, 124, 125, 162, 164, 171–72, 181, 197, 200, 234

255

Uzbeg Khan 78
Uzbekistan 6, 7, 8, 13, 14, 21, 24, 31, 39, 52, 75, 77, 91, 120, 139, 149–50, 163, 165, 187, 199, 201, 245

vegetables *see also* specific vegetables
   torshi (Iranian pickled vegetables) 83
vodka 168–69, 236
von Richthofen, Ferdinand 10

walnuts 32, 244
   an Azeri tomato salad 32
   qurutob (Tajik bread salad) 31
   Silk Roads stuffed fish 135
   sour cherry & walnut shortbread 244–45
   spiced walnut blondies 229
   walnut jam 240
watermelons 6
watermelon rind jam 239
wine 121, 209

Xanadu 188
Xanadu of dumpling fillings 188–90
Xian 8, 11, 46, 54, 60, 104, 163, 173, 177 *see also* Chang'an
Xinjiang Province 13, 117, 124, 203

Yang Guifei 54
yangrou chuan Uyghur lamb chops 124
yangrou paomo (torn-bread-and-lamb soup) 54–55
Yaşil Bazaar 75
yogurt 72–74, 75, 77
   almond bundt cake 227–28
   doogh (Iranian yogurt spritzer) 78
   dovga (Azeri warm yogurt soup) 63
   jujeh brick chicken thighs 121–23
   khingal (Azeri noodles with crispy minced lamb) 168–69
   no-waste beetroot *borani* (Iranian yogurt dip) 84
   qurutob (Tajik bread salad) 31
   suzma (Uzbek strained yogurt) 77
   tachin (Iranian chicken & rice cake) 151–53
   Turkmen fish rice 157–58
Yunnan Province 22, 87, 112

Zevin, Gabrielle 178
Zingerman's Deli 87
ziran doufu (Uyghur cumin tofu) 108
zulbia 232

Publisher's Acknowledgments
DK would like to thank Kristine Jakobsson for assistance with food styling and Kate Reeves-Brown for proofreading.

Bibliography
To access a full list of research citations supporting the information in this book, please visit: https://www.dk.com/uk/information/silk-roads-biblio/

Picture Credits
The publisher would like to thank the following for their kind permission to reproduce their photographs:
Anna Ansari: 2, 4, 7, 8, 11, 12, 15, 17, 18, 21, 42, 46, 52, 60, 67, 70, 73, 75, 88, 91, 104, 110, 113, 120, 123, 130, 136, 139, 150, 160, 163, 165, 182, 185, 201, 214, 217, 219, 228, 245; **Kirstin Perers:** 251.

DK **[RED]** | Penguin Random House

DK LONDON
Editorial Director Cara Armstrong
Senior Editor Lucy Sienkowska
Senior Designer Jordan Lambley
Senior Production Editor Tony Phipps
Senior Production Controller Stephanie McConnell
DTP and Design Coordinator Heather Blagden
Jackets and Sales Material Coordinator Emily Cannings
Publishing Director Stephanie Jackson
Art Director Maxine Pedliham

DK DELHI
Art Editor Devina Pagay
Senior Art Editor Ira Sharma
Managing Art Editor Neha Ahuja Chowdhry
Pre-Production Designer Satish Gaur
Pre-Production Coordinator Pushpak Tyagi

Editorial Tara O'Sullivan
Design Dave APE
Photography Laura Edwards
Food Styling Sam Dixon
Prop Styling Charlie Phillips

First published in Great Britain in 2025 by DK RED, an imprint of Dorling Kindersley Limited 20 Vauxhall Bridge Road, London SW1V 2SA

The authorised representative in the EEA is Dorling Kindersley Verlag GmbH. Arnulfstr. 124, 80636 Munich, Germany

Copyright © 2025 Dorling Kindersley Limited A Penguin Random House Company
Text copyright © Anna Ansari 2025
Photographs copyright © Laura Edwards, 2025 except the following:
Photographs on pages 2, 4, 7, 8, 11, 12, 15, 17, 18, 21, 42, 46, 52, 60, 67, 70, 73, 75, 88, 91, 104, 110, 113, 120, 123, 130, 136, 139, 150, 160, 163, 165, 182, 185, 201, 214, 217, 219, 228, and 245 © Anna Ansari; photograph on page 251 © Kristin Perers.
Anna Ansari has asserted her right to be identified as the author of this work.

10 9 8 7 6 5 4 3 2 1
001–342781–Oct/2025

All rights reserved.
No part of this publication may be reproduced, stored in or introduced into a retrieval system, or transmitted, in any form, or by any means (electronic, mechanical, photocopying, recording, or otherwise), without the prior written permission of the copyright owner.
DK values and supports copyright. Thank you for respecting intellectual property laws by not reproducing, scanning or distributing any part of this publication by any means without permission. By purchasing an authorised edition, you are supporting writers and artists and enabling DK to continue to publish books that inform and inspire readers. No part of this publication may be used or reproduced in any manner for the purpose of training artificial intelligence technologies or systems. In accordance with Article 4(3) of the DSM Directive 2019/790, DK expressly reserves this work from the text and data mining exception.

A CIP catalogue record for this book is available from the British Library.
ISBN: 978-0-2416-9437-4

Printed and bound in Malaysia

www.dk.com

MIX Paper | Supporting responsible forestry
FSC® C018179

This book was made with Forest Stewardship Council™ certified paper – one small step in DK's commitment to a sustainable future. Learn more at www.dk.com/uk/information/sustainability

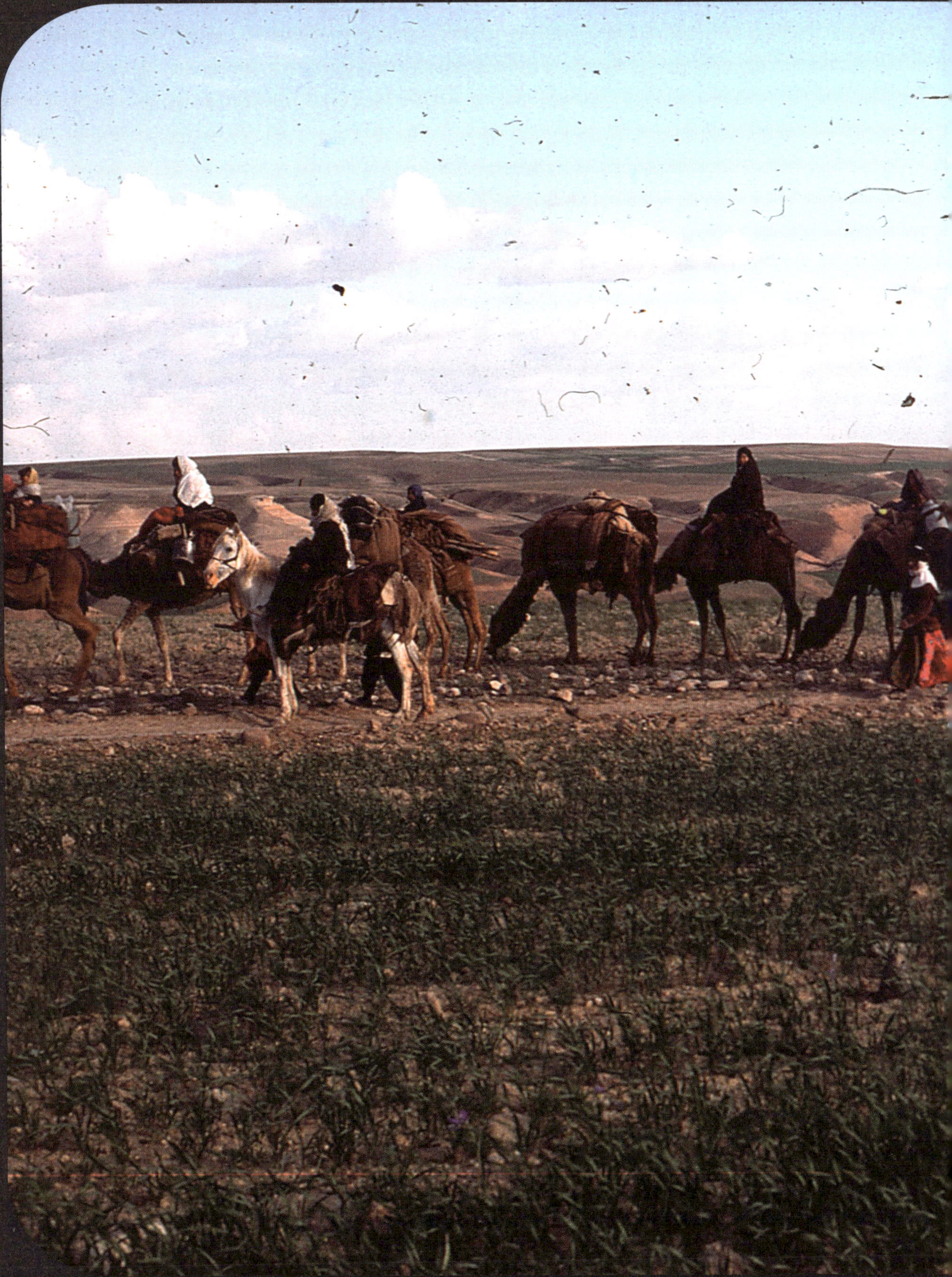